FIRST IMPRESSIONS

FIRST IMPRESSIONS

Edited by
NALINI AMBADY
JOHN J. SKOWRONSKI

THE GUILFORD PRESS
New York   London

© 2008 The Guilford Press
A Division of Guilford Publications, Inc.
72 Spring Street, New York, NY 10012
www.guilford.com

Printed in the United States of America

This book is printed on acid-free paper.

Last digit is print number: 9 8 7 6 5 4 3 2 1

Library of Congress Cataloging-in-Publication Data

Ambady, Nalini.
  First impressions / Nalini Ambady, John J. Skowronski.
     p. cm.
  ISBN 978-1-59385-716-5 (hardcover : alk. paper)
  1. Impression formation (Psychology) 2. Body language. I. Skowronski, John
Joseph. II. Title.
  BF637.C45A5188 2008
  155.9′27—dc22

                                                        2008010071

About the Editors

Nalini Ambady, PhD, is Professor and Neubauer Faculty Fellow at Tufts University. Previously, she taught at Holy Cross College and Harvard University, where she was the John and Ruth Hazel Associate Professor of the Social Sciences. Her research interests focus on the accuracy of social, emotional, and perceptual judgments; how personal and social identities affect cognition and performance; and nonverbal and cross-cultural communication. She examines these phenomena from multiple perspectives, ranging from the biological to the sociocultural. Dr. Ambady is a recipient of the Presidential Early Career Award for Scientists and Engineers (1999), the American Association for the Advancement of Science, Behavioral Science Research Award (1993), and the American Psychological Association Division 5 (Evaluation, Measurement, and Statistics) Dissertation Award (1994).

John J. Skowronski, PhD, is Presidential Research Professor at Northern Illinois University. He has published numerous studies exploring impression formation and social cognition, and has also published extensively in the area of autobiographical memory. Dr. Skowronski has served as Associate Editor of *Social Cognition*, is currently Associate Editor of the *Journal of Experimental Social Psychology*, and currently serves on the editorial board of the *Journal of Personality and Social Psychology*.

Contributors

Reginald B. Adams, Jr., PhD, Department of Psychology, The Pennsylvania State University, University Park, Pennsylvania

Nalini Ambady, PhD, Department of Psychology, Tufts University, Medford, Massachusetts

Susan A. Andrzejewski, MA, Department of Psychology, Northeastern University, Boston, Massachusetts

Hillel Aviezer, MA, Department of Psychology, Hebrew University, Jerusalem, Israel

Simon Baron-Cohen, PhD, Autism Research Centre, Developmental Psychiatry Section, University of Cambridge, Cambridge, United Kingdom

Shlomo Bentin, PhD, Department of Psychology and Center of Neural Computation, Hebrew University, Jerusalem, Israel

Donal E. Carlston, PhD, Department of Psychological Sciences, Purdue University, West Lafayette, Indiana

Bhismadev Chakrabarti, PhD, Autism Research Centre, Developmental Psychiatry Section, University of Cambridge, Cambridge, United Kingdom

Kristin N. Dukes, MS, Department of Psychology, Tufts University, Medford, Massachusetts

Klaus Fiedler, PhD, Psychology Institute, University of Heidelberg, Heidelberg, Germany

Sam Gaddis, BA, Department of Psychology, University of Texas, Austin, Texas

Christopher P. Garris, MA, Department of Psychology, University of Kentucky, Lexington, Kentucky

Samuel D. Gosling, PhD, Department of Psychology, University of Texas, Austin, Texas

Heather M. Gray, PhD, Health and Disability Research Institute, Boston University, Boston, Massachusetts

Judith A. Hall, PhD, Department of Psychology, Northeastern University, Boston, Massachusetts

Monica J. Harris, PhD, Department of Psychology, University of Kentucky, Lexington, Kentucky

Jessica Hartnett, MA, Department of Psychology, Northern Illinois University, DeKalb, Illinois

Ran R. Hassin, PhD, Department of Psychology, Hebrew University, Jerusalem, Israel

Ursula Hess, PhD, Department of Psychology, University of Quebec at Montreal, Montreal, Quebec, Canada

David A. Kenny, PhD, Department of Psychology, The University of Connecticut, Storrs, Connecticut

Robert E. Kleck, PhD, Department of Psychological and Brain Sciences, Dartmouth College, Hanover, New Hampshire

Keith B. Maddox, PhD, Department of Psychology, Tufts University, Medford, Massachusetts

Joann M. Montepare, PhD, Department of Psychology, Emerson College, Boston, Massachusetts

Nicholas O. Rule, AB, Department of Psychology, Tufts University, Medford, Massachusetts

Mark Schaller, PhD, Department of Psychology, University of British Columbia, Vancouver, British Columbia, Canada

John J. Skowronski, PhD, Department of Psychology, Northern Illinois University, DeKalb, Illinois

Yaacov Trope, PhD, Department of Psychology, New York University, New York, New York

Christian Unkelbach, PhD, School of Psychology, University of New South Wales, Sydney, Australia

Simine Vazire, PhD, Department of Psychology, Washington University, St. Louis, Missouri

Max Weisbuch, PhD, Department of Psychology, Tufts University, Medford, Massachusetts

Tessa V. West, MA, Department of Psychology, The University of Connecticut, Storrs, Connecticut

Leslie A. Zebrowitz, PhD, Department of Psychology, Brandeis University, Waltham, Massachusetts

Contents

FIRST IMPRESSIONS

First Impressions

Rationales and Roadmap

JOHN J. SKOWRONSKI
NALINI AMBADY

What's she like? Will he like me? How could she do that to me? Would he be a good fit for this organization? These are the kinds of questions that one often asks oneself or that one often hears in the course of conversation. Such questions reflect what we believe to be a fundamental human motivation: to understand the unobservable characteristics, intentions, traits, motives, goals, and needs of others. These first impressions matter, especially today. Consider the Internet. People, places, products, and services are all evaluated rapidly over the web. For example, on September 26, 2007, the *New York Times* ran a story (Sec. D, p. 5) about chefs under pressure to provide good food as well as to deliver favorable first impressions—managing the product as well as their images. Mr. Greco, a chef in New York, was quoted as saying, "Now, half our customers come from the Internet, and a negative experience on a blog can affect thousands of potential customers." This book reviews research and theory that explores perceivers' proclivities to make such inferences.

In bringing the area into focus, this book reflects an attempt to depict the current "state of the art" with regard to these first impressions.

1

Accordingly, we asked authors to contribute whose own research, in our opinion, was at or near the state of the art, and who we thought could do a good job of conveying the state of the art that was not reflected in their own research program. Accordingly, one of the strengths of this volume is that it is filled with work that has a contemporary focus. This may leave the book open to criticism that we have ignored more traditional approaches to first impressions, but this is a criticism that we can live with. Our explicit goal was to reflect current research in psychology that explores the topic of first impressions, and such a focus may have inevitably caused us to downplay the long history of research in this area.

A second goal underlying this book was breadth. One of the criticisms of modern researchers is that we often become too compartmentalized, being enmeshed in our own research programs, failing to step back and see the big picture. Well, the big picture is that research relevant to first impressions is thriving. It is especially exciting to see that first impression research is coming from very different research traditions and from people in very different areas of psychology. As editors of this volume, we saw an opportunity to provide a service to the field by making parts of the big picture easily accessible and digestible. Indeed, we both can attest to the fact that although we are supposed experts in impression formation, we have both learned an immense amount from reading and editing the chapters included in this volume and have both begun to think about our own research in different ways. It is our hope that such cross-fertilization may serve as a similar stimulus to new ideas in others and to new research.

How fundamental is the tendency of people to form first impressions? This tendency is absolutely fundamental to the processes of person perception and social cognition. The chapters in this volume attest to its ubiquity. Perceivers form impressions of others from a host of cues that originate from both appearance and behavior. We construe the term "behavior" broadly. For example, the tendency of perceivers to draw impressions about people from the nature of the environments that they inhabit, documented in Chapter 14 by Samuel D. Gosling, Sam Gaddis, and Simine Vazire, might be construed as inferences from behavior. Even in the absence of direct observation of an actor, dispositions can be inferred from observed aftereffects (e.g., a room, such as author John S.'s office, that uses the "piles of crud everywhere" method of storage might signal to a perceiver that the author is either dispositionally lazy or extremely busy!).

The fundamental nature of first impressions (and of impression formation in general) may even be tied to processes of evolution. That is, it has been argued that human evolution occurred in a social context in which rules and roles and relationships and alliances and enemies were always in flux. In his chapter, Mark Schaller (see Chapter 1) argues that one consequence of this lack of a constant social hierarchy, of this constant social flux, is that one of the driving forces of human evolution was the need to understand others. Why would fulfilling this need produce evolutionary benefits? Obviously, coming to an accurate understanding of others can substantially aid one's ability to function in a group—for instance, in judging who would be a partner that one could trust (or alternatively, that one could safely swindle). Moreover, accuracy in such perceptions could help the group as a whole to function, allowing people to be appropriately fit to the various roles (e.g., hunter or negotiator) that might emerge during group interactions (see Schaller, Park, & Kenrick, 2007).

Of course, some might quibble with locating the need and capacity to understand others in the context of evolution. One difficulty with evolutionary arguments is that the available data are often open to alternative explanations. For example, one might argue that human thinking abilities developed independently of social selection pressures (e.g., as a consequence of living in difficult environments in which finding food and self-protection were constant challenges). Hence, selection pressures deriving from social interactions with others may have had absolutely nothing to do with the development of human cognitive abilities. Nonetheless, one implication of these abilities is that, once developed, they could be applied to other humans. Human social thinking may not have been shaped by evolution, but once developed, human thinking abilities could certainly have been applied to others.

We do not offer a counterpoint to Schaller's theoretical position because we disagree with him—we are actually fellow advocates of an evolutionary position. Our point is to simply note that at this time it is very easy to tell alternative stories about the emergence of the human species' tendency to spontaneously "go beyond the information given" to think about others. This is why we heartily endorse Schaller's plea for additional research, especially research that can be diagnostic among alternative explanations for the emergence of human social thought capabilities. Moreover, even if such evidence is ultimately not diagnostic of the role that evolution might have played in prompting people to routinely make inferences about others, it certainly would be useful to know whether such inference-making tendencies represent a facet of cognition that is separate from—or, rather, related to—other forms of cognition.

One source of evidence with regard to the separateness question comes from studies relating brain structures to social inference making. As reflected in the study of social neuroscience, this area of study continues to add substantially to our understanding of social inference making.

For example, one approach is to show that social thinking uses different brain structures or substrates than nonsocial thinking. Several research teams are proceeding along these lines. The increasingly large amount of research in this area makes it impractical to cover it all in a single chapter. However, in our view, there would be a substantial deficiency in a contemporary book devoted to first impressions that did not provide a flavor of some of the ways that the study of neural mechanisms informs our understanding of social inference making. Toward this end, in Chapter 2 Nicholas O. Rule and Nalini Ambady provide examples of how understanding underlying neurological mechanisms might contribute to our understanding of first impressions derived from perceptual cues.

Of course, data supportive of the "special" status of social inference making could also come from studies showing functional specificity in human cognitive capacities—that social inference making seems to work differently than nonsocial inference-making. This can be done at different levels of analysis. For example, one kind of evidence can come from tasks demonstrating selectivity in learning or performance. Indeed, such data may exist. Logical reasoning tasks, such as the Wason selection task, are seemingly solved much more easily when placed in the context of human social hypothesis testing than when presented in more abstract terms (see Fiddick, Cosmides, & Tooby, 2000).

One other indicator of the relatively special nature of human social inference making might come from the examination of specific kinds of abnormalities. Specific and recurring cognitive and behavior patterns that deviate from the norm can often suggest abnormalities in the neural substrates that underlie thought, and some of those abnormalities may be unique to the social domain. Attention in mainstream social psychology has only recently begun to be directed toward the kinds of systematic deviances that may suggest such specificity while at the same time providing evidence as to the neural substrates of social thought (see Klein & Kihlstrom, 1998; Sacks, 1995). One promising area of examination is prosopagnosia, a disorder that involves the loss of the ability to recognize familiar others without a more general loss of perceptual or pattern-recognition abilities (e.g., see McKone, Kanwisher, & Duchaine, 2007). Another disorder that has similar implications is Williams syndrome, a rare genetic disorder characterized by intellectual impairment and deficits in visual-spatial cognition but relatively undiminished language and face recognition and a strong appetitive drive toward social interaction.

Yet another area, the study of autism, has led to the emergence of a corpus of research findings that has implications for the specificity of social inference making relative to other forms of cognition. We are happy to include the chapter by Bhismadev Chakrabarti and Simon Baron-

Cohen (Chapter 3), who describe theory and research relevant to empathy: the ability to identify others' emotions and thoughts and to respond to these with appropriate emotion. One argument that these authors make is that appropriate empathic responding presupposes insight into the mental state of others (a capacity that is often absent in autistics). Empathic responses may involve structures and processes that go beyond such inferences, but to be able to empathize one clearly must be able to accurately infer another's mental state. The authors describe a mind reading (e.g., social inference) system model that enables one to infer others' mental states. The two detectors described in the model by Chakrabarti and Cohen link up to two of the main themes represented in other chapters in this volume.

For example, the Intentionality Detector system reflects the emergence of notions of intentionality in inferences. This system reflects our ability to "know" from others' actions what they might be trying to do. A link to this system exists in social psychology research showing that inference making is often geared toward understanding the goals of others (Magliano, Skowronski, Britt, Guss, & Forsythe, 2008). Moreover, a second key theme in social psychological research on first impressions is that such inferences are often made spontaneously, without prompting. The spontaneity theme is explored by John J. Skowronski, Donal E. Carlston, and Jessica Hartnett in Chapter 13.

Chakrabarti and Cohen also postulate a gaze detection system that is sensitive to the gaze direction of others. The Eye Detector system reflects an individual's ability to use nonverbal cues to draw inferences about the content of others' thoughts. Such ideas are strongly echoed by research in social psychology. In fact, social psychological research describing the use of nonverbal cues in such inference making in adults is reviewed in Chapter 4, written by Judith A. Hall and Susan A. Andrzejewski.

One notable omission from the model described in the Chakrabarti and Cohen chapter concerns the use of appearance cues as a source of impressions about others. This is one area in which psychologists have contributed several important insights, and several of the chapters in this volume reflect such insights. For example, Chapter 8 by Leslie A. Zebrowitz and Joann M. Montepare reflects many of the themes that have been pursued by researchers in this area. One of these themes concerns the use of relatively "static" facial cues as grist for first impressions. Major questions here have focused on the cues (or cue combinations) that contribute to impressions of others. Chapter 8 splendidly describes the findings with regard to how such cues are used to produce impressions of attractiveness and maturity. Zebrowitz and Montepare also discuss the issue of impressions from emotional facial expressions, which have an explicit theoretical link to evolution. From this view, it has been suggested that facial expressions can suggest to perceivers how happy, angry, or afraid a target person may feel, and that such information might be functional in allowing a perceiver to infer whether the target my act in a dominant or affiliative manner and whether the perceiver should approach or avoid the target. The research described by Zebrowitz and Montepare is fairly consistent with these Darwinian speculations about the information value of emotion expression.

Ursula Hess, Reginald B. Adams, Jr., and Robert E. Kleck (Chapter 10) also address the issue of the perceived meaning of facial expressions and recapitulate some of these Darwinian themes. This chapter, however, makes a particularly important point with respect to the Darwinian argument, one that is reinforced in Chapter 11, written by Hillel Aviezer, Ran R. Hassin, Shlomo Bentin, and Yaacov Trope. This point is that the interpretation of facial expressions does not rely solely on the cues presented by the face alone. Instead, the broader environmental context in which these cues are emitted also contributes substantially to the inferences that are derived from facial expressions of emotion. For example, the research documented by both Hess et al. and Aviezer et al. suggests that inferences drawn from facial expressions may vary, depending on a perceiver's past experiences, goals, concerns, motivations, and stereotypes. Such flexibility might be seen as inconsistent with one kind of Darwinian view of the interpretation of emotional expressions, a view that sees genetically determined reactions as relatively "fixed." However, this in only one such view; other views allow for considerable flexibility in the expression of inherited characteristics. For example, humans may generally be disposed to make inferences about others, but the nature and content of those inferences might be flexibly responsive to immediate situational influences. This is certainly not a radical idea, at least from the perspective of those reasonably well versed in how genetics become expressed in phenotypes. To such individuals, the idea that appropriate situations may trigger the expression of certain traits (e.g., inference making) is second nature.

The importance of the environment in influencing first impressions is carefully detailed by Max Weisbuch, Christian Unkelbach, and Klaus Fiedler (Chapter 12), who discuss how recent environmental history (or priming) affects first impressions. Environmental cues encountered before the formation of first impressions can influence the impression through processes of assimilation or contrast. Not only do factors in the environment affect first impressions, but also factors within individuals have an impact. Accordingly, Weisbuch et al. also consider how some of the factors that individuals bring to the situation, such as their theories and communicative goals, might affect first impressions.

An additional point that can be derived from the Hess et al. and Aveizer et al. chapters is central to this volume's message. First impression research has often been fractionated, with researchers generally coalescing into different "camps." In part, this has occurred because theorizing across different areas often took different forms. For example, research on appearance cues and facial expressions was dominated by ecological and Darwinian views, while research on first impressions from trait descriptions was dominated by information processing views. One of the goals of the present volume is to attempt to weaken the isolationism that has characterized first impression research by providing summaries of outcomes in various areas of relevant research and by highlighting conceptual and empirical similarities across areas. Accordingly, in our view one of the prime lessons to be derived from the Hess et al. and Aveizer et al. chapters is that there is an essential unity that we believe links these research areas.

The benefits of being aware of theoretical ideas from different camps can be illustrated in Chapter 9, written by Keith B. Maddox and Kristin N. Dukes. This chapter describes research that is similar to other face perception research in that it examines how people use facial cues in the formation of prejudice. However, the chapter examines what are essentially competing theoretical views of how this prejudice comes about. One theoretical perspective is explicitly derived from the tradition of research that tried to explain how people "go from acts to dispositions." That perspective often focused on how perceivers place actors in trait or motive categories based on the actors' behaviors. Interestingly, Maddox and Dukes examine that position and find it wanting. Their analysis suggests that prejudice is not necessarily a result of using a constellation of cues to categorize a target (e.g., he's African American), with a prejudiced response following from that categorization (e.g., I don't like African Americans). Instead, they suggest that facial cues can directly influence prejudice, bypassing the categorization stage of processing. To some, this may not be a new idea. After all, over 25 years ago Robert Zajonc asserted that preferences need no inferences (Zajonc, 1980), and a prejudice can be perceived as nothing more than an evaluative preference. Nonetheless, the point made by Maddox and Dukes in their chapter is crucial, reminding researchers in this area to be very careful about assuming that categorization moderates the relation between facial cues and subsequent responses, particularly when those responses are evaluative in nature.

David A. Kenny and Tessa V. West, in Chapter 6, describe a program of research revolving around the social relations model, showing that consensus among observers about a trait possessed by an actor is often reasonably high, particularly for traits (extraversion and conscientiousness) that are exemplified by cues—such as appearance cues—that seem to strongly exemplify an underlying trait. On the other hand, other traits (e.g., emotional stability) do not seem to be directly exemplified by a class of cues; so, behaviors related to emotional stability traits appear to be open to idiosyncratic interpretations that lower the consensus among observers.

The Kenny and West chapter also explores the fascinating issue of accuracy in first impressions. Certainly, accuracy takes on even more importance when considered in the context of the evolutionary explanation of inference making. The evolutionary explanation presupposes that there is some degree of accuracy in inference making. After all, without accuracy, which presumably guides adaptive social behavior, why would the tendency to make social inferences be functional (functionality is also emphasized in this volume in Chapter 4, by Hall and Andrzejewski)? Kenny and West review data showing that there is accuracy in person perceptions subsequent to brief interactions with others—perhaps enough accuracy to satisfy the requirements of evolutionary approaches. For example, Kenny and West note that in their brief-interaction, zero-acquaintance studies perceivers were able to accurately predict how targets would behave with others in general but not with others in particular. The fact that there is at least some accuracy in first impressions—even impressions that are derived from small behavior samples—also fits with conclusions from "thin-slice" studies in which perceivers can seemingly make accurate inferences about others from only a brief or obscured snippet of their behavior (Ambady & Rosenthal, 1992). Again, however, one must be careful not to extrapolate such findings to an extreme. Thin-slice accuracy-in-perception effects are stronger for some internal states and traits than others (Ambady, Bernieri, & Richeson, 2000).

In their chapter, Kenny and West rue the fact that they did not give sufficient attention to individual differences in perception accuracy. Happily, however, Hall and Andrzejewski (in Chapter 4) consider this issue. They conclude that there are, indeed, significant differences in the extent to which people are accurate in their perceptions of others. However, to what should we attribute these individual differences? Again, we return to the theme of the "specialness" of impression formation. Hall and Andrzejewski add their voice to the chorus on this theme when they note that accuracy in the formation of first impressions is not just another way of estimating a person's general intelligence. Instead, accuracy in the formation of first impressions is a skill, proficiency at which seems to be independent of other cognitive skills. While the origins of this skill remain unclear, we agree with them that multiple variables, and multiple causal paths among those variables, are likely related to skill development. However, the Hall and Andrzejewski analysis holds out the intriguing possibility that perceivers can be trained to be more accurate in their perceptions of others. As people who are in an occupation (university professors) in which such social sensitivity can come in awfully handy (is this student honest or merely dissembling about missing the homework assignment?), we stand ready to sign up for training programs when they achieve sufficient power to be viable in practical terms.

The theme of accuracy in the perception of others, and the degree of accuracy, is also taken up by Heather M. Gray (Chapter 5). Gray expands on the one basic theme of Hall and Andrzejewski (and of Kenny, as well): that accuracy is only a sometime thing. Gray outlines the conditions under which accuracy seems to occur and those under which it does not. In this manner, the chapter serves as a nice complement to the Kenny and West chapter, which focuses on results from the social relations model's methodology and perspective. Kenny and West's conclusions can be perceived as limited to the methodologies that they describe; Gray's chapter shows that many of those conclusions generalize to the research world at large.

Gray also reminds researchers that while the study of accuracy as an outcome is important, it is also the case that the mental structures and processes that contribute to accuracy represent topics that are very much understudied. In that sense, the chapter makes a plea for more of the kind of research embodied in certain chapters (Hess et al.; Avezier et al; Maddox & Dukes; Skowronski & Carlston) that are as concerned with the processes by which we come to first impressions as with the outcomes of those impression formation processes.

Finally, it seems reasonable to comment about some of the reasons underlying all of this interest in first impressions. Of course, we are academics, so the study of topics that fascinate us is within our purview. However, there is also a practical reason to study first impressions—namely, that they substantially affect "downstream" processing. Indeed, Monica J. Harris and Christopher P. Garris (Chapter 7) review the ways in which prior expectations can influence subsequent perceptions of others. Expectations derived from first impressions can lead to biases in processing as well as self-fulfilling prophecies. Moreover, inaccurate or biased first impressions may have serious implications for later affect, cognition, and behavior. More specifically, the first impression that may seem fleeting now may actually persist in an individual's mental representation of others and may subsequently affect: (1) the kinds of information that are subsequently sought out about that other; (2) the information that is attended to in the array of other relevant information that is received; (3) how received information is encoded or interpreted; (4) the affective responses to new information; (5) how information is stored; (6) how information is retrieved and reconstructed from memory; and (7) how one ultimately acts toward the target. Given the widespread possible scope of effects that can be produced from first impressions, it seems important to know whether and when such effects emerge and also how long they last. Interestingly, we know relatively little about how first impressions operate to affect later thought and behavior about others, especially in the real-life contexts that are so often dominated by consequential interpersonal interactions.

Of course, there is much more to this volume than can be described in the few words that we have available in this overview chapter. Each of the chapters brings new and interesting perspectives to the study of first impressions, and each contains ideas and insights that should inform and delight diligent readers. At this point, it is worth reiterating one of our earlier comments. Both of us, as volume editors, were supposed "experts" in this area. However, both of us have been both awed and overjoyed at the new learning experienced from reading these chapters and at the new thoughts prompted by such reading. It is our hope and our expectation that readers of this volume will have the same experience. Enjoy it.

REFERENCES

Ambady, N., Bernieri, F. J., & Richeson, J. A. (2000). Toward a histology of social behavior: Judgmental accuracy from thin slices of the behavioral stream. In M. P. Zanna (Ed.), *Advances in experimental social psychology* (Vol. 32, pp. 201–271). San Diego: Academic Press.

Ambady, N., & Rosenthal, R. (1992). Thin slices of expressive behavior as predictors of interpersonal consequences: A meta-analysis. *Psychological Bulletin, 111*, 256–274.

Fiddick, L., Cosmides, L., & Tooby, J. (2000). No interpretation without representation: The role of domain-specific representations in the Wason selection task. *Cognition, 77*, 1–79.

Klein, S. B., & Kihlstrom, J. F. (1998). On bridging the gap between social–personality psychology and neuropsychology. *Personality and Social Psychology Review, 2*, 228–242.

Magliano, J. P., Skowronski, J. J., Britt, M.A., Guss, D., & Forsythe, J. C. (2008). What do you want? How perceivers use cues to make goal inferences about others. *Cognition, 106*, 594–632.

McKone, E., Kanwisher, N., & Duchaine, B. C. (2007). Can generic expertise explain special processing for faces? *Trends in Cognitive Sciences, 11*, 8–15.

Sacks, O. (1995). *An anthropologist on Mars: Seven paradoxical tales.* New York: Knopf.

Schaller, M., Park, J. H., & Kenrick, D. T. (2007). Human evolution and social cognition. In R. I. M. Dunbar & L. Barrett (Eds.), *The Oxford handbook of evolutionary psychology* (pp. 491–504). New York: Oxford University Press.

Zajonc, R. B. (1980). Feeling and thinking: Preferences need no inferences. *American Psychologist, 35,* 151–175.

PART I

BIOLOGICAL ASPECTS

CHAPTER 1

Evolutionary Bases of First Impressions

MARK SCHALLER

Why do we form first impressions at all? What kinds of information are especially likely to influence our first impressions, and what specific impressions are inspired by that information? Under what conditions are we especially likely to form specific kinds of first impressions? What specific psychological mechanisms are responsible for producing these inferential phenomena?

These are fundamental questions in the study of first impressions. A lot of different theoretical perspectives can be applied to address those questions. This chapter focuses on the metatheoretical perspective supplied by evolutionary psychology. I discuss various ways in which the logic of evolutionary inquiry can be applied fruitfully to the study of first impressions.

THE PROSPECTS AND PERILS OF SOCIAL LIFE

Underlying most exercises in human evolutionary psychology is the assumption that the human genome (and the brain anatomy that it produces) evolved in response to chronic features of the local ecology. Conspecifics (i.e., our fellow human beings or, in more deeply historical times, fellow members of species ancestral to *Homo sapiens*) have made up a fundamental part of that local ecology. Specific kinds of behavioral responses to these conspecifics are likely to have had specific implications for reproductive fitness. This has consequences for cognition. Many features of human cognition may have evolved to facilitate specific forms of fitness-enhancing social behavior.

Consider a few examples. Most obviously, perhaps, social interaction provides a necessary means toward sexual reproduction. But not all mates exert equal impact on reproductive fitness. Thus, there may have evolved specific aspects of human cognition that help solve the problem of selecting a mate (or mates) bearing characteristics that are advantageous to the perceiver's reproductive fitness. Reproductive fitness is influenced not only by the successful production of offspring but also by the extent to which one's offspring, and other close kin, successfully reproduce. Because of this, there may have evolved specific aspects of human cognition that help individuals distinguish among different degrees of kinship and incline them to allocate resources differentially in favor of closer kin. These two examples illustrate specific fitness-relevant opportunities associated with the presence of others. Implicitly, they also illustrate a broader point about the opportunities afforded by social life: because loners and outcasts are relatively unlikely to have access to desirable mates, or to receive the material benefits of kinship, simply being an accepted member of any social group has fitness-relevant advantages. Thus, there may have evolved specific aspects of human cognition that help promote sociality in general.

Of course, social interactions not only are a source of potential benefit; they can sometimes be the source of specific fitness-relevant threats as well. Some conspecifics, for a variety of reasons (e.g., competition for mates or material resources) may have the intention of doing harm. If one falls prey to these malevolent intentions (if one is killed, for instance), the cost to reproductive fitness can be enormous. Consequently, specific aspects of human cognition may have evolved that facilitate detection of, and defensive responses to, potential harm doers. Even well-meaning conspecifics may pose a threat to health and reproductive fitness—if those individuals are infected with communicable, disease-causing pathogens. Thus, specific aspects of human cognition may have evolved that facilitate detection and physical avoidance of disease-bearing conspecifics. A third form of peril arises in the form of conspecifics who cheat, steal, or other otherwise fail to uphold social contracts. Thus, specific aspects of human cognition may have evolved that facilitate the detection and punishment of such norm violators.

This is hardly an exhaustive list (for a longer list, see Schaller, Park, & Kenrick, 2007). It is merely illustrative of the kinds of enduring fitness-relevant "problems"—prospects to be achieved or perils to be avoided—associated with the presence of conspecifics. The key point is that, because these problems have endured across vast stretches of ancestral time, they may have exerted nontrivial selection pressures on the evolution of human social cognition. An extensive body of research is consistent with this general line of speculation (for a set of extensive reviews and discussions, see Schaller, Simpson, & Kenrick, 2006). More importantly, this body of research documents dozens of novel psychological discoveries that have emerged from the rigorous testing of specific hypotheses deduced within this evolutionary framework. Some of these discoveries bear directly on our understanding of first impressions.

ADAPTIVE SPONTANEITY OF FIRST IMPRESSIONS

Let's start with one of the most fundamental facts about first impressions: the fact that people form them spontaneously and with minimal cognitive effort (Carlston & Skowronski, 2005; Gilbert & Malone, 1995; Newman & Uleman, 1989). The relatively effortless formation of first impressions can be produced by repeated practice and overlearning (Bargh & Chartrand, 1999; Palmeri, 1999). However, there are good reasons to suppose that there's something more going on here as well—that people may be adaptively predisposed to form immediate impressions of others.

When detecting the fitness-relevant features of others, it is often essential to act fast. If someone is untrustworthy—if he or she intends to injure me—I'd better detect that trait immediately; or if he or she intends to cheat me, I'd better detect that intention immediately as well. Because, if I don't, I'll probably end up injured or cheated. Similarly, if another person nearby has an infectious disease, I'd better figure that out as soon as possible. If I don't and I fail to take precautions, I'm likely to fall ill myself. Accordingly, there may have been substantial adaptive advantages associated with any mechanism that promotes instant inferences about the threat-relevant characteristics of other people.

Inferential speed is probably most essential to the avoidance of social dangers. But it's not irrelevant to the attainment of social opportunities as well. When mating opportunities arise, for instance, it may be necessary to make an immediate decision whether to pursue that opportunity—because if one dithers and deliberates, that window of opportunity may close. Thus, there may have been adaptive advantages associated with mechanisms that promote the immediate discrimination between fit and unfit mates.

The upshot is that there is an inferential need for speed. In many other domains of human decision making, it has been compellingly asserted there were evolutionary advantages associated with psychological mechanisms that are fast and frugal—mechanisms that promote inferences immediately and with a minimum expenditure of cognitive resources (e.g., Gigerenzer, Todd, & the ABC Research Group, 1999). So, too, it is with person perception. It seems likely that trait inferences and other first impressions emerge spontaneously because, over a long stretch of human evolutionary history, this spontaneity was adaptive.

Spontaneous first impressions can be adaptive even if these impressions are fallible and imperfect. As long as immediate impressions are even minimally diagnostic, it may be more advantageous to form these first impressions than to dither and deliberate. "Minimally diagnostic" is a standard easily surpassed by many immediate inferences. Exposure to a person for just a few seconds produces first impressions that are often remarkably accurate (Ambady, Bernieri, & Richeson, 2000). Given this state of affairs, one could argue that it would defy the basic logic of evolutionary biology if people didn't form immediate impressions of others.

Of course, the fact remains that some inferential errors are inevitable. Importantly, different kinds of errors may have different implications for reproductive fitness. When it comes to avoiding social perils, the fitness implications follow what Nesse (2005) has called the "smoke detector principle": the failure to detect a real danger (a false-negative error) typically has implications that are far more costly than the detection of a danger that doesn't really exist (a false-positive error). Consequently, just as smoke detectors are calibrated to err on the side on false-positive errors (to trigger an alarm at the merest hint of smoke, even if it that smoke is associated with no real threat whatsoever), psychological mechanisms may have evolved to implicitly err on the side of making false-positive errors when inferring the potentially dangerous traits or intentions of others.

For other kinds of fitness-relevant problems, the relative costs of false-positive and false-negative errors may be very different. For instance, in the realm of mating, there is a profound sex difference in the number of offspring than men and women can produce; consequently, a poor mating decision (i.e., the choice of a genetically unfit mate) has greater fitness costs to a woman than it does to a man. It follows that, when inferring whether a potential mate might be desirable, women are more likely than men to err on the side of false-negative errors. In other words, among women, the immediate impression of any potential male suitor may be that he is potentially unsuitable as a mate. In contrast, among men, the immediate impression of any women may be that she might be just fine as a mate. In several recent overviews of "error management theory," Haselton and her colleagues review implications that an evolutionarily informed signal-detection analysis has for this and other kinds of impression formation phenomena (Haselton & Funder, 2006; Haselton & Nettle, 2006).

It is with considerations like these in mind that Haselton and Funder (2006) suggested the existence of an evolved "personality judgment instinct." If such an instinct exists, they argue, the tendency to form spontaneous trait inferences should appear very early in childhood, and it appears that it does. Moreover, proficiency in drawing personality judgments should be ubiquitous, and it appears that this is the case as well. Indeed, Haselton and Funder (2006, pp. 30–31) observed that "consistent individual differences in judgmental ability have been surprisingly difficult to establish. . . . Perhaps this is because personality judgment is such an essential life skill that nearly everyone can do it well enough to get by." Also consistent with the notion of a personality judgment instinct is some evidence showing that trait inferences—as opposed to other kinds of social inferences—are associated with activity in specific regions of the brain (Heberlein & Saxe, 2005). Bear in mind, of course, that it's extraordinarily tricky to draw conclusions about evolutionary adaptations—especially those that might actually qualify as instincts—solely on the basis of contemporary psychological observations (Conway & Schaller, 2002; Schmitt & Pilcher, 2004). Still, it's within the realm of possibility that our tendency to form fast and frugal first impressions is not merely a product of practice; it may actually be instinctual.

INFERENCES ABOUT WHAT: THE CONTENTS OF FIRST IMPRESSIONS

OK, so we form first impressions; but just what do we form these impressions about? What specific kinds of inferences do we draw? We know, of course, that our minds are agile and responsive to whatever objective information is picked up by our sensory systems; and so we can, conceivably, form first impressions that focus on just about any kind of trait at all. But if our mind evolved to facilitate fitness-enhancing behavior, then we may be predisposed to be on the lookout especially for information bearing on the potential perils and prospects of social life. Accordingly, we may also be adaptively predisposed to form impressions more readily about certain kinds of traits than about others.

From an evolutionary perspective, the ultimate goal is the reproduction of one's genes. Behaviors that promote genetic reproduction (mating, provision of resources to offspring, etc.) are more difficult to produce if one is injured, destitute, dying, or dead. For that reason, some of the most evolutionarily fundamental psychological goals pertain to the avoidance of (or defense against) other people who might harm us, cheat us, or kill us. That requires that we know—or at least make a reasonable first guess—whether someone is nasty or nice. From an evolutionary perspective, no other kind of inference probably matters quite so much.

The implication for the contents of first impressions is obvious. This implication is one of the classic findings in the study of first impressions: the most basic evaluative dimension is that of interpersonal warmth and agreeableness (Kelley, 1950; Peeters & Czapinski, 1990; see also Cottrell, Neuberg, & Li, 2007).

This adaptive perspective not only predicts the evaluative dimension along which first impressions are most likely to be formed, it also suggests that these first impressions are likely to be pulled especially easily toward the negative end of this dimension. Recall the smoke detector principle again (Nesse, 2005). There may be grave fitness costs to me if you're really nasty but I think you're nice; there are more modest costs if you're really nice but I think you're nasty. The inferential implication is that a strongly negative interpersonal impression ("What a jerk!") may be formed on the basis of very little information, whereas a strongly positive impression ("What a wonderful guy!") may require a greater amount of informational input. In addition, a positive first impression may be easily reversed by additional information to the contrary, but a negative first impression may persist even in the face of contradictory information. These implications are borne out by extensive empirical evidence (Baumeister, Bratslavsky, Finkenauer, & Vohs, 2001; Rothbart & Park, 1986; Rozin & Royzman, 2001; Skowronski & Carlston, 1992).

One's fitness is potentially influenced not only by others' intentions (whether they are nasty or nice) but also by their abilities to carry out those intentions. If two people want to kill me, the one who poses the greatest actual threat to me is the one who is smartest and most capable; not so much the malicious idiot. (Similarly, if two people want to do nice things for me, I will probably get more real benefit from the generous genius than from the equally generous fool.) The implication is that there should also be a second evaluative dimension—one that focuses on capability—along which people will be especially likely to form first impressions. This implication too is borne out by an enormous body of research. When boiled down to their simplest essence, impressions of people are located within a two-dimensional space anchored by the evaluative dimensions of interpersonal warmth and agency (Judd, James-Hawkins, Yzerbyt, & Kashima, 2005; Rosenberg, Nelson, & Vivekananthan, 1968).

Another implication emerges from this line of reasoning as well. If indeed greater fitness consequences follow from other individuals' capability rather than their incapability, then—in contrast to the negativity bias that occurs in impressions of agreeableness and warmth—a positivity bias may occur in impressions of capability. For instance, first impressions of incapability may be relatively easily reversed by information to the contrary, but first impressions of capability may be more resistant to change. There is now considerable empirical support for this hypothesis (Skowronski, 2002; Skowronski & Carlston, 1992).

These last few paragraphs reveal some of the useful insights that can emerge when applying an evolutionary perspective to the study of first impressions. We've known for a long time that warmth and agency are the fundamental dimensions of impression formation and that different kinds of impressions are more easily formed (and more resistant to revision). The evolutionary perspective helps us understand why that is. Moreover, it suggests that these classic findings (the dimensional structure, negativity and positivity biases) are not the conceptually distinct phenomena that they might superficially appear to be; they may be interrelated consequences of the same adaptive mechanisms.

Beyond these general insights, evolutionary theorizing is proving to be productive in generating additional discoveries bearing on the specific contents of first impressions. Many of these discoveries have emerged from deductions about (1) specific kinds of features in others to which we might be adaptively hypersensitive and (2) specific inferences that, for fitness-relevant reasons, may be spontaneously implied by the perception of those features.

For instance, in order to avoid falling prey to malicious or untrustworthy conspecifics, it would have been adaptive to be extraordinarily sensitive to any cue that might signal another person's potential maliciousness or untrustworthiness. This appears to be the case. Compared with other kinds of facial expressions, angry faces are especially likely to grab and/or hold attention (Fox et al., 2000; Schupp et al., 2004). Angry facial expressions are presumably predictive of aggressive inclinations and so are diagnostic of potential danger. Other superficial cues may be more fallible; but because of their history of diagnosticity in ancestral environments, they may still inspire immediate inferences implying danger. Membership in a coalitional out-group may serve as one such cue. Throughout much of human evolutionary history, in-groups have been sources of support and safety, whereas encounters with out-group members presented a potential threat to personal welfare (Schaller & Neuberg, 2008). Consequently, out-group members may be especially likely to inspire first impressions that are tilted toward distrust. Consistent with this reasoning is evidence that people find it easier to learn (and harder to unlearn) aversive responses to out-group faces (e.g., Olsson, Ebert, Banaji, & Phelps, 2005).

Similarly, because of the powerful fitness costs associated with parasitic infection, it is likely that people are sensitive to cues signaling the possibility that another person is the carrier of an infectious disease. A wide variety of morphological anomalies (e.g., pustules, rashes, and other disfigurements) may have been symptomatic of parasitic infections over the long course of human evolutionary history. Consequently, our minds may be hypervigilant to any kind of perceptible disfigurement or morphological oddity; and, when perceived, those anomalies may inspire negative inferences. There is now a growing body of evidence consistent with this reasoning (Perrett et al., 1999; Schaller & Duncan, 2007). Moreover, consistent with the spontaneous and associative nature of many first impressions (e.g., Carlston & Skowronski, 2005; Skowronski, Carlston, Mae, & Crawford, 1998), some of this evidence indicates that these negative inferences are formed even when perceivers know that the perceived anomaly is misleading. For instance, in a study by Duncan (2005), participants were provided with photographs and brief biographical sketches of two men. One man had a superficial birthmark on his face but was described as strong and healthy. The other man looked just fine but was described as being infected with a strain of drug-resistant tuberculosis. Participants then responded to a computer-based reaction time task that assessed which of the two men was more strongly associated with the semantic concept "disease." Results revealed a tendency to associate disease with the facially disfigured man (who was known to be healthy) more strongly than the man who was actually known to be diseased (but who looked normal). In short, even when rational appraisal explicitly indicates otherwise, anomalous morphological features may implicitly inspire negative first impressions.

This line of reasoning also implies that physical unattractiveness of any kind may serve as a sort of crude heuristic cue for ill health, and thus lead to aversive trait inferences (Schaller & Duncan, 2007; Zebrowitz, Fellous, Mignault, & Andreoletti, 2003). A conceptually different piece of adaptive logic leads to a similar prediction. This additional line of reasoning focuses not on *un*attractiveness as disease cue but rather on attractiveness as cue for genetic fitness. The subjective assessment of facial attractiveness is based substantially on elements of facial physiognomy (prototypicality, symmetry) that may be diagnostic signals of genetic fitness (Fink & Penton-Voak, 2002; Thornhill & Gangestad, 1999a). There are clear adaptive advantages to mating (and perhaps affiliating more generally) with individuals who have a high degree of genetic fitness. Consequently, when people exhibit these desirable traits (i.e., when they appear subjectively to be physical attractive), they may inspire positive inferences of the sort that promote approach-oriented behavior. This clearly is the case: first impressions of physically attractive people are more positive, along many different trait dimensions, than first impressions of unattractive people (Eagly, Ashmore, Makhijani, & Longo, 1991).

Other specific kinds of features may inspire other specific kinds of initial impressions for yet other adaptive reasons. Recall that reproductive fitness depends, in part, on the likelihood that one's own offspring survive long enough to successfully reproduce themselves. This fact, coupled with the fact that newborn primates are helpless and dependent on others for survival, highlights the adaptive importance of providing care to one's own infant offspring (and to the infant offspring of close kin as well). Thus, our minds may be hypersensitive to superficial facial features that are diagnostic of infancy (e.g., round faces, big eyes, small noses); and when perceived, those features may trigger functionally correspondent inferences. If indeed this is a spontaneous and associative process, these inferences may emerge even when the perceived person isn't an infant at all. There is abundant evidence attesting to exactly this phenomenon. Compared to other adults, babyfaced adults are more likely to inspire impressions suggesting ignorance and incapability (Zebrowitz & Montepare, 1992).

In the preceding paragraph I made a parenthetical allusion to kinship— a topic with substantial adaptive implications of its own. Fitness benefits follow from the differential allocation of resources in favor of closer kin, for instance, and fitness costs follow from sexual intercourse with close kin. Because of these and other fitness implications, many animal species employ superficial cues—such as phenotypic similarity—that help them distinguish close kin from more distant kin (Hepper, 1991; Rendall, 2004). These cue-based kin recognition mechanisms are evolutionarily ancient. And so, despite the fact that humans have more recently evolved additional mechanisms (such as those involved in language use and symbolic thought) that allow us to accurately know who our close kin are, our inferences may be implicitly influenced by evolutionarily ancient cue-based mechanisms as well. There is plenty of evidence that people respond to phenotypically similar individuals in a more kin-like way— even if those individuals objectively are strangers. Perceived facial similarity leads to impressions connoting greater trustworthiness, but, importantly, it does not lead to increased sexual attractiveness (DeBruine 2002, 2005). Another study found that perceived self–other attitudinal similarity activates semantic cognitions connoting kinship (Park & Schaller, 2005). This finding suggests that the evolved psychology of kin detection may help explain the classic effect whereby attitude similarity leads to greater liking (Byrne et al., 1971). It also accounts for the observation that the similarity-liking effect emerges more strongly when similarity occurs along attitudes that are more highly heritable—and thus more highly diagnostic of actual kinship (Tesser, 1993).

FUNCTIONAL FLEXIBILITY AND THE
MODULATION OF ADAPTIVE INFERENCES

Evolved mechanisms of social inference may often operate spontaneously and with a minimum of cognitive effort, but that doesn't mean that they are inflexible in their operation. The opposite is true. These mechanisms—and their implications for first impressions—are highly flexible and predictably influenced by fitness-relevant regulatory cues in the immediate environment.

We must assume that evolved cognitive mechanisms are (or at least used to be, in ancestral environments) associated with specific fitness benefits. But their actual operation typically entails some costs as well. Any psychological response to perceptual stimuli consumes some metabolic resources. This is the case especially when psychological responses precipitate behavioral responses, as they often do. Plus, the engagement of one adaptive activity (e.g., avoidance of danger) often inhibits an organism's ability to engage in other kinds of adaptive activity (e.g., mating). For these reasons, many evolved mechanisms are functionally flexible. They are more likely to be engaged when additional information in the immediate environment indicates that the fitness-relevant benefits outweigh the costs; they are less likely to be engaged when additional information indicates either lower benefits or higher costs.

This broadly applicable line of reasoning has many specific implications for how the outputs of social inference mechanisms may differ across cultures, individuals, and situations (Schaller et al., 2007). Some of these implications are directly relevant to the formation of first impressions. To illustrate, I'll revisit some of the phenomena discussed above and discuss how these inferences may be moderated by input variables bearing on an evolutionary cost–benefit calculus.

Start with the phenomenon in which a distrustful first impression emerges simply from the perception that another person is a member of a coalitional out-group. According to the principle of functional flexibility, this effect should be more likely to emerge under circumstances in which people feel more vulnerable to harm and less likely under circumstances in which perceivers feel relatively invulnerable. What sorts of things might influence perceivers' sense of personal vulnerability or invulnerability? Lots of things—including chronic individual difference variables (some people are more tempermentally anxious and worried about interpersonal threats), as well as temporary features within the local ecology (e.g., being alone, or in the dark, or in a strange and unpredictable environment). Do these kinds of variables have the predicted influence on first impressions? It appears that they do. In one set of studies, Maner et al. (2005) assessed perceivers' beliefs about the emotional states of target individuals who, in fact, were not displaying any real emotional signals at all. Some of these target individuals were ethnic in-group members, and some were out-group members. Results revealed that perceivers who chronically worried about interpersonal danger were especially likely to perceive anger (but not other emotions) erroneously in the faces of out-group members (but not in-group members). Similarly, if perceivers had been made to feel temporarily fearful through entirely artificial methods (by watching a scary scene from a popular movie), they also were more likely to perceive anger (and anger only) in the faces of out-group (but not in-group) members.

A similar sort of modulation can be seen in the phenomenon whereby morphologically anomalous physical features (which may serve as heuristic cues to parasitic infection) inspire negative associations (Schaller & Duncan, 2007). In one study (Park, Faulkner, & Schaller, 2003), physically handicapped people were more likely to be associated with negative semantic concepts, and this effect was especially pronounced among individuals who either tended to feel especially vulnerable to infectious diseases or who were especially liable to experience disgust (an emotional cue for potential infection). Building on this evidence, it is interesting to consider the possibility that actual variation in the functioning of the immune system might also have effects of this sort. For instance, a natural form of immunosuppression occurs in women during the first few weeks of pregnancy, and there is evidence that this has predictable effects on emotional experiences and social attitudes (e.g., greater sensitivity to disgust, greater ethnocentrism; Fessler, Eng, & Navarrete, 2005; Navarrete, Fessler, & Eng, 2007). It's possible that among newly pregnant women and other immunosuppressed individuals (e.g., organ transplantees) the natural tendency to respond aversively to perceived morphological anomalies might also be exaggerated.

Inferential outcomes relevant to mating are also likely to be variable, depending on the extent to which perceivers are interested in pursuing mating goals. In one of their studies on emotion inference, Maner et al. (2005) found that men erroneously inferred exaggerated levels of sexual arousal from the objectively neutral facial expressions of physically attractive women. This effect was especially pronounced among men who reported a chronically active mating motive. The effect was also especially pronounced among men for whom a mating motive had been made temporarily salient by exposing them to a romantically evocative scene from a popular movie. An even better demonstration of functional flexibility in the realm of mating-related inferences is found in evidence that the female menstrual cycle moderates the strength of adaptive inferences to specific fitness-relevant stimulus features in men. A particularly fascinating phenomenon involves the inferences that women draw from the odors of men whose bodies are variable in their bilateral symmetry. There is evidence that morphological symmetry may be a signal of genetic fitness (Thornhill & Moller, 1997). There is also a basis to believe that genetic fitness (and therefore symmetry) is also signaled by body odor cues. Women are sensitive to these olfactory cues, and this has consequences on impression formation. On the basis of body odor alone, women infer that symmetrical men are sexier; and women are most sensitive to the scent of symmetry under circumstances in which the differentiation between genetically fit and unfit mates has the greatest bearing on their reproductive fitness. That is, when women are in the fertile part of their menstrual cycle, they are especially likely to infer—on the basis of odor alone—that symmetrical men are sexier (Gangestad & Thornhill, 1998; Thornhill & Gangestad, 1999b).

Fitness-relevant circumstances may also moderate the extent to which kin-connoting impressions are implicitly inferred on the basis of superficial phenotypic similarities. An evolutionary cost–benefit analysis reveals that a tendency to make false-positive kin recognition errors (judging non-kin to be kin) leads to higher fitness costs when the actual base rate of kin in the local population is lower and leads to lower fitness costs when the actual base rate of kin is higher (Reeve, 1998). One possible implication is that individuals may be more likely to make false-positive kin recognition errors when contextual information implies a relatively high base rate of kin (e.g., rural environments, large families). If there is any merit to this speculation, then the similarity-liking effect may be especially pronounced among people in rural environments or those who grew up in large families.

I don't want to drift into mere speculation just yet; so, I'll end this section of the chapter by highlighting one more empirically documented example of functional flexibility in the realm of first impression formation. This line of research takes as its starting point the fundamental fitness benefits associated with being an accepted member of a social group (Baumeister & Leary, 1995; Brewer & Caporael, 2006). Given these benefits of belongingness, it would have been adaptive to respond toward others in such ways that social connections are maintained. Moreover, should this fundamental need for social connection be threatened (through some act of social exclusion, for instance), it would have been adaptive to respond in ways that maximize the likelihood of re-establishing social connections. Is reconnection facilitated by being fearful, disdainful, or otherwise negatively inclined toward others? No, it's facilitated by social optimism and positive regard for others. The implication is that, while social exclusion may lead individuals (quite logically) to form negative impressions of those who actually do the rejecting, it may also dispose those same individuals to form unusually positive first impressions of other people—if those other people are perceived to be potential sources of social connection. A recent set of set of studies supports this set of evolutionarily informed hypotheses (Maner, DeWall, Baumeister, & Schaller, 2007). When threatened with social exclusion, people express greater interest in making new friends, they increase their desire to work with others, and (here's the finding that is most pertinent to the theme of this chapter) they form more positive first impressions of novel interaction partners. Importantly, these effects occur only when those novel target persons really are perceived to be realistic sources of social connection—a result implicating the functional nature of this bias in person perception.

DIGGING DEEPER

For the most part, evolutionary inquiries into person perception have followed an epistemic strategy analogous to that of behavioral ecology. Evolutionary logic is employed to deduce hypotheses about phenotypic outcomes (e.g., impressions, attitudes, and other cognitive knowledge structures); these hypotheses are then tested against observable data. It is understood, of course, that evolutionary processes don't produce cognitive outcomes in any direct way. Evolutionary processes operate on genes, after all, and the causal relationship between genes and cognitions involves lots of steps and is extraordinarily complicated. But if one takes an evolutionary approach seriously, one must eventually start to ask such questions as: If these impression formation phenomena are the product of evolutionary processes, just what actually evolved? Exactly what was selected for that produces these specific kinds of social inference phenomena?

Great questions. As yet, we're not even close to having satisfying answers. However, it's not too early to discuss, in a very general sort of way, the kinds of answers that are (and are not) likely to emerge over the next few decades of research. At the very least, it may be useful to do this because it is easy to be misled about just what is (and is not) logically implied by an evolutionary perspective on social cognition.

First, let's talk about learning mechanisms. There remains a common misconception that evolutionary psychological processes are independent of developmental processes in general and learning processes in particular. Nothing could be further from the truth. Genes are instrumental in guiding developmental processes as they unfold, and genes produce the many different mechanisms through which individual organisms learn (Carroll, 2005; Marcus, 2004; Moore, 2004). Reciprocally, the phenotypic expressions of many genes are influenced by the developmental context and so can be influenced by specific contextual information that is acquired through the operation of learning mechanisms (e.g., Godwin, Luckenbach, & Borski, 2003; for additional examples, see Ridley, 2003). Plus, many lines of psychological research on specific kinds of allegedly evolved response tendencies (e.g., the fear of snakes) suggest that one of the things that may have evolved is a predispostion—a sort of biological preparedness—to learn those specific tendencies in an unusually fast and efficient manner (Öhman & Mineka, 2001). This has clear implications for the way we might think about evolutionary influences on first impressions. Learning mechanisms may be integral to the allegedly evolved mechanisms through which a particular kind of fitness-relevant feature spontaneously produces a particular kind of first impression. Specifically, one of the things that may have evolved is a preparedness to learn—very quickly and efficiently—that particular association between social stimulus and adaptive response. As we dig more deeply into the question of what exactly evolved to produce specific kinds of social cognitive phenomena, we would probably be wise not to overlook the important role of evolved learning mechanisms.

Some learning mechanisms are specific to certain domains of information acquisition (e.g., when a taste aversion is acquired through one-trial learning, it is the result of a highly specific form of associative conditioning; Moore, 2004). Other learning mechanisms are much more general in their application. Many speculations about the evolutionary bases of cognition focus on the alleged domain specificity of the underlying mechanisms (e.g., Kanazawa, 2004). These speculations are often accompanied by speculations about specific regions of brain anatomy that might be dedicated to these psychological adaptations. In proposing an evolved module of fear learning, for instance, Öhman and Mineka (2001) point to neuroscience evidence indicating the presence of neural circuitry dedicated specifically to fear learning. Similarly, in speculating about the existence of an evolved personality judgment instinct, Haselton and Funder (2006) suggest that such an instinct, if it exists, would be characterized by a dedicated neural structure.

Neuroanatomical evidence certainly can inform our understanding of evolutionary processes that lie at the root of psychological phenomena. However, this does not mean that every evolutionary speculation about cognition must be accompanied by the corollary assumption that some neural structure be dedicated uniquely to its operation. Evolutionary processes typically produce phenotypic "improvements" not by inventing whole new anatomical structures but by tinkering with existing ones. Just as birds' beaks may evolve to be longer (in response to changes in the local ecological conditions), existing cognitive mechanisms may evolve to be responsive to a wider range of eliciting stimuli. Mechanisms that once served primarily to facilitate the detection and avoidance of dangerous nonsocial objects (e.g., snakes) might have evolved, over time, in such a way that they are now activated also in the social domain, to facilitate the detection and avoidance of potentially dangerous conspecifics (e.g., coalitional out-group members). This kind of adaptation may involve modest changes in only a very few genes and is unlikely to be associated with any sort of uniquely dedicated neural structure (at least not of the sort that can be detected with the methods of contemporary cognitive neuroscience). Nonetheless, if such a response truly is an adaptation, evidence should be found at a more subtle—genetic—level of analysis.

So, now we're talking about genes. Here again it is important to think sensibly about what a genetic influence on social inference might (or might not) mean. The effects of genes on phenotypic responses are often not the result of the presence (or absence) of some specific gene (or set of genes) but rather whether that gene (or set of genes)—even if present—is switched on or off; and that depends on a lot of other factors in the immediate environment (Carroll, 2005). How might this be relevant to the study of social inference? Consider the fact that there is plenty of evidence attesting to sex differences in social inference processes, and many scholars have speculated about the evolutionary bases of these sex differences (e.g., Haselton & Nettle, 2006). It's tempting to assume that this speculation implies that there must be a specific set of genes associated with each specific social inference phenomenon, and that these specific genes differ between men and women. Well, perhaps. But it is also entirely plausible that, if any specific set of genes is associated with these specific social inference phenomena, those genes are equally present in both men and women. What may have evolved is the tendency for those genes to be turned on (or off) in response to specific kinds of bodily signals (e.g., hormone levels) that are diagnostic of the perceiver's sex.

Again, this is just crude speculation. I claim no expertise whatsoever when discussing evolutionary processes at this genetic level of analysis. Nor can I claim any expertise on learning mechanisms or neuroanatomy. I broach these topics simply to illustrate three more general points. First, if one is to take seriously an evolutionary perspective on social inference, one must eventually begin to ask difficult questions about what exactly might have evolved to produce the phenomena we witness at a behavioral level of analysis. Second, in order to try to address those questions, we have to dig deeper and consider events operating on many additional levels of scientific analysis. And third, if we are to ever successfully provide answers to those questions, we cannot just gesture vaguely (which is all I've done here) toward those additional level of analysis; we will have to pay serious attention to advances in fields such as cognitive neuroscience, psychoneuroendocrinology, developmental biology, and functional genomics.

Yes, it's a serious challenge. And, yes, it will take considerable collective effort. But the scientific payoff should be substantial. There is already abundant evidence attesting to the intellectual benefits associated with an evolutionary approach to first impressions. An evolutionary perspective provides a rigorous means of generating insights into the ancient roots of contemporary social inference phenomena. This helps to build coherent conceptual bridges to other exciting scientific disciplines. An evolutionary perspective also provides a means of coherently linking together many superficially distinct kinds of social inference phenomena. In this chapter, for instance, I have discussed a wide variety of phenomena pertaining to first impressions (e.g., spontaneous trait inferences, the dimensional structure of person perception, the effect of attitude similarity on liking). These phenomena are typically treated by textbooks as conceptually independent factoids. But they are not. An evolutionary framework helps connect the conceptual dots between these different facts. Finally, and perhaps most importantly, an evolutionary perspective can be extraordinarily generative. When employed smartly, these logical tools promise to yield an enormous set of novel hypotheses and brand-new discoveries about first impressions.

REFERENCES

Ambady, N., Bernieri, F. J., & Richeson, J. A. (2000). Toward a histology of social behavior: Judgmental accuracy from thin slices of the behavioral stream. *Advances in Experimental Social Psychology, 32,* 201–271.

Bargh, J. A., & Chartrand, T. L. (1999). The unbearable automaticity of being. *American Psychologist, 54,* 462–479.

Baumeister, R. F., Bratslavsky, E., Finkenauer, C., & Vohs, K. D. (2001). Bad is stronger than good. *Review of General Psychology, 5,* 323–370.

Baumeister, R. F., & Leary, M. R. (1995). The need to belong: Desire for interpersonal attachments as a fundamental human motivation. *Psychological Bulletin, 117,* 497–529.

Brewer, M. B., & Caporael, L. (2006). An evolutionary perspective on social identity: Revisiting groups. In M. Schaller, J. A. Simpson, & D. T. Kenrick (Eds.), *Evolution and social psychology* (pp. 143–161). New York: Psychology Press.

Byrne, D., Gouaux, C., Griffitt, W., Lamberth, J., Murakawa, N., Prasad, M. B., et al. (1971). The ubiquitous relationship: Attitude similarity and attraction: A cross-cultural study. *Human Relations, 24,* 201–207.

Carlston, D. E., & Skowronski, J. J. (2005). Linking versus thinking: Evidence for the different associative and attributional bases of spontaneous trait transference and spontaneous trait inference. *Journal of Personality and Social Psychology, 89,* 884–898.

Carroll, S. B. (2005). *Endless forms most beautiful.* New York: Norton.

Conway, L. G., III, & Schaller, M. (2002). On the verifiability of evolutionary psychological theories: An analysis of the psychology of scientific persuasion. *Personality and Social Psychology Review, 6,* 152–166.

Cottrell, C. A., Neuberg, S. L., & Li, N. P. (2007). What do people desire in others? A sociofunctional perspective on the importance of different valued characteristics. *Journal of Personality and Social Psychology, 92,* 208–231.

DeBruine, L. M. (2002). Facial resemblance enhances trust. *Proceedings of the Royal Society B, 269,* 1307–1312.

DeBruine, L. M. (2005). Trustworthy but not lust-worthy: Context-specific effects of facial resemblance. *Proceedings of the Royal Society B, 272,* 919–922.

Duncan, L. A. (2005). *Heuristic cues automatically activate disease cognitions despite rational knowledge to the contrary.* Unpublished master's thesis, University of British Columbia, Vancouver, BC, Canada.

Eagly, A. H., Ashmore, R. D., Makhijani, M. G., & Longo, L. C. (1991). What is beautiful is good, but . . . : A meta-analytic review of research on the physical attractiveness stereotype. *Psychological Bulletin, 110,* 109–128.

Fessler, D. M. T., Eng, S. J., & Navarrete, C. D. (2005). Elevated disgust sensitivity in the first trimester of pregnancy: Evidence supporting the compensatory prophylaxis hypothesis. *Evolution and Human Behavior, 26,* 344–351.

Fink, B., & Penton-Voak, I. (2002). Evolutionary psychology of facial attractiveness. *Current Directions in Psychological Science, 11,* 154–158.

Fox, E., Lester, V., Russo, R., Bowles, R. J., Pichler, A., & Dutton, K. (2000). Facial expressions of emotion: Are angry faces detected more efficiently? *Cognition and Emotion, 14,* 61–92.

Gangestad, S. W., & Thornhill, R. (1998). Menstrual cycle variation in women's preference for the scent of symmetrical men. *Proceedings of the Royal Society B, 262,* 727–733.

Gigerenzer, G., Todd, P. M., & the ABC Research Group. (1999). *Simple heuristics that make us smart.* New York: Oxford University Press.

Gilbert, D. T., & Malone, P. S. (1995). The correspondence bias. *Psychological Bulletin, 117,* 21–38.

Godwin, J., Luckenbach, J. A., & Borski, R. J. (2003). Ecology meets endocrinology: Environmental sex determination in fishes. *Evolution and Development, 5,* 40–49.

Haselton, M. G., & Funder, D. (2006). The evolution of accuracy and bias in social judgment. In M. Schaller, J. A. Simpson, & D. T. Kenrick (Eds.), *Evolution and social psychology* (pp. 15–37). New York: Psychology Press.

Haselton, M. G., & Nettle, D. (2006). The paranoid optimist: An integrative evolutionary model of cognitive biases. *Personality and Social Psychology Review, 10,* 47–66.

Heberlein, A. S., & Saxe, R. R. (2005). Dissociation between emotion and personality judgments: Convergent evidence from functional neuroimaging. *NeuroImage, 28,* 770–777.

Hepper, P. G. (Ed.). (1991). *Kin recognition.* New York: Cambridge University Press.

Judd, C. M., James-Hawkins, L., Yzerbyt, V., & Kashima, Y. (2005). Fundamental dimensions of social judgment: Understanding the relations between judgments of competence and warmth. *Journal of Personality and Social Psychology, 89,* 899–913.

Kanazawa, S. (2004). General intelligence as a domain-specific adaptation. *Psychological Review, 111,* 512–523.

Kelley, H. H. (1950). The warm–cold variable in first impressions of persons. *Journal of Personality, 18,* 431–439.

Maner, J. K., DeWall, C. N., Baumeister, R. F., & Schaller, M. (2007). Does social exclusion motivate interpersonal reconnection? Resolving the "porcupine problem." *Journal of Personality and Social Psychology, 92,* 42–55.

Maner, J. K., Kenrick, D. T., Becker, D. V., Robertson, T. E., Hofer, B., Neuberg, S., et al. (2005). Functional projection: How fundamental social motives can bias interpersonal perception. *Journal of Personality and Social Psychology, 88,* 63–78.

Marcus, G. (2004). *The birth of the mind.* New York: Basic Books.

Moore, B. R. (2004). The evolution of learning. *Biological Review, 79,* 301–335.

Navarrete, C. D., Fessler, D. M. T., & Eng, S. J. (2007). Elevated ethnocentrism in the first trimester of pregnancy. *Evolution and Human Behavior, 28,* 60–65.

Nesse, R. M. (2005). Natural selection and the regulation of defenses: A signal detection analysis of the smoke detector principle. *Evolution and Human Behavior, 26,* 88–105.

Newman, L. S., & Uleman, J. S. (1989). Spontaneous trait inference. In J. S. Uleman & J. A. Bargh (Eds.), *Unintended thought* (pp. 155–188). New York: Guilford Press.

Öhman, A., & Mineka, S. (2001). Fears, phobias, and preparedness: Toward an evolved module of fear and fear learning. *Psychological Review, 108,* 483–522.

Olsson, A., Ebert, J. P., Banaji, M. R., & Phelps, E. A. (2005). The role of social groups in the persistence of learned fear. *Science, 309,* 785–787.

Palmeri, T. J. (1999). Theories of automaticity and the power law of practice. *Journal of Experimental Psychology: Learning, Memory, and Cognition, 25,* 543–551.

Park, J. H., Faulkner, J., & Schaller, M. (2003). Evolved disease-avoidance processes and contemporary anti-social behavior: Prejudicial attitudes and avoidance of people with physical disabilities. *Journal of Nonverbal Behavior, 27,* 65–87.

Park, J. H., & Schaller, M. (2005). Does attitude similarity serve as a heuristic cue for kinship?: Evidence of an implicit cognitive association. *Evolution and Human Behavior, 26,* 158–170.

Peeters, G., & Czapinski, J. (1990). Positive–negative asymmetry in evaluations: The distinction between affective and informational negativity effects. *European Review of Social Psychology, 1*, 33–60.

Perrett, D. I., Burt, D. M., Penton-Voak, I. S., Lee, K. J., Rowland, D. A., & Edwards, R. (1999). Symmetry and human facial attractiveness. *Evolution and Human Behavior, 20*, 295–307.

Reeve, H. K. (1998). Acting for the good of others: Kinship and reciprocity with some new twists. In C. Crawford & D. L. Krebs (Eds.), *Handbook of evolutionary psychology: Ideas, issues, and applications* (pp. 43–85). Mahwah, NJ: Erlbaum.

Rendall, D. (2004). "Recognizing" kin: Mechanisms, media, minds, modules, and muddles. In B. Chapais & C. M. Berman (Eds.), *Kinship and behavior in primates* (pp. 295–316). Oxford, UK: Oxford University Press.

Ridley, M. (2003). *The agile gene.* Toronto: HarperCollins.

Rosenberg, S., Nelson, C., & Vivekananthan, P. S. (1968). A multidimensional approach to the structure of personality impressions. *Journal of Personality and Social Psychology, 9*, 283–294.

Rothbart, M., & Park, B. (1986). On the confirmability and disconfirmability of trait concepts. *Journal of Personality and Social Psychology, 50*, 131–142.

Rozin, P., & Royzman, E. (2001). Negativity bias, negativity dominance, and contagion. *Personality and Social Psychology Review, 5*, 296–320.

Schaller, M., & Duncan, L. A. (2007). The behavioral immune system: Its evolution and social psychological implications. In J. P. Forgas, M. G. Haselton, & W. von Hippel (Eds.), *Evolution and the social mind: Evolutionary psychology and social cognition* (pp. 293–307). New York: Psychology Press.

Schaller, M., & Neuberg, S. L. (2008). Intergroup prejudices and intergroup conflicts. In C. Crawford & D. L. Krebs (Eds.), *Foundations of evolutionary psychology: Ideas, issues, and applications* (pp. 399–412). Mahwah, NJ: Erlbaum.

Schaller, M., Park, J. H., & Kenrick, D. T. (2007). Human evolution and social cognition. In R. I. M. Dunbar & L. Barrett (Eds.), *Oxford handbook of evolutionary psychology* (pp. 491–504). Oxford, UK: Oxford University Press.

Schaller, M., Simpson, J. A., & Kenrick, D. T. (2006). *Evolution and social psychology.* New York: Psychology Press.

Schmitt, D. P., & Pilcher, J. J. (2004). Evaluating evidence of psychological adaptation: How do we know one when we see one? *Psychological Science, 15*, 643–649.

Schupp, H. T., Öhman, A., Junghofer, M., Weike, A. I., Stockburger, J., & Hamm, A. O. (2004). The facilitated processing of threatening faces: An ERP analysis. *Emotion, 4*, 189–200.

Skowronski, J. J. (2002). Honesty and intelligence judgments of individuals and groups: The effects of entity-related behavior diagnosticity and implicit theories. *Social Cognition, 20*, 136–169.

Skowronski, J. J., & Carlston, D. E. (1992). Caught in the act: When impressions based on highly diagnostic behaviours are resistant to contradiction. *European Journal of Social Psychology, 22*, 435–452.

Skowronski, J. J., Carlston, D. E., Mae, L., & Crawford, M. T. (1998). Spontaneous trait transference: Communicators take on the qualities they describe in others. *Journal of Personality and Social Psychology, 74,* 837–848.

Tesser, A. (1993). The importance of heritability in psychological research: The case of attitudes. *Psychological Review, 100,* 129–142.

Thornhill, R., & Gangestad, S. W. (1999a). Facial attractiveness. *Trends in Cognitive Sciences, 3,* 452–460.

Thornhill, R., & Gangestad, S. W. (1999b). The scent of symmetry: A human sex pheromone that signals fitness? *Evolution and Human Behavior, 20,* 175–201.

Thornhill, R., & Moller, A. P. (1997). Developmental stability, disease, and medicine. *Biological Reviews, 72,* 497–548.

Zebrowitz, L. A., Fellous, J. M., Mignault, A., & Andreoletti, C. (2003). Trait impressions as overgeneralized responses to adaptively significant facial qualities: Evidence from connectionist modeling. *Personality and Social Psychology Review, 7,* 194–215.

Zebrowitz, L. A., & Montepare, J. M. (1992). Impressions of babyfaced males and females across the lifespan. *Developmental Psychology, 28,* 1143–1152.

CHAPTER 2

First Impressions

Peeking at the
Neural Underpinnings

Nicholas O. Rule
Nalini Ambady

The chapters in this book provide considerable insight as to the sources of information that contribute to first impressions, the cognitive and mental processes that comprise first impressions, how first impressions affect interpersonal interactions, as well the ways in which we use first impressions in our social world. In this chapter, we examine insights from social and cognitive neuroscience to address the question of the neural underpinnings of first impressions.

We define first impressions as the initial perception and formation of thoughts about another. Our overarching goal is to sketch how the process of forming a first impression occurs at the neural level. We do so in a temporally linear fashion for the sake of simplicity while recognizing that some of the processes we discuss might occur concurrently. We begin with the initial perception of a person, a face, or an object from the environment. Although initial perception can occur by means of input from all five senses, it usually takes place via vision and/or hearing. We then move to the initial, most primitive, subcortical structures (e.g., the amygdala), where this information is first filtered and formed into what we might consider social thought. From there, we go on to the upper cortex—that part of the brain that most separates us humans from other primates and in which the information takes on a meaning that is truly social. Finally, we end with the processing of this information in the frontal and prefrontal cortices. This is where the information drawn in from the outside world becomes fully processed and crosses the barrier into what we think of as consciousness and the mind. At that point, our impression of another is formed, and this is where we begin to have access to that impression via our conscious thought. At consciousness, the rest of what is discussed in this book begins—our impressions of others and the concomitant, and resultant, behaviors, processes, and complex relationships that color our social world.

SIGHT AND SOUND: THE ORIGINS OF FIRST IMPRESSIONS

The first step in the person perception process begins with perceptions derived from various sensory systems. Although the neural correlates of touch (Deibert, Kraut, Kremen, & Hart, 1999), taste (Norgren, Hajnal, & Mungarndee, 2006), and smell (Shepherd, 2006) have all been explored, arguably the principal senses for perceiving other *people* are sight and sound. Therefore, we consider the starting point of person perception and first impressions to lie within the domains of the visual and auditory cortices, with both human behavior and the neuroimaging research tending to focus on the former (sight) over the latter (sound).

Seeing Others

Explorations of the visual system and person perception have focused on the fusiform face area (FFA). This is an area of the fusiform cortex that appears to respond selectively to faces (though this is debated—see Tarr & Gauthier, 2000). Very few neural structures can boast the sort of specificity demonstrated by the FFA. Despite attempts at domain-specific assignment of behavioral functions to discrete brain regions, none has been as successful as the assignment of face responsiveness to the FFA.

However, person perception can be even better understood when placed in the context of the entire visual system. Our first representation of others occurs in the primary visual cortex (also known as the striate cortex and typically focused on area V1). The visual cortex shows differentiation of objects versus people very early in the perceptual process (e.g., Wang et al., 1999). Signals from the eyes, essentially representing colors, feed to the visual cortex straight to area V1. These colors are then assembled into patterns and the patterns assembled into shapes. The shapes are then interpreted and sorted for transport out of the striate cortex along two paths. One, the dorsal or "where/how" stream, primarily deals with motion—sending the semirefined visual information in a dorso-cortical direction toward areas in the parietal and temporal cortices, such as the middle temporal and posterior parietal areas (Claeys et al., 2004; Servos, Osu, Santi, & Kawato, 2002; Wang et al., 1999). The other, ventral or "what," stream primarily deals with objects, body parts, and faces, with such perceptions resulting in the identification of others (Downing, Jiang, Shuman, & Kanwisher, 2001; Herholz et al., 2001; Kanwisher, 2000; Kanwisher, McDermott, & Chun, 1997; Sperling et al., 2001; Wang et al., 1999; but see also Gauthier, Tarr, Anderson, Skudlarski, & Gore, 1999; Tarr & Gauthier, 2000).

On leaving the striate cortex, the first stop along the ventral stream is the extrastriate. The extrastriate contains two areas of particular interest regarding person perception and first impressions. The first of these is the extrastriate body area (EBA; Downing et al., 2001), which deals with the perception of both human and nonhuman body parts (with the exception of the face) and is distinctly sensitive to biological forms. For instance, transcranial magnetic stimulation (TMS) delivered to the EBA causes a temporary lesion to the area that results in the impairment of body part perception while leaving object part perception unaffected (Urgesi, Berlucchi, & Aglioti, 2004). Moreover, unlike higher-order cortical structures that code for the *actions* of body parts, the EBA is preferentially responsive to the perception of *static* aspects of the human form, such as identity (Downing, Peelen, Wiggett, & Tew, 2006; Urgesi, Candidi, Ionta, & Aglioti, 2007). Hence, the EBA plays an important role in perceiving others.

The second extrastriate structure is the fusiform gyrus. The fusiform shows specificity for both perceptual expertise (Tarr & Gauthier, 2000) as well as responsiveness to faces (Kanwisher, 2000), suggesting that humans are expert face processors.[1] Hence, the face-selective area of the fusiform gyrus is known as the fusiform *face* area (see Wojciulik, Kanwisher, & Driver, 1998) and is one of the most important neural structures in the formation of first impressions.

The FFA is most likely the first place in which face stimuli are processed, when faces are intact. When faces are not intact and only parts of faces are perceived, the EBA shows preferential activation (though the EBA does not respond to fully intact faces, thereby distinguishing it in function from the FFA). In addition to the FFA and EBA, an area within the striate cortex also shows activation to face stimuli: the face-responsive occipital region (FROR) within the inferior occipital gyrus. The FROR is believed to respond prior to the FFA and may possibly serve as a relay station for sending confirmed face stimuli to the FFA for further processing (see Winston, Henson, Fine-Goulden, & Dolan, 2004). The FFA plays an important role in determining the identity of a perceived target. This conclusion comes from research that examines how brain areas differentially respond to spatial frequency information in faces (e.g., Vuilleumier, Armony, Driver, & Dolan, 2003; see Figure 2.1). The term "spatial frequency information" refers to the manner in which gray-scale values change relative to their neighbors within an image. Slowly varying changes in gray scale across an image constitute the low spatial frequencies. Pixel values that vary radically from adjacent pixels in an image make up the high spatial frequencies. High spatial frequencies are important for carrying information about identity, whereas low spatial frequencies are important for carrying information about other qualities of the face, such as emotion. The FFA responds to high spatial frequencies, whereas low spatial frequency information bypasses the FFA and, instead, travels more dorsally to the thalamus (Vuilleumier, Henson, Driver, & Dolan, 2002).

Along the ventral stream of visual information processing, the immediate next stop after the FFA is the amygdala. The amygdala is a structure that is critical for, among other things, the interpretation of socially relevant signals such as affective valence and threat (e.g., Phelps, 2006). Although we will provide a full explanation of the amygdala's role in first impression formation later in this chapter, for the purposes of the FFA it is important to know that the amygdala and FFA are directly linked. It is supposed that the FFA feeds information about faces and facial identity directly to the amygdala, which then processes the stimulus for cues to threat and/or familiarity (Vuilleumier et al., 2003). Interestingly, the connections between the amygdala and FFA appear to work in both directions: the amygdala receives input from visual areas but also sends information back, influencing visual processing (e.g., Winston, Strange, O'Doherty, & Dolan, 2002; Vuilleumier, Richardson, Armony, Driver, & Dolan, 2004). Indeed, the influence of the amygdala on the visual cortex seems to be greater than the visual cortex's influence on the amygdala (Iidaka et al., 2001).

Despite the presence of direct links between the FFA and the amygdala, recent evidence suggests that the FFA does not communicate information about emotional expressions directly to the amygdala. Rather, high spatial frequencies are sent forward to the FFA and serve to establish identity, whereas low spatial frequencies take a slight dorsal detour just above the FFA to the thalamus. It is believed that the thalamus recognizes these low spatial frequencies and sends the information directly downward to the amygdala, where the low spatial frequency informa-

Low-spatial frequencies   Full Spectrum   High-spatial frequencies

FIGURE 2.1. Visual information about faces is processed in distinct neural areas based on spatial frequency. Low-spatial frequency information (left of center) encodes aspects of the face such as emotional expression. This information is carried to the thalamus and then on to the amygdala. High-spatial frequency information (right of center) contains the features necessary for determining identity. This information is fed from the striate cortex to the fusiform and then to the amygdala.

tion about emotion is integrated with the high spatial frequency information about identity (see Vuilleumier et al., 2003). It has also been suggested that low spatial frequency information from the optic nerve may feed into the thalamus, where it is relayed to the amygdala (see Vuilleumier et al., 2003; Vuilleumier & Pourtois, 2007). This process is thought to occur *prior* to the provision of visual information from the occipital cortex, possibly influencing early visual representations. But the precise timing of these processes is not known, as imaging technology cannot noninvasively track such low-level neuroelectrical activity in these regions.

Although we may tend to assume that our perception of the world is like a camera, feeding directly to our consciousness, growing evidence shows that this is not the case. For example, the concept of "blindsight" refers to patients with damage to visual cortex whose capacity for retino-optical perception is unimpaired. Although these individuals may experience the world as blind, they nonetheless take in visual information from their eyes, which provide input to the brain and cortex (Vuilleumier et al., 2004). Thus, patients with blindsight show activation to threatening stimuli in the amygdala. Although these patients do not report the conscious experience of seeing anything, they show amygdala responses to threatening stimuli similar to the way that individuals with intact visual cortices do (Vuilleumier et al., 2004). Blindsight patients also report fairly accurate intuitive guesses about the physical properties or valence of stimuli (Tong,

2003; Vuilleumier et al., 2004). For them, this experience seems like pure guesswork, but the higher-than-random accuracy rates of such guesses suggest that, despite the absence of processing in the striate cortex, visual information transmitted via this secondary, retino-thalamic pathway can also be passed on to higher-level cortical structures, such as the orbito-frontal and cingulate cortices, allowing for reason and decision making. Insights from blindsight patients regarding nonconscious visual information processing have important implications for intuitive judgments, which often form the basis of first impressions.

Although the face is extremely important in the formation of first impressions, other channels of communication also provide visual information that is processed when perceiving others. Returning again to the striate cortex, particular regions (such as V1, V2, and V3; Servos et al., 2002) are important for the perception of shape and motion. Indeed, biological motion seems to be specially recognized in the brain, and evidence from neuroimaging studies shows that shape and motion cues can be of particular importance in forming impressions about others.

For example, the superior temporal sulcus has been shown to exhibit increased activity in response to human action and in the extraction of information about biological motion (e.g., Beauchamp, Lee, Haxby, & Martin, 2003). Studies in this area use point-light displays to examine biological motion (see Kozlowski & Cutting, 1977). Point-light displays use reflectors attached to the joints of individuals wearing dark clothes while being filmed in a dark room. All that is seen from the person's movement are the points of light as floating dots moving about. At first, the dots appear to be nothing more than an array of scrambled points against a dark background. However, once the individual begins to move, it becomes quickly apparent that the dots represent motion. This movement activates the superior temporal sulous (STS) and is believed to represent an area especially attuned to social meaning.[2]

That the STS is involved with social meaning is further supported by the finding that the STS becomes active during experiments involving the inference of thoughts and intentions. Theory of mind refers to the ability to infer the thoughts of others either by taking their perspective and imagining oneself in their shoes ("simulation theory") or by reasoned observation wherein one extrapolates the behaviors of others as might a naive scientist reasoning about a phenomenon ("theory theory"; see Gallagher & Frith, 2003, for a review; see also Chapter 3 in this volume). Since the STS is involved in perceiving biological movement, and because movement is one of the best cues in inferring someone's intentions and thoughts, it makes sense that the STS should be involved in thinking about the intentions of others. Similarly, the STS has been implicated in detecting eye gaze, which also signals intention and focus of attention (Hoffman & Haxby, 2000; Pelphrey, Viola, & McCarthy, 2004; Pourtois et al., 2004).[3]

Hearing Others

The tone of voice has been consistently shown in behavioral studies to signal cues to identity (e.g., Gaudio, 1994), emotion (e.g., Johnstone, van Reekum, Oakes, & Davidson, 2006), and intent and thought (see Schiffrin, Tannen, & Hamilton, 2001). Hence, perceptions of others' voices play an important role in forming first impressions, as well.

The social and cognitive neuroscience of vision has received much more attention than the social and cognitive neuroscience of audition, largely owing to the technological limitations of imaging auditory activation in the noisy environment of the fMRI scanner. The studies that have been done have shown some very interesting findings. For instance, emotional prosody (tone of voice), as contrasted with neutral and nonemotional speech, activates the right-middle and superior temporal gyri (see also Grandjean et al., 2005; Mitchell, Elliott, Barry, Cruttenden, & Woodruff, 2003). These activations are distinct from language processing, which typically occurs in the left temporal gyrus. One implication of such studies is that the middle temporal gyrus is active for complex emotional processing, whereas the superior temporal gyrus is active for semantic prosody. Even more importantly, these studies suggest that certain parts of the brain may be especially attuned to particular types of sounds produced by other people.

Sander, Roth, and Scheich (2003) explored how the brain responds to nonverbal vocalizations of laughing and crying. Using a low-noise fMRI scanner, they were able to locate differences between the perception of laughing and crying in the amygdala, insula, and auditory cortex. Activation was greater for laughing in the auditory cortex than for crying, and activation in the amygdala during the control task (detecting pitch shifts in the stimuli) was reported as evidence for amygdala activation independent of the emotional aspects of the stimuli. In another study, Nakamura et al. (2001)—using PET scanning, which does not pose the noise constraints of fMRI—explored how the brain responds differently to familiar versus unfamiliar voices. They found that the left frontal pole and right temporal pole were principally active in response to familiar voices and that activity in these areas was related to memory for voices. Pourtois, de Gelder, Bol, and Crommelinck (2005), also using PET scanning, expanded on this work by demonstrating that combinations of audio (voices) and visual (faces) information activated the left lateral temporal cortex more than either auditory or visual stimuli alone. Similarly, happy voices showed greater activation in middle temporal gyri and the inferior frontal gyrus than did angry voices (Johnstone et al., 2006).

While the body of research examining how the brain responds to social auditory information may not be as extensive as the literature examining visual stimuli, this work has much to offer to our understanding of the perception of others and the formation of first impressions. Particularly relevant is the implication that the brain is "tuned" to receive and respond to social vocalizations. Such tuning suggests a biological basis for the idea that people form impressions of others from the vocal cues that those others emit.

INTEGRATING IMPRESSIONS AT THE AMYGDALA

We turn now to another level of brain involvement in impression formation: the integration of information at the amygdala. Although the role of the amygdala in impression formation is somewhat debated, most researchers agree that the amygdala is responsive to a range of emotional stimuli, particularly fear (Fitzgerald, Angstadt, Jelsone, Nathan, & Phan, 2006). The amygdala is necessary for both the acquisition as well as the expression of conditioned fear responses (Phelps, 2006). For example, amygdala lesions impair fear recognition, causing unfriendly faces to be perceived as friendly (Adolphs, Baron-Cohen, & Tranel, 2002; Adolphs, Tranel, & Damsio, 1998; see also Ochsner, 2006). The amygdala responds even to subliminal presentations of fearful faces and to eyes expressing fear (Whalen et al., 1998; Whalen et al., 2004).[4] In addition, heightened amygdala activity has been shown to correspond to higher emotional intensity (Cunningham, Raye, & Johnson, 2004).

Responsiveness in the amygdala across a variety of social tasks has led scientists to ascribe different purposes to the amygdala. For example, some claim that the amygdala is responsive to variations in familiarity, wherein less familiar stimuli (which may be inherently more threatening at first perception) trigger greater amygdala activation (e.g., Whalen et al., 2001). Others, however, have suggested that the amygdala is responsive to changes in the environment (Knight, Smith, Cheng, Stein, & Helmstetter, 2004; LaBar, Crupain, Voyvodic, & McCarthy, 2003; see also Winston et al., 2002). Although we cannot resolve this debate in this chapter, a similar theme that is highly relevant to the formation of first impressions exists among each of these theories. Specifically, fear, familiarity, and stimulus change all appear related to threat and affect. Indeed, as we have noted in our prior discussion of both visual and auditory perceptions, amygdala activation is important in the perception of threatening and affective stimuli that are important in forming first impressions of others, whether they be faces, bodies, or voices.

The amygdala has also been implicated in judgments of trustworthiness. Winston et al. (2002) have shown that the amygdala bilaterally responds to untrustworthy faces. Although unilateral damage to the amygdala does not disrupt trustworthiness judgments (suggesting that either right or left amygadalae are sufficient to produce responses to untrustworthy faces), damage to the ventral-medial prefrontal cortex (vmPFC), which is projected to by the amygdala, does produce deficits in such judgments. In addition, both explicit and implicit assessments of trustworthiness are associated with orbitofrontal cortex (OFC) activation, presumably because of the connections between the amygdala, the OFC, and the ventral anterior cingulate cortex (vACC; Williams et al., 2006; Winston et al., 2002). Similarly, feedback from the amygdala to hippocampal and visual areas results in increased memory and perception, respectively, for emotionally salient stimuli (Cahill, Uncapher, Kilpatrick, Alkire, & Turner, 2004).

Detecting emotions in other individuals is critical to forming impressions of their mental states, and connection patterns between the amygdala and other brain areas attest to the amygdala's importance in this regard. For example, the amygdala has direct neural projections to the OFC, an area of the frontal cortex that is largely responsible for higher-level emotional processing. The amygdala also has direct connections to the vACC, possibly constituting the final leg of the ventral processing stream that originated in the striate cortex (Cassell & Wright, 1986; Porrino, Crane, & Goldman-Rakic, 1981; Rolls, 2007). One implication of this connection pattern is that information about a target's emotional state may be passed on to higher brain centers even before the striate cortex has completed its visual analysis of the stimulus. As noted earlier in this chapter, information from a target's face may be transmitted rapidly from the amygdala to the vmPFC, possibly by virtue of a retinothalamic pathway that feeds to the amygdala directly from the optic nerve (Vuilleumier et al., 2003; Williams et al., 2006). However, also projecting from the amygdala is a dorsal stream (see Palermo & Rhodes, 2007), which ultimately terminates in the dorsal frontal cortex (dFC; including dorsal ACC), the area most responsible for reasoning and decision making. The fact that the amygdala plays an important role in the communication of emotional stimuli to both OFC and dFC regions fits with the observation that the amygdala is a key player in the formation of impressions of others (Adolphs et al., 1998; Adolphs et al., 2002; Engell, Haxby, & Todorov, 2007; Winston et al., 2004). However, although the amygdala is highly involved in such social inferences and subserves frontal activations, damage to the amygdala does not entirely eliminate social acuity, suggesting that multiple systems are involved in the process of understanding others (Adolphs, 2006).

Despite the consistent relations of these patterns of brain activation to person perception, there is increasing evidence that individual differences influence neural activation. For example, whereas the amygdala and FFA show decreased activation in response to happy faces among depressed patients, they show increased activation in response to happy faces among healthy controls (Surguladze et al., 2005).[5] Amygdala activation is also attenuated by participant and target gender such that men show greater left amygdala activation in response to women's faces, whereas women show no difference in the extent to which target gender activates the amygdala in either hemisphere (Fischer et al., 2004). Moreover, women show greater activation in the sublenticular extended amygdala and rostral anterior cingulate cortex (racc) when viewing negatively valenced versus positively valenced images, whereas men show no difference in activation across image type (Klein et al., 2003; see also Kesler-West et al., 2001). Similar differences are found for amygdala activation involved in emotional memories. Recall of emotionally arousing events increases activation of the left amygdala in women and the right amygdala in men (Cahill et al., 2004). Finally, personality traits, too, may moderate amygdala activation such that extraverted persons show increased activation in the amygdala, caudate, and putamen to positive stimuli whereas neurotic persons show decreased activation to such stimuli (Canli et al., 2001).

GETTING TOGETHER IN THE FRONTAL CORTEX

The frontal cortex serves as the terminus for both dorsal and ventral streams from the amygdala and serves as a final point of integration for information derived from the senses. More specifically, projections from the amygdala ventrally to the OFC are primarily responsible for communicating emotional information, which is then carried superiorly to the rACC. Projections from the amygdala dorsally, however, also terminate in the anterior cingulate cortex (ACC), but in the dorsal areas. From the ACC, information is distributed to areas of the frontal cortex for higher-level thought. The anterior rostral ACC (arACC) is connected to the OFC and reacts to information about the emotional characteristics of a stimulus. The posterior rostral ACC (prACC), however, is the site associated with attention and the monitoring and detection of error. This area is activated when an interruption to continuous processing occurs, such as pain, errors, or the violation of expectations (Adolphs, 2006; Amodio & Frith, 2006). Similarly, the dorsal ACC is implicated in control (Keri, Decety, Roland, &

Gulyas, 2004). Thus, the ACC has primarily been implicated in decision making and the integration of more "rational" cognitive processes with more "irrational" emotional processes (see also Fichtenholtz et al., 2004; Northoff et al., 2004). Similarly, the OFC monitors the outcomes of events, such as rewards and punishments (Amodio & Frith, 2006).

Moreover, although the majority of direct connections are between the amygdala and OFC (at least in terms of emotion), reciprocal paths between the OFC and ventral and dorsal prefrontal cortex (PFC) are also important for emotion regulation (Hariri, Mattay, Tessitore, Fera, & Weinberger, 2003). For instance, activity in the right ventral PFC and the ACC appear to modulate activity in the amygdala, suggesting a feedback control mechanism from such frontally oriented activities as labeling emotional expressions (Hariri et al., 2003). Emotional valence also seems to implicate distinct neural regions, at least for facial expressions. For instance, although all emotional expressions may activate the amygdala, PFC, and FFA, facial expressions of negative emotions appear to activate the right OFC whereas facial expressions of positive emotions appear to activate the right angular gyrus (Iidaka et al., 2001).

Other regions of the frontal cortex also contribute to understanding the neural substrates of first impressions. For example, the dorsal-medial prefrontal cortex (dmPFC), has been shown to be active during judgments of others when one's own affective experience is necessary to make the evaluation (Gusnard, Akbudak, Shulman, & Raichle, 2001) and for impression formation, generally (Mitchell, Macrae, & Banaji, 2004). Moreover, information that is diagnostic of a target, such as the statement "has a bad temper" paired with a face, activates the dmPFC automatically. However, nondiagnostic information does not automatically activate the dmPFC but only activates the dmPFC if the information is somehow relevant to forming an impression, indicating that the dmPFC is implicated in thinking about others with the goal of forming an impression (Mitchell, Cloutier, Banaji, & Macrae, 2006).

The prACC monitors actions, and the arACC is involved in theory-of-mind tasks. Specifically, thoughts about the self activate the most inferior portion of the arACC, whereas thoughts about others activate the most superior portion of the arACC. Such overlapping activations suggest that we make sense of unfamiliar others cognitively by predicting their actions, yet think about ourselves and similar others emotionally by predicting and estimating their feelings (Amodio & Frith, 2006; see also Mitchell, Macrae, & Banaji, 2006).[6] Another instance of such delineation within the ACC shows a similar pattern: the caudal ACC is involved in the more cognitive aspects of pain perception, whereas the prACC is involved in the more emotional aspects of pain perception. Hence, the ACC appears to be laid out on a spectrum by which emotional processing is greatest near the border with the OFC and becomes more cognitively oriented as one travels posteriorly toward the PFC.

The ACC is clearly a very important structure for forming first impressions about others. Within milliseconds, information from the sensory organs has traveled through the perceptual cortices, been routed by the amygdala, and is present in the ACC, where thought and consciousness begin to occur. At this final destination for stimulus information, other areas of the prefrontal cortex become active to form thoughts and impressions and to plan actions in regard to perceived others. The area stretching from the ACC forward to the frontal pole (referred to as the paracingulate cortex) is where most of our conscious impression formation of others occurs (Amodio & Frith, 2006). Perhaps the most well-studied part of this area is the medial prefrontal cortex (mPFC). The mPFC may well be the brain region most implicated in social cognition and is largely involved in self-referential thought, self-reflection (Macrae, Moran, Heatherton, Banfield, & Kelley, 2004; Mitchell, Mason, Macrae, & Banaji, 2006), and thinking about others (e.g., Ochsner et al., 2004; Seger, Stone, & Keenan, 2004).[7] This area is implicated both in theory-of-mind tasks, as thoughts about oneself and others are integrated, and has also been found to be active when comparing thoughts about oneself to thoughts about others. However, the anterior rostral portion of the ACC is thought to be the seat of person perception (e.g., Seitz, Nickel, & Azari, 2006). It is in this area that inferences about others are believed to primarily occur.

Information from these areas, though, is not linearly unidirectional. Rather, much as the amygdala feeds back toward the FFA, information within the frontal cortex feeds back to the ACC and then from the ACC back to other structures. One obvious link is that between the STS and ACC, both of which are involved in theory of mind and mentalizing about others. Consistent communication between the amygdala, STS, ACC, FFA, and temporal poles, then, cumulatively gives rise to the way that we are able to form impressions about others (Amodio & Frith, 2006). Note that although we have described this process in a feed-forward manner, originating in the most posterior regions of the brain (striate cortex) and traveling forward to the most anterior regions (prefrontal cortex), the brain is less like a flowchart and more like a roundtable discussion (but see Figure 2.2).

It is this interconnected nature of the brain that explains perhaps the most interesting aspect of first impressions: intuitive judgment.[8] Although we have already explained how blindsight patients report seeing nothing, though nevertheless possessing knowledge of what it is that their eyes are exposed to, similar processes occur in higher-level cognitive areas (see Tong, 2003). For instance, the OFC responds to both

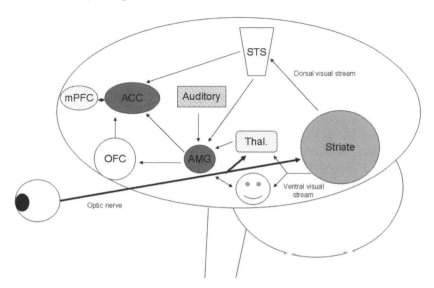

FIGURE 2.2. A conceptual diagram summarizing the formation of first impressions in the brain. Visual information from the optic nerve travels to the striate cortex and also feeds directly to the thalamus. From the striate cortex, visual information travels either dorsally to the superior temporal sulcus (providing information about motion—the "where/how" path) or ventrally to the fusiform face area (FFA) and thalamus. Low spatial frequency information passes from the striate cortex to the thalamus, whereas high spatial frequency information passes from the striate cortex to the FFA. Information from all three regions, and also from the auditory cortex, converges at the amygdala to ascertain the emotional relevance of the stimuli. This information is then projected upward to the orbitofrontal cortex (OFC), medial prefrontal cortex (mPFC), and anterior cingulate cortex (ACC). Information from the superior temporal sulcus (STS) is also passed to the ACC along a dorsal route. That said, each of these connections is believed to be reciprocal—exchanging and refining information—rather than purely feed-forward in character.

blindsight and subliminal presentations of emotional stimuli (Vuilleumier et al., 2002). Promising work by Tong and colleagues has shown that the fixation of someone's attention to visual stimuli can be read from neuroimaging data of their early visual cortex (striate cortex/V1; Kamitani & Tong, 2005; Meng, Remus, & Tong, 2005; Tong, 2003).[9] In addition, behaviorally observed phenomena such as the McGurk effect (McGurk & MacDonald, 1976) show that the integration of visual and auditory information can lead to perceptual illusions of which perceivers are not even aware. Hence, much processing occurs outside of consciousness. Indeed, it has been suggested that the *vast majority* of the mind's activities are outside of consciousness. Much like the blindsight patient whose skin conductance changes in response to the fearful face that he cannot see, we form our impressions of others and the environment without necessarily having access to all the information and processing that subserves those thoughts (see Vuilleumier et al., 2002).

LOOKING FURTHER

In this chapter we have largely focused on the cognitive neuroscience of first impressions by examining evidence from neuroimaging techniques with high spatial resolution (e.g., fMRI and PET). However, there are, of course, other methods by which one can observe brain function in response to behavioral tasks. Each of these has its benefits. For instance, ERP (evoked reaction potentials) use EEG (electroencephalograph) technology to measure postsynaptic electrical potentials as neurons fire during tasks. While the spatial resolution of ERPs are relatively poor as compared to methods such as fMRI, this method has the advantage of providing fairly good temporal resolution, allowing one to discern "what regions of the cerebral cortex are active when" (see Ito, Urland, Willadsen-Jensen, & Correll, 2006, for a review of ERPs in social neuroscience and person perception).

In addition, lesion studies, such as those providing knowledge of the effects of blindsight, also provide valuable and critical information for understanding neurocognitive function. Again, though contributions from work with patients with lesions and normals with temporary lesions delivered via transcranial magnetic stimulation (TMS) have not been covered extensively in this chapter, they provide unique insights to understanding brain function. Thus, further information about the formation of first impressions may also be gleaned from studies of prosopagnosia, or "split-brain" callosectomy patients, as well as from psychopathological (e.g., Shin et al., 2005) and neurophysiological work (e.g., Harrison, Singer, Rotshtein, Dolan, & Critchley, 2006).

SUMMARY AND CONCLUSION

Throughout this chapter, we have attempted to review the process by which we perceive and form initial thought about others in our social world. Figure 2.2 attempts to provide an illustrative summary of this process; however, it presents only a rough depiction. The current chapter is not an exhaustive review of the literature on cognitive or social neuroscience (see Lieberman, 2007, for a recent review of the field), but it presents a schema for how the brain perceives and forms impressions about others in light of what is contemporarily known. The process of person perception occurs incredibly rapidly, and once the information feeds forward in the manner we have described, a process of reciprocation is already under way by which the principal areas of the brain begin exchanging and conferring more and more information about the stimulus. Hence, it is the interconnected nature and the mutual and reciprocal exchange of information in our neural structures that forms the neural basis for first impressions.

NOTES

1. Distinctions have been made between the detection of a face and ascribing identity to a face (see de Gelder & Rouw, 2001). For instance, Winston et al. (2004) have shown that the FFA is involved in establishing face identity, whereas other areas (such as the superior temporal sulcus; STS) code for emotion and other changeable aspects of the face that involve movement (see also Henson et al., 2003; Hoffman & Haxby, 2000; Sato, Kochiyama, Yoshikawa, Naito, & Matsumura, 2004). Hence, as face-selective cells appear to exist in areas outside of the FFA—such as the STS, the amygdala, the face-responsive occipital region (FROR), and even the prefrontal cortex—it is believed that these may serve different roles in the perception of faces and the matching of identity and emotion to a face as a visual stimulus. de Gelder and Rouw (2001), however, report that the FROR within the inferior occipital gyrus is the structure responsible for simple face detection.
2. Notably, STS activation is stronger for videos than for the more impoverished point-light displays. The medial temporal area appears to be involved in motion processing, whereas biological motion activates the area anterior and superior to the medial temporal gyrus—namely, the STS—and videos and point-light displays of nonbiological movement activate the medial temporal area and the area just below it in the inferior temporal sulcus (ITS; see Beauchamp et al., 2003).
3. STS response to eyes appears to be automatic. When participants see a stimulus that can be manipulated to look like a pair of eyes versus the wheels of a car, the STS is active only when the phenomenon is perceived as eyes. Participants' reflexive orienting to the image (a measure of attention), however, does not differ (Kingstone, Tipper, Ristic, & Ngan, 2004).
4. Adams, Gordon, Baird, Ambady, and Kleck (2003) offer an alternative explanation. In their work, they found an interaction between eye gaze and facial expression for amygdala activity. They argue that, ecologically, fear is an aversion-related response and anger is an approach-related response. Similarly, averted eye gaze signals aversive intentions, while direct eye gaze signals intentions to approach. Therefore, by combining fear and anger expressions with averted and direct eye gaze, they concluded that left amygdala activation is greater for ambiguously threatening expressions, that is, anger with averted gaze and fear with direct gaze. Noting this, they point to a possible confound

in the earlier work on fear in the amygdala, as most or all of the previous studies have used fear faces with direct eye gaze, which is ambiguously threatening. Therefore, the reason that the amygdala responds differentially to fear versus anger may be due to a difference in the nature of the signals: congruent (anger with direct gaze) versus incongruent (fear with direct gaze).

5. Notably, the amygdala and FFA of depressed patients also show an increased response to sad faces.

6. Kaplan, Freedman, and Iacoboni (2007) even found mPFC activation for participants' favored political candidate prior to a U.S. presidential election, reflecting identification of the favored candidate with the self.

7. Mason, Banfield, and Macrae (2004) asked participants to imagine actions if performed by a dog or by a person. They found that thinking about humans activated areas within the PFC (e.g., mPFC, ACC) but that thinking about dogs activated occipital regions. Hence, we appear to reason about human actions using the frontal cortex, whereas visualizing nonhuman (dog) actions results in occipital activation. This is not the case if thinking about the dog's mental state, though—then the mPFC is used for both the dog and the human (Mitchell, Banaji, & Macrae, 2005).

8. Leube, Erb, Grodd, Bertels, and Kircher, (2003) have suggested that the intuitive feeling of familiarity involves the dorsal visual stream, as contrasted with the ventral visual stream, which processes identity—for example, the sense that someone seems familiar without being able to recognize who the person is, or the opposite phenomenon (the Capgras delusion), in which individuals can identify a face but do not feel that it is a familiar one.

9. Similarly, Ress and Heeger (2003) have shown that activation in the visual cortex is greater for misses than for false alarms in a signal-detection paradigm, indicating that early visual processing corresponds to *perceived* rather than physically presented (purely visual) stimuli.

REFERENCES

Adams, R. B., Jr., Gordon, H. L., Baird, A. A., Ambady, N., & Kleck, R. E. (2003). Effects of gaze on amygdala sensitivity to anger and fear faces. *Science, 300,* 1536.

Adolphs, R. (2006). What is special about social cognition? In J. T. Cacioppo, P. S. Visser, & C. L. Pickett (Eds.), *Social neuroscience: People thinking about thinking people* (pp. 269–285). Cambridge, MA: MIT Press.

Adolphs, R., Baron-Cohen, S., & Tranel, D. (2002). Impaired recognition of social emotions following amygdala damage. *Journal of Cognitive Neuroscience, 14,* 1264–1274.

Adolphs, R., Tranel, D., & Damsio, A. R. (1998). The human amygdala in social judgment. *Nature, 393,* 470–474.

Amodio, D. M., & Frith, C. D. (2006). Meeting of minds: The medial frontal cortex and social cognition. *Nature Reviews Neuroscience, 7,* 268–277.

Beauchamp, M. S., Lee, K. E., Haxby, J. V., & Martin, A. (2003). fMRI responses to video and point-light displays of moving humans and manipulable objects. *Journal of Cognitive Neuroscience, 15*, 991–1001.

Cahill, L., Uncapher, M., Kilpatrick, L., Alkire, M. T., & Turner, J. (2004). Sex-related hemispheric lateralization of amygdala function in emotionally influenced memory: An fMRI investigation. *Learning and Memory, 11*, 261–266.

Canli, T., Zhao, Z., Desmond, J. E., Kang, E., Gross, J., & Gabrieli, J. D. E. (2001). An fMRI study of personality influences on brain reactivity to emotional stimuli. *Behavioral Neuroscience, 115*, 33–42.

Cassell, M. D., & Wright, D. J. (1986). Topography of projections from the medial prefrontal cortex to the amygdala in the rat. *Brain Research Bulletin, 17*, 321–333.

Claeys, K. G., Dupont, P., Cornette, L., Sunaert, S., Van Hecke, P., De Schutter, E., et al. (2004). Color discrimination involves ventral and dorsal stream visual areas. *Cerebral Cortex, 14*, 803–822.

Cunningham, W. A., Raye, C. L., & Johnson, M. K. (2004). Implicit and explicit evaluation: fMRI correlates of valence, emotional intensity, and control in the processing of attitudes. *Journal of Cognitive Neuroscience, 16*, 1717–1729.

de Gelder, B., & Rouw, R. (2001). Beyond localisation: A dynamical dual route account of face recognition. *Acta Psychologica, 107*, 183–207.

Deibert, E., Kraut, M., Kremen, S., & Hart, J., Jr. (1999). Neural pathways in tactile object recognition. *Neurology, 52*, 1413–1417.

Downing, P. E., Jiang, Y., Shuman, M., & Kanwisher, N. (2001). A cortical area selective for visual processing of the human body. *Science, 293*, 2470–2473.

Downing, P. E., Peelen, M. V., Wiggett, A. J., & Tew, B. D. (2006). The role of the extrastriate body area in action perception. *Social Neuroscience, 1,* 52–62.

Engell, A. D., Haxby, J. V., & Todorov, A. (2007). Implicit trustworthiness decisions: Automatic coding of face properties in human amygdala. *Journal of Cognitive Neuroscience, 19*, 1508–1519.

Fichtenholtz, H. M., Dean, H. L., Dillon, D. G., Yamasaki, H., McCarthy, G., & LaBar, K. S. (2004). Emotion-attention network interactions during a visual oddball task. *Cognitive Brain Research, 20*, 67–80.

Fischer, H., Sandblom, J., Herlitz, A., Fransson, P., Wright, C. I., & Backman, L. (2004). Sex-differential brain activation during exposure to female and male faces. *Neuroreport, 15*, 235–238.

Fitzgerald, D. A., Angstadt, M. Jelsone, L. M., Nathan, P. J., & Phan, K. L. (2006). Beyond threat: Amygdala reactivity across multiple expression of facial affect. *NeuroImage, 30*, 1441–1448.

Gallagher, H. L., & Frith, C. D. (2003). Functional imaging of "theory of mind." *Trends in Cognitive Sciences, 7*, 77–83.

Gaudio, R. (1994). Sounding gay: Pitch properties in the speech of gay and straight men. *American Speech, 69*, 30–57.

Gauthier, I., Tarr, M. J., Anderson, A. W., Skudlarski, P., & Gore, J. C. (1999). Activation of the middle fusiform "face area" increases with expertise in recognizing novel objects. *Nature Neuroscience, 2*, 568–573.

Grandjean, D., Sander, D., Pourtois, G., Schwartz, S., Seghier, M. L., Scherer, K. R., et al. (2005). The voices of wrath: Brain responses to angry prosody in meaningless speech. *Nature Neuroscience, 8,* 145–146.

Gusnard, D. A., Akbudak, E., Shulman, G. L., & Raichle, M. E. (2001). Medial prefrontal cortex and self-referential mental activity: Relation to a default mode of brain function. *Proceedings of the National Academy of Sciences, 98,* 4259–4264.

Hariri, A. R., Mattay, V. S., Tessitore, A., Fera, F., & Weinberger, D. R. (2003). Neocortical modulation of the amygdala response to fearful stimuli. *Biological Psychiatry, 53,* 494–501.

Harrison, N. A., Singer, T., Rotshtein, P., Dolan, R. J., & Critchley, H. D. (2006). Pupillary contagion: Central mechanisms engaged in sadness processing. *Social, Cognitive, and Affective Neuroscience, 1,* 5–17.

Henson, R. N., Goshen-Gottstein, Y., Ganel, T., Otten, L. J., Quayle, A., & Rugg, M. D. (2003). Electrophysiological and haemodynamic correlates of face perception, recognition and priming. *Cerebral Cortex, 13,* 793–805.

Herholz, K., Ehlen, P., Kessler, J., Strotmann, T., Kalbe, E., & Markowitsch, H. (2001). Learning face-name associations and the effect of age and performance: A PET activation study. *Neuropsychologia, 39,* 643–650.

Hoffman, E. A., & Haxby, J. V. (2000). Distinct representations of eye gaze and identity in the distributed human neural system for face perception. *Nature Neuroscience, 3,* 80–84.

Iidaka, T., Omori, M., Murata, T., Kosaka, H., Yonekura, Y., Tomohisa, O., et al. (2001). Neural interaction of the amygdala with the prefrontal and temporal cortices in the processing of facial expressions as revealed by fMRI. *Journal of Cognitive Neuroscience, 13,* 1035–1047.

Ito, T. A., Urland, G. R., Willadsen-Jensen, E., & Correll, J. (2006). The social neuroscience of stereotyping and prejudice: Using event-related brain potentials to study social perception. In J. T. Cacioppo, P. S. Visser, & C. L. Pickett (Eds.), *Social neuroscience: People thinking about thinking people* (pp. 189–212). Cambridge, MA: MIT Press.

Johnstone, T., van Reekum, C. M., Oakes, T. R., & Davidson, R. J. (2006). The voice of emotion: An fMRI study of neural responses to angry and happy vocal expressions. *Social, Cognitive, and Affective Neuroscience, 1,* 242–249.

Kamitani, Y., & Tong, F. (2005). Decoding the visual and subjective contents of the human brain. *Nature Neuroscience, 8,* 679–685.

Kanwisher, N. (2000). Domain specificity in face perception. *Nature Neuroscience, 3,* 759–763.

Kanwisher, N., McDermott, J., & Chun, M. M. (1997). The fusiform face area: A module in human extrastriate cortex specialized for face perception. *Journal of Neuroscience, 17,* 4302–4311.

Kaplan, J. T., Freedman, J., & Iacoboni, M. (2007). Us versus them: Political attitudes and party affiliation influence neural response to faces of presidential candidates. *Neuropsychologia, 45,* 55–64.

Keri, S., Decety, J., Roland, P. E., & Gulyas, B. (2004). Feature uncertainty activates anterior cingulate cortex. *Human Brain Mapping, 21,* 26–33.

Kim, H., Somerville, L. H., Johnstone, T., Alexander, A. L., & Whalen, P. J. (2003).

Inverse amygdala and medial prefrontal cortex responses to surprised faces. *NeuroReport, 14*, 2317–2322.

Kingstone, A., Tipper, C., Ristic, J., & Ngan, E. (2004). The eyes have it!: An fMRI investigation. *Brain and Cognition, 55*, 269–271.

Klein, S., Smolka, M. N., Wrase, J., Gruesser, S. M., Mann, K., Braus, D. F., et al. (2003). The influence of gender and emotional valence of visual cues on fMRI activation in humans. *Pharmacopsychiatry, 36*, S191–S194.

Knight, D. C., Smith, C. N., Cheng, D. T., Stein, E. A., & Helmstetter, F. J. (2004). Amygdala and hippocampal activity during acquisition and extinction of human fear conditioning. *Cognitive, Affective & Behavioral Neuroscience, 4*, 317–325.

Kozlowski, L. T., & Cutting, J. E. (1977). Recognizing the sex of a walker from a dynamic point-light display. *Perception and Psychophysics, 21*, 575–580.

LaBar, K. S., Crupain, M. J., Voyvodic, J. T., & McCarthy, G. (2003). Dynamic perception of facial affect and identity in the human brain. *Cerebral Cortex, 13*, 1023–1033.

Leube, D. T., Erb, M., Grodd, W., Bartels, M., & Kircher, T. T. J. (2003). Successful episodic memory retrieval of newly learned faces activates a left fronto-parietal network. *Cognitive Brain Research, 18*, 97–101.

Lieberman, M. D. (2007). Social cognitive neuroscience: A review of core processes. *Annual Review of Psychology, 58*, 259–289.

Macrae, C. N., Moran, J. M., Heatherton, T. F., Banfield, J. F., & Kelley, W. M. (2004). Medial prefrontal activity predicts memory for self. *Cerebral Cortex, 14*, 647–654.

Mason, M. F., Banfield, J. F., & Macrae, C. N. (2004). Thinking about actions: The neural substrates of person knowledge. *Cerebral Cortex, 14*, 209–214.

McGurk, H., & MacDonald, J. (1976). Hearing lips and seeing voices. *Nature, 264*, 746–748.

Meng, M., Remus, D. A., & Tong, F. (2005). Filling-in of visual phantoms in the human brain. *Nature Neuroscience, 8*, 1248–1254.

Mitchell, J. P., Banaji, M. R., & Macrae, C. N. (2005). General and specific contributions of the medial prefrontal cortex to knowledge about mental states. *NeuroImage, 28*, 757–762.

Mitchell, J. P., Cloutier, J., Banaji, M. R., & Macrae, C. N. (2006). Medial prefrontal dissociations during processing of trait diagnostic and nondiagnostic person information. *Social, Cognitive and Affective Neuroscience, 1*, 49–55.

Mitchell, J. P., Macrae, C. N., & Banaji, M. R. (2004). Encoding-specific effects of social cognition on the neural correlates of subsequent memory. *The Journal of Neuroscience, 24*, 4912–4917.

Mitchell, J. P., Macrae, C. N., & Banaji, M. R. (2006). Dissociable medial prefrontal contributions to judgments of similar and dissimilar others. *Neuron, 50*, 655–663.

Mitchell, J. P., Mason, M. F., Macrae, C. N., & Banaji, M. R. (2006). Thinking about others: The neural substrates of social cognition. In J. T. Cacioppo, P. S. Visser, & C. L. Pickett (Eds.), *Social neuroscience: People thinking about thinking people* (pp. 63–82). Cambridge, MA: MIT Press.

Mitchell, R. L. C., Elliott, R., Barry, M., Cruttenden, A., & Woodruff, P. W. R. (2003). The neural response to emotional prosody, as revealed by functional magnetic resonance imaging. *Neuropsychologia, 41*, 1410–1421.

Nakamura, K., Kawashima, R., Sugiura, M., Kato, T., Nakamura, A., Hatano, K., et al. (2001). Neural substrates for recognition of familiar voices: A PET study. *Neuropsychologia, 39*, 1047–1054.

Norgren, R., Hajnal, A., & Mungarndee, S. S. (2006). Gustatory reward and the nucleus accumbens. *Physiology & Behavior, 89*, 531–535.

Northoff, G., Heinzel, A., Bermpohl, F., Niese, R., Pfennig, A., Pascual-Leone, A., et al. (2004). Reciprocal modulation and attenuation in the prefrontal cortex: An fMRI study on emotional-cognitive interaction. *Human Brain Mapping, 21*, 202–212.

Ochsner, K. N. (2006). Characterizing the functional architecture of affect regulation: Emerging answers and outstanding questions. In J. T. Cacioppo, P. S. Visser, & C. L. Pickett (Eds.), *Social neuroscience: People thinking about thinking people* (pp. 245–268). Cambridge, MA: MIT Press.

Ochsner, K. N., Knierim, K., Ludlow, D. H., Hanelin, J., Ramachandran, T., Glover, G., et al. (2004). Reflecting upon feelings: An fMRI study of neural systems supporting the attribution of emotion to self and other. *Journal of Cognitive Neuroscience, 16*, 1746–1772.

Palermo, R., & Rhodes, G. (2007). Are you always on my mind? A review of how face perception and attention interact. *Neuropsychologia, 45*, 75–92.

Pelphrey, K. A., Viola, R. J., & McCarthy, G. (2004). When strangers pass: Processing of mutual and averted social gaze in the superior temporal sulcus. *Psychological Science, 15*, 598–603.

Phelps, E. A. (2006). Emotion and cognition: Insights from studies of the human amygdala. *Annual Review of Psychology, 57*, 27–53.

Porrino, L. J., Crane, A. M., & Goldman-Rakic, P. S. (1981). Direct and indirect pathways from the amygdala to the frontal lobe in rhesus monkeys. *Journal of Comparative Neurology, 198*, 121–136.

Pourtois, G., de Gelder, B., Bol, A., & Crommelinck, M. (2005). Perception of facial expressions and voices and of their combination in the human brain. *Cortex, 41*, 49–59.

Pourtois, G., Sander, D., Andres, M., Grandjean, D., Reveret, L., Olivier, E., et al. (2004). Dissociable roles of the human somatosensory and superior temporal cortices for processing social face signals. *European Journal of Neuroscience, 20*, 3507–3515.

Ress, D., & Heeger, D. J. (2003). Neural correlates of perception in early visual cortex. *Nature Neuroscience, 6*, 414–420.

Rolls, E. T. (2007). The representation of information about faces in the temporal and frontal lobes. *Neuropsychologia, 45*, 124–143.

Sander, K., Roth, P., & Scheich, H. (2003). Left-lateralized fMRI activation in the temporal lobe of high repressive women during the identification of sad prosodies. *Cognitive Brain Research, 16*, 441–456.

Sato, W., Kochiyama, T., Yoshikawa, S., Naito, E., & Matsumura, M. (2004). Enhanced neural activity in response to dynamic facial expressions of emotion: An fMRI study. *Cognitive Brain Research, 20*, 81–91.

Schiffrin, D., Tannen, D., & Hamilton, H. E. (2001). *The handbook of discourse analysis*. Malden, MA: Blackwell.

Seger, C. A., Stone, M., & Keenan, J. P. (2004). Cortical activations during judgments about the self and another person. *Neuropsychologia, 42,* 1168–1177.

Seitz, R. J., Nickel, J., & Azari, N. P. (2006). Functional modularity of the medial prefrontal cortex: Involvement in human empathy. *Neuropsychology, 20,* 743–751.

Servos, P., Osu, R., Santi, A., & Kawato, M. (2002). The neural substrates of biological motion perception: An fMRI study. *Cerebral Cortex, 12,* 772–782.

Shepherd, G. M. (2006). Smell images and the flavour system in the human brain. *Nature, 444,* 316–321.

Shin, L. M., Wright, C. I., Cannistraro, P. A., Wedig, M. M., McMullin, K., Martis, B., et al. (2005). A functional magnetic resonance imaging study of amygdala and medial prefrontal cortex responses to overtly presented fearful faces in posttraumatic stress disorder. *Archives of General Psychiatry, 62,* 273–281.

Sperling, R. A., Bates, J. F., Cocchiarella, A. J., Schacter, D. L., Rosen, B. R., & Albert, M. S. (2001). Encoding novel face-name associations: A functional MRI study. *Human Brain Mapping, 14,* 129–139.

Surguladze, S., Brammer, M. J., Keedwell, P., Giampietro, V., Young, A. W., Travis, M. J., et al. (2005). A differential pattern of neural response toward sad versus happy facial expressions in major depressive disorder. *Biological Psychiatry, 57,* 201–209.

Tarr, M. J., & Gauthier, I. (2000). FFA: A flexible fusiform area for subordinate-level visual processing automatized by expertise. *Nature Neuroscience, 3,* 764–769.

Tong, F. (2003). Primary visual cortex and visual awareness. *Nature Reviews Neuroscience, 4,* 219–229.

Urgesi, C., Berlucchi, G., & Aglioti, S. M. (2004). Magnetic stimulation of extrastriate body area impairs visual processing of nonfacial body parts. *Current Biology, 14,* 2130–2134.

Urgesi, C., Candidi, M., Ionta, S., & Aglioti, S. M. (2007). Representation of body identity and body actions in extrastriate body area and ventral premotor cortex. *Nature Neuroscience, 10,* 30–31.

Vuilleumier, P., Armony, J. L., Driver, J., & Dolan, R. J. (2003). Distinct spatial frequency sensitivities for processing faces and emotional expressions. *Nature Neuroscience, 6,* 624–631.

Vuilleumier, P., Henson, R. N., Driver, J., & Dolan, R. J. (2002). Multiple levels of visual object constancy revealed by event-related fMRI of repetition priming. *Nature Neuroscience, 5,* 491–499.

Vuilleumier, P., & Pourtois, G. (2007). Distributed and interactive brain mechanisms during emotion face perception: Evidence from functional neuroimaging. *Neuropsychologia, 45,* 174–194.

Vuilleumier, P., Richardson, M. P., Armony, J. L., Driver, J., & Dolan, R. J. (2004). Distant influences of amygdala lesion on visual cortical activation during emotional face processing. *Nature Neuroscience, 7,* 1271–1278.

Wang, J., Zhou, T., Qiu, M., Du, A., Cai, K., Wang, Z., et al. (1999). Relationship between ventral stream for object vision and dorsal stream for spatial vision: An fMRI + ERP study. *Human Brain Mapping, 8*, 170–181.

Whalen P. J., Kagan, J., Cook, R. G., Davis, F. C., Kim H., Polis, S., et al. (2004). Human amygdala responsivity to masked fearful eye whites. *Science, 306*, 2061.

Whalen, P. J., Rauch, S. L., Etcoff, N. L., McInerney, S. C., Lee, M. B., & Jenike, M. A. (1998). Masked presentations of emotional facial expressions modulate amygdala activity without explicit knowledge. *Journal of Neuroscience, 18*, 411–418.

Whalen, P. J., Shin, L. M., McInerney, S. C., Fischer, H., Wright, C. I., & Rauch, S. L. (2001). A functional MRI study of human amygdala responses to facial expressions of fear versus anger. *Emotion, 1*, 70–83.

Williams, L. M., Liddell, B. J., Kemp, A. H., Bryant, R. A., Meares, R. A., Peduto, A. S., et al. (2006). Amygdala–prefrontal dissociation of subliminal and supraliminal fear. *Human Brain Mapping, 27*, 652–661.

Winston, J. S., Henson, R. N. A., Fine-Goulden, M. R., & Dolan, R. J. (2004). fMRI-adaptation reveals dissociable neural representations of identity and expression in face perception. *Journal of Neurophysiology, 92*, 1830–1839.

Winston, J. S., Strange, B. A., O'Doherty, J., & Dolan, R. J. (2002). Automatic and intentional brain responses during evaluation of trustworthiness of faces. *Nature Neuroscience, 5*, 277–283.

Wojciulik, E., Kanwisher, N., & Driver, J. (1998). Covert visual attention modulates face-specific activity in the human fusiform gyrus: fMRI study. *Journal of Neurophysiology, 79*, 1574–1578.

CHAPTER 3

The Biology
of Mind Reading

BHISMADEV CHAKRABARTI
SIMON BARON-COHEN

When we form a first impression of another person, or when they form one of us, what happens? Specifically, what social information is processed by the brain, and where in the brain does this take place? In this chapter, we argue that in the typical brain an empathy system is constantly active when looking at someone else's face or when interpreting another's actions. This system involves some key component mechanisms that we describe in the first part of this chapter. Empathy also varies in terms of individual differences, the clearest of these being evident in typical sex differences in the general population, which we describe in the second part of the chapter. In the extreme, clinical groups such as those with autism may involve very atypical development of empathy, and that is discussed next. Finally, we review the literature on emotion processing from neuroimaging studies that suggest that perception of discrete basic emotions is subserved by different neural regions and networks (Panksepp, 1998). We end by describing a recent study that investigates how an individual's level of empathy affects how his or her brain processes discrete emotions.

TRIGGERING EMPATHY

In the normal case, we start to empathize as soon as we make eye contact with another person, or as we look at their posture, actions, and the context. Empathizing is the drive to identify another person's emotions and thoughts and to respond to these with an appropriate emotion (Davis, 1994). We use the term "drive" but recognize that it also overlaps with the concept of a skill or ability. Empathizing doesn't just entail the cold calculation of what someone else thinks and feels (or what is sometimes called mind reading). Psychopaths can do that much. Empathizing is also about having an appropriate emotional reaction inside you, an emotion triggered by the other person's emotion. Empathizing is done in order to understand another person, predict his or her behavior, and to connect or resonate with the person emotionally. Imagine you recognize that "Jane is in pain," but this perception left you cold, or detached, or happy, or preoccupied. This would not be empathizing. Now, imagine you don't just see Jane's pain, but you also automatically feel concern, wincing yourself, and experience a desire to run across and help alleviate her pain. That is empathizing. And empathizing extends to recognizing and responding to any emotion or state of mind, not just the more obvious ones, like pain. Empathy is a skill (or a set of skills). As with any other skill, such as athleticism or mathematical or musical ability, this skill varies across individuals. In the same way that we can think about why someone is talented or average or even disabled in these other areas, so we can think about individual differences in empathy.

Empathy is a defining feature of human relationships. Empathy stops you from doing things that would hurt another person's feelings. Empathy also stops you from inflicting pain on a person or animal. Empathy allows you to tune into someone else's world, setting aside your own world—your perceptions, knowledge, assumptions, or feelings. It allows you to see another side of an argument easily. Empathy drives you to care for, or offer comfort to, another person even if they are unrelated to you and you stand to gain nothing in return. Empathy also makes real communication possible. Talking "at" a person is not real communication—it is a monologue. Real conversation is sensitive to *this* listener at *this* time. Empathy also provides a framework for the development of a moral code. Moral codes are built out of fellow-feeling and compassion.

FRACTIONATING EMPATHY

Philosophical (Stein, 1989) and evolutionary (Brothers, 1990; Levenson, 1996; Preston & de Waal, 2002) accounts have suggested that empathizing is not a unitary construct. Possible constituent "fractions" of empathy include (1) "emotional contagion/affective empathy," (2) "cognitive empathy," and (3) sympathy. Cognitive empathy is involved in explicit understanding of another's feelings and switching to take their perspective. Piaget referred to empathy as "decentering," or responding nonegocentrically (Piaget & Inhelder, 1956). More recent developmental psychologists refer to this aspect of empathy in terms of using a "theory of mind," or "mind reading" (Astington, Harris, & Olson, 1988; Whiten, 1991). Essentially, the cognitive component of empathizing entails setting aside your own current perspective, attributing a mental state (sometimes called an "attitude") to the other person, and then inferring the likely content of their mental state, given their experience. The cognitive element also enables you to predict the other person's mental state or behavior.

The second aspect to empathy is the "affective" component (Hobson, 1993). A similar component in other accounts has been called "emotional contagion," defined as the tendency to automatically mimic and synchronize facial expressions, vocalizations, postures, and movements with those of another person and, consequently, to converge emotionally (Hatfield, Cacioppo, & Rapson, 1992). This may be the most primitive component of empathy. For example, when witnessing someone else in a state of fear, the observer may "catch" a similar state of fear. Such a mechanism can act as a "quick-and-easy" route to alerting observers to environmental dangers without having to face the dangers themselves.

A third component involves a "concern mechanism" (Nichols, 2001) often associated with a prosocial/altruistic component, also termed "sympathy." This is distinct from emotional contagion in not necessarily involving matched states between the observer and the person experiencing the emotion, and being possibly specific to a certain class of emotions (sadness and pain, but not disgust or happiness) in the other person. It represents a case where the observer feels both an emotional response to someone else's distress and a desire to alleviate their suffering.

DEVELOPMENT OF EMPATHY

In 1994 Baron-Cohen proposed a model to specify the neurocognitive mechanisms that constitute the "mindreading system" (Baron-Cohen, 1994, 1995). Mind reading is defined as the ability to interpret one's own or another agent's actions as driven by mental states. The model was proposed in order to explain (1) ontogenesis of a theory of mind and (2) neurocognitive dissociations that are seen in children with or without autism. The model, shown in Figure 3.1, contains four components: ID, or the Intentionality Detector; EDD, or the Eye Direction Detector; SAM, or the Shared Attention Mechanism; and finally ToMM, or the Theory of Mind Mechanism.

ID and EDD build "dyadic" representations of simple mental states. ID automatically represents or interprets an agent's self-propelled movement as a desire or goal-directed movement, a sign of its agency, or an entity with volition (Premack, 1990). For example, ID interprets an animate-like moving shape as "it wants x" or "it has goal y." EDD automatically interprets or represents eye-like stimuli as "looking at me" or "looking at something else." That is, EDD picks out that an entity with eyes can perceive. Both ID and EDD emerge earlier in development than the other two mechanisms and are active early in infancy, if not from birth.

SAM is developmentally more advanced. SAM automatically represents or interprets if the self and another agent are (or are not) perceiving the same event. SAM does this by building "triadic" representations. For example, while ID can build the dyadic representation "Mother wants the cup," and EDD can build the dyadic representation "Mother sees the cup," SAM can build the triadic representation "Mother sees that I see the cup." As is apparent, triadic representations involve embedding or recursion. (A dyadic representation ["I see a cup"] is embedded within another dyadic representation ["Mum sees the cup"] to produce this triadic representation.) SAM takes its input from ID and EDD, forming triadic representations from dyadic representations. SAM typically emerges between 9 and 14 months of age and allows "joint-attention" behaviors such as protodeclarative pointing and gaze monitoring (Scaife & Bruner, 1975).

ToMM is the mechanism in the 1994 model of the mind reading system that has received the most research attention. It allows epistemic mental states to be represented (e.g., "Mother thinks this cup contains water" or "Mother pretends this cup contains water"), and it integrates the full set of mental state concepts (including emotions) into a theory. ToMM develops between 2 and 4 years of age, and allows pretend play (Leslie, 1987), understanding of false belief (Wimmer & Perner, 1983), and understanding of the relationships between mental states (Wellman, 1990). An example of the latter is the seeing-leads-to-knowing principle (Pratt & Bryant, 1990), by which the typical 3-year-old can infer that if someone has seen an event, then the other person will know about it.

The model shows the ontogenesis of a theory of mind in the first 4 years of life. The four components are justified by observations of developmental competence and neuropsychological dissociation. In terms of

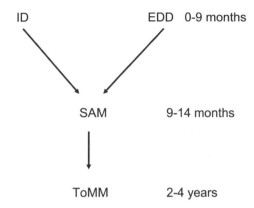

FIGURE 3.1. Baron-Cohen's (1994) model of mind reading. IDD, Intentionality Detector; EDD, Eye Direction Detector; SAM, Shared Attention Mechanism; ToMM, Theory of Mind Mechanism.

developmental competence, joint attention does not appear possible until 9–14 months of age, and joint attention appears to be a necessary but not sufficient condition for understanding epistemic mental states (Baron-Cohen, 1991; Baron-Cohen & Swettenham, 1996). There appears to be a developmental lag between acquiring SAM and ToMM, suggesting that these two mechanisms are dissociable. In terms of neuropsychological dissociation, congenitally blind children can ultimately develop joint (auditory or tactile) attention (i.e., SAM), using the amodal ID rather than the visual EDD route. They can therefore go on to develop ToMM. Children with autism appear able to represent the dyadic mental states of seeing and wanting, but show delays in shared attention (Baron-Cohen, 1989b) and in understanding false belief (Baron-Cohen, 1989a; Baron-Cohen, Leslie, & Frith, 1985)—that is, in acquiring SAM and ultimately ToMM. It is this specific developmental delay that suggests that SAM and ToMM are dissociable from EDD.

The 1994 model of the mind reading system was revised in 2005 because of certain omissions and an overly narrow focus in the original model. The key omission in the original model was that information about *affective* states, available to the infant perceptual system, has no dedicated neurocognitive mechanism. Figure 3.2 shows the revised model (Baron-Cohen, 2003). The model now includes a new fifth component: TED, or The Emotion Detector. Moreover, the focus of the new model has changed from the earlier one. The concept of mind reading (or theory of mind) that the original model attempted to capture made no reference to the affective state in the observer triggered by recognition of another's mental state. This is a particular problem for any account of

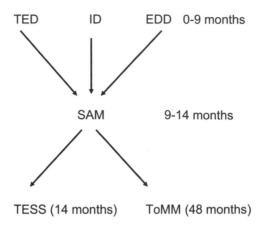

FIGURE 3.2. Baron-Cohen's (2003) model of empathizing. TED, The Emotion Detector; TESS, The Empathizing SyStem; other abbreviations as in Figure 3.1.

the distinction between autism and psychopathy. For this reason, the new model is designed to capture "empathizing" instead of mind reading. The focus on empathy is emphasized by the inclusion of a sixth component in the new model, TESS, or The Empathizing SyStem. Where the 1994 mind reading system was a model of a passive observer (because all the components had simple decoding functions), the 2005 Empathizing SyStem is a model of an observer impelled toward action (because an emotion is triggered in the observer which typically motivates the observer to respond to the other person).

As with the other infancy perceptual input mechanisms of ID and EDD, the new component of TED can build dyadic representations of a special kind, namely, it can represent affective states. An example would be "Mother is unhappy, " or even "Mother is angry with me." Formally, we can describe this as agent-affective state-proposition. We know that infants can represent affective states from as early as 3 months of age (Walker, 1982). As with ID, TED is amodal, in that affective information can be picked up from facial expression, or vocal intonation, "motherese" being a particularly rich source of the latter (Field, 1979). Another's affective state is presumably also detectable from their touch (e.g., tense vs. relaxed), which implies that congenitally blind infants should find affective information accessible through both auditory and tactile modalities. TED allows the detection of the basic emotions (Ekman & Friesen, 1969). The development of TED is probably aided by simple imitation that is typical of infants (e.g., imitating the caregiver's expressions), which in itself would facilitate emotional contagion (Meltzoff & Decety, 2003).

When SAM becomes available, at 9–14 months of age, it can receive inputs from any of the three infancy mechanisms, ID, EDD, or TED. Here, we focus on how a dyadic representation of an affective state can be converted into a triadic representation by SAM. An example would be that the dyadic representation "Mother is unhappy" can be converted into a triadic representation "I am unhappy that Mother is unhappy," or "Mother is unhappy that I am unhappy," etc. Again, as with perceptual or volitional states, SAM's triadic representations of affective states have this special embedded, or recursive, property.

ToMM has been discussed for the past 20 years in research in developmental psychology (Leslie, 1987; Whiten, 1991; Wimmer, Hogrefe, & Perner, 1988). ToMM is of major importance in allowing the child to represent the full range of mental states, including epistemic ones (such as false belief), and is important in allowing the child to pull mentalistic knowledge into a useful theory with which to predict behavior (Baron-Cohen, 1995; Wellman, 1990). But TESS allows more than behavioral explanation and prediction (itself a powerful achievement). TESS allows an empathic reaction to another's emotional state. This is, however, not to say that these two modules do not interact. Knowledge of mental states of others made possible by ToMM could certainly influence the way in which an emotion is processed and/or expressed by TESS. TESS also allows for sympathy. It is this element of TESS that gives it the adaptive benefit of ensuring that organisms feel a drive to help one another.

To see the difference between TESS and ToMM, consider this example: I see you are in pain. Here, ToMM is needed to interpret your facial expressions and writhing body movements in terms of your underlying mental state (pain). But now consider this further example: I am devastated that you are in pain. Here, TESS is needed, since an appropriate affective state has been triggered in the observer by the emotional state identified in the other person. And while ToMM employs M-(mental) Representations (Leslie, 1995) of the form agent–attitude–proposition (e.g., Mother–believes–Johnny took the cookie), TESS employs a new class of representations, which we can call E-(empathy) Representations of the form self-affective state–[self-affective state–proposition] (e.g. "I feel sorry that–Mom feels sad about–the news in the letter") (Baron-Cohen, 2003). The critical feature of this E-Representation is that the self's affective state is appropriate to and triggered by the other person's affective state. Thus, TESS can represent [I am horrified–that you are in pain], or [I am concerned–that you are in pain], or [I want to alleviate–that you are in pain], but it cannot represent [I am happy–that you are in pain]. At least, it cannot do so if TESS is functioning normally. One could imagine an abnormality in TESS leading to the triggering of inappropriate emotional states, or one could imagine them arising from other systems (such as a competition system, or a sibling-rivalry system), but these would not be evidence of TESS per se.

This new model has both conceptual and empirical advantages over the older one. First, emotional states are an important class of mental states to detect in others, but the earlier model focused only on volitional, perceptual, informational, and epistemic states. Moreover, adding TED and TESS to the model helps make sense of data that have emerged from various forms of pathology. For example, in autism TED may function, but the ability to detect others' emotions may be delayed (Baron-Cohen, Spitz, & Cross, 1993; Baron-Cohen, Wheelwright, & Jolliffe, 1997; Hobson, 1986). Even high-functioning people with autism or Asperger syndrome have difficulties both in ToMM (when measured with mental-age appropriate tests) (Baron-Cohen, Jolliffe, Mortimore, & Robertson, 1997; Baron-Cohen, Wheelwright, Hill, Raste, & Plumb, 2001; Happe, 1994) and TESS (Attwood, 1997; Baron-Cohen, O'Riordan, Jones, Stone, & Plaisted, 1999; Baron-Cohen, Richler, Bisarya, Gurunathan, & Wheelwright, 2003; Baron-Cohen & Wheelwright, 2004; Baron-Cohen, Wheelwright, Stone, & Rutherford, 1999). This suggests TED and TESS may be fractionated.

In contrast, the psychiatric condition of psychopathy may entail an intact TED and ToMM, along with an impaired TESS. The psychopath (or sociopath) can represent that you are in pain, or that you believe that he is the gas utility reader, thereby gaining access to your house. The psychopath can go on to hurt you or cheat you without having the appropriate affective reaction to your affective state. In other words, he or she doesn't care about your affective state (Blair, Jones, Clark, & Smith, 1997; Mealey, 1995). Lack of guilt or shame or compassion in the presence of another's distress are diagnostic of psychopathy (Cleckley, 1977; Hare et al., 1990). Separating TESS and ToMM thus allows a functional distinction to be drawn between the neurocognitive causes of autism and psychopathy.

Developmentally, one can also distinguish TED from TESS. We know that at 3 months of age infants can discriminate facial and vocal expressions of emotion (Trevarthen, 1989; Walker, 1982) but that it is not until about 14 months that they can respond with appropriate affect (e.g., a facial expression of concern) to another's apparent pain (Yirmiya, Kasari, Sigman, & Mundy, 1989) or show "social referencing." Clearly, this account is skeletal in not specifying how many emotions TED is capable of recognizing. Our recent survey of emotions identifies that there are 412 discrete emotion concepts that the adult English language user recognizes (Baron-Cohen, Wheelwright, Hill, & Golan, 2008). How many of these are recognized in the first year of life is not clear. It is also not clear exactly how empathizing changes during the second year of life. We have assumed that the same mechanism that enables social referencing at 14 months old also allows sympathy and the growth of empathy across development. This is the most parsimonious model, though it may be that future research will justify the specification of further mechanisms that affect the development of empathy.

SEX DIFFERENCES IN EMPATHIZING

The study of individual differences is important, because few human abilities if any are all-or-none, but come by degrees. Some of the best evidence for individual differences in empathizing comes from the study of sex differences, where many studies converge on the conclusion that there is a female superiority in empathizing. Sex differences are best viewed as summated individual differences on multiple dimensions that include genetic and epigenetic factors. Some of the observed behavioral differences are reviewed here.

1. *Sharing and turn taking.* On average, girls show more concern for fairness, whilst boys share less. In one study, boys showed 50 times more competition, while girls showed 20 times more turn taking (Charlesworth & Dzur, 1987).

2. *Rough and tumble play*, or "rough housing" (wrestling, mock fighting, etc.). Boys show more of this than girls do. Although there's a playful component, it can hurt or be intrusive, so it needs lower empathizing to carry it out (Maccoby, 1999).

3. *Responding empathically* to the distress of other people. Girls from 1 year old onward show greater concern through more sad looks, sympathetic vocalizations, and comforting. More women than men also report frequently sharing of the emotional distress of their friends. Women also show more comforting, even of strangers, than men do (Hoffman, 1977).

4. *Using a "theory of mind."* By 3 years old, little girls are already ahead of boys in their ability to infer what people might be thinking or intending (Happe, 1995). This sex difference appears in some but not all studies (Charman, Ruffman, & Clements, 2002).

5. *Sensitivity to facial expressions.* Women are better at decoding nonverbal communication, picking up subtle nuances from tone of voice or facial expression, or judging a person's character (Hall, 1978).

6. *Questionnaires measuring empathy.* Many of these find that women score higher than men (Davis, 1994).

7. *Values in relationships.* More women value the development of

altruistic reciprocal relationships, which by definition require empathizing. In contrast, more men value power, politics, and competition (Ahlgren & Johnson, 1979). Girls are more likely to endorse cooperative items on a questionnaire and to rate the establishment of intimacy as more important than the establishment of dominance. Boys are more likely than girls to endorse competitive items and to rate social status as more important than intimacy (Knight, Fabes, & Higgins, 1989).

8. *Disorders of empathy* (such as psychopathic personality disorder, or conduct disorder) are far more common among males (Blair, 1995; Dodge, 1980).

9. *Aggression*, even in normal quantities, can only occur with reduced empathizing. Here, again, there is a clear sex difference. Males tend to show far more "direct" aggression (pushing, hitting, punching, etc.) while females tend to show more "indirect" (or "relational," covert) aggression (gossip, exclusion, bitchy remarks, etc.). Direct aggression may require an even lower level of empathy than indirect aggression. Indirect aggression needs better mind-reading skills than does direct aggression, because its impact is strategic (Crick & Grotpeter, 1995).

10. *Murder* is the ultimate example of a lack of empathy. Daly and Wilson (1988) analyzed homicide records dating back over 700 years from a wide range of societies. They found that "male-on-male" homicide was 30–40 times more frequent than "female-on-female" homicide.

11. *Establishing a "dominance hierarchy."* Males are quicker to establish these. This, in part, may reflect their lower empathizing skills, because often a hierarchy is established by one person pushing others around, to become the leader (Strayer, 1980).

12. *Language style.* Girls' speech is more cooperative, reciprocal, and collaborative. In concrete terms, this is also reflected in girls being able to keep a conversational exchange with a partner going for longer. When girls disagree, they are more likely to express their different opinion sensitively, in the form of a question rather than an assertion. Boys' talk is more "single-voiced discourse" (the speaker presents his own perspective alone). The female speech style is more "double-voiced discourse" (girls spend more time negotiating with the other person, trying to take the other person's wishes into account) (Smith, 1985).

13. *Talk about emotions.* Women's conversation involves much more talk about feelings, while men's conversations with one another tend to be more object- or activity-focused (Tannen, 1991).

14. *Parenting style.* Fathers are less likely than mothers to hold their infant in a face-to-face position. Mothers are more likely to follow through on the child's choice of topic in play, while fathers are more

likely to impose their own topic. And mothers fine-tune their speech more often to match what the child can understand (Power, 1985).

15. *Face preference and eye contact.* From birth, females look longer at faces, and particularly at people's eyes, and males are more likely to look at inanimate objects (Connellan, Baron-Cohen, Wheelwright, Ba'tki, & Ahluwalia, 2001).

16. *Language ability.* Finally, females have also been shown to have better language ability than males. It seems likely that good empathizing would promote language development (Baron-Cohen, Baldwin, & Crowson, 1997) and vice versa, so these may not be independent.

Leaving aside sex differences as one source of evidence for individual differences, one can see that empathy is normally distributed within the population. Figure 3.3 shows the data from the Empathy Quotient (EQ), a validated 60-item self-report questionnaire (Baron-Cohen & Wheelwright, 2004). It has been factor-analyzed in two independent studies (Lawrence, Shaw, Baker, Baron-Cohen, & David, 2004; Muncer & Ling, 2006) to suggest the existence of three distinct components. These three components roughly correspond to the three-component model of empathy. Scores on the EQ show a continuous distribution in

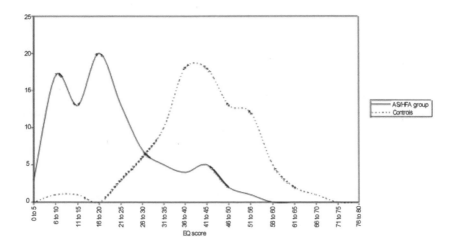

FIGURE 3.3. EQ scores in AS/HFA group and controls. The quasi-normal distribution of empathy in the population (dotted line). Also shown is the distribution of empathy scores from people with Asperger syndrome (AS) or high-functioning autism (HFA). From Baron-Cohen and Wheelwright (2004). Copyright 2004 by Springer. Reprinted by permission.

several populations, with scores from people with ASC clustering toward the lower end (see Figure 3.3). The EQ is associated with significant sex differences (Goldenfeld, Baron-Cohen, Wheelwright, Ashwin, & Chakrabarti, 2007).

NEUROIMAGING STUDIES OF EMPATHIZING
AND EMOTION PERCEPTION

One of the aspects of the new model that we have been exploring is the assumption that the components of the model have a physical reality. That is, we believe that there are physical and neural systems that are dedicated to performing the inferential and empathetic functions described by the model. One recent line of research has pursued this idea by examining activity in various brain areas that are associated with engagement in the various mental activities embodied in the model. For example, neuroimaging studies, conducted mostly on adults, have implicated the following different brain areas in performing tasks that tap components of the model of empathy proposed above, presented in order of their development.

1. Studies of *emotional contagion* have demonstrated involuntary facial mimicry (Dimberg, Thunberg, & Elmehead, 2000) as well as activity in regions of the brain where the existence of "mirror" neurons has been suggested, for example, the inferior frontal gyrus, inferior parietal lobule, and superior temporal sulcus (Carr, Iacoboni, Dubeau, Mazziotta, & Lenzi, 2003; Jackson, Meltzoff, & Decety, 2005; Wicker et al., 2003). Dapretto et al. (2006) have recently demonstrated that children with autism spectrum conditions (ASC), when compared to typically developing controls, show a lower response in inferior frontal gyrus both during observation and explicit imitation of facial expressions of emotion.

2. *ID* has been tested (Brunet, Sarfati, Hardy-Bayle, & Decety, 2000) in a PET study in a task involving attribution of intentions to cartoon characters versus predicting physical causality using the same set of characters. Significantly activated regions included the right medial prefrontal (Brodmann Area [BA] 9) and inferior frontal (BA 47) cortices, the superior temporal gyrus (BA 42) and the bilateral anterior cingulate cortex. In an elegant set of experiments that required participants to attribute intentions to animations of simple geometric shapes (Castelli, Happe, Frith, & Frith, 2000), it was found that the "intentionality" score attributed by the participants to individual animations was positively correlated to the activity in the superior temporal sulcus (STS), the

temporo-parietal junction, and the medial prefrontal cortex. A subsequent study (Castelli, Frith, Happe, & Frith, 2002) demonstrated a group difference in activity in the same set of structures between people with ASC and typical controls.

3. *EDD* has been studied in several neuroimaging studies on gaze direction perception (Calder et al., 2002; Pelphrey, Singerman, Allison, & McCarthy, 2003; Grosbras, Laird, & Paus, 2005). These studies suggest that the posterior STS is involved in EDD bilaterally. This evidence, taken together with similar findings from primate literature (Perrett & Emery, 1994), suggests this area to be a strong candidate for the anatomical equivalent of the EDD.

4. A recent imaging study (Williams, Waiter, Perra, Perrett, & Whiten, 2005) investigated the neural correlates of shared attention mechanism (SAM) in a joint attention task. When compared to a control task involving nonjoint attention, heightened activation was observed bilaterally in the anterior cingulate (BA 32, 24), the medial prefrontal cortex (BA 9, 10), and the body of the caudate nucleus (Frith & Frith, 2003).

5. Traditional *"theory of mind"* (cognitive empathy) tasks have consistently shown activity in the medial prefrontal cortex, superior temporal gyrus, and the temporo-parietal junctions (Frith & Frith, 2003; Saxe, Carey, & Kanwisher, 2004). This could be equated to the brain basis of ToMM.

6. *Sympathy* has been relatively less investigated, with one study implicating the left inferior frontal gyrus, among a network of other structures (Decety & Chaminade, 2003). Work on "moral" emotions has suggested the involvement of a network comprising the medial frontal gyrus, the medial orbitofrontal cortex, and the STS (Moll et al., 2002).

An increasing body of evidence from lesion, neuroimaging, and electrophysiological studies suggests that these affect programs might have discrete neural bases (Calder, Lawrence, & Young, 2001). *Fear* is possibly the single most well-investigated emotion. Passive viewing of fear expressions as well as experiencing fear (as induced through recalling a fear memory, or seeing fear stimuli) reliably activates the amygdala, orbitofrontal cortex, and anterior cingulate cortex (Blair, Morris, Frith, Perrett, & Dolan, 1999; Hariri, Mattay, Tessitore, Fera, & Weinburger, 2003). There is considerable evidence from nonhuman primates (Kalin, Shelton, & Davidson, 2001) and rats (LeDoux, 2000) to suggest a crucial role for these regions in processing fear. Passive viewing of *disgust* faces as well as experiencing disgust oneself is known to evoke a response in the anterior insula and globus pallidus, as reported in several studies (Wicker et al., 2003; Phillips et al., 1997; Calder et al., 2001). An increasing consensus on the role of the ventral striatum in processing reward from different sensory domains (receiving food rewards [O'Doherty, Deichmann, Critchley, & Dolan, 2002], viewing funny cartoons [Mobbs, Greicius, Abdel-Azim, Menon, & Reiss, 2003], remembering happy events [Damasio et al., 2000]) concurs well with studies that report activation of this region in response to viewing *happy* faces (Lawrence et al., 2004; Phillips, Baron-Cohen, & Rutter, 1998).

Perception of *angry* expressions have been shown to evoke a response in the premotor cortex and the striatum (Grosbras & Paus, 2006) as well as the lateral orbitofrontal cortex (Blair & Cipolotti, 2000; Blair et al., 1999). The results of studies on the processing of *sad* expressions are comparatively less consistent. The perception of sad faces and the induction of sad mood are both known to be associated with an increased response in the subgenual cingulate cortex (Liotti et al., 2000; Mayberg et al., 1999), the hypothalamus in humans (Malhi et al., 2004) and rats (Shumake, Edwards, & Gonzalez-Lima, 2001) as well as in the middle temporal gyrus (Eugene et al., 2003). There have been very few studies on the passive viewing of *surprise*. One study by Schroeder et al. (2004) reported bilateral activation in the parahippocampal region, which is known for its role in novelty detection from animal research literature.

While the discrete emotions model holds well for these relatively "simple" emotions, the dimensional models (Rolls, 2002) become increasingly relevant as we consider the more socially complex emotion—for example, pride, shame, and guilt—since it would not be economical to have discrete neural substrates for the whole gamut of emotions. Dimensional models do not assume a discrete neural mechanism for every emotion but, rather, view different emotions as lying at different points on a continuum. These two models, however, need not be in conflict, since the more complex emotions can be conceptualized as being formed from a combination of the basic ones (i.e., with each of the "basic" emotions representing a dimension in emotion space).

Two major meta-analytic studies of neuroimaging literature on emotions highlight the role of discrete regions in primarily visual processing of different basic emotions (Murphy, Nimmo-Smith, & Lawrence, 2003; Phan, Wager, Taylor, & Liberzon, 2002). Some studies using other sensory stimuli—olfactory (Anderson et al., 2003), gustatory (Small et al., 2003), auditory (Lewis et al., 2005)—have shown the possibly dissociable role for the amygdala and the orbitofrontal cortex in processing emotions along the two dimensions of valence and arousal.

The relative absence of neuroimaging studies of "complex" emotions could be due to the increased cultural variability of the elicitors as well as the display rules that these expressions entail. Among the few exceptions, guilt and embarrassment have been investigated by Takahashi et al. (2004), who reported activation in the ventromedial prefrontal cortex, the left superior temporal sulcus (STS), and higher visual cortices when participants read sentences designed to evoke guilt or embarrassment. This, taken together with the areas underlying the ToMM system, suggests an increased role of "theory-of-mind" to make sense of these emotions. In summary, then, there is now growing evidence that each of the six processes that we propose in our model is associated with heightened activity in specific brain areas.

EMPATHIZING WITH DISCRETE EMOTIONS

Returning to the concept of individual differences in empathizing, this poses an interesting question for the brain basis of perception of discrete emotions. Do we use a centralized "empathy circuit" to make sense of all emotions? If so, can one detect differences in how discrete emotions are processed among individuals at different points on the EQ continuum?

A direct approach to investigate individual differences in empathizing has been to test for sex differences in the perception of emotions. Using facial EMG, one study (Helland, 2005) observed that females tend to show increased facial mimicry to facial expressions of happiness and anger as compared to males. In a metareview of neuroimaging results on sex differences on emotion perception, (Phan et al., 2002) report that females show increased bilaterality in emotion-relevant activation as compared to males, though this is not always found (Lee et al., 2002; Schienle, Schaefer, Stark, Walter, & Vaitl, 2005). One of the reasons for this might have been the fact that sex differences are summated individual differences. Instead of such a broad category-based approach (as in sex-difference studies), an approach based on individual differences in self-report personality scores (Canli, Sivers, Whitfield, Gotlib, & Gabrieli, 2002) or genetic differences (e.g., Hariri et al., 2002) may be more finely tuned.

To test this model of individual variability, we asked if an individual's score on the EQ predicted his or her response to four basic emotions (happiness, sadness, anger, disgust). If empathizing was modulated by a unitary circuit, then individual differences in empathizing would correlate with activity in the same structures for all basic emotions. Twenty-five adult volunteers (13 female, 12 male) selected across the EQ space were scanned in a 3T fMRI scanner on a passive viewing task using dynamic facial expressions as stimuli. It was found that activity in different brain regions correlated with EQ scores for different basic emotions (Chakrabarti, Baron-Cohen, & Bullmore, 2005).

Using a whole-brain analysis with permutation-based techniques (XBAMM, *www-bmu.psychiatry.cam.ac.uk/software/docs/xbamm/*), we found that different brain regions were maximally correlated with the EQ for different emotions. Specifically, for perception of happy faces, a parahippocampal-ventral striatal cluster response was positively correlated with the EQ. The role of this region in reward processing is well known (O'Doherty, 2004). This suggests that the more empathic a person is, the higher is his or her reward response to a happy face. Interestingly, the response from the same region correlated negatively with the EQ during perception of sad faces. This fits perfectly with the earlier results, that is, the more empathic a person is, the lower is his or her reward response to a sad face.

For happy and sad faces, therefore, empathizing seems to involve mirroring. The higher a person's EQ, the stronger the reward response to happy faces, and vice versa for sad faces. This is in concordance with suggestions from earlier studies on pain perception (Singer et al., 2004) and disgust perception (Wicker et al., 2003), where observation and experience have been shown to be mediated by the same set of structures. One of the issues with the previous studies is a possible confound between "personal distress" and empathizing. The novel element in our study is that we explicitly tested for the personality trait of empathizing in relation to perception of specific emotions.

However, empathizing does not appear to be purely an index of mirroring. For perception of angry faces, EQ correlated positively to clusters centered on the precuneus/ inferior parietal lobule, the superior temporal gyrus, and the dorsolateral prefrontal cortex. The posterior cingulate region is known to be involved in self–other distinction (Vogt, 2005), and the superior temporal gyrus is known for its role in theory of mind tasks (Saxe et al., 2004). This suggests that higher EQ corresponds to higher activation in areas related to the distinction of self versus other, as well as those that are recruited to determine another person's intentions. The dorsolateral prefrontal cortex is known for its role in decision making and context evaluation (Rahm et al., 2006). Higher EQ would therefore predict better evaluation of the threat from an angry expression. Since expressions of anger are usually more socially urgent for attention than those of either sadness or happiness, it is essential that highly empathic persons not merely "mirror" the expression. A high empathizer's perception of an angry face would therefore need to be accompanied by an accurate determination of the intentions of the person as well as an evaluation of the posed threat.

In response to disgust faces, a cluster containing the dorsal anterior cingulate cortex and medial prefrontal cortices is negatively correlated with EQ, suggesting that the areas involved in attribution of mental states (primarily required for deciphering the "complex" emotions) are selectively recruited less by people of high EQ. This is what might be expected, because disgust as an emotion is less interpersonal than anger or sadness; so, resources for decoding complex emotional signals need not be utilized. Another cluster that includes the right insula and inferior frontal gyrus (IFG) is negatively correlated with EQ. Given the well-established role of this region in processing disgust, this was a surprising result. We expected that an increased ability to empathize would result in an increased disgust response to facial expressions of disgust. The negative correlation suggests that people with high EQ had a lower insula–IFG response to disgust expressions. A reexamination of the behavioral literature on disgust sensitivity reveals a similar result, since Haidt, McCauley, and Rozin (1994) suggested that increased socialization leads to lower disgust sensitivity. Individuals with high EQ may socialize more than those with low EQ.

The results suggest that empathizing with different basic emotions involves distinct brain regions. While some of the emotions involve more "mirroring" (the same areas show activation during recognition and experience, e.g., the striatal response to happy faces correlating positively with EQ), others require an increased distinction between one's own emotional state and another's (e.g., the STG and IPL–precuneus response to angry faces correlating with EQ). While this explanation fits the discrete emotions model, it did not explicitly test whether there was any region that was common to all four correlation maps. To explore this, we performed a conjunction analysis for all four (emotionneutral) versus EQ correlation plots. Using a hypothesis-driven region-of-interest analysis, we found a significant overlap in the left IFG–premotor cortex. This region was positively correlated with EQ for all four (emotion-neutral) contrasts. Interestingly, a recent study by Lee et al. (2006) shows a similar emotion-specific pattern in the brain regions underlying overt imitation of different facial expressions of emotion.

The IFG–premotor cortex is a fundamental part of the "mirror systems" discussed earlier (Keysers & Perrett, 2004; Rizzolatti & Craighero, 2004). Several studies have shown involvement of "mirror systems" during perception of facial expressions (Buccino et al., 2001; Carr et al., 2003; Dapretto et al., 2006) and actions (Johnson-Frey et al., 2003; Molnar-Szakacs, Iacoboni, Koski, & Mazziotta, 2005) in humans. This fits well with predictions from heuristic models that integrate perception and action (Hurley, 2005). The lower IFG–premotor response to all expressions as a function of trait empathy corroborates similar findings (Dapretto et al., 2006; Nishitani, Avikainen, & Hari, 2004). How-

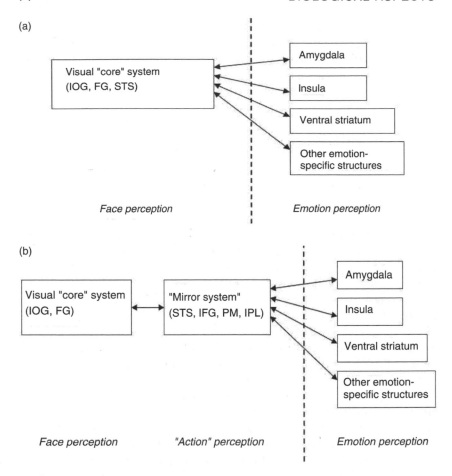

FIGURE 3.4. (a). The original model for face perception proposed by Haxby, Hoffman, and Gobbini (2000) applied to a discrete-emotions framework. Haxby et al. (2000). Copyright 2000 by Psychology Press UK. Adapted by permission. (b). Suggested modifications to the model, specifically for perception of facial expressions of emotion, incorporating a module for "action perception." See text for discussion.

ever, some studies (Carr et al., 2003; Dapretto et al., 2006) have used paradigms involving perception and explicit imitation of facial expressions and did not report any analysis for possible differences among emotions. Our analysis takes these possible differences into account, and the IFG–premotor cluster emerges as a candidate region that correlates with empathy, independent of which emotion is being perceived.

This result provides a putative biomarker for empathy, a trait distributed continuously across the general population, with people with autism spectrum conditions (ASC) clustering toward the low end (Baron-Cohen & Wheelwright, 2004).

COMMON AND DISCRETE NEURAL SUBSTRATES OF EMPATHY

Comparing the results from the conjunction analysis (showing a common neural substrate of EQ across different emotions) with those from the whole brain analysis (showing varying spatial patterns of correlation of EQ with different emotions) shows that there are both common regions that underlie empathy across different emotions and regions specific to certain emotions.

We interpret this by using a model of face processing (Haxby, Hoffman, & Gobbini, 2000) applied to a discrete-emotions framework (see Figure 3.4a). At its simplest, the model proposes a core visual system for face perception. This constitutes the inferior occipital gyrus (for low-level facial feature analysis), the lateral fusiform gyrus (for higher-order invariant aspects of faces such as identity), and the superior temporal sulcus (for variable aspects of faces such as lip movement and speech comprehension). This then interacts with an extended system, which involves different structures for different emotions (Haxby, Hoffman, & Gobbini, 2002). Focusing specifically on perception of dynamic facial expressions of emotion, we propose that an intermediate module for action perception is involved, in line with similar suggestions from others (Gallese, 2003; Keysers & Perrett, 2004; Preston & de Waal, 2002; Rizzolatti & Craighero, 2004) (see Figure 3.4b).

Focusing on the left of the dotted line in Figure 3.4b shows the processes that are equally influenced by trait empathy across all emotions. This includes the regions involved in face perception and the fundamental "mirror" systems used for action perception. This is revealed by the conjunction analysis, which shows a cluster that includes the inferior frontal gyrus–premotor cortex. The common element between different facial expressions of emotion is the fact that they involve the movement of eyes and the mouth, which are possibly coded for by generic "mirror systems" used for action perception. However, on investigating the interaction of each emotion with empathy, we move over to the right-hand side of the dotted line, which gives us emotion-specific correlation maps, in accordance with the discrete emotions model. We interpret these in light of their evolutionary function. It is worth noting though that we do not propose a strict temporal sequence of activation from left to right in this model; nor do we represent subcortical pathways from the visual areas to the emotion-related structures. As in the original model, several of these regions are reciprocally connected, and the temporal progression of activation could be mediated through reafferent projections (Iacoboni et al., 2001). These can be investigated through methods that allow better temporal resolution (e.g., MEG) and forward-model based connectivity analysis (e.g., dynamic causal modeling [Friston, Harrison, & Penny, 2003]).

In sum, the neuroimaging data collected to date show how empathy at the neural level is subtle and complex: various elements in neural networks are activated by the perception of discrete emotions and seem to be related to the various cognitive and behavioral components that are involved in empathetic responding. Moreover, these activation patterns can be modulated by an observer's EQ. At the molecular level, empathy is likely to be determined by other individual differences, such as fetal testosterone (Knickmeyer, Baron-Cohen, Reggatt, & Taylor, 2005), genetic variation (Chakrabarti, Kent, Suckling, Bullmore, & Baron-Cohen, 2006; Skuse et al., 1997), as well as early care or neglect (Fonagy, Steele, Steele, & Holder, 1997). We conclude that more basic neuroscience research into empathy will enrich our understanding of this most fundamental human quality.

ACKNOWLEDGMENTS

Simon Baron-Cohen was supported by the Medical Research Council and the Lurie Marks Family Foundation during the period of this work. Bhismadev Chakrabarti was supported by Trinity College, Cambridge. Parts of this chapter are reprinted from elsewhere (Goldenfeld et al., 2007; Chakrabarti et al., 2006).

REFERENCES

Ahlgren, A., & Johnson D. W. (1979). Sex differences in cooperative and competitive attitudes from the 2nd to the 12th grades. *Developmental Psychology, 15,* 45–49.

Anderson, A., Christoff, K., Stappen, I., Panitz, D., Ghahremani, D., et al. (2003). Dissociated neural representations of intensity and valence in human olfaction. *Nature Neuroscience, 6,* 196–202.

Astington, J., Harris, P., & Olson, D. (1988). *Developing theories of mind.* New York: Cambridge University Press.

Attwood, T. (1997). *Asperger's syndrome.* London, UK: Kingsley.

Baron-Cohen, S. (1989a). The autistic child's theory of mind: A case of specific developmental delay. *Journal of Child Psychology and Psychiatry, 30,* 285–298.

Baron-Cohen, S. (1989b). Perceptual role taking and protodeclarative pointing in autism. *British Journal of Developmental Psychology*, 7, 113–127.

Baron-Cohen, S. (1991). Precursors to a theory of mind: Understanding attention in others. In A. Whiten (Ed.), *Natural theories of mind* (pp. 233–251). Oxford, UK: Blackwell.

Baron-Cohen, S. (1994). The Mindreading System: New directions for research. *Current Psychology of Cognition*, 13, 724–750.

Baron-Cohen, S. (1995). *Mindblindness: An essay on autism and theory of mind*. Boston: MIT Press/Bradford.

Baron-Cohen, S. (2003). *The essential difference: Men, women and the extreme male brain*. London: Penguin.

Baron-Cohen, S., Baldwin, D., & Crowson, M. (1997). Do children with autism use the Speaker's Direction of Gaze (SDG) strategy to crack the code of language? *Child Development*, 68, 48–57.

Baron-Cohen, S., Jolliffe, T., Mortimore, C., & Robertson, M. (1997). Another advanced test of theory of mind: Evidence from very high functioning adults with autism or Asperger syndrome. *Journal of Child Psychology and Psychiatry*, 38, 813–822.

Baron-Cohen, S., Leslie, A. M., & Frith, U. (1985). Does the autistic child have a "theory of mind"? *Cognition*, 21, 37–46.

Baron-Cohen, S., O'Riordan, M., Jones, R., Stone, V., & Plaisted, K. (1999). A new test of social sensitivity: Detection of faux pas in normal children and children with Asperger syndrome. *Journal of Autism and Developmental Disorders*, 29, 407–418.

Baron-Cohen, S., Richler, J., Bisarya, D., Gurunathan, N., & Wheelwright, S. (2003). The systemizing quotient (SQ): An investigation of adults with Asperger syndrome or high functioning autism and normal sex differences. *Philosophical Transactions of the Royal Society B*, 358, 361–374.

Baron-Cohen, S., Spitz, A., & Cross, P. (1993). Can children with autism recognize surprise? *Cognition and Emotion*, 7, 507–516.

Baron-Cohen, S., & Swettenham, J. (1996). The relationship between SAM and ToMM: The lock and key hypothesis. In P. Carruthers & P. Smith (Eds.), *Theories of theories of mind* (pp. 156–168). Cambridge, UK: Cambridge University Press.

Baron-Cohen, S., & Wheelwright, S. (2004). The Empathy Quotient (EQ). An investigation of adults with Asperger syndrome or high functioning autism, and normal sex differences. *Journal of Autism and Developmental Disorders*, 34, 163–175.

Baron-Cohen, S., Wheelwright, S., Hill, J., & Golan, O. (2008). A taxonomy of human emotions.

Baron-Cohen, S., Wheelwright, S., Hill, J., Raste, Y., & Plumb, I. (2001). The "Reading the Mind in the eyes" test revised version: A study with normal adults, and adults with Asperger syndrome or high-functioning autism. *Journal of Child Psychiatry and Psychiatry*, 42, 241–252.

Baron-Cohen, S., Wheelwright, S., & Jolliffe, T. (1997). Is there a "language of the eyes"?: Evidence from normal adults and adults with autism or Asperger syndrome. *Visual Cognition*, 4, 311–331.

Baron-Cohen, S., Wheelwright, S., Stone, V., & Rutherford, M. (1999). A mathematician, a physicist, and a computer scientist with Asperger syndrome: Performance on folk psychology and folk physics test. *Neurocase, 5*, 475–483.

Blair, R. J. (1995). A cognitive developmental approach to morality: Investigating the psychopath. *Cognition, 57*, 1–29.

Blair, R. J., & Cipolotti, L. (2000). Impaired social response reversal—A case of "acquired" sociopathy. *Brain, 123*, 1122–1141.

Blair, R. J., Jones, L., Clark, F., & Smith, M. (1997). The psychopathic individual: A lack of responsiveness to distress cues? *Psychophysiology, 34*, 192–198.

Blair, R. J., Morris, J., Frith, C., Perrett, D. I., & Dolan, R. J. (1999). Dissociable neural responses to facial expressions of sadness and anger. *Brain, 122*, 883–893.

Brothers, L. (1990). The neural basis of primate social communication. *Motivation and Emotion, 14*, 81–91.

Brunet, E., Sarfati, Y., Hardy-Bayle, M.-C., & Decety, J. (2000). A PET investigation of the attribution of intentions with a non-verbal task. *NeuroImage, 11*, 157–166.

Buccino, G., Binkofski, F., Fink, G., Fadiga, L., Fogassi, L., et al. (2001). Action observation activates premotor and parietal areas in a somatotopic manner: An fMRI study. *European Journal of Neuroscience, 13*, 400–404.

Calder, A. J., Lawrence, A. D., Keane, J., Scott, S. K., Owen, A. M., et al. (2002). Reading the mind from eye gaze. *Neuropsychologia, 40*, 1129–1138.

Calder, A. J., Lawrence, A. D., & Young, A. W. (2001). Neuropsychology of fear and loathing. *Nature Reviews Neuroscience, 2*, 352–363.

Canli, T., Sivers, H., Whitfield, S. L., Gotlib, I., & Gabrieli, J. (2002). Amygdala response to happy faces as a function of extraversion. *Science, 296*, 2191.

Carr, L., Iacoboni, M., Dubeau, M.-C., Mazziotta, J., & Lenzi, G. (2003). Neural mechanisms of empathy in humans: A relay from neural systems for imitation to limbic areas. *Proceedings of the National Academy of Sciences, 100*, 5497–5502.

Castelli, F., Frith, C., Happe, F., & Frith, U. (2002). Autism, Asperger syndrome and brain mechanisms for the attribution of mental states to animated shapes. *Brain, 125*, 1839–1849.

Chakrabarti, B., Baron-Cohen, S., & Bullmore, E. T. (2005). *"Empathizing" with discrete emotions: An fMRI study.* Presented at the Society for Neuroscience annual conference, Washington, DC.

Chakrabarti, B., Kent, L., Suckling, J., Bullmore, E. T., & Baron-Cohen, S. (2006). Variations in human cannabinoid receptor (CNR1) gene modulate striatal response to happy faces. *European Journal of Neuroscience, 23*, 1944–1948.

Charlesworth, W. R., & Dzur, C. (1987). Gender comparisons of preschoolers' behavior and resource utilization in group problem-solving. *Child Development, 58*, 191–200.

Charman, T., Ruffman, T., & Clements, W. (2002). Is there a gender difference in false belief development. *Social Development, 11*, 1–10.

Cleckley, H. M. (1977). *The mask of sanity: An attempt to clarify some issues about the so-called psychopathic personality.* St Louis, MO: Mosby.

Connellan, J., Baron-Cohen, S., Wheelwright, S., Ba'tki, A., & Ahluwalia, J.

(2001). Sex differences in human neonatal social perception. *Infant Behavior and Development, 23,* 113–118.

Crick, N. R., & Grotpeter, J. K. (1995). Relational aggression, gender, and social-psychological adjustment. *Child Development, 66,* 710–722.

Daly, M., & Wilson, M. (1988). *Homicide.* New York: Aldine de Gruyter.

Damasio, A. R., Grabowski, T. J., Bechara, A., Damasio, H., Ponto, L. L. B., et al. (2000). Subcortical and cortical brain activity during the feeling of self-generated emotions. *Nature Neuroscience, 3,* 1049–1056.

Dapretto, M., Davies, M., Pfeifer, J., Scott, A., Sigman, M., et al. (2006). Understanding emotions in others: Mirror neuron dysfunction in children with autism spectrum disorders. *Nature Neuroscience, 9,* 28–30.

Davis, M. H. (1994). *Empathy: A social psychological approach.* Boulder, CO: Westview Press.

Decety, J., & Chaminade, T. (2003). Neural correlates of feeling sympathy. *Neuropsychologia, 41,* 127–138.

Dimberg, U., Thunberg, M., & Elmehead, K. (2000). Unconscious facial reactions to emotional facial expressions. *Psychological Science, 11,* 86 89.

Dodge, K. (1980). Social cognition and children's aggressive behavior. *Child Development, 51,* 162–170.

Ekman, P., & Friesen, W. (1969). The repertoire of non-verbal behavior: Categories, origins, usage, and coding. *Semiotica, 1,* 49–98.

Eugene, F., Levesque, J., Mensour, B., Leroux, J.-M., Beaudoin, G., et al. (2003). The impact of individual differences on the neural circuitry underlying sadness. *NeuroImage, 19,* 354–364.

Field, T. (1979). Visual and cardiac responses to animate and inanimate faces by term and preterm infants. *Child Development, 50,* 188–194.

Fonagy, P., Steele, H., Steele, M., & Holder, J. (1997). Attachment and theory of mind: Overlapping constructs? *Association for Child Psychology and Psychiatry Occasional Papers, 14,* 31–40.

Friston, K., Harrison, L., & Penny, W. (2003). Dynamic causal modelling. *NeuroImage, 19,* 1273–1302.

Frith, U., & Frith, C. (2003). Development and neurophysiology of mentalizing. *Philosophical Transactions of the Royal Society B, 358,* 459–473.

Gallese, V. (2003). The roots of empathy: The shared manifold hypothesis and the neural basis of intersubjectivity. *Psychopathology, 36,* 171–180.

Goldenfeld, N., Baron-Cohen, S., Wheelwright, S., Ashwin, C., & Chakrabarti, B. (2007). Empathizing and systemizing in males and females, and in autism spectrum conditions. In T. Farrow & P. W. R. Woodruff (Eds.), *Empathy in mental illness* (pp. 322–334). Cambridge, UK: Cambridge University Press.

Grosbras, M.-H., Laird, A. R., & Paus, T. (2005). Cortical regions involved in eye movements, shifts of attention and gaze perception. *Human Brain Mapping, 25,* 140–154.

Grosbras, M.-H., & Paus, T. (2006). Brain networks involved in viewing angry hands or faces. *Cerebral Cortex, 16,* 1087–1096.

Haidt, J., McCauley, C., & Rozin, P. (1994). Individual differences in sensitivity to disgust: A scale sampling seven domains of disgust elicitors. *Persononality and Individual Differences, 16,* 701–713.

Hall, J. A. (1978). Gender effects in decoding nonverbal cues. *Psychological Bulletin*, 845–848.

Happe, F. (1994). An advanced test of theory of mind: Understanding of story characters' thoughts and feelings by able autistic, mentally handicapped, and normal children and adults. *Journal of Autism and Development Disorders*, 24, 129–154.

Happe, F. (1995). The role of age and verbal ability in the theory of mind task performance of subjects with autism. *Child Development*, 66, 843–855.

Hare, R. D., Hakstian, T. J., Ralph, A., Forth, A., Hart, S., & Newman, S. (1990). The Revised Psychopathy Checklist: Reliability and factor structure. *Psychological Assessment*, 2, 338–341.

Hariri, A. R., Mattay, V. S., Tessitore, A., Fera, F., & Weinberger, D. R. (2003). Neocortical modulation of the amygdala response to fearful stimuli. *Biological Psychiatry*, 53, 494–501.

Hariri, A. R., Mattay, V. S., Tessitore, A., Kolachana, B., Fera, F., et al. (2002). Serotonin transporter genetic variation and the response of the human amygdala. *Science*, 297, 400–403.

Hatfield, E., Cacioppo, J. T., & Rapson, R. (1992). Primitive emotional contagion. In M. Clark (Ed.), *Review of personality and social psychology: Emotion and behavior* (pp. 151–177). Newbury Park, CA: Sage.

Haxby, J. V., Hoffman, E. A., & Gobbini, M. I. (2000). The distributed human neural system for face perception. *Trends in Cognitive Sciences*, 4, 223–233.

Haxby, J. V., Hoffman, E. A., & Gobbini, M. I. (2002). Human neural systems for face recognition and social communication. *Biological Psychiatry*, 51, 59–67.

Helland, S. (2005). *Gender differences in facial imitation.* Bachelor's thesis. University of Lund, Sweden.

Hobson, R. P. (1986). The autistic child's appraisal of expressions of emotion. *Journal of Child Psychology and Psychiatry*, 27, 321–342.

Hobson, R. P. (1993). *Autism and the development of mind.* Mahweh, NJ: Erlbaum.

Hoffman, M. L. (1977). Sex differences in empathy and related behaviors. *Psychological Bulletin*, 84, 712–722.

Hurley, S. L. (2005). Active perception and perceiving action: The shared circuits hypothesis. In T. Gendler & J. Hawthorne (Eds.), *Perceptual experience* (pp. 205–259). New York: Oxford University Press.

Iacoboni, M., Koski, L., Brass, M., Bekkering, H., Woods, R., et al. (2001). Reafferent copies of imitated actions in the right superior temporal cortex. *Proceedings of the National Academy of Sciences*, 98, 13995–13999.

Jackson, P., Meltzoff, A., & Decety, J. (2005). How do we perceive the pain of others?: A window into the neural processes involved in empathy. *NeuroImage*, 24, 771–779.

Johnson-Frey, S., Maloof, F., Newman-Norlund, R., Farrer, C., Inati, S., & Grafton, S. (2003). Actions or hand–object interactions?: Human inferior frontal cortex and action observation. *Neuron*, 39, 1053–1058.

Kalin, N. H., Shelton, S. E., & Davidson, R. J. (2001). The primate amygdala mediates acute fear but not the behavioral and physiological components of anxious temperament. *Journal of Neuroscience*, 21, 2067–2074.

Keysers, C., & Perrett, D. I. (2004). Demystifying social cognition: A Hebbian perspective. *Trends in Cognitive Science, 8,* 501–507.

Knickmeyer, R., Baron-Cohen, S., Raggatt, P., & Taylor, K. (2005). Foetal testosterone, social cognition, and restricted interests in children. *Journal of Child Psychology and Psychiatry, 46,* 198–210.

Knight, G. P., Fabes, R. A., & Higgins, D. A. (1989). Gender differences in the cooperative, competitive, and individualistic social values of children. *Motivation and Emotion, 13,* 125–141.

Lawrence, E. J., Shaw, P., Baker, D., Baron-Cohen, S., & David, A. S. (2004). Measuring empathy—reliability and validity of the empathy quotient. *Psychological Medicine, 34,* 911–919.

LeDoux, J. (2000). Emotion circuits in the brain. *Annual Review of Neuroscience, 23,* 155–184.

Lee, T.-W., Josephs, O., Dolan, R. J., & Critchley, H. D. (2006). Imitating expressions: Emotion-specific neural substrates in facial mimicry. *Social Cognitive Affective Neuroscience, 1*(2), 122–135.

Lee, T., Liu, H.-L., Hoosain, R., Liao, W.-T., Wu, C.-T., et al. (2002). Gender differences in neural correlates of recognition of happy and sad faces in humans assessed by functional magnetic resonance imaging. *Neuroscience Letters, 333,* 13–16.

Leslie, A. (1995). ToMM, ToBy, and Agency: Core architecture and domain specificity. In L. Hirschfeld & S. Gelman (Eds.), *Domain specificity in cognition and culture.* New York: Cambridge University Press.

Leslie, A. M. (1987). Pretence and representation: The origins of "theory of mind." *Psychological Review, 94,* 412–426.

Levenson, R. (1996). Biological substrates of empathy and facial modulation of emotion: Two facets of the scientific legacy of John Lanzetta. *Motivation and Emotion, 20,* 185–204.

Lewis, P., Critchley, H. D., Rotshtein, P., & Dolan, R. J. (2005). *Processing valence and arousal in affective words.* Presented at the Society for Neuroscience annual conference, Washington, DC.

Liotti, M., Mayberg, H., Brannan, S., McGinnis, S., Jerabek, P., & Fox, P. (2000). Differential limbic-cortical correlates of sadness and anxiety in healthy subjects: Implications for affective disorders. *Biological Psychiatry, 48,* 30–42.

Maccoby, E. (1999). *The two sexes: Growing up apart, coming together.* Cambridge, MA: Harvard University Press.

Malhi, G., Lagopoulos, J., Ward, P., Kumari, V., Mitchell, D., et al. (2004). Cognitive generation of affect in bipolar depression: An fMRI study. *European Journal of Neuroscience, 19,* 741–754.

Mayberg, H., Liotti, M., Brannan, S., McGinnis, M. Y., Mahurin, R., et al. (1999). Reciprocal limbic-cortical function and negative mood: Converging PET findings in depression and normal sadness. *American Journal of Psychiatry, 156,* 675–682.

Mcaley L. (1995). The sociobiology of sociopathy: An integrated evolutionary model. *Behavioral and Brain Sciences, 18,* 523–599.

Meltzoff, A. N., & Decety, J. (2003). What imitation tells us about social cognition: A rapprochement between developmental psychology and cognitive neuroscience. *Philosophical Transactions of the Royal Society B, 358*, 491–500.

Mobbs, D., Greicius, M. D., Abdel-Azim, E., Menon, V., & Reiss, A. L. (2003). Humor modulates the mesolimbic reward centres. *Neuron, 40*, 1041–1048.

Moll, J., de Oliveira-Souza, R., Eslinger, P., Bramati, I., Mourao-Miranda, J., et al. (2002). The neural correlates of moral sensitivity: A functional magnetic resonance imaging investigation of basic and moral emotions. *Journal of Neuroscience, 22*, 2730–2736.

Molnar-Szakacs, I., Iacoboni, M., Koski, L., & Mazziotta, J. C. (2005). Functional segregation within pars opercularis of the inferior frontal gyrus: Evidence from fMRI studies of imitation and action observation. *Cerebral Cortex, 15*(7), 986–994.

Muncer, S., Ling, J. (2006). Psychometric analysis of the empathy quotient (EQ) scale. *Personality and Individual Differences, 40*, 1111–1119.

Murphy, F. C., Nimmo-Smith, I., & Lawrence, A. D. (2003). Functional neuroanatomy of emotions: A meta-analysis. *Cognitive, Affective and Behavioral Neuroscience, 3*, 207–233.

Nichols, S. (2001). Mindreading and the cognitive architecture underlying altruistic motivation. *Mind and Language, 16*, 425–455.

Nishitani, N., Avikainen, S., & Hari, R. (2004). Abnormal imitation-related cortical activation sequences in Asperger's syndrome. *Annals of Neurology, 55*, 558–562.

O'Doherty, J. (2004). Reward representations and reward-related learning in the human brain: Insights from neuroimaging. *Current Opinion in Neurobiology, 14*, 769–776.

O'Doherty, J., Deichmann, R., Critchley, H. D., & Dolan, R. J. (2002). Neural responses during anticipation of a primary taste reward. *Neuron, 33*, 815–826.

Panksepp, J. (1998). *Affective neuroscience: The foundations of human and animal emotions.* New York: Oxford University Press.

Pelphrey, K. A., Singerman, J. D., Allison, T., & McCarthy, G. (2003). Brain activation evoked by perception of gaze shifts: The influence of context. *Neuropsychologia, 41*, 156–170.

Perrett, D. I., & Emery, N. (1994). Understanding the intentions of others from visual signals: Neurophysiological evidence. *Current Psychology of Cognition, 13*, 683–694.

Phan, K. L., Wager, T., Liberzon, I., & Taylor, S. F. (2003). Valence, gender, and lateralization of functional brain anatomy in emotion: A meta-analysis of findings from neuroimaging. *NeuroImage, 19*(3), 513–531.

Phan, K. L., Wager, T., Taylor, S. F., & Liberzon, I. (2002). Functional neuroanatomy of emotion: A meta-analysis of emotion activation studies in PET and fMRI. *NeuroImage, 16*, 331–348.

Phillips, W., Baron-Cohen, S., & Rutter, M. (1998). Understanding intention in normal development and in autism. *British Journal of Developmental Psychology, 16*, 337–348.

Phillips, M., Young, A., Senior, C., Brammer, M., Andrew, C., Caldeer, A., et al.

(1997). A specific neural substrate for perceiving facial expressions of disgust. *Nature*, *389*, 495–498.

Piaget, J., & Inhelder, B. (1956). *The child's conception of space*. London: Routledge and Kegan Paul.

Power, T. G. (1985). Mother– and father–infant play: A developmental analysis. *Child Development*, *56*, 1514–1524.

Pratt, C., & Bryant, P. (1990). Young children understand that looking leads to knowing (so long as they are looking into a single barrel). *Child Development*, *61*, 973–983.

Premack, D. (1990). The infant's theory of self-propelled objects. *Cognition*, *36*, 1–16.

Preston, S. D., & de Waal, F. B. M. (2002). Empathy: Its ultimate and proximate bases. *Behavioral and Brain Sciences*, *25*, 1–72.

Rahm, B., Opwis, K., Kaller, C., Spreer, J., Schwarzvald, R., et al. (2006). Tracking the subprocesses of decision-based action in the human frontal lobes. *Neuro-Image*, *30*(2), 656–667.

Rizzolatti, G., & Craighero, L. (2004). The Mirror Neuron System. *Annual Review of Neuroscience*, *27*, 169–192.

Rolls, E. T. (2002). Neural basis of emotions. In N. Smelsner & P. Baltes (Eds.), *International encyclopedia of the social and behavioral sciences* (pp. 4444–4449). Amsterdam: Elsevier.

Saxe, R., Carey, S., & Kanwisher, N. (2004). Understanding other minds: Linking developmental psychology and functional neuroimaging. *Annual Review of Psychology*, *55*, 87–124.

Scaife, M., & Bruner, J. (1975). The capacity for joint visual attention in the infant. *Nature*, *253*, 265–266.

Schienle, A., Schafer, A., Stark, R., Walter, B., & Vaitl, D. (2005). Gender differences in the processing of disgust- and fear-inducing pictures: An fMRI study. *Neuroreport*, *16*, 277–280.

Schroeder, U., Hennenlotter, A., Erhard, P., Haslinger, B., Stahl, R., et al. (2004). Functional neuroanatomy of perceiving suprised faces. *Human Brain Mapping*, *23*, 181–187.

Shumake, J., Edwards, E., & Gonzalez-Lima, F. (2001). Hypermetabolism of para ventricular hypothalamus in the congenitally helpless rat. *Neuroscience Letters*, *311*, 45–48.

Singer, T., Seymour, B., O'Doherty, J., Kaube, H., Dolan, R., & Frith, C. (2004). Empathy for pain involves the affective but not sensory components of pain. *Science*, *303*, 1157–1167.

Skuse, D. H., James, R. S., Bishop, D. V. M., Coppins, B., Dalton, P., et al. (1997). Evidence from Turner's syndrome of the imprinted x-linked locus affecting cognitive function. *Nature*, *287*, 705–708.

Small, D., Gregory, M., Mak, Y., Gitelman, D., Mesulam, M., & Parrish, T. (2003). Dissociation of neural representation of intensity and affective valuation in human gustation. *Neuron*, *39*, 701–711.

Smith, P. M. (1985). *Language, the sexes and society*. Oxford, UK: Blackwell.

Stein, E. (1989). *On the problem of empathy (1917)*. Washington, DC: ICS Publications.

Strayer, F. F. (1980). Child ethology and the study of preschool soical relations. In H. C. Foot, A. J. Chapman, & J. R. Smith (Eds.), *Friendship and social relations in children*. New York: Wiley.

Takahashi, H., Yahata, N., Koeda, M., Matsuda, T., Asai, K., & Okubo, Y. (2004). Brain activation associated with evaluative process of guilt and embarrassment: An fMRI study. *NeuroImage, 23*, 967–974.

Tannen, D. (1991). *You just don't understand: Women and men in conversation*. London: Virago.

Trevarthen, C. (1989). The relation of autism to normal socio-cultural development: The case for a primary disorder in regulation of cognitive growth by emotions. In G. Lelord, J. Muk, & M. Petit (Eds.), *Autisme et troubles du développment global de l'enfant*. Paris: Expansion Scientifique Francaise.

Vogt, B. (2005). Pain and emotion interactions in subregions of the cingulate gyrus. *Nature Reviews Neuroscience, 6*, 533–544.

Wager, T., Phan, K. L., Liberzon, I., & Taylor, S. (2003). Valence gender and lateralization of functional brain anatomy: A meta-analysis of findings from neuroimaging. *NeuroImage, 19*, 513–531.

Walker, A. S. (1982). Intermodal perception of exptessive behaviors by human infants. *Journal of Experimental Child Psychology, 33*, 514–535.

Wellman, H. (1990). *Children's theories of mind*. Cambridge, MA: MIT Press.

Whiten, A. (1991). *Natural theories of mind*. Oxford, UK: Blackwell.

Wicker, B., Keysers, C., Plailly, J., Royet J.-P., Gallese, V., & Rizzolatti, G. (2003). Both of us disgusted in *my* insula: The common neural basis of seeing and feeling disgust. *Neuron, 40*, 655–664.

Williams, J. H. G., Waiter, G. D., Perra, O., Perrett, D. I., & Whiten A. (2005). An fMRI study of joint attention experience. *NeuroImage, 25*, 133–140.

Wimmer, H., Hogrefe, J., & Perner, J. (1988). Children's understanding of informational access as a source of knowledge. *Child Development, 59*, 386–396.

Wimmer, H., & Perner, J. (1983). Beliefs about beliefs: Representation and constraining function of wrong beliefs in young children's understanding of deception. *Cognition, 13*, 103–128.

Yirmiya, N., Kasari, C., Sigman, M., & Mundy, P. (1989). Facial expressions of affect in autistic, mentally retarded, and normal children. *Journal of Child Psychology and Psychiatry, 30*(5), 725–735.

PART II

FUNCTIONALITY

CHAPTER 4

Who Draws Accurate First Impressions?

*Personal Correlates
of Sensitivity to Nonverbal Cues*

JUDITH A. HALL
SUSAN A. ANDRZEJEWSKI

Forming first impressions of people is a phenomenon that is both ubiquitous and irresistible in daily life. The human proclivity to perceive, and generalize from, covariations between behavior or appearance and other personal qualities provides a sense of order and predictability in social interaction. By applying judgment policies based on these generalizations as well as stereotypes and folk knowledge learned from the wider society, people are able to make inferences about new people even with little information to go on. This vast collection of knowledge and beliefs enables us to answer questions such as: Is that car salesman telling me the truth? Is my future mother-in-law really happy to meet me? Is that person going to try to interact with me? Should I go out with that cute person I chatted with only briefly? Though many of these quick inferences are easy and accurate, many are difficult and ambiguous. At the same time, the consequences of being accurate or not can be great.

Because first impressions are made all the time and carry important consequences, researchers have long tried to find out whether some people are especially correct, or incorrect, in drawing conclusions about strangers based on very little information (which we call accuracy of first impressions, or AFI), and what the personal correlates of such accuracy might be. This chapter is concerned with summarizing research on the characteristics of people who have higher or lower AFI. The first impressions measured in this research were based chiefly, or entirely, on judgments of information revealed through nonverbal cues of the face, body, or voice, with the latter being either entirely nonverbal (voice tone only) or accompanied by verbal cues intended to be ambiguous enough so that their presence does not make the task too easy.

Researchers have routinely captured excerpts of behavior in some recorded medium, such as videotape, so that the same excerpts can be shown to different perceivers. Keeping the stimuli constant in this manner means that a given perceiver's accuracy in drawing a first impression can be validly compared to other perceivers' accuracy, revealing a range of accuracy scores that can be attributed to the perceivers' relative abilities to make such judgments rather than to the confounded effects of the target persons' attributes.

Many studies reviewed in this chapter are based on standardized interpersonal sensitivity tests or on widely used stimulus sets, notably the Diagnostic Analysis of Nonverbal Accuracy (DANVA; Nowicki & Duke, 1994), the Interpersonal Perception Task (IPT; Costanzo & Archer, 1989), the Pictures of Facial Affect (POFA; Ekman & Friesen, 1976), and the Profile of Nonverbal Sensitivity (PONS; Rosenthal, Hall, DiMatteo, Rogers, & Archer, 1979). Other tests that are less widely used are also included, such as the Communication of Affect Receiving Ability Test (CARAT; Buck, 1976) and the Japanese and Caucasian Brief Affect Recognition Test (JACBART; Matsumoto et al., 2000). In addition some tests were developed for one-time use in a specific study.

The instruments represented in our review vary across a number of dimensions. The cues being judged are, predominantly, about affective states—often facial expressions of basic emotions such as anger, sadness, or happiness—or personality traits. Some instruments present still photographs, while others show movement via videotape. Some depict the face, some the body, and some the total person. Some instruments depict only visual cues, while others include voice with the visual cues, or only the voice. Verbal content may be masked by, for example, the use of electronic filtering or standard content. Excerpts may be shown for less than 1 second to a minute or more. The stimulus persons in these tests may be engaging in deliberate portrayals or may be behaving spontaneously, as in a conversation.

All such tests have in common that the perceiver must make a judgment about the stimulus person based on limited information and that the judgment can be scored for accuracy by calculating agreement with scoring criteria developed by the researcher. These scoring criteria are operational definitions of the construct in question and vary widely across instruments for measuring AFI. Examples are posed expressions of emotion (e.g., anger, sadness), posed enactments of scenarios (e.g., talking to a lost child, expressing gratitude), expressors' retrospective reports of their thoughts and feelings, objectively measured situational characteristics (e.g., whether the expressors were watching funny or frightening movies), objectively measured personal characteristics (e.g., occupational or relationship status of the expressors), and psychometrically measured personality variables (e.g., self or peer ratings of personality). Different criteria bring their own problems of reliability and validity that, in turn, impact the measurement of accuracy, and therefore any conclusions about correlates of AFI are strengthened if a variety of different testing instruments is represented, as is indeed often the case.

Many perceiver characteristics have been examined in relation to AFI. Because we are interested in enduring personal characteristics, we exclude most studies of transient or experimentally manipulated influences (such as mood; Ambady & Gray, 2002). We will develop the profile of the person who is good in drawing accurate first impressions (has high AFI), with primary focus on late adolescents and adults. Because of space constraints and limited evidence for construct-specific trends (for an exception see Marsh, Kozak, & Ambady, 2007), for the most part we refer to AFI in general, without distinguishing among the various constructs that were judged in different studies (e.g., emotions in general, specific emotions, personality, status, intelligence, etc.).

ARE FIRST IMPRESSIONS ACCURATE?

Although this is a very reasonable question to ask before summarizing correlates of AFI, it does not have an easy answer. For starters, one must define what being "accurate" means for researchers. When researchers say a given construct (such as an emotion or a personality trait) can be accurately judged, they do not necessarily mean that everyone is 100% accurate in judging it. Typically, they mean that the average accuracy score exceeds the level that would be obtained if perceivers were just guessing, according to a statistical test. Indeed, a test on which everyone was 100% accurate would not be a good test because it could not differentiate among people with different accuracy levels. Researchers often deliberately construct their tests to be neither too easy nor too hard. They can, for example, adjust the amount of information presented to perceivers (by degrading or abbreviating the signal), or they can adjust the difficulty of the discriminations perceivers make. As an example of the latter, when judging a fearful facial expression, it is easier to be right if the choice is between "happy" and "fearful" than if the choice is between "surprised" and "fearful." The fact that researchers can engineer the difficulty of their tests presents an obstacle to reaching a firm conclusion about overall accuracy levels. Nevertheless, some general conclusions are warranted. Researchers find that accuracy in judging truthful versus deceptive cues, though significantly above the guessing level, is actually only barely above that level (Bond & DePaulo, 2006). In contrast, perceivers are typically extremely accurate at judging prototypical facial expressions of basic emotions, such as happiness, sadness, or disgust (Ekman, Sorenson, & Friesen, 1969), and they are significantly (i.e., above random choice) accurate even when they are exposed to emotional facial expressions that last only a fraction of a second (Matsumoto et al., 2000). Indeed, studies that successfully use facial expressions as subliminal primes demonstrate that perceivers can make unconscious accurate inferences about faces they do not even know they have seen (Murphy & Zajonc, 1993).

Accuracy can also be very high for judging certain group characteristics, an obvious example being the judgment of whether a person self-identifies as male or female, though even here there is sometimes ambiguity. Ranging widely between these high and low extremes of accuracy are the many other characteristics that one might judge from first impressions, such as subtle emotions, personality traits, intelligence, ethnic/minority group membership, the relationships between people, and status.[1]

CONCEPTUAL MODELS

Because most of the studies we will review are correlational, there is usually no way to know definitively about cause–effect relations. Assume, hypothetically, that a person's AFI is positively related to how much other people like her (or him). Does this mean that being likable causes her AFI to improve? Or does it mean that having high AFI causes other people to like her? The nature of cause–effect relations may differ across variables, such that for some variables AFI might be a causal antecedent and for other variables AFI might be a consequence. Additionally, the relation could be spurious, meaning that there is no causal relation even though there is a correlation. Imagine, for example, that being more physically attractive produces high AFI and also produces high liking by others. In this case, AFI and being liked would likely be correlated with each other but not causally related.

Research can be designed to establish, or at least rule out, different causal possibilities, but unfortunately this is rarely done. Therefore, we can mainly just speculate about what model seems more or less likely. In some instances, one path is much more plausible than another. For example, it is plausible that assignment to the social categories "male" and "female" at birth leads causally to differences in AFI (through mechanisms such as societal expectations and social learning), whereas the reverse is not very plausible. Other relations are usually much more ambiguous than this one, however. In this chapter we will be cautious about causal interpretations, but we will also suggest plausible paths.

IS AFI A UNITARY SKILL?

If Nancy is a good judge of strangers' emotional states, will she also be a good judge of their other qualities, such as their intelligence or their personality? Similarly, if she can judge emotions well from others' faces, does this mean she is equally good when only hearing their voices? In general, how well are different AFI tests correlated with one another? Mostly, such correlations are small and often negligible, as observed for decades (e.g., Buck, 1976; Vernon, 1933) and as reviewed by Hall (2001). The reasons for these low correlations have not been definitively established and may stem in part from the low reliability of some such testing instruments (Hall, 2001). Thus, though the reasons for the low correlation among different AFI tests are still unclear, it is justified to say that different tests of AFI are far from interchangeable. Knowing a person's measured AFI in one domain is not a good predictor of that person's measured AFI in other domains. This opens up the possibility that specific correlates of AFI may not generalize across different ways of measuring AFI. A case in point is Marsh et al.'s (2007) finding that accuracy at judging fear expressions predicted prosocial tendencies better than did accuracy at judging other emotions. Not much insight exists at present into the generalizability question.

GROUP DIFFERENCES

The most widely documented group difference in AFI is for perceivers' sex (as operationally defined by self-classification as male or female): women generally score higher than men on tests of AFI (Hall, 1978, 1984, 2006). This is also true of elementary school children and young adolescents (McClure, 2000; Rosenthal et al., 1979). Females' advantage holds for judgments of face, body, and voice (Hall, 1978), and it is evident cross-culturally (e.g., Biehl et al., 1997; Izard, 1971; Rosenthal et al., 1979). Little is known about the origins of this difference though, as suggested above, a likely contributor is socialization (e.g., societal expectations) that serves to increase females' knowledge of nonverbal cue meanings. Indeed, women do score higher on a paper-and-pencil test of nonverbal cue knowledge than men do (Rosip & Hall, 2004). The domain of judgment is important as well; women's advantage is very evident for judging emotions (a female-stereotypical domain), whereas women have a much less consistent advantage in a more male-stereotypical domain (such as judging the relative status of two people; Schmid Mast & Hall, 2004), and they have no advantage for the arguably gender-neutral domain of lie detection (Aamodt & Custer, 2006). Situational factors may contribute to the sex differences as well (Horgan & Smith, 2006; Ickes, Gesn, & Graham, 2000; Klein & Hodges, 2001) by increasing and/or decreasing motivation to be accurate, depending on the purported gender relevance of the task. The relative contributions of knowledge, content domain, and motivation are not yet well understood.

Other groups whose AFI is elevated include married women with preverbal toddlers (compared to similar women without children; Rosenthal et al., 1979), homosexuals (when judging whether a person is homosexual or not; Ambady, Hallahan, & Conner, 1999), individuals who are in people-oriented occupations (compared to people in object-oriented occupations; Trimboli & Walker, 1993); and people from higher social class families (Hall, Halberstadt, & O'Brien, 1997). One can only speculate about whether this elevated skill stems from adaptive requirements, level of motivation, or acquired knowledge among individuals in the stated group. The mother with the toddler who can't talk yet might learn about judging nonverbal cues from having to read the toddlers' feelings and intentions from nonverbal cues, and similarly the homosexual person would be strongly motivated to know the minimal cues that allow for differentiation between heterosexual and homosexual strangers. On the other hand, selection factors could be involved; for example, people who are already good in AFI might self-select into occupations that require interaction with people.

Low AFI often characterizes members of groups identified as having a wide variety of clinical disorders such as schizophrenia, mania, depression, alcoholism, and autism (e.g., Edwards, Jackson, & Pattison, 2002; Lembke & Ketter, 2002; McGee & Morrier, 2003; Philippot, Kornreich, & Blairy, 2003). Some of these studies lack control tasks that would allow for the demonstration that clinical groups have trouble processing social cues as distinct from difficulties with any kind of test. There may also be confounding factors such as medications. It is important, therefore, to look at milder and more everyday forms of personal dysfunction, as we do shortly.

PERSONAL CORRELATES

Social Functioning

Is high AFI related to how well one gets along in the social world? Extensive evidence indicates "yes" to this question. Several aspects of social functioning can be discussed.

It is a reasonable assumption that people value interpersonal sensitivity in others, and furthermore interpersonal sensitivity is a valued aspect of certain occupational roles. Evidence suggests that peers, spouses, or supervisors in people-related occupations such as mental health counseling can identify who is more and less interpersonally sensitive, as indicated by positive correlations between sensitivity ratings of targets and those targets' scores on an AFI test (Costanzo & Archer, 1989; Rosenthal et al., 1979). In all likelihood, those individuals thus identified as higher in AFI will reap social benefits. Also, perhaps because others value interpersonal sensitivity, both children and adults with high AFI are more popular, according to peer reports (sociometric ratings) (Nowicki & Duke, 1994; Rosenthal et al., 1979). High-AFI adults report themselves to be less lonely (Pitterman & Nowicki, 2004) and to have higher relationship well-being (Carton, Kessler, & Pape, 1999). Perhaps a contributor to these effects is the high-AFI person's heightened prosocial tendencies, mentioned earlier (Marsh et al., 2007). High-AFI women (not men) were more loved by their romantic partners in Sabatelli, Buck, and Dreyer's study (1980), and the more happily married individuals in Schweinle, Ickes, and Bernstein's (2002) all-male sample scored higher on an AFI test. People with higher AFI also have more positive attachment styles (more secure and preoccupied, less dismissive and fearful) than those with lower AFI (Cooley, 2005). But of course these relations may not be direct. For example, the Schweinle et al. (2002) study also showed that high-AFI men reported using more reasoning tactics in marital conflict. Perhaps their more effective approach to conflict is what made for marital satisfaction rather than their AFI per se. Either way, high AFI appears to be associated with an adaptive interpersonal style.

Some aspects of social functioning have been measured in work settings. Those with higher AFI received higher salary raises (Byron, Teranova, & Nowicki, 2007) and tended to be in higher ranks within a university (Hall & Halberstadt, 1994). Elfenbein and Ambady (2002) found that individuals higher in AFI received higher performance ratings from senior staff and peers. Similar findings have emerged for foreign service officers (Rosenthal et al., 1979). The causal processes in such situations will be interesting to explore. Perhaps those with higher AFI are able to impress their superiors irrespective of objective performance indicators (see Halberstadt & Hall, 1980, for evidence that this occurred with teachers' ratings of children's intelligence). Alternatively, higher AFI may directly influence performance, so that those higher in AFI actually do a better job (e.g., in a job requiring interpersonal sensitivity). Research finding that physicians with higher AFI (especially for judging body movement cues) had patients who were more satisfied with them may exemplify this causal process (DiMatteo, Taranta, Friedman, & Prince, 1980). Yet another possibility is that success and/or higher rank in an organization place interpersonal demands on a person that have the effect of increasing his or her interpersonal sensitivity over time.

PERSONALITY

Among individuals in the normal (i.e., not clinically diagnosed) range of functioning, those who experience fewer depressive symptoms have higher AFI (Ambady & Gray, 2002; Carton et al., 1999; Shah, 2001, as cited in Pitterman & Nowicki, 2004). Those with higher AFI also report less social anxiety, shyness, and communication apprehension (Pitterman & Nowicki, 2004; Schroeder, 1995); they report higher social competence (Barnes & Sternberg, 1989); and they describe themselves as functioning better on self-report personality scales labeled "interpersonal adequacy" and "maturity" (Rosenthal et al., 1979).

Individuals with high AFI have higher internal locus of control than those with low AFI (Baum & Nowicki, 1998; Pitterman & Nowicki, 2004) and are more open to new experiences (Matsumoto et al., 2000; Realo et al., 2003), both of which suggest a confident, mentally healthy approach to the world. They also score higher on conscientiousness (Matsumoto et al., 2000).

The previous section on social functioning would lead us to expect that personality traits that have an interpersonal focus would be especially related to AFI, and the evidence strongly confirms this expectation. People with higher AFI report being more generally interested in, and attuned to, the social environment (Riggio & Carney, 2003); they report themselves as being higher in expressiveness (DiMatteo, Hays, & Prince, 1986; Miczo, Segrin, & Allspach, 2001; Riggio & Carney, 2003); and they report themselves to have better conversational skills (Miczo et al., 2001).

Those with high AFI report a higher need for social belonging (Pickett, Gardner, & Knowles, 2004), describe themselves as high on communion (e.g., warm, sociable, seeking closeness to others; Vogt & Colvin, 2003), and are reported by friends as seeking reassurance from others (Funder & Harris, 1986). Those with high AFI sometimes score higher on self-monitoring, but the effect seems to be carried by the acting and extraversion components of self-monitoring (Ames & Kammrath, 2004; Barnes & Sternberg, 1989; Costanzo & Archer, 1989; DiMatteo et al., 1986; Funder & Harris, 1986; Snyder, 1974). Consistent with the latter, extraversion generally predicts higher AFI (Matsumoto et al., 2000; Realo et al., 2003). The trend of these findings suggests that persons who are high in AFI may be particularly attuned to decoding the cues of others in order to be accepted and liked by others. Alternatively, their greater comfort around other people and the rewards that follow may promote the acquisition of interpersonal accuracy. Individuals high in AFI are also more empathic (Barnes & Sternberg, 1989; Funder & Harris, 1986; Pitterman & Nowicki, 2004), though (as with nearly all of the generalizations reported in this chapter) there are exceptions (e.g., Hall, 1979).

Funder and Harris (1986) gathered ratings from close friends rather than relying only on self-reports. Those who scored higher on an AFI test were seen by their friends as being sought out for advice and reassurance. They were also seen as warm, compassionate, and capable of close relationships; as sympathetic and considerate; as low on hostility and deceitfulness; and as low on rebelliousness and nonconformity. These results converge well with the self-report findings listed above.

One study took a longitudinal approach, relating childhood and parental variables collected early in life to AFI measured at age 31 (Hodgins & Koestner, 1993). Those with higher AFI were rated at age 5 by the mother as having a less difficult infant temperament; they also had fathers who exercised an intermediate (as opposed to low or high) level of strictness, and they had parents who agreed more with each other about childrearing practices. The authors suggested that an easy temperament, combined with a harmonious and moderately structured household, formed an optimal environment for the development of interpersonal sensitivity. Such an environment may promote interpersonal attunement and autonomy (internal locus of control).

Self-Insight

If people had a very accurate sense of their own AFI, researchers would have a much easier time, because, instead of giving time-consuming cue judgment tests, they could just ask people to describe their own accuracy. Unfortunately, self-insight into AFI is relatively weak (meta-analysis by Hall, Andrzejewski, & Yopchick, 2008; see also review by Riggio & Riggio, 2001). Individuals do have some idea of how skilled they are at test-specific nonverbal decoding ability and general nonverbal decoding ability. However, the relationships are not strong enough to justify using self-ratings of AFI as a substitute for giving participants an AFI test. Why self-insight for this skill is only mediocre is an interesting question. Perhaps in real life, people do not get enough timely feedback on their AFI to develop accurate self-awareness. Perhaps much of this phenomenon is due to those at the lower end of measured AFI, as these individuals should, by definition, lack insight into how well they can judge others and they may not be able to make good use of others' feedback.

Cognitive Aptitude and Other Kinds of Knowledge

For both theoretical and methodological reasons it is important to ask how AFI tests relate to objective measures of cognitive aptitude, such as intelligence tests or other standardized cognitive tests. Is high AFI just a manifestation of being generally smart? If this were the case, AFI would be a much less interesting topic of inquiry. Numerous studies have investigated this question and collectively have found a positive correlation that is small and often negligible in magnitude (see reviews by Davis & Kraus, 1997; Halberstadt & Hall, 1980). Thus, there is little reason to be concerned that AFI reflects "just" general intelligence.

In contrast, measures of knowledge, aptitude, or cognitive style that are geared specifically toward the social realm are often related to AFI. Higher AFI is positively related to knowledge of nonverbal communication as measured on an objectively scored pencil-and-paper test (Davitz, 1964; Rosip & Hall, 2004); knowledge of psychological gender differences as measured on an objectively scored pencil-and-paper test (Hall & Carter, 1999); knowledge of friends' interpersonal sensitivity as measured objectively based on friends' actual sensitivity (Carney & Harrigan, 2003); and having more interpersonal cognitive and attributional complexity (Woods, 1996). Thus, it would seem that measures that fall broadly under the heading of social intelligence predict AFI.

An intriguing study by Bernieri (1991) suggested that the ability to learn in a face-to-face situation may be influenced by one's AFI. High school students ("teachers") taught nonsense words to a partner ("learners"). The learner's (but not the teacher's) AFI was strongly correlated with how many words were learned, with a correlation substantially stronger than that generally found between overall cognitive ability and

AFI. This suggests that the ability to learn in a face-to-face situation may draw on quick social judgment skills (for example, to notice and learn the teacher's nonverbal reinforcement cues). It is also possible that the quicker learning on the part of high-AFI participants in Bernieri's study may be related to cognitive style rather than cognitive ability per se. Hall and Carter (1999) found that AFI was positively related to higher need for cognition, that is, the desire to think and be challenged mentally.

Social Power, Dominance, and Status

Earlier, we reported that higher AFI is associated with higher social class and higher ranks within a university. Other research suggests that higher AFI is also related to higher personality dominance (Hall et al., 1997). Most research on AFI is based on standardized nonverbal tests, with the power/dominance/status variable also defined in trait terms. A few studies have defined both in situational terms, with the power construct defined in terms of assigned roles and AFI defined in terms of dyad members' judgments of each other. Results for the trait and situational approaches at first appear to be contradictory because in the latter studies decoding accuracy is higher in the low-power group (Hall, Rosip, Smith LeBeau, Horgan, & Carter, 2006; Snodgrass, 1992). However, this has been shown to be due not to the low-power group's decoding accuracy per se (spurred, for example, by their motive to be accurate) but rather to the fact that the low-power role produces deficient nonverbal expressions in those assigned to that group, compared to those assigned to the high-power group, leading to relatively weak decoding by those in the high-power group (Hall et al., 2006; Snodgrass, Hecht, & Ploutz-Snyder, 1998). Thus, in the dyadic power paradigm, low-power individuals are more accurate decoders of nonverbal cues because their own expressions are relatively difficult for their high-power partners to decode.

Social Attitudes

Individual differences also exist in a person's attitudes about other people in general. Are there particular social attitudes that accompany being good at drawing first impressions? Hall and Carter (1999) conducted research that suggests that those who are good at AFI use less gender stereotyping and score lower on social dominance orientation scales (i.e., they do not endorse the belief that some groups are superior to others).

Research on the topic of AFI and prejudice shows that people who are better at decoding affective states are less prejudiced than those who have lower accuracy scores (Andrzejewski, in press). Those researchers also found that people who scored higher on a test of judging emotional meanings in African Americans' faces were less prejudiced against African Americans. Research on the identification of Jewish ethnicity based on facial cues shows that those who are more accurate at such a task also exhibit less anti-Semitic attitudes (Andrzejewski, Hall, & Salib, under review). These findings are consistent with other research that suggests that those who are more interpersonally sensitive tend to be more democratic and less dogmatic (Rosenthal et al., 1979).

WHAT DOES IT ADD UP TO?

A large amount of research shows that it is good to be able to draw accurate inferences about people based on first impressions. Indeed, though not all studies in this literature produced significant differences, the net trends were overwhelmingly positive. AFI seems to have ramifications in relationships and in workplaces and is related to an array of positive personality characteristics, particularly those that are interpersonal in nature. Accuracy of drawing first impressions is related to social adjustment and mental health. It is not strongly enough related to general cognitive ability to suggest that AFI is just another way of estimating a person's general intelligence. AFI is, however, related to several different kinds of social and interpersonal knowledge. In spite of the evident importance of AFI in daily life, people cannot report their AFI very well, though they are more accurate than chance. Therefore, tests are needed. Though many such testing instruments exist, there is much room for improvement both in the range of sensitivities being tested and in terms of the psychometric properties of the instruments.

One can easily imagine the practical implications of having high AFI. These include enhanced ability to detect compatibility with potential dating partners, employers' ability to detect whether or not someone would be a good fit for their company, and greater ease of interaction with the people one meets on a daily basis. Perhaps the high-AFI person can more easily discriminate friend from foe and be more productive in occupations and personal lives. Indeed, higher AFI is associated with tangible rewards such as increased raises and higher performance ratings on the job. And, for people who are high in AFI, the social world may simply be a somewhat less confusing place.

Considering the evidence for adaptive potential of AFI, it should be a high priority to understand where high (and low) AFI comes from. No firm answers are available for this question. Hodgins and Koestner's (1993) longitudinal study implicated both temperamental and home environment factors, suggesting that optimal development may depend on a combination of person and situation. Certain developmental experiences are associated with greater AFI. Individuals who reported spending more time traveling abroad scored higher on AFI (Swenson & Casmir, 1998), suggesting that the travel experience may expand interpersonal sensitivity because of the need to communicate in spite of language barriers.[2]

There is evidence that specific learning experiences can enhance AFI. Thompson, Schellenberg, and Husain (2004) found that college students with higher AFI reported a higher level of previous music study; those authors also performed an experiment demonstrating that providing music and drama lessons improved AFI in children as compared to a control group. Pitterman and Nowicki (2004) found that college dancers had higher AFI than a comparison group of nondancers, suggesting a causal path from dancing to AFI. Feldman, Coats, and Spielman (1996) also found that children who watched more television were more accurate in judging the meanings of facial expressions. Though television viewing is not generally considered a beneficial activity, perhaps it provides good practice at emotional decoding. Experiences such as those outlined in this paragraph may cause people to be more attuned to others' nonverbal nuances or may even enhance the knowledge base required for AFI.

Research that provides people with training opportunities in nonverbal cue recognition has achieved some measure of success, though it is not known how lasting or how generalizable such effects are (Beck & Feldman, 1989; Costanzo, 1992; Davitz, 1964; Ekman & Friesen, 1975; Grinspan, Hemphill, & Nowicki, 2003). Certain experiences in the workplace could similarly have the effect of promoting the development of AFI. A person working in human relations or supervising others on the job might acquire a higher level of AFI than a worker who spends the day underneath automobiles or looking at a computer screen. Whether such gains would be limited to the kinds of cues needing to be decoded in that particular context, or would generalize to performance in other AFI contexts, would be important to ascertain.

Cause–effect issues pose a difficult challenge to further progress in understanding the role of AFI in daily life. The many interpretational ambiguities discussed in this chapter call out for experimental and longitudinal designs, as well as efforts to control for possible confounders and to test mediational models. In addition, research should attempt to put AFI into perspective vis-à-vis other causal variables. For example, if higher AFI leads to better workplace outcomes, one should also ask how this relationship compares to other possible causal influences on such outcomes such as general aptitude, other job-related skills and knowledge, or mental health.

NOTES

1. "Accuracy" in the present context is, as noted in the text, limited to the operational definitions used by researchers in developing scoring criteria. This in no way reifies the existence of constructs such as gender, race, and personality, but merely demonstrates that perceivers vary in the extent to which their judgments concur with the operational criteria for determining what is a "right answer" on the test.
2. Of course, other causal paths for this result are possible. For example, a person who is more interpersonally oriented may opt for foreign travel, and the correlation between travel and AFI is the spurious result of the correlation between interpersonal orientation and AFI. Or, those who travel more may be from higher socioeconomic groups, whose AFI has been shown to be elevated. These distinctly different causal possibilities highlight the ambiguities inherent to the simple correlational approach that is the mainstay of this research literature.

REFERENCES

Aamodt, M. G., & Custer, H. (2006). Who can best catch a liar?: A meta-analysis of individual differences in detecting deception. *Forensic Examiner, 15*, 6–11.

Ambady, N., & Gray, H. M. (2002). On being sad and mistaken: Mood effects on the accuracy of thin-slice judgments. *Journal of Personality and Social Psychology, 83*, 947–961.

Ambady, N., Hallahan, M., & Conner, B. (1999). Accuracy of judgments of sexual orientation from thin slices of behavior. *Journal of Personality and Social Psychology, 77*, 538–547.

Ames, D. R., & Kammrath, L. K. (2004). Mind-reading and metacognition: Narcissism, not actual competence, predicts self-estimated ability. *Journal of Nonverbal Behavior, 28*, 187–209.

Andrzejewski, S. A. (in press). *Interpersonal sensitivity and prejudicial attitudes: A meta-analysis.* Manuscript submitted for publication.

Andrzejewski, S. A., Hall, J. A., & Salib, E. R. (under review). *Anti-Semitism and accuracy in identifying Jewish faces: An examination of how time affects the relation.* Manuscript submitted for publication.

Barnes, M. L., & Sternberg, R. J. (1989). Social intelligence and decoding of nonverbal cues. *Intelligence, 13*, 263–287.

Baum, K. M., & Nowicki, S. (1998). Perception of emotion: Measuring decoding accuracy of adult prosodic cues varying in intensity. *Journal of Nonverbal Behavior, 22*, 89–107.

Beck, L., & Feldman, R. S. (1989). Enhancing children's decoding of facial expression. *Journal of Nonverbal Behavior, 13*, 269–278.

Bernieri, F. J. (1991). Interpersonal sensitivity in teaching interactions. *Personality and Social Psychology Bulletin, 17*, 98–103.

Biehl, M., Matsumoto, D., Ekman, P., Hearn, V., Heider, K., Kudoh, T., et al. (1997). Matsumoto and Ekman's Japanese and Caucasian Facial Expressions of Emotion (JACFEE): Reliability data and cross-national differences. *Journal of Nonverbal Behavior, 21*, 3–21.

Bond, C. F., Jr., & DePaulo, B. M. (2006). Accuracy of deception judgments. *Personality and Social Psychology Review, 10*, 214–234.

Buck, R. (1976). A test of nonverbal receiving ability: Preliminary studies. *Human Communication Research, 2*, 162–171.

Byron, K., Terranova, S., & Nowicki, S., Jr. (2007). Nonverbal emotion recognition and salespersons: Linking ability to perceived and actual success. *Journal of Applied Social Psychology, 27*, 2600–2619.

Carney, D. R., & Harrigan, J. A. (2003). It takes one to know one: Interpersonal sensitivity is related to accurate assessments of others' interpersonal sensitivity. *Emotion, 3*, 194–200.

Carton, J. S., Kessler, E. A., & Pape, C. L. (1999). Nonverbal decoding skills and relationship well-being in adults. *Journal of Nonverbal Behavior, 23*, 91–100.

Cooley, E. L. (2005). Attachment style and decoding of nonverbal cues. *North American Journal of Psychology, 7*, 25–34.

Costanzo, M. (1992). Training students to decode verbal and nonverbal cues: Effects on confidence and performance. *Journal of Educational Psychology, 84*, 308–313.

Costanzo, M., & Archer, D. (1989). Interpreting the expressive behavior of others: The Interpersonal Perception Task. *Journal of Nonverbal Behavior, 13*, 225–245.

Davis, M. H., & Kraus, L. A. (1997). Personality and empathic accuracy. In W. J. Ickes (Ed.), *Empathic accuracy* (pp. 144–168). New York: Guilford Press.

Davitz, J. R. (1964). *The communication of emotional meaning.* New York: McGraw-Hill.

DiMatteo, M. R., Hays, R. D., & Prince, L. M. (1986). Relationship of physician's nonverbal communication skill to patient satisfaction, appointment noncompliance, and physician workload. *Healthy Psychology, 5*, 581–594.

DiMatteo, M. R., Taranta, A., Friedman, H. S., & Prince, L. M. (1980). Predicting patient satisfaction from physicians' nonverbal communication skills. *Medical Care, 18*, 376–387.

Edwards, J., Jackson, H. J., & Pattison, P. E. (2002). Emotion recognition via facial expression and affective prosody in schizophrenia: A methodological review. *Clinical Psychology Review, 22*, 789–832.

Ekman, P., & Friesen, W. V. (1975). *Unmasking the face.* Englewood Cliffs, NJ: Prentice-Hall.

Ekman, P., & Friesen, W. V. (1976). *Pictures of facial affect.* Palo Alto, CA: Consulting Psychologists Press.

Ekman, P., Sorenson, E. R., & Friesen, W. V. (1969). Pan-cultural elements in facial displays of emotions. *Science, 164*, 86–88.

Elfenbein, H. A., & Ambady, N. (2002). Predicting workplace outcomes from the ability to eavesdrop on feelings. *Journal of Applied Psychology, 87*, 963–971.

Elfenbein, H. A., Foo, M. D., White, J., Tan, H. H., & Aik, V. C. (2007). Reading your counterpart: The benefit of emotion recognition accuracy for effectiveness in negotiation. *Journal of Nonverbal Behavior, 31*, 205–223.

Feldman, R. S., Coats, E. J., & Spielman, D. A. (1996). Television exposure and children's decoding of nonverbal behavior. *Journal of Applied Social Psychology, 26*, 1718–1733.

Funder, D. C., & Harris, M. J. (1986). On the several facets of personality assessment: The case of social acuity. *Journal of Personality, 54*, 528–550.

Grinspan, D., Hemphill, A., & Nowicki, S., Jr. (2003). Improving the ability of elementary school-age children to identify emotion in facial expression. *Journal of Genetic Psychology, 164*, 88–100.

Halberstadt, A. G., & Hall, J. A. (1980). Who's getting the message?: Children's nonverbal skill and their evaluation by teachers. *Developmental Psychology, 16*, 654–673.

Hall, J. A. (1978). Gender effects in decoding nonverbal cues. *Psychological Bulletin, 85*, 845–857.

Hall, J. A. (1979). Gender, gender roles, and nonverbal communication skills. In R. Rosenthal (Ed.), *Skill in nonverbal communication: Individual differences* (pp. 32–67). Cambridge, MA: Oelgeschlager, Gunn, & Hain.

Hall, J. A. (1984). *Nonverbal sex differences: Communication accuracy and expressive style.* Baltimore: The Johns Hopkins University Press.

Hall, J. A. (2001). The PONS test and the psychometric approach to measuring interpersonal sensitivity. In J. A. Hall & F. J. Bernieri (Eds.), *Interpersonal sensitivity: Theory and measurement* (pp. 143–160). Mahwah, NJ: Erlbaum.

Hall, J. A. (2006). Men's and women's nonverbal communication: Similarities, differences, stereotypes, and origins. In V. Manusov & M. L. Patterson (Eds.), *The Sage handbook of nonverbal communication* (pp. 201–218). Thousand Oaks, CA: Sage.

Hall, J. A., Andrzejewski, S. A., & Yopchick, J. E. (2008). *Psychosocial correlates of interpersonal sensitivity: A meta-analysis.* Manuscript under review.

Hall, J. A., & Carter, J. D. (1999). Gender-stereotype accuracy as an individual difference. *Journal of Personality and Social Psychology, 77*, 350–359.

Hall, J. A., & Halberstadt, A. G. (1994). "Subordination" and sensitivity to nonverbal cues: A study of married working women. *Sex Roles, 31*, 149–165.

Hall, J. A., Halberstadt, A. G., & O'Brien, C. E. (1997). "Subordination" and nonverbal sensitivity: A study and synthesis of findings based on trait measures. *Sex Roles, 37*, 295–317.

Hall, J. A., Rosip, J. C., Smith LeBeau, L., Horgan, T. G., & Carter, J. D. (2006). Attributing the sources of accuracy in unequal-power dyadic communication: Who is better and why? *Journal of Experimental Social Psychology, 42*, 18–27.

Hodgins, H. S., & Koestner, R. (1993). The origins of nonverbal sensitivity. *Personality and Social Psychology Bulletin, 19*, 466–473.

Horgan, T. G., & Smith, J. L. (2006). Interpersonal reasons for interpersonal perceptions: Gender-incongruent purpose goals and nonverbal judgment accuracy. *Journal of Nonverbal Behavior, 30*, 127–140.

Ickes, W., Gesn, P. R., & Graham, T. (2000). Gender differences in empathic accuracy: Differential ability or differential motivation? *Personal Relationships, 7*, 95–109.

Izard, C. E. (1971). *The face of emotion.* New York: Appleton-Century-Crofts.

Klein, K. J., & Hodges, S. D. (2001). Gender differences, motivation, and empathic accuracy: When it pays to understand. *Personality and Social Psychology Bulletin, 27*, 720–730.

Lembke, A., & Ketter, T. A. (2002). Impaired recognition of facial emotion in mania. *American Journal of Psychiatry, 159*, 302–304.

Marsh, A. A., Kozak, M. N., & Ambady, N. (2007). Accurate identification of fear facial expressions predicts prosocial behavior. *Emotion, 7*, 239–251.

Matsumoto, D., LeRoux, J., Wilson-Cohn, C., Raroque, J., Kooken, K., Ekman, P., et al. (2000). A new test to measure emotion recognition ability: Matsumoto and Ekman's Japanese and Caucasian Brief Affect Recognition Test (JACBART). *Journal of Nonverbal Behavior, 24*, 179–209.

McClure, E. B. (2000). A meta-analytic review of sex differences in facial expression processing and their development in infants, children, and adolescents. *Psychological Bulletin, 126*, 424–453.

McGee, G., & Morrier, M. (2003). Clinical implications of research in nonverbal behavior of children with autism. In P. Philippoy, R. S. Feldman, & E. J. Coats (Eds.), *Nonverbal behavior in clinical settings.* Oxford, UK: Oxford University Press.

Miczo, N., Segrin, C., & Allspach, L. E. (2001). Relationship between nonverbal sensitivity, encoding, and relational satisfaction. *Communication Reports, 14*, 39–48.

Murphy, S. T., & Zajonc, R. B. (1993). Affect, cognition, and awareness: Affective priming with optimal and suboptimal stimulus exposures. *Journal of Personality and Social Psychology, 64*, 723–739.

Nowicki, S., & Duke, M. P. (1994). Individual differences in the nonverbal communication of affect: The Diagnostic Analysis of Nonverbal Accuracy Scale. *Journal of Nonverbal Behavior, 18*, 9–35.

Philippot, P., Kornreich, C., & Blairy, S. (2003). Nonverbal deficits and interpersonal regulation in alcoholics. In P. Philippot, R. S. Feldman, & E. J. Coats (Eds.), *Nonverbal behavior in clinical settings.* Oxford, UK: Oxford University Press.

Pickett, C. L., Gardner, W. L., & Knowles, M. (2004). Getting a cue: The need to belong enhances sensitivity to social cues. *Personality and Social Psychology Bulletin, 30*, 1095–1107.

Pitterman, H., & Nowicki, S., Jr. (2004). A test of the ability to identify emotion in human standing and sitting postures: The Diagnostic Analysis of Nonverbal

Accuracy-2 Posture Test (DANVA2-POS). *Genetic, Social, and General Psychology Monographs, 130*, 146–162.

Realo, A., Allik, J., Nolvak, A., Valk, R., Ruus, T., Schmidt, M., et al. (2003). Mind-reading ability: Beliefs and performance. *Journal of Research in Personality, 37*, 420–445.

Riggio, R. E., & Carney, D. R. (2003). *Social skills inventory manual* (2nd ed.). Redwood City, CA: Mind Garden.

Riggio, R. E., & Riggio, H. R. (2001). Self-report measurement of interpersonal sensitivity. In J. A. Hall & F. J. Bernieri (Eds.), *Interpersonal sensitivity: Theory and measurement* (pp. 127–142). Mahwah, NJ: Erlbaum.

Rosenthal, R., Hall, J. A., DiMatteo, M. R., Rogers, P. L., & Archer, D. (1979). *Sensitivity to nonverbal communication: The PONS test*. Baltimore: Johns Hopkins University Press.

Rosip, J. C., & Hall, J. A. (2004). Knowledge of nonverbal cues, gender, and nonverbal decoding accuracy. *Journal of Nonverbal Behavior, 28*, 267–286.

Sabatelli, R. M., Buck, R., & Dreyer, A. (1980). Communication via facial cues in intimate dyads. *Personality and Social Psychology Bulletin, 6*, 242–247.

Schmid Mast, M., & Hall, J. A. (2004). Who is the boss and who is not? Accuracy of judging status. *Journal of Nonverbal Behavior, 28*, 145–165.

Schroeder, J. E. (1995). Interpersonal perception skills: Self-concept correlates. *Perceptual and Motor Skills, 80*, 51–56.

Schweinle, W. E., Ickes, W., & Bernstein, I. H. (2002). Empathic inaccuracy in husband to wife aggression: The overattribution bias. *Personal Relationships, 9*, 141–158.

Shah, N. (2001). *The association between nonverbal communication skill and depression and anxiety*. Unpublished master's thesis, Department of Psychology, Emory University, Atlanta, GA.

Smith, H. J., Archer, D., & Costanzo, M. (1991). "Just a hunch": Accuracy and awareness in person perception. *Journal of Nonverbal Behavior, 15*, 3–18.

Snodgrass, S. E. (1992). Further effects of role versus gender on interpersonal sensitivity. *Journal of Personality and Social Psychology, 62*, 154–158.

Snodgrass, S. E., Hecht, M. A., & Ploutz-Snyder, R. (1998). Interpersonal sensitivity: Expressivity or perceptivity? *Journal of Personality and Social Psychology, 74*, 238–249.

Snyder, M. (1974). Self-monitoring of expressive behavior. *Journal of Personality and Social Psychology, 30*, 526–537.

Swenson, J., & Casmir, F. L. (1998). The impact of culture-sameness, gender, foreign travel, and academic background on the ability to interpret facial expression of emotion in others. *Communication Quarterly, 46*, 214–230.

Thompson, W. F., Schellenberg, E. G., & Husain, G. (2004). Decoding speech prosody: Do music lessons help? *Emotion, 4*, 46–64.

Trimboli, A., & Walker, M. (1993). The CAST test of nonverbal sensitivity. *Journal of Language and Social Psychology, 12*, 49–65.

Vernon, P. E. (1933). Some characteristics of the good judge of personality. *Journal of Social Psychology, 4,* 42–58.

Vogt, D. S., & Colvin, R. C. (2003). Interpersonal orientation and the accuracy of personality judgments. *Journal of Personality, 71,* 267–295.

Woods, E. (1996). Associations of nonverbal decoding ability with indices of person-centered communicative ability. *Communication Reports, 9,* 13–22.

CHAPTER 5

To What Extent, and under What Conditions, Are First Impressions Valid?

HEATHER M. GRAY

On November 12, 2004, a 12-person jury in Redwood City, California, found Scott Peterson guilty of killing his pregnant wife, Laci. A month later, they recommended that Peterson receive the death penalty for his crime. How did the jury come to these conclusions, and what evidence did they weigh most heavily? There was a lack of physical evidence tying Peterson to the killing of his wife and unborn baby. Instead, the jurors relied on a web of circumstantial clues—including Peterson's demeanor during the trial. They noted that in the course of 6 months of graphic testimony Peterson only cried "once or twice." They referred to his "blank stare" and his failure to show an "expression of caring." One juror explained her decision to recommend the death penalty in this way: "For me, a big part of it was at the end, the verdict—no emotion, no anything. That spoke a thousand words" (CNN.com, 2004).

The jurors made, quite literally, a life-or-death decision about Peterson. But in the course of everyday life, we all make important decisions about other people. Like the jurors in the Peterson case, we form impressions of people's personal character, motives, emotions, and capacity to deceive, and we take note of the state of their relationships with other people. And like the jurors, in forming all of these impressions we pay a great deal of attention to nonverbal behavior. How accurate are these impressions, and what conditions improve or diminish our accuracy? The goal of this chapter is to survey the literature and attempt to provide answers to these questions.

The relative accuracy of interpersonal perceptions is hotly debated in the field of social psychology. On one hand, some scholars point to common errors in social judgment and conclude that, overall, first impressions are generally inaccurate. Demonstrations of the "fundamental attribution error" reveal that when behavior is shaped entirely by situational forces, perceivers will still attribute that behavior, in part, to stable dispositions (e.g., Jones & Harris, 1967; Ross, Amabile, & Steinmetz, 1977). However, other scholars suggest that in everyday interactions this "error" may actually allow perceivers to function quite effectively (Krueger & Funder, 2004). For instance, people more prone to making the fundamental attribution error tend to be more socially engaged and competent as well as more emotionally well adjusted and satisfied with their lives (Block & Funder, 1986). Block and Funder (1986) suggest that in most real-life situations attributing behavior to a mixture of *both* dispositional and situational forces may well be an appropriate strategy of inference. Another common error of social judgment is egocentrism, the tendency for perceivers to falsely assume that others share their knowledge, preferences, and attitudes (e.g., Keysar, Ginzel, & Bazerman, 1995; Ross, Greene, & House, 1977). But, like the fundamental attribution error, egocentrism may be beneficial in real-life relationships when people *do* have similar knowledge, preferences, and attitudes (e.g., Murray, Holmes, Bellavia, Griffin, & Dolderman, 2002).

Clearly, the question of whether interpersonal perceptions are generally accurate or inaccurate is a complex one. I suggest that, in addition to considering accuracy and other *outcomes* of social judgments, it may be fruitful to also consider the mental *processes* that produce judgments. This could be accomplished by considering the conditions under which judgments are rendered more or less accurate. In this chapter, I discuss relative levels of accuracy in first impressions of personality, thoughts, feelings, capacity to deceive, and social relations. For each, I review two kinds of moderators of accuracy: information-level factors (characteristics of stimuli that tend to foster or inhibit accuracy) and person-level factors (characteristics of particular judges that render them especially accurate or inaccurate).

I begin with personality. Perceivers are clearly prone to use personality to make sense of behavior. It seems important to ask, therefore, how accurate are perceptions of personality, and what conditions foster or impair accuracy?

PERSONALITY

The ability to gauge an individual's personality quickly and on the basis of limited information is of critical importance. Consider the job interview, the blind date, or the first meeting with a potential roommate. In each of these situations, the validity of early impressions has lasting consequences for a perceiver's ability to create positive relationships. Forming impressions of personality traits occurs spontaneously, without intention or even awareness (e.g., Uleman, Newman, & Moskowitz, 1996). But to what extent are these impressions valid?

In order for researchers to establish the base rates of accuracy in personality judgments, they must tackle the thorny issue of defining accuracy in the context of such an intangible construct. As outlined by Kruglanski (1989), there are at least three ways to define accuracy. First, one could access the degree of correspondence between a judgment (such as a perceiver's impression of personality) and a criterion (such as a target's self-assessment of personality). Alternatively, one could access interpersonal consensus: the degree to which perceivers independently come to the same conclusion regarding a target's personality. A third option is to somehow measure the pragmatic utility of a judgment—such as whether a personality judgment accurately predicts a target's behavior in a given situation. The majority of researchers in this area have chosen to adopt the first or second criterion.

Using the first criterion, researchers have highlighted the ease with which judgments can be made about enduring personality traits. In perhaps the first study of its kind, Estes (1938) compared perceivers' impressions of personality with targets' self-reported assessments. After viewing 2-minute film clips of people engaged in expressive movement, perceivers formed valid impression of emotionality, inhibition, and apathy. Half a century later, Borkenau and Liebler (1992) systematically examined accuracy in perceptions of the five factors believed to summarize individual differences in personality (extraversion, agreeableness, conscientiousness, neuroticism, and openness; McCrae & Costa, 1987). Perceivers viewed 90-second video clips of targets performing standardized behavior. Their perceptions of extraversion and conscientiousness showed the highest correspondence with self-assessments; correlations were 0.42 and 0.25, respectively. Neuroticism, agreeableness, and openness were less well judged. Concerned with the use of self-assessments as the sole criterion for accuracy, Borkenau and Liebler (1993) also asked targets' romantic partners or family members to provide descriptions of targets' personality. When these informant reports were used as the criterion for accuracy, extraversion and conscientiousness again emerged as the most discernible traits.

Some researchers have called for the use of more naturalistic paradigms in the study of accuracy in personality assessment. For instance, Kenny, Horner, Kashy, and Chu (1992, p. 96) suggested that researchers should "move back and forth between controlled laboratory ratings and more naturalistic interactions between people" in order to develop a more complete picture of accuracy in personality assessment. Recently, Gray and Ambady (2006) examined the accuracy of personality impressions stemming from naturalistic interactions. This experiment consisted of several phases. First, upon entering the lab, participants were led into a small room and were asked to view scenes from popular movies. After the scenes ended, an experimenter entered the room and explained that the materials needed for the next phase of the study were not yet available. The experimenter then sat down and engaged the participant in a short conversation about college courses, life on campus, and plans for the upcoming summer break. After about 5 minutes, the experimenter left the room and returned with a surprise task: the challenge of describing the experimenter's personality, solely on the basis of the previous 5-minute conversation. Accuracy was defined as the degree of participants' correspondence with self-reports and with reports provided by knowledgeable informants (the experiments' close friends and family members). Results revealed that participants' reports showed a high level of correspondence with these criteria; average correlations for extraversion, agreeableness, conscientiousness, and neuroticism were all above 0.64. Participants had much more difficultly inferring openness; the average correlation for this domain was only 0.18. Results also revealed that participants' impressions tended to overlap more with those provided by the experimenters' close friends (average correlation = 0.65) and less with the experimenters' self-assessments (average correlation = 0.51). This suggests that during the brief conversation the experimenters expressed a "version" of themselves—in their verbal statements, facial displays, and countless other channels of communication—that was most similar to the one they show their close friends.

Another stream of research has adopted Kruglanski's (1989) second criterion for accuracy. The conclusion, at least at this point, is again optimistic: unacquainted judges can exhibit a surprisingly high degree of consensus in their impressions of a stranger's personality. In an early study, Norman and Goldberg (1966) examined consensus in judgments of personality as a function of acquaintance. They found that, although consensus increased with increased exposure, consensus at "zero acquaintance" was not zero. In other words, independent perceivers show some agreement regarding a target's personality even in the absence of interaction with that target.

Several years later, Albright, Kenny, and Malloy (1988) followed up on this work. They, too, gave perceivers no opportunity to interact with the target of their judgment. Therefore, in order to make personality judgments, they were forced to rely primarily on physical appearance. Albright and colleagues (1988) reasoned that consensus at zero acquaintance would result from the use of shared implicit theories about the link between observable physical appearance characteristics and underlying personality (for example, that good grooming and neat clothing are valid signs of conscientiousness). Results largely supported this hypothesis: on two dimensions of personality—extraversion and conscientiousness—a significant proportion of variance in perceivers' impressions (41% and 25%, respectively) was due to the stimulus target.

Many potential moderators of accuracy in personality judgment have been identified. One information-level moderator concerns the type of personality trait being judged. Across many studies, extraversion has emerged as the facet of personality that is most easily judged by naive observers (Albright et al., 1988; Borkenau & Liebler, 1992, 1993; Kenny et al., 1992). What makes this factor so transparent? Funder and Dobroth (1987) found that the behaviors that express extraversion (e.g., being cheerful and talkative) tend to be revealed relatively directly in social behavior, whereas the behaviors that express other traits, particularly neuroticism and openness, are much less visible. In most social situations, it is easy to determine whether someone is socially poised and gregarious; it is much more difficult to assess the tendency to daydream or experience anxiety. In some special situations, however, these less transparent traits begin to emerge more clearly. For instance, situations that express relative levels of creativity and cognitive complexity—like discussing philosophical issues or musical preferences—reveal openness (Borkenau, Mauer, Riemann, Spinath, & Angleitner, 2004; Funder & Sneed, 1993; Rentfrow & Gosling, 2006).

Another stream of research has examined how much information is necessary for forming an accurate impression of personality. Although research into this question has yielded a complex pattern of results, it *is* clear that with increasing acquaintance comes increasing accuracy—at least when self-assessments are used as the gold standard (Bernieri, Zuckerman, Koestner, & Rosenthal, 1994; Biesanz, West, & Millevoi, 2007; Paulhus & Bruce, 1992). This probably results from increased exposure to the target person in a range of diverse environments. However, although our naive intuition that increasing exposure yields increased accuracy may be correct, it is also true—as revealed by the zero-acquaintance paradigm—that perceivers can be surprisingly accurate in their impressions even without the benefit of direct interaction. In a meta-analysis of the accuracy of predictions of a wide range of outcomes, Ambady and Rosenthal (1992) found that impressions formed after very brief observations were as accurate as those based on 5-minute observations. They attributed this finding to the fact that personality is often revealed in very "thin slices" of expressive behavior (see also Colvin & Funder, 1991; Funder & Sneed, 1993). And, as demonstrated by Gosling, Gaddis, and Vazire (see Chapter 14), a surprising amount of information about personality is revealed solely in the environments we construct—whether real or virtual.

Another exciting line of inquiry concerns the extent to which temporary changes in the perceiver's cognitive orientation influence the ability to infer personality. For instance, early on, Estes (1938) speculated that judges were most successful in forming impressions of personality when they relied on relatively effortless thinking. Ambady (2001) directly tested this notion by asking some participants to deliberate carefully before producing their judgments. In line with Estes's early speculation, participants who were asked to deliberate carefully produced less valid assessments than did those who were allowed to use their "gut reactions." This suggests that in some cases relying on cognitive strategies that are not consciously mediated may facilitate accuracy.

Motivation also influences accuracy. People who are more highly motivated to understand others often produce more accurate judgments of personality, probably because they behave in ways that make their interaction partner feel more comfortable in divulging relevant cues to personality (Letzring, Greve, & Funder, 2005). Somewhat paradoxically, sad mood may have the same effect. In the Gray and Ambady (2006) study discussed above, the film clips participants viewed during the first phase of the study were actually used to induce either sadness or a relatively neutral mood. Those who viewed sad clips and were therefore more sad than usual during the conversation with the experimenter subsequently produced more valid first impressions. As displayed in Figure 5.1, this pattern extended to all five facets of personality judged. Why did sad mood have a beneficial impact? It appears that sadness increases the motivation to form and maintain social connections (Keller & Nesse, 2005).

To summarize, perceivers spontaneously form impressions of personality, and these impressions—even when based on very minimal information—are surprisingly accurate. At the same time, situational and person-level factors help to shape accuracy levels. People who rely on their "gut reactions" when forming impressions tend to be more accurate, as do those who have the skill to draw out more diagnostic infor-

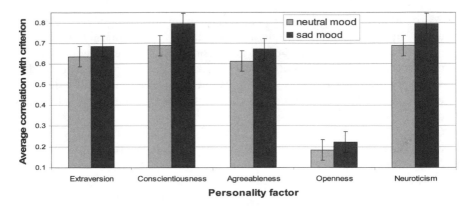

FIGURE 5.1. Accuracy in personality judgments as a function of the mood state of the perceiver and the personality factor being judged. Bars represent standard error of the mean.

mation from their interaction partners. Accuracy generally increases with exposure and acquaintanceship, but expressive behavior reveals a great deal even in small doses.

There are substantial benefits to forming valid first impressions of personality. People who are successful in this endeavor are granted the ability to predict a wide range of behaviors, including job performance (Barrick & Mount, 1991; Thoresen, Bradley, Bliese, & Thoresen, 2004), suitability as a spouse (Botwin, Buss, & Shackelford, 1997), and even preferred tactics of manipulation (Buss, 1992). However, the roots of behavior go beyond personality traits. Behavior is also governed by relatively transient constructs. In the next section I focus on whether and when perceivers can infer two such constructs—thoughts and feelings.

THOUGHTS AND FEELINGS

About 2 million years ago, the brain size of our hominid ancestors began to increase exponentially. Because brain tissue is metabolically very expensive, this dramatic growth likely served an important purpose. At around the same time in our evolutionary history, people began living in larger, more complex, groups. The social brain hypothesis (Dunbar, 1998) links these two events: it suggests that our large brains reflect the computational demands of life within complex social groups.

We use the computational capacity afforded by our big brains in the service of sophisticated social skills, including deception, deception detection, and forming coalitions. These skills require mind reading: the capacity to recognize that other people have mental states—like thinking, believing, and wanting—that are different from one's own and that do not necessarily reflect reality. Mental states must be inferred on the basis of external cues such as facial expressions, because they are not directly observable (Siegal & Varley, 2002). Because people act on their *beliefs* about the world—rather than the true state of the world—perceiving mental states is crucial for predicting behavior.

The frequent need for mind reading could easily place an overwhelming demand on our limited supply of cognitive resources. However, recent research has established that perceivers can form inferences about mental states without usurping cognitive resources. Specifically, perceivers make inferences about goals and intentions unintentionally, without awareness, and in the absence of experimental instructions (Hassin, Bargh, & Uleman, 2002; Hassin, Aarts, & Ferguson, 2005). Upon seeing Jane chasing a taxi, for instance, most perceivers would spontaneously conclude that Jane would like a ride—*not* that she is trying to get some exercise (Hassin et al., 2005). Perceivers are so hungry for this kind of information that they spontaneously ask and answer questions about what drives behavior (e.g., Heider & Simmel, 1944). Developmental psychologists have discovered that children begin to have "first-order beliefs" between the ages of 4–6 (Wimmer & Perner, 1983). That is, they begin to understand that other people have their own distinct mental representations of the world (e.g., "John thinks that the toy is in the box").[1] A few years later they begin to develop competence in understanding second-order, or embedded, beliefs (e.g., "John thinks that Mary thinks the toy is in the box"). These kinds of inferences underlie much of our sophisticated social reasoning and behavior.

Although most individuals succeed in complex mind reading by the time they are school-age, some disorders, including autism, disrupt the development of competence. Individuals with autism show a selective impairment in the ability to use nonverbal behavior, particularly eye movements, to infer mental states (Baron-Cohen, Wheelwright, Hill, Raste, & Plumb, 2001). Abnormalities in the neural network known as the "social brain" (which consists of the medial, inferior frontal and superior temporal cortices, and the amygdala) may be responsible for these deficits (Golan, Baron-Cohen, Hill, & Golan, 2006; Brothers & Ring, 1992). Whatever its cause, an ability to infer mental states makes the social world seem unpredictable and incomprehensible. Confusion and withdrawal likely contribute to the social impairment often apparent in autism spectrum disorders (e.g., Hill & Frith, 2003).

On the other hand, biological processes can sometimes *facilitate* the ability to infer mental states. Recognizing that the hormone oxytocin plays a key role in prosocial behavior and affiliation (e.g., Young &

Wang, 2004), and that affiliation results, in part, from having a clear understanding of social situations, Domes, Heinrichs, Michel, Berger, and Herpertz (2007) studied whether oxytocin facilitates the inference of mental states. Consistent with this hypothesis, Domes and colleagues found that a single dose of oxytocin substantially improved men's ability to interpret subtle facial cues to mental states. The authors speculate that oxytocin enhances the reward of social encounters, thus promoting the motivation to understand others and to engage in social interactions (Insel & Young, 2001). In sum, person-level biological factors can powerfully impact social connections by altering the motivation and knowledge necessary for reading minds.

Understanding others and predicting their behavior demands an accurate reading not only of their beliefs and other mental states but also of their feelings. Emotion recognition—the ability to identify subtle cues to affective states like sadness, happiness, and anger—is a necessary first step toward successful interaction (Custrini & Feldman, 1989). The bulk of reliable information about emotional state is transmitted through nonverbal cues, particularly facial displays and vocal tone (Nowicki & Duke, 2001).

Skill in interpreting these signals confers the ability to avoid life-threatening situations and discover opportunities for growth and joy. It is not surprising, therefore, that most healthy adults are experts in emotion recognition from the face (e.g., Isaacowitz et al., 2007) and the voice (Johnstone & Scherer, 2000). Our expertise is endowed: researchers have identified biologically programmed systems that govern the automatic and effortless recognition of emotional displays (e.g., Dimberg, 1997; Dimberg, Thunberg, & Elmehed, 2000; Whalen et al., 1998), and the so-called "basic" emotions are recognized at above-chance accuracy across cultures, both literature and preliterate (Ekman, 1972; Izard, 1971).

As with mind reading, some factors do influence emotion recognition expertise. Person-level factors include age and health. Preverbal children depend entirely on nonverbal communication in order to interact with the social world. To aid in their survival, they can interpret facial signs of emotion as early as 3 months—even earlier if the emotion is expressed by the infant's own mother (for a review, see Walker-Andrews, 1997). Preschoolers can verbally label facial expressions of emotion at above-chance levels (e.g., Widen & Russell, 2003), but they do not acquire full proficiency until about age 10 (Walker-Andrews, 1997).

Adults with certain developmental disorders and psychiatric illnesses experience some of the same difficulties. Autism seems to present a particular challenge in recognizing sadness (Boraston, Blakemore, Chilvers, & Skuse, 2007), and people with schizophrenia (Feinberg,

Rifkin, Schaffer, & Walker, 1986), social anxiety (Montagne et al., 2006), and depression (Feinberg et al., 1986) all struggle with both emotion recognition and social adjustment. The neural systems that underlie emotion recognition may be abnormal in persons with these disorders.

One information-level moderator of emotion recognition is the match, in terms of cultural group membership, between the target and the perceiver. Although there is evidence for cross-cultural recognition of emotions (e.g., Ekman, 1972; Izard, 1971), it appears that emotional expressions may lose some of their meaning when translated across cultural boundaries. In a meta-analysis of the available data, Elfenbein and Ambady (2002) found that emotions tend to be more accurately understood by perceivers who are members of the same national, ethnic, or regional group as the individual who expressed the emotion. Subtle variations in expressive style and underlying emotion concepts may be responsible. Elfenbein and Ambady (2002) specifically point to culture-specific elements of emotional behavior that must be learned, mostly by growing up in the culture but also through exposure to the culture via television or other mediums.

To summarize, we generally develop an expertise in inferring mental and emotional states by late childhood, and for good reason. Understanding others' thoughts and feelings is essential to understanding the social world and building vital social support systems. However, biological events can influence the activation of the neural systems that are dedicated to these tasks, thus impairing or facilitating accuracy. Less drastic changes to the nature of the available stimuli, such as the cultural group membership of the target, produce more subtle effects on accuracy.

Although I have discussed mental state and emotional state attribution separately, perceivers spontaneously form inferences of both thoughts and feelings (Ickes, Stinson, Bissonnette, & Garcia, 1990). Next, I explore what happens when targets actively try to hide their true thoughts or feelings. How effective are their attempts to mislead perceivers, and under what conditions can perceivers accurately detect lies?

DECEPTION

Lying is a ubiquitous part of social life. As DePaulo and colleagues (DePaulo, Kashy, Kirkendol, Wyer, & Epstein, 1996) note, most lies are relatively harmless, told in order to avoid friction and maintain harmony in relationships. "Little white lies," including those about the attractiveness of a friend's new haircut, are good examples. Other lies, however, are less innocuous. Consider the false denial of marital infidelity, or the deliberate misreporting of a company's assets. In these kinds of cases, the successful deceiver can maliciously manipulate individuals and organizations in order to advance his or her particular self-interests. So, it seems reasonable to ask: how successful are perceivers in distinguishing truths from lies?

Unfortunately for the perceiver, it appears that skills in detecting deception lag behind skills in perpetrating deception. A growing body of literature—including at least 100 estimates of lie detection ability—finds that the typical perceiver often fails to detect lies. The average accuracy rate is 54%, only slightly better than that afforded by chance guessing (Bond & DePaulo, 2006).

Why are base rates of accuracy so low? There are several possible explanations. First, perceivers often fail to receive prompt and accurate feedback regarding their detection performance (DePaulo & Pfeifer, 1986). As a result, they cannot assess and refine their judgmental strategies. Second, detecting deception requires a lot of cognitive flexibility. One must gather all observable cues—from the verbal and nonverbal streams of behavior—and then reconsider this evidence in light of information about the deceiver's goals, pursuits, and personal character. Perceivers often find it difficult to step this far outside their own perspective (e.g., Keysar, 1994). And finally, the cues to deception may be too idiosyncratic for perceivers to develop a general judgmental strategy that applies to a whole group of targets. Over time, and with increased exposure, it may be possible to identify a close friend's deceptive behavior patterns by comparing behavior expressed during deception with behavior expressed typically; however, these behaviors may not apply to one's colleague or friendly acquaintance.

The relationship between the liar and the lie detector is indeed emerging as one potential moderator of accuracy in the detection of lies. In a longitudinal study, Anderson, DePaulo, and Ansfield (2002) examined how lie detection accuracy changes over the course of relationships. They recruited pairs of same-sex friends, measured perceived closeness, and asked one member to tell truthful and fabricated stories. The other member's job was to distinguish truths from lies. Overall, accuracy did not improve significantly over the course of 5 months. However, change over time was moderated by relationship closeness; close friends showed a substantial and significant improvement in lie detection accuracy (accuracy increased from 47% to 61%), but less close friends showed a small *decrease* in accuracy. The authors speculate that close friends are more motivated to learn to interpret cues to deception (and potentially many other internal states) more accurately over time.

One might expect expertise, experience, and formal training to bolster lie detection accuracy. On the contrary, in a meta-analysis of the literature, Aamodt and Custer (2006; see also Vrij, 1993; Vrij & Semin,

1996) found that "professional lie catchers" (such as police officers, detectives, judges, secret service agents, and parole officers) were no more accurate at detecting deception than were students and other citizens. The professionals had an average accuracy rate (56%) only slightly higher than novices (54%). It could be that formal training disrupts the normal ways in which we learn to recognize cues to deception. More specifically, formal training may focus our attention on "salient and plausible," but nondiagnostic cues (Wilson & Schooler, 1991, p. 182; Kassin & Fong, 1999).

By contrast, one particular group of individuals may be especially accurate in recognizing deception. According to Coyne's (1976) interpersonal model of depression, depressed people may be more sensitive than healthy individuals to a special class of deception: phoniness. According to the model, people struggling with depression are especially hungry for support and reassurance from others. Their appeals for support and reassurance are often met with a mixed reaction, a form of sympathy combined with irritation. A friend or family member may respond by professing a desire to help, but this verbal message may be combined with subtle nonverbal signs of hostility. The model states that depressed people can see through the false reassurances and become even more depressed, thus perpetuating the cycle. Consistent with this, Lane and DePaulo (1999) found that people with elevated levels of depression symptoms were *more* accurate than healthy controls at spotting false reassurances and phoniness. It is unclear whether increased sensitivity to insincerity is a cause or a consequence of depression, or some combination of the two.

When perceivers *do* successfully distinguish truths and lies, they rely heavily on streams of expressive behavior, including facial displays, gestures, and tones of voice. Are any of these channels particularly revealing of deception? Some work has explored this potential moderator of accuracy. Ekman and Friesen (1969) postulated a hierarchy of "leakiness," or uncontrollability. Verbal statements are believed to be the most controllable and therefore the least leaky channel of communication, followed by facial displays, gestures, and vocal tone. Vocal tone may be the leakiest channel of communication because the speaker's perception differs from that of the listener; because the voice sounds different to the speaker and the listener, the speaker has difficulty monitoring and modulating it (Ekman, 1992). Indeed, deception is easiest to detect from changes in the tone of voice (e.g., DePaulo, Lassiter, & Stone, 1982; Heinrich & Borkenau, 1998).

The bulk of research on deception detection comes from carefully controlled laboratory studies, when the liar's motivation to be successful may be minimal. However, in a meta-analysis of the literature, DePaulo and colleagues (2003) examined whether the cues to deception become more transparent during "high-stakes" lies, when the liar has more motivation to be successful. Their analysis revealed that when liars are more motivated to succeed, they become tenser; specifically, they use less eye contact and a higher pitched voice. Similar results were reported by Mann, Vrij, and Bull (2004) in a study of people's behavior during real-life high-stakes situations, including police interrogations. It is as yet unclear whether this greater transparency during higher-stakes situations results in greater accuracy on the part of perceivers.

SOCIAL RELATIONS

Up to this point, I have discussed whether, and under what conditions, naive observers can glean insight into another individual's thoughts, feelings, and personal character. I have noted the utility of first impressions—how accurate judgments foster the ability to understand and predict an individual's behavior. Thoughts, feelings, and personal character are all constructs that exist *within* people. At the same time, it also is important for perceivers to understand constructs that exist *between* people (Bernieri & Gillis, 2001). Throughout our evolutionary history, we have had a basic need to make quick and accurate assessments of others' relationship patterns. This is essential for identifying, for instance, whether a certain group of individuals is forming an alliance that may be threatening to one's safety or resource availability. Even nonhuman primates show an ability to quickly scan the social environment and recognize relationship patterns (Cheney & Seyfarth, 1990).

Among humans, how observable are the signals to relationship type? Costanzo and Archer (1989) explored this question by presenting study participants with a series of short video clips portraying people interacting in a variety of natural situations. Participants were asked to answer interpretative questions about things like kinship (e.g., "Who is the child of the two adults?"), relationships (e.g., "Are these individuals friends or romantic partners?"), and status (e.g., "Which person is the other person's boss?"). No obvious clues to the correct answer were included in the video clips, and so accurate responses depended on a correct interpretation of available verbal and nonverbal cues. Average performance on this measure, the Interpersonal Perception Task, is well above chance levels (Costanzo & Archer, 1989). This suggests that perceivers can categorize relationship type with only minimal information at their disposal.

In addition to identifying the type of relationship people share, perceivers are also often faced with the task of making inferences about the *quality* of people's relationships. Imagine being romantically interested in someone who is currently involved in another relationship. It would be important, in this case, to know whether that relationship is flourishing or faltering. Rapport is defined as the extent to which a relationship is pleasant, engaging, and harmonious (Bernieri & Gills, 2001). When two people feel rapport toward each other, they express it in their attention toward each other, the positivity of their behavior, and the coordination of their movements (Tickle-Degnen & Rosenthal, 1990).

How well can perceivers interpret these cues? Bernieri, Gillis, Davis, and Grahe (1996) explored this question by asking participants to view brief (50-second) video clips of opposite-sex strangers interacting. They asked the perceivers to infer the degree of rapport felt by the interaction partners, and they compared these responses with the interaction partners' own level of felt rapport. They also systematically coded a variety of nonverbal behaviors expressed during the conversations. Bernieri and colleagues (1996) first determined that a small subset of behaviors did reliably express interaction partners' level of rapport, confirming that a great deal of information is revealed in "thin slices" of expressive behavior (Ambady & Rosenthal, 1992). However, the outside observers did not appear to correctly use this information. Correlations between perceivers' and interactants' judgments of rapport were modest, averaging at 0.19 in one study and 0.35 in another. (In these studies, judgmental accuracy was considered to be greater than that expected by chance alone if it was above 0.28.) Why were the correlations so modest? The authors speculate that rapport, "defined as a relational variable between two or more individuals, may be too complex and difficult to perceive, assess, and quantify with a single number" (p. 123). While perceivers have little difficulty categorizing the type of relationship that two people share, they have trouble quantifying the quality of that relationship.

As with judgments of personality, mental states, emotional states, and deception, several factors moderate the ability to make valid inferences about social relations. In the rapport study discussed above, about a third of the perceivers achieved a level of accuracy significantly higher than chance (Bernieri et al., 1996). What separates these perceivers from their less accurate counterparts? Individual differences in some facets of personality may be involved (Bernieri & Gillis, 1995), although variation in perceivers' motivation to perform well likely plays a more substantial role. For instance, people who are more motivated to understand others—as reflected in higher ratings of social skill and competence—perform better on the Interpersonal Perception Task (e.g., Costanzo & Archer, 1989; Schroeder, 1995). On the other hand, people who are highly preoccupied with themselves and their perceived shortcomings perform worse on the same task (Aube & Whiffen, 1996). Knowledge about social relations is also an important person-level moderator. People who have had advanced theatrical training score higher on the Interpersonal Perception Task, perhaps because their theatrical training sensitizes them to the meaning of particular gestures, facial displays, and vocal patterns (Bush & Marshall, 1999; see also Costanzo, 1992).

Information-level moderators of the ability to infer social relations have also been identified. In general, conditions that promote the expression of subtle nonverbal cues to rapport and relationship type will enhance accuracy. For instance, it is difficult to infer the level of rapport felt between two people when they are engaged in an activity that heavily constrains their behavior (Puccinelli, Tickle-Degnen, & Rosenthal, 2004). In these kinds of situations, behavior is governed more by social norms than by true feelings and beliefs. More diagnostic information is available in situations that do not constrain behavior. Diagnostic information is also more reliably expressed in nonverbal channels of communication. Using an early version of the Interpersonal Perception Task, Archer and Akert (1977) compared the performance among perceivers who viewed video clips or simply read transcripts of the conversations. Those who viewed video clips—and who therefore were exposed to dynamic facial displays, gestures, and other body movements—made more accurate judgments of relationship type.

CONCLUSION

When it comes to perceiving other people, we all make mistakes. We tend to project our own thoughts, feelings, and beliefs onto the canvas of another's mind. We often lack the motivation or ability to sufficiently adjust from this perspective, which results in impressions that are egocentrically biased. We can also be blind to the situational forces that shape other people's behavior, preferring to attribute that behavior to stable dispositions.

But along with these mistakes comes an ability to use available information—particularly in the form of facial displays, gestures, and other nonverbal cues—to infer states and traits that are not directly broadcast to us. Although perceivers may be biased toward attributing behavior to personality, their impressions of personality are often remarkably accurate (Ambady, Bernieri, & Richeson, 2000). With only a brief glimpse at expressive behavior, perceivers can determine to what extent another individual is generally extraverted or introverted, conscientious or careless. This accuracy extends to more fleeting states; starting even in infancy, perceivers develop an ability to read the nonverbal signs of thoughts and feelings. Only when an individual actively tries to portray *deceptive* thoughts and feelings does our accuracy falter. And when it comes to impressions of social relations, we are adept at categorizing the type of relationship that other people share but not at describing—at least verbally—the quality of that relationship.

To better understand the wide range of moderators of accuracy, it may be helpful first to break down the process of social judgment into its component parts.[2] According to Funder's Realistic Accuracy Model (1995, 1999), there are four stages of social inference. First, the construct being judged must produce a behavioral effect. These behavioral effects are said to be *relevant* to the trait being judged. To use one of Funder's (1995) examples, the act of saving a family from a burning house is a dramatic example of a behavioral cue that is relevant to the trait of courageousness. Second, this behavior must be made *available* to the perceiver. Although the act of saving people from a burning house may be a highly relevant sign of courageousness, it is a rare occurrence, not ordinarily available for a perceiver to witness. Next, the perceiver must *detect* the relevant available information. If the perceiver is distracted or simply uninterested in witnessing an act of heroism, behavioral information that *is* emitted will not be factored into a first impression. Finally, the relevant, available, and detected cues must be *utilized,* or correctly interpreted. At this stage, the perceiver must decide whether the act of heroism is truly a sign of courageousness or the cynical attempt of a future politician to woo the news media.

The *information-level moderators* I have discussed in this review have their impact during Funder's first two stages of social inference. Regarding deception, high-stakes situations may increase a perceiver's ability to distinguish truth from lies, because they increase the tendency to produce relevant cues, such as decreased eye contact and a higher-pitched voice (DePaulo et al., 2003). All five facets of personality are associated with relevant behavioral cues, but the cues to Extraversion and Conscientiousness tend to be more readily available in typical social situations. As a result, perceivers are more adept at inferring these aspects of personality (Albright et al., 1988; Borkenau & Liebler, 1992, 1993; Kenny et al., 1992). The same is true for judgments of social relations. There are several behavioral signs of rapport, but situations that heavily constrain behavior do not present much opportunity for people to behave in ways that reveal their rapport. As a result, perceivers are less adept at judging rapport in these situations (Puccinelli et al., 2004).

The *person-level moderators* I have discussed have their impact during Funder's (1995, 1999) final two stages. In many cases, I have discussed factors that influence a perceiver's motivation to detect and interpret relevant and available cues. Sadness appears to make perceivers more motivated to detect and interpret behavioral cues to personality (Gray & Ambady, 2006). By increasing the reward value of social encounters, oxytocin increases the motivation to understand other minds (Domes et al., 2007). Close friends are more motivated to learn to interpret each other's cues to deception (Anderson et al., 2002). Similarly, as compared to people who are highly self-involved, sociable people are more highly motivated to detect and utilize behavioral cues to social relations (e.g., Costanzo & Archer, 1989; Schroeder, 1995). Knowledge is another factor that has a widespread influence on detection and utilization. Formal training can bolster the ability to categorize social relations by providing information about behavioral signs of kinship and intimacy (Costanzo, 1992). On the other hand, it can impair the ability to detect lies by focusing perceivers' attention on cues that are not relevant (Kassin & Fong, 1999). Finally, autism, depression, schizophrenia, and other psychological disorders likely diminish interpersonal sensitivity by decreasing both motivation *and* knowledge. Feeling that the world is a confusing and hostile place must not encourage the motivation necessary for acquiring knowledge.

In sum, first impressions are sometimes accurate and sometimes inaccurate. Accuracy depends partly on the construct being judged, partly on the information available to the perceiver, partly on the perceiver's motivation and ability to understand others, and partly on a host of other factors not covered in this review. Research that explores *both* the outcomes and the process of first impressions—as exemplified in this volume—will set the stage for a deeper understanding of the accuracy of first impressions.

ACKNOWLEDGMENT

Preparation of this chapter was supported by a grant from the National Institute on Disability and Rehabilitation Research (U.S. Department of Education; Grant No. H133P050001).

NOTES

1. New research, using paradigms that do not rely on a child's ability to respond verbally to questions tapping belief attribution, suggests that mental state attribution may actually begin to emerge as early as age 1 (Surian, Caldi, & Sperber, 2007) or 2 (Southgate, Senju, & Csibra, 2007).
2. Funder's model primarily refers to the process of forming impressions of personality; this review applies it more generally to the process of social inference.

REFERENCES

Aamodt, M. G., & Custer, H. (2006). Who can best catch a liar? A meta-analysis of individual differences in deception detection. *The Forensic Examiner, 15*, 6–11.

Albright, L., Kenny, D. A., & Malloy, T. E. (1988). Consensus in personality judgments at zero acquaintance. *Journal of Personality and Social Psychology, 55*, 387–395.

Ambady, N., (2001). *The perils of pondering: Distraction, deliberation, and thin-slice judgments*. Manuscript in preparation.

Ambady, N., Bernieri, F., & Richeson, J. (2000). Towards a histology of social behavior: Judgmental accuracy from thin slices of behavior. In M. P. Zanna (Ed.), *Advances in experimental social psychology* (Vol. 32, pp. 201–272).

Ambady, N., & Rosenthal, R. (1992). Thin slices of expressive behavior as predictors of interpersonal consequences: A meta-analysis. *Psychological Bulletin, 111*(2), 256–274.

Anderson, D. E., DePaulo, B. M., & Ansfield, M. E. (2002). The development of deception detection skill: A longitudinal study of same-sex friends. *Personality and Social Psychology Bulletin, 28*, 536–545.

Archer, D., & Akert, R. M. (1977). Words and everything else: Verbal and nonverbal cues in social interpretation. *Journal of Personality and Social Psychology, 35*(6), 443–449.

Aube, J., & Whiffen, V. E. (1996). Depressive styles and social acuity: Further evidence for distinct interpersonal correlates of dependency and self-criticism. *Communication Research, 23*, 407–424.

Baron-Cohen, S., Wheelwright, S., Hill, J. J., Raste, Y., & Plumb, I. (2001). The "Reading the Mind in the Eyes" Test revised version: A study with normal adults, and adults with Asperger's syndrome or high-functioning autism. *Journal of Child Psychology and Psychiatry, 42*, 241–251.

Barrick, M. R., & Mount, M. K. (1991). The big five personality dimensions and job performance: A meta-analysis. *Personnel Psychology, 44*, 1–25.

Bernieri, F. J., & Gillis, J. S. (1995). Personality correlates of accuracy in a social perception task. *Perceptual and Motor Skills, 81*, 168–170.

Bernieri, F. J., & Gillis, J. S. (2001). Judging rapport: Employing Brunswik's lens model to study interpersonal sensitivity. In J. A. Hall & F. J. Bernieri (Eds.), *Interpersonal sensitivity: Theory and measurement* (pp. 67–88). Mahwah, NJ: Erlbaum.

Bernieri, F. J., Gillis, J. S., Davis, J. M., & Grahe, J. E. (1996). Dyad rapport and the accuracy of its judgment across situations: A lens model analysis. *Journal of Personality and Social Psychology, 71*, 110–129.

Bernieri, F. J., Zuckerman, M., Koestner, R., & Rosenthal, R. (1994). Measuring person perception accuracy: Another look at self–other agreement. *Personality and Social Psychology Bulletin, 20*, 367–378.

Biesanz, J. C., West, S. G., & Millevoi, A. (2007). What do you learn about someone over time? The relationship between length of acquaintance and consensus and self–other agreement in judgments of personality. *Journal of Personality and Social Psychology, 92,* 119–135.

Block, J., & Funder, D. C. (1986). Social roles and social perception: Individual differences in attribution and error. *Journal of Personality and Social Psychology, 51,* 1200–1207.

Bond, C. F., & DePaulo, B. M. (2006). Accuracy of deception judgments. *Personality and Social Psychology Review, 10,* 214–234.

Boraston, Z., Blakemore, S., Chilvers, R., & Skuse, D. (2007). Impaired sadness recognition is linked to social interaction deficit in autism. *Neuropsychologia, 45,* 1501–1510.

Borkenau, P., & Liebler, A. (1992). Trait inferences: Sources of validity at zero acquaintance. *Journal of Personality and Social Psychology, 62,* 645–657.

Borkenau, P., & Liebler, A. (1993). Convergence of stranger ratings of personality and intelligence with self-ratings, partner ratings, and measured intelligence. *Journal of Personality and Social Psychology, 65,* 546–553.

Borkenau, P., Mauer, N., Riemann, R., Spinath, F. M., & Angleitner, A. (2004). Thin slices of behavior as cues of personality and intelligence. *Journal of Personality and Social Psychology, 86,* 599–614.

Botwin, M., Buss, D. M., & Shackelford, T. (1997). Personality and mate preferences: Five factor in mate selection and marital satisfaction. *Journal of Personality, 65,* 107–136.

Brothers, L., & Ring, B. (1992). A neuroethological framework for the representation of other minds. *Journal of Cognitive Neuroscience, 4,* 107–118.

Bush, J., & Marshall, P. (1999). *The inter-relationship between self-monitoring, interpersonal perception, and acting training.* Unpublished manuscript.

Buss, D. M. (1992). Conflict in married couples: Personality predictors of anger and upset. *Journal of Personality, 59,* 663–688.

Cheney, D. L., & Seyfarth, R. M. (1990). *How monkeys see the world: Inside the mind of another species.* Chicago: University of Chicago Press.

Colvin, R. C., & Funder, D. C. (1991). Predicting personality and behavior: A boundary on the acquaintanceship effect. *Journal of Personality and Social Psychology, 60,* 884–894.

Costanzo, M. (1992). Training students to decode verbal and nonverbal cues: Effects on confidence and performance. *Journal of Educational Psychology, 84,* 308–313.

Costanzo, M., & Archer, D. (1989). Interpreting the expressive behavior of others: The Interpersonal Perception Task. *Journal of Nonverbal Behavior, 13,* 225–245.

Coyne, J. C. (1976). Toward an interactional description of depression. *Psychiatry: Journal for the Study of Interpersonal Processes, 39,* 28–40.

CNN.com. (2004, December 14). Jurors: Evidence, Peterson's demeanor "spoke for itself." Retrieved July 24, 2007, from *www.cnn.com/2004/LAW/12/13/jury.reax/.*

Custrini, R. J., & Feldman, R. S. (1989). Children's social competence and nonverbal encoding and decoding of emotions. *Journal of Clinical Child Psychology, 18,* 336–342.

DePaulo, B. M., Kashy, D. A., Kirkendol, S. E., Wyer, M. M., & Epstein, J. A.

(1996). Lying in everyday life. *Journal of Personality and Social Psychology,* 70, 979–995.

DePaulo, B. M., Lassiter, G. D., & Stone, J. I. (1982). Attentional determinants of success at detecting deception and truth. *Personality and Social Psychology Bulletin, 8,* 273–279.

DePaulo, B. M., Lindsay, J. L., Malone, B. E., Muhlenbruck, L., Charlton, K., & Cooper, H. (2003). Cues to deception. *Psychological Bulletin, 129,* 74–118.

DePaulo, B. M., & Pfeifer, R. L. (1986). On–the-job experience and skill at detecting deception. *Journal of Applied Social Psychology, 16,* 249–267.

Dimberg, U. (1997). Psychophysiological reactions to facial expressions. In U. Segerstrale & P. Molnar (Eds.), *Nonverbal communication: Where nature meets culture* (pp. 47–60). Mahwah, NJ: Erlbaum.

Dimberg, U., Thunberg, M., & Elmehed, K. (2000). Unconscious facial reactions to emotional facial expressions. *Psychological Science, 11*(1), 86–89.

Domes, G., Heinrichs, M., Michel, A., Berger, C., & Herpertz, S. C. (2007). Oxytocin improves "mind-reading" in humans. *Biological Psychiatry, 61,* 731–733.

Dunbar, R. I. M. (1998). The social brain hypothesis. *Evolutionary Anthropology, 6,* 178–190.

Ekman, P. (1972). Universals and cultural differences in facial expressions of emotion. In J. K. Cole (Ed.), *Nebraska symposium on motivation, 1971* (pp. 207–283). Lincoln: University of Nebraska Press.

Ekman, P. (1992). *Telling lies.* New York: Norton.

Ekman, P., & Friesen, W. V. (1969). Nonverbal leakage and cues to deception. *Psychiatry, 32,* 88–106.

Elfenbein, H. A., & Ambady, N. (2002). On the universality and cultural specificity of emotion recognition: A meta-analysis. *Psychological Bulletin, 128,* 203–235.

Estes, S. G. (1938). Judging personality from expressive behavior. *Journal of Abnormal and Social Psychology, 33,* 217–236.

Feinberg, T. E., Rifkin, A., Schaffer, C., & Walker, E. (1986). Facial discrimination and emotional recognition in schizophrenia and affective disorders. *Archives of General Psychiatry, 43,* 276–279.

Funder, D. C. (1995). On the accuracy of personality judgment: A realistic approach. *Psychological Review, 102*(4), 652–670.

Funder, D. C. (1999). *Personality judgment: A realistic approach to person perception.* San Diego, CA: Academic Press.

Funder, D. C., & Dobroth, K. M. (1987). Differences between traits: Properties associated with interjudge agreement. *Journal of Personality and Social Psychology, 52,* 409–418.

Funder, D. C., & Sneed, C. D. (1993). Behavioral manifestations of personality: An ecological approach to judgmental accuracy. *Journal of Personality and Social Psychology, 64,* 479–490.

Golan, O., Baron-Cohen, S., Hill, J. J., & Golan, Y. (2006). The "Reading the Mind in the Films" Task: Complex emotion recognition in adults with and without autism spectrum conditions. *Social Neuroscience, 1,* 111–123.

Gray, H. M., & Ambady, N. (2006). *When sadness spurs social acuity: Insights from a dyadic interaction paradigm.* Manuscript under revision.

Hassin, R. R., Aarts, H., & Ferguson, M. (2005). Automatic goal inferences. *Journal of Experimental Social Psychology, 41,* 129–140.

Hassin, R. R., Bargh, J. A., & Uleman, J. S. (2002). Spontaneous causal inferences. *Journal of Experimental Social Psychology, 38,* 515–522.

Heider, F., & Simmel, M. (1944). An experimental study of apparent behavior. *American Journal of Psychology, 57,* 243–259.

Heinrich, C. U., & Borkenau, P. (1998). Deception and deception detection: The role of cross-modal inconsistency. *Journal of Personality, 66,* 687–712.

Hill, E. F., & Frith, U. (2003). Understanding autism: Insights from mind and brain. In U. Frith & E. F. Hill (Eds.), *Autism: Mind and brain* (pp. 1–19). New York: Oxford University Press.

Insel, T. R., & Young, L. J. (2001). The neurobiology of attachment. *Nature Reviews Neuroscience, 2,* 129–136.

Isaacowitz, D. M., Lockenhoff, C. E., Lane, R. D., Wright, R., Sechrest, L., Riedel, R., et al. (2007). Age differences in recognition of emotion in lexical stimuli and facial expressions. *Psychology and Aging, 22,* 147–159.

Ickes, W., Stinson, L., Bissonnette, V., & Garcia, S. (1990). Naturalistic social cognition: Empathic accuracy in mixed-sex dyads. *Journal of Personality and Social Psychology, 59,* 730–742.

Izard, C. E. (1971). *The face of emotion.* New York: Appleton-Century-Crofts.

Johnstone, T., & Scherer, K. R. (2000). Vocal communication of emotion. In M. Lewis & J. Haviland (Eds.), *Handbook of emotion* (2nd ed., pp. 220–235). New York: Guilford Press.

Jones, E. E., & Harris, V. A. (1967). The attribution of attitudes. *Journal of Experimental Social Psychology 3,* 1–24.

Kassin, S. M., & Fong, C. T. (1999). "I'm innocent!": Effects of training on judgments of truth and deception in the interrogation room. *Law and Human Behavior, 23,* 499–516.

Keller, M. C., & Nesse, R. M. (2005). Subtypes of low mood provide evidence of its adaptive significance. *Journal of Affective Disorders, 86,* 27–35.

Kenny, D. A., Horner, C., Kashy, D. A., & Chu, L. (1992). Consensus at zero acquaintance: Replication, behavioral cues, and stability. *Journal of Personality and Social Psychology, 62,* 88–97.

Keysar, B. (1994). The illusory transparency of intention: Linguistic perspective taking in text. *Cognitive Psychology, 23,* 165–208.

Keysar, B., Ginzel, L. E., & Bazerman, M. H. (1995). States of affairs and states of mind: The effect of knowledge of beliefs. *Organizational Behavior and Human Decision Processes, 64,* 283–293.

Kruglanski, A. W. (1989). The psychology of being "right": The problem of accuracy in social perception and cognition. *Psychological Bulletin, 106,* 395–409.

Krueger, J. I., & Funder, D. C. (2004). Towards a balanced social psychology: Causes, consequences, and cures for the problem-seeking approach to social behavior and cognition. *Behavioral and Brain Sciences, 27,* 313–327.

Lane, J. D., & DePaulo, B. M. (1999). Completing Coyne's cycle: Dysphorics' ability to detect deception. *Journal of Research in Personality, 33,* 311–329.

Letzring, T. D., Greve, L. A., & Funder, D. C. (2005). *Behaviors of accurate judges of personality.* Paper presented at the 6th annual conference for the Society for Personality and Social Psychology, New Orleans.

Mann, S., Vrij, A., & Bull, R. (2004). Detecting true lies: Police officers' ability to detect suspects' lies. *Journal of Applied Psychology, 89,* 137–149.

McCrae, R. R., & Costa, P. T. (1987). Validation of the five-factor model of personality across instruments and observers. *Journal of Personality and Social Psychology, 52,* 81–90.

Montagne, B., Schutters, S., Westenberg, H. G. M., van Honk, J., Kessels, R. P. C., & de Haan, E. H. F. (2006). Reduced sensitivity in the recognition of anger and disgust in social anxiety disorder. *Cognitive Neuropsychiatry, 11,* 389–401.

Murray, S. L., Holmes, J. G., Bellavia, G., Griffin, D. W., & Dolderman, D. (2002). Kindred spirits? The benefits of egocentrism in close relationships. *Journal of Personality and Social Psychology, 82,* 563–581.

Norman, W. T., & Goldberg, L. R. (1966). Raters, ratees, and randomness in personality structure. *Journal of Personality and Social Psychology, 4,* 681–691.

Nowicki, S., & Duke, M. P. (2001). Nonverbal receptivity: The diagnostic analysis of nonverbal accuracy (DANVA). In J. A. Hall & F. J. Bernieri (Eds.), *Interpersonal sensitivity.* Mahwah, NJ: Erlbaum.

Paulhus, D. L., & Bruce, M. N. (1992). The effect of acquaintanceship on the validity of personality impressions: A longitudinal study. *Journal of Personality and Social Psychology, 63,* 816–824.

Puccinelli, N., Tickle-Degnen, L., & Rosenthal, R. (2004). Effect of target position and target task on judge sensitivity to felt rapport. *Journal of Nonverbal Behavior, 28,* 211–220.

Rentfrow, P. J., & Gosling, S. D. (2006). Message in a ballad: The role of music preferences in interpersonal perception. *Psychological Science, 17,* 236–242.

Ross, L. D, Amabile, T. M., & Steinmetz, J. L. (1977). Social roles, social control, and biases in social-perception processes. *Journal of Personality and Social Psychology, 35,* 485–494.

Ross, L., Greene, D., & House, P. (1977). The false consensus effect: An egocentric bias in social perception and attribution processes. *Journal of Experimental Social Psychology, 13,* 279–301.

Schroeder, J. E. (1995). Self-concept, social anxiety, and interpersonal perception skills. *Personality and Individual Differences, 19,* 955–958.

Siegal, M., & Varley, R. (2002). Neural systems involved in "theory of mind." *Nature Reviews Neuroscience, 3,* 463–471.

Southgate, V., Senju, A., & Csibra, G. (2007). Action anticipation through attribution of false belief by 2-year-olds. *Psychological Science, 18,* 587–592.

Surian, L., Caldi, S., & Sperber, D. (2007). Attribution of beliefs by 13-month-old infants. *Psychological Science, 18,* 580–586.

Tickle-Degnen, L., & Rosenthal, R. (1990). The nature of rapport and its nonverbal correlates. *Psychological Inquiry, 1,* 285–293.

Thoresen, C. J., Bradley, J. C., Bliese, P. D., & Thoresen, J. D. (2004). The big five personality traits and individual job performance growth trajectories in maintenance and transitional job stages. *Journal of Applied Psychology, 89,* 835–853.

Uleman, J. S., Newman, L. S., & Moskowitz, G. B. (1996). People as flexible interpreters: Evidence and issues from spontaneous trait inference. In M. P. Zanna (Ed.), *Advances in experimental social psychology* (Vol. 28, pp. 211–279). Boston: Academic Press.

Vrij, A. (1993). Credibility judgments of detectives: The impact of nonverbal behavior, social skills, and physical characteristics on impression formation. *Journal of Social Psychology, 133,* 601–610.

Vrij, A., & Semin, G. R. (1996). Lie experts' beliefs about nonverbal indicators of deception. *Journal of Nonverbal Behavior, 20*(1), 65–80.

Walker-Andrews, A. S. (1997). Infants' perception of expressive behaviors: Differentiation of multimodal information. *Psychological Bulletin, 121,* 437–456.

Whalen, P. J., Rauch, S. L., Etcoff, N. L., McInerney, S. C., Lee, M. B., & Jenike, M. A. (1998). Masked presentations of emotional facial expressions modulate amygdala activity without explicit knowledge. *Journal of Neuroscience, 18*(1), 411–418.

Widen, S. C., & Russell, J. A. (2003). A closer look at preschoolers' freely produced labels for facial expressions. *Developmental Psychology, 39,* 114–128.

Wilson, T. D., & Schooler, J. W. (1991). Thinking too much: Introspection can reduce the quality of preferences and decisions. *Journal of Personality and Social Psychology, 60,* 181–192.

Wimmer, H., & Perner, J. (1983). Beliefs about beliefs: Representation and constraining function of wrong beliefs in young children's understanding of deception. *Cognition, 13,* 103–128.

Young, L. J., & Wang, Z. (2004). The neurobiology of pair bonding. *Nature Neuroscience, 7,* 1048–1054.

CHAPTER 6

Zero Acquaintance

*Definitions, Statistical Model,
Findings, and Process*

DAVID A. KENNY
TESSA V. WEST

Zero-acquaintance research began with a study by Norman and Goldberg in 1966, using data that were originally published by Passini and Norman (1966). In the study, 12 groups, numbering 6–9 members in each, were created on the first day of class at the University of Michigan. Students were previously unacquainted and were asked to rate one another "without any information" across a set of variables, which have come to be known as the Big Five personality traits. Given that perceivers had very little information about targets, the expectation was that perceivers would not agree with one another in their perceptions and that the ratings of personality at zero acquaintance would have little or no validity. Norman and Goldberg (1966) surprisingly found agreement or consensus in the perceptions of personality, and, moreover, agreement correlated with self-ratings of the targets' personality. We think Norman and Goldberg were rather embarrassed by the high levels of consensus and self–other agreement at zero acquaintance. We have heard reports that Norman regretted ever gathering the Passini and Norman data.

The first author of this chapter, David A. Kenny, read the Norman and Goldberg (1966) study in 1969 and was fascinated by the findings. However, it was not until the mid-1980s that Kenny began to research basic questions in interpersonal perception (Kenny, 1988). It occurred to him that the Norman and Goldberg paper was very relevant, because he was interested in how interpersonal perception changed over time, but Kenny had forgotten who had written that paper. That year Kenny was visiting Arizona State and asked Steve West about the paper. He gave him the citation and Kenny reread the paper, nearly 20 years after he had first read the paper. Kenny was fascinated and was eager to replicate the study. He returned to Connecticut and conducted three studies that were eventually published in an article by Albright, Kenny, and Malloy (1988).

Many researchers, especially those studying personality, found Albright et al. (1988) troubling. For instance, Paunonen (1991) published a paper in which he discussed "the apparent accuracy of strangers' ratings" (p. 471). He also referred to perceivers in these studies as "so-called strangers" (p. 472). At that time, the belief was that it took time for people to get to know someone. Acquaintance was viewed as a slow and gradual process, comparable to the peeling away of layers of an onion (Altman & Taylor, 1973). Albright et al. (1988) were also dubious of the phenomenon, and that was why they replicated the phenomenon three times. This book is testimony that there is a great deal of information, some of which is valid, concerning first impressions.

In this chapter, we begin by defining zero acquaintance and compare it to "thin slices." We then describe a statistical model for social perception data that is closely tied to many zero-acquaintance research studies. We then review the major findings of zero-acquaintance research. Finally, we briefly discuss the process that leads to accuracy in the zero-acquaintance situation.

WHAT IS ZERO ACQUAINTANCE?

The person–perception literature often uses the terms "zero acquaintance," "thin slices," and "first impressions" interchangeably. Explicit distinctions among these types of studies have never been made; for the purposes of our review, we separately define each term in turn.

When first impressions are made in everyday contexts, there is typically some interaction between the perceiver and the target. One common element of both the zero-acquaintance and thin-slices paradigms is that, unlike the situation in everyday person perceptions, the perceiver does not interact with the target prior to making judgments. However, in many zero-acquaintance studies, perceivers and targets make perceptions while they are face-to-face; there is the possibility of nonverbal dyadic behavior between the perceiver and the target. For example, the target may directly smile at or make eye contact with the perceiver. Research using controlled procedures (Borkenau & Liebler, 1992; Kenny, Horner, Kashy, & Chu, 1992), such as videotapes of targets where there is no possibility of perceiver–target interaction, has shown essentially the same pattern as studies using less controlled procedures.

The key feature of a thin-slices study, as the name suggests, is that information that is communicated is brief and in some cases degraded (e.g., content-filtered audio). The key feature of a zero-acquaintance study is that the information given to perceivers is presumably unrelated to the judgment task. We realize that the phrase "presumably unrelated" is somewhat vague and open to interpretation. In addition, when information that is hypothesized to be "presumably unrelated" leads to valid personality judgments, researchers no longer consider such information as "unrelated." For example, Rentfrow and Gosling (2006) had perceivers infer targets' personality from target-reported musical preferences. Perceivers listened to lists of songs that targets most enjoyed and then made ratings of the Big Five personality factors. The appeal of Rentfrow and Gosling is that musical preferences are not intuitively predictable cues of personality characteristics. However, when Rentfrow and Gosling found evidence for consensus and accuracy of personality based on such preferences, future person-perception researchers would likely consider music preferences as indicators of personality characteristics. Gosling and others have also conducted studies in which "presumably irrelevant" cues to personality are found in offices, bedrooms (Gosling, Ko, Mannarelli, & Morris, 2002), and even handshakes (Chaplin, Phillips, Brown, Clanton, & Stein, 2000).

It is important to note that, given our definitions, some zero-acquaintance studies also qualify as thin-slices studies. For instance, in Ambady, Hallahan, and Conner's study (1999) perceivers judged sexual orientation after watching brief video clips of gestures or viewing stills of targets. Ambady et al.'s (1999) research can be considered both a zero-acquaintance and a thin-slices study, because the perceivers did not interact with targets, the information has presumably not directly related to judgments, and the perceivers were presented with only brief snippets of behaviors. In addition, Ambady and Rosenthal (1993) also qualifies as both a thin-slices and zero-acquaintance study because perceivers viewed short video clips of teachers and made trait judgments, which were presumably irrelevant to the criterion, end-of-semester teaching evaluations.

The most typical zero-acquaintance paradigm, following the Norman and Goldberg study (1966), involves face-to-face judgments. Groups of strangers are formed from classes or as part of an experiment (DiPilato, West, & Chartier, 1988), and most zero-acquaintance studies instruct participants not to speak, although some do (Borkenau & Liebler, 1992; Levesque & Kenny, 1993). Several studies, one as early as 1938 by Estes, have used film materials. In addition, numerous studies have involved photo judgments that qualify as zero-acquaintance studies, given our definition. However, space precludes our reviewing these studies, and we therefore refer the reader to Zebrowitz and Collins (1997) for a review of perceptions based on photographs.

USING THE SOCIAL RELATIONS MODEL
TO STUDY ZERO-ACQUAINTANCE RESEARCH

Several studies have examined perceptions made at zero acquaintance using Kenny and La Voie's (1984) Social Relations Model (SRM), which is a two-way random effects analysis of variance model. Imagine a study in which multiple perceivers make ratings of multiple targets at zero acquaintance, as was the case in Norman and Goldberg's study (1966). This design is referred to as a *round-robin design*. Consider the perception that Irene has of Jane. Irene's perception can be decomposed into the following four components:

Irene's Perception of Jane = Group Mean + Irene's Perceiver Effect
+ Jane's Target Effect
+ Relationship Effect of Irene toward Jane

The mean refers to how people generally see others on the trait in question; the perceiver effect refers to how Irene generally sees others; the target effect refers to how Jane is generally seen by others; and the relationship effect refers to how Irene uniquely sees Jane, above and beyond how Irene sees others and how Jane is seen by others. The relationship effect can be viewed as the interaction of perceiver and target.

In most zero-acquaintance and more generally first-impression studies, the key component of a Social Relations Analysis is the target effect, which assesses the degree to which a target is perceived consistently across perceivers. Reliable target variance indicates that perceivers agree in their ratings of targets (i.e., there is reliable consensus in the perceptions of targets), and such perceptions vary from target to target—for example, the perceivers agree that Jane is outgoing and that Irene is shy.

Not all researchers who are interested in consensus of perceptions at zero acquaintance use the SRM as a statistical model. When targets are rated by multiple perceivers, the average of perceivers' judgments is sometimes used to obtain a measure of consensus (e.g., Gosling et al., 2002). While an average is generally not problematic, from an SRM perspective there are three issues worth discussing. First, the mean rating is an estimate of the target effect, not the actual target effect, because it contains an additional variance component measured by the SRM, the relationship effect. Relationship variance assesses the idiosyncratic perceptions that perceivers have of targets, controlling for both the target and the perceiver effects. Second, because the mean perception of a target contains the relationship effect, it is necessary to compute the reliability, or the degree of consensus in ratings of a target. For many studies, a conventional reliability measure, such as Cronbach's alpha, can be computed. We strongly recommend that researchers report the reliability of the target effect. Additionally, following the advice of Norman and Goldberg (1966), we urge that researchers also report the extent to which two perceivers agree with each other, which is analogous to the interitem correlation. Third, for specialized designs, such as the round-robin design in which perceivers serve also as targets, the mean across perceivers is a biased measure of the target effect, and more complicated methods are needed to adjust for such biases (see Kenny, 1994).

In most studies of first impressions, researchers use a criterion variable to estimate the target's actual standing on a trait. We can examine accuracy as the correlation between the target effect and the criterion measure. Many researchers treat self-judgments as the criterion variable; yet, in several studies (e.g., Gosling et al., 2002) multiple informants provide information about the target, and so the degree of consensus of highly acquainted others then serves as the criterion measure. When there are multiple informants, we can again perform an SRM decomposition of the criterion measure. The same issues that we raised about the measurement of judgment also apply to the criterion.

Very typically, studies report the correlation between the estimated target effect of the judgment with the estimated target effect on the criterion. For example, we can correlate the target effect in strangers' perceptions of Jane's intelligence (i.e., the degree to which everyone perceives Jane as intelligent at zero acquaintance) with the target effect in well-acquainted others' perceptions of Jane's intelligence. We denote that correlation as r_{nm} because there are n perceivers and m informants per target, which gives the correlation between estimated target effects. We can represent the correlation between the theoretical target effects as $r_{\infty\infty}$, which represents the correlation between estimated target effects if there were a large number of judges. To estimate $r_{\infty\infty}$, we would divide r_{nm} by the square root of the product of the reliabilities of the judgment and the criterion. The correlation $r_{\infty\infty}$ is said to be *corrected for attenuation*, and it would be larger than r_{nm}. It estimates the correlation between the two means if there were an infinite number of perceivers and informants. The other correlation is the correlation between a single perceiver and a single informant, or r_{11}. That correlation would equal $r_{\infty\infty}$ times the square root of the reliability of a single perceiver times the reliability of a single perceiver. The reliability of a single perceiver (informant) is the same as the correlation between two perceivers (informants). Note that r_{11} would be much smaller than the value r_{nm}.

It is very possible that $r_{\infty\infty}$ can be relatively large whereas r_{11} can be very small. For instance, a very typical value for r in zero-acquaintance and thin-slices studies is .39 (Ambady & Rosenthal, 1992). If we assume the reliability for perceptions is .85 and for the criterion is .80, the value of $r_{\infty\infty}$ would be an impressive .473. However, the typical value of the reliability of a single judge and a single informant is only .25, making r_{11} equal to only .118. Note the two correlations of .473 and .118 differ by a factor of four.

FINDINGS

Thus far, we have provided a definition of zero acquaintance. In addition, we have examined one statistical model that can be used to examine perceptions at zero acquaintance, the SRM. Here, we review the major findings of zero-acquaintance research. Although our review is structured around findings that are typically discussed in studies that use the SRM, we have included in our review studies that did not utilize that model. We begin with the discussion of agreement among perceivers of a target; we examine consensus or agreement between perceivers' judgments and self–other agreement, or agreement between the perceivers' judgment and the target's self-judgment. We then discuss different forms of accuracy in perception. Next we examine how perceptions made at zero acquaintance can be extended to the study of metaperceptions, or perceptions that individuals have of the perceptions that perceivers make of them. Finally, we consider the stability of zero-acquaintance perceptions.

Consensus

Beginning with Norman and Goldberg (1966), zero-acquaintance research initially concentrated on agreement of personality measures using the Big Five. The level of consensus in personality is theoretically relevant to personality psychologists, where there has been debate about the degree to which consistency in targets' traits is predictive of behavior (e.g., Kenrick & Funder, 1988). In a review of studies that examined consensus of perceptions at zero acquaintance, Kenny, Albright, Malloy, and Kashy (1994) presented the results of nine zero-acquaintance studies. In seven of the nine studies, perceptions were made using a round-robin design where individuals in small groups all made perceptions of one another. In these studies, targets and perceivers potentially engaged in nonverbal interaction when perceptions were made. For example, in Albright et al. (1988), participants who were previously unacquainted were placed into groups numbering four to six members. Individuals then made perceptions of all group members (i.e., all participants were both perceivers and targets) across the Big Five personality factors. The majority of studies in Kenny et al.'s (1994) review used a research paradigm that was the same as the one used by Albright et al. (1988). Across the nine studies, consensus was highest for perceptions of Extraversion; nearly 30% of the variance in perceptions was attributed to the target effect. Conscientiousness demonstrated the next highest level of consensus; around 15% of the variance was attributed to the target effect. Small levels of consensus were found for Emotional Stability, Culture, and Agreeableness.

In one study reviewed by Kenny et al. (1994), judges made perceptions of videotaped targets (Kenny et al., 1992). As argued by Paunonen (1991) and Kenny et al. (1992), some nonverbal communication between targets and perceivers likely occurred during zero-acquaintance studies that use a design where perceivers and targets make perceptions face-to-face. In order to control for the possibility that consensus was driven by nonverbal communication between targets and perceivers, in Study 1 of Kenny et al. (1992) targets were videotaped without their knowledge while waiting for the experimenter to enter the room. A set of judges later viewed portions of the videos during which the target faced the camera. Results of Study 1 in Kenny et al. (1992) were consistent with those found in Kenny et al.'s (1994) review. The authors found that 22% of the variance in perceptions of extraversion and 13% of the variance in perceptions of conscientiousness were due to the target.

In Borkenau and Liebler's study (1992), perceivers also made judgments based on videos of targets. Targets were videotaped while sitting down at a table and reading a script about the weather. Borkenau and Liebler were primarily interested in how the varying amounts of information that judges had on which to base perceptions influenced consensus at zero acquaintance. Judges were assigned to make perceptions of personality in one of four conditions: they watched the complete tape with both audio and visual information, listened to an audio clip only, viewed a silent video, or viewed a still photo derived from the videotape. Consensus, especially for emotional stability, was lowest in the still condition. Interestingly, consensus was not systematically lower across traits in the audio-only or the video-only conditions as compared to the condition where perceivers received both audio and video information. This result is consistent with thin-slices research, which indicates that perceivers need relatively little information on which to base perceptions of targets (Ambady, Bernieri, & Richeson, 2000; Ambady et al., 1995). An additional refinement present in the Borkenau and Liebler study (1992) is the use of a community sample for the targets instead of college students. They found nearly three times the level of consensus found in the studies reviewed by Kenny et al. (1992). Thus, with a more representative sample of targets, the levels of consensus are higher.

Recent research has expanded the study of perceptions made at zero acquaintance from using cues provided directly by the target to perceptions of personality not based on face-to-face interactions. Gosling and colleagues have examined perceptions of personality based on bedrooms, offices, and recently, musical preferences (see Chapter 14 for a review of this research). In Gosling et al.'s study (2002), groups of perceivers made ratings of targets' personality on the Big Five after they examined the bedrooms and offices of targets. All photographs of targets were removed prior to the judges' entering the rooms. In addition, targets and judges never interacted. The authors found that, for perceptions based on offices, the consensus was greatest for perceptions of openness (roughly comparable to culture in Kenny et al.'s 1994 study), followed by conscientiousness and extraversion. Agreeableness showed some consensus, and the least amount of consensus was found for emotional stability. For perceptions made based on bedrooms, results were consistent with perceptions of the targets' offices. Consensus was highest for openness and conscientiousness, followed by extraversion and agreeableness; little consensus was found for emotional stability.

Rentfrow and Gosling (2006) examined perceptions of personality based on music preferences. Targets gave lists of their top 10 favorite songs; several perceivers then made personality ratings, using the 44-item Big Five Inventory (John & Srivastava, 1999) of each target after listening to the songs. The authors ensured that perceivers had no contact with the targets. Because perceivers and targets did not rate one another, consensus was computed as the intraclass correlation between the eight judges (Shrout & Fleiss, 1979). Perceptions of openness to experience, conscientiousness, and agreeableness showed the strongest consensus, followed by extraversion. Consistent with Kenny et al. (1994), the least amount of consensus was found for perceptions of emotional stability.

Evidence indicates that consensus is consistently found at zero acquaintance, using a variety of methodological approaches to studying such perceptions. Early work in the area used round-robin designs where perceivers and targets all made perceptions of each other face-to-face, based on Norman and Goldberg's (1966) paradigm. Recent work has demonstrated how consensus is found for perceptions of videotaped targets, targets' living spaces, and even their musical preferences. Thus, personality is evident in a variety of contexts, even at zero acquaintance. Overall, consensus is largest for perceptions of extraversion and conscientiousness, and smallest for perceptions of emotional stability. It has been argued that consensus is highest for levels of extraversion at zero acquaintance because extraversion and conscientiousness correlate highly with cues of physical appearance. In particular, Albright et al. (1988) found that perceptions of extraversion correlated significantly with perceptions of attractiveness, and perceptions of conscientiousness correlated highly with perceptions of how neatly and formally dressed targets were. Physical appearance cues are readily available cues utilized in face-to-face perception making. However, in Gosling and colleagues' work (2002), perceivers never observed the targets. Thus, perceptions of personality for which high consensus is consistently found cannot be explained solely by physical appearance cues.

There have been relatively few studies that have examined consensus at zero acquaintance in non-Western cultures. Albright et al. (1997) studied zero acquaintance in China and found somewhat lower consensus for extraversion but higher levels of consensus for the other factors.

Self–Other Agreement

In addition to consensus, one area of research that has attracted zero-acquaintance researchers in general and personality researchers in particular is the degree to which targets' self-judgments agree with the perceptions that strangers make of them. Perhaps the most surprising result in Norman and Goldberg's study (1966) was the finding that ratings of targets at zero acquaintance correlated with targets' self-ratings. The authors found that perceiver ratings of extraversion (i.e., sociable), conscientiousness (i.e., responsible) and culture (i.e., intellectual) all correlated positively with targets' self-ratings. Norman and Goldberg (1966) did not examine perceptions using a componential approach; self–other correlations are correlations between self-ratings and mean peer ratings.

When an SRM analysis of perception data is performed, self–other agreement is assessed as the correlation between the target effect and self-perception. Albright et al. (1988) used the SRM and found results consistent with Norman and Goldberg (1966). Self-target correlations for extraversion and conscientiousness were statistically reliable. Kenny et al. (1992) found generally consistent results with Albright et al. (1988). In Studies 2 and 3 of Kenny et al. (1992), self-target correlations were substantial for extraversion and conscientiousness (.33 and .62, respectively). However, in Study 1, self-target correlations were essentially zero. It is not clear why the self-target correlations were so weak in this one study. However, Borkenau and Liebler (1992) did find reliable self–other agreement, especially for Extraversion, when videotape information was presented. In addition, Rentfrow and Gosling (2006) also found that self–other agreement is relatively high for Extraversion, and perceptions were based on music preferences, where there was no possibility of interaction between targets and perceivers.

Self–other agreement for perceptions of other Big Five factors is consistently small to essentially zero in zero-acquaintance research. Recall that consensus for perceptions of Emotional Stability, in particular, is especially low. When there is not sufficient variance in an SRM component—in this case, the target effect—the correlation between the target effect and self-perceptions cannot be examined. In general, perceptions that demonstrate the highest levels of consensus almost always demonstrate the highest levels of self–other agreement.

We need to realize that self–other agreement does not necessarily imply accuracy, for two different reasons. First, targets may wish to communicate their self-image to perceivers, but that self-image may be false. For example, a target may believe that he or she is athletic, and he or she might communicate that self-image by wearing sweats, a headband, and running shoes; yet, the target may actually not be athletic. Second, people might use the same false stereotype in the ratings of self and others. For example, people might think that blonds are unintelligent, but that stereotype might not be true. If both perceivers and self have the same belief (e.g., blonds are unintelligent), then there would be self–other agreement that was not based on reality.

Target Accuracy

There has been much debate among person perception researchers on how to appropriately measure the accuracy of perceptions, specifically, in defining the criterion measure for accuracy (e.g., Funder & Colvin, 1988). Some researchers define accuracy as the correlation between self-perception and consensus (e.g., Blackman & Funder, 1998). Although self-perceptions are the clear criterion for accuracy in some contexts (e.g., sexual orientation), in perceptions of general personality traits, there are additional criteria that can be considered. For example, researchers have defined accuracy as the correlation between peer ratings and observer ratings, or interjudge agreement (Funder, 1987). However, as discussed by Funder and Colvin (1988), consensus of peer ratings does not necessarily imply accuracy. Peers may agree with one another, but they may be inaccurate if agreement is based on shared stereotypes among perceivers.

An additional approach is to define the criterion for accuracy as the combined perceptions of self and peer (e.g., Gosling et al., 2002). In examining the degree of accuracy of perceptions of personality based on bedrooms and offices, Gosling et al. (2002) created a combined score of the perceptions of close acquaintances and self-ratings (the average correlation between peer and self reports was .40), and then correlated the combined ratings with the perceptions of strangers.

Perhaps the least controversial criterion measure for accuracy of personality traits is behavior. Although not all personality traits map clearly onto behaviors, accuracy for perceptions of extraversion can be examined by correlating perceptions with a behavioral measure of extraversion. Levesque and Kenny (1993) instructed participants to first complete personality ratings at zero acquaintance, in groups of four. Participants were then asked to make behavioral predictions for each of the targets, both when the target interacted with the perceiver him- or herself and when the target interacted with others. Perceptions were made for talking, voice animation, gazing, smiling, nervousness, gesturing, and body posture. Participants then took turns engaging in 5-minute unstructured dyadic conversations while being videotaped. The tapes were coded by outside observers for the behaviors of talking, voice animation, gazing, smiling, nervousness, gesturing, and body posture. Results indicated significant generalized accuracy (but not dyadic accuracy) for perceptions of extraversion for all of the behavioral predictions. Perceivers were able to accurately predict how targets would behave with others in general but not with others in particular. Self-ratings of personality also correlated very highly with actual behaviors during interaction, in general across interaction partners.

In sum, evidence indicates that perceptions at zero acquaintance do map onto behaviors and that zero-acquaintance perceptions reliably correlate with perceptions that well-acquainted individuals make of targets. We next discuss a different form of accuracy, meta-accuracy of perceptions at zero acquaintance.

Meta-Accuracy

A key interest in the field of interpersonal perception is the study of metaperceptions, or the perceptions that individuals think that others make of them (Kenny, 1994; Laing, Phillipson, & Lee, 1966). In some first-impressions contexts, for example, in job interviews and on first dates, meta-accuracy is of strong interest. In zero-acquaintance studies, metaperceptions are understudied because presumably targets have little information on which to metaperceive. In zero-acquaintance studies where perceivers are provided with videotapes or photographs of perceivers, targets have no information about particular perceivers on which to base their metaperceptions. It is likely that when targets make metaperceptions of strangers, they rely heavily on two sources of information: feedback they have received from outside of the laboratory on their standing on a trait and self-perceptions. Previous work has found a consistently high correlation between self-perceptions and metaperceptions (Kenny & DePaulo, 1993).

Marcus and Miller (2003) examined metaperceptions of physical attractiveness, using a round-robin design with groups of men and women strangers.[1] The authors were primarily interested in the degree to which consensus and meta-accuracy are moderated by the gender of the target and the perceiver. The authors found statistically reliable self–other agreement for perceptions of physical attractiveness for both male and female targets and perceivers. Thus, men's self-judgments agreed with how attractive they were perceived by both men and women, and women's self-judgments also agreed with how attractive they were viewed by men and women. Self-judgments were also highly correlated with metaperceptions. Women who considered themselves to be attractive believed that they were consistently viewed as attractive by most people, and those who considered themselves as unattractive believed they were consistently viewed as unattractive by most people. In addition, the authors found a considerable degree of generalized meta-accuracy (i.e., perceivers knew how attractive others viewed them in general). Thus, there is evidence that meta-accuracy can be achieved at zero acquaintance. Next, we turn to an example of metaperceptions of personality measures.

Jung (2006), as reported in Kenny and West (2007), examined perceptions and metaperceptions of personality, using a Korean sample of students. Using the Albright et al. (1988) paradigm, participants each rated one another, themselves, and made metaperceptions on 20 personality traits. Jung found statistically significant generalized meta-accuracy for the traits bold, sloppy, intelligent, sincere, and tough, with the average correlation being .42. As expected, there was little or no evidence of dyadic meta-accuracy, the average correlation being .03. Self–other agreement was found for perceptions of bold and tough. This study provides evidence that meta-accuracy is not always driven by self-perception, at least in a non-Western context. Although self–other agreement was found for two of the variables for which meta-accuracy was found, it was not found for the other three.

Stability of Perceptions

There is a common belief that first impressions are lasting impressions. Within the SRM, we can measure the stability of the target and the relationship effect. The stability of the target refers to the extent to which the consensual part of the first impression is stable. The stability of the relationship effect refers to the stability of unique or idiosyncratic impressions of the target. It would seem reasonable that both components are stable, with the target being more stable than the relationship.

In Table 6.1, we present the results from Kenny et al. (1992), as well as the results from one additional study. We see that the target effect is very stable, averaging to .77, and most of the stabilities are statistically different from zero. The relationship correlations are much weaker, and only one of five is statistically different from zero. The following conclusion across the three studies seems warranted, despite the fact that we have limited data: judgments at zero acquaintance that are consensual tend to be very stable after the perceivers have interacted with the targets; however, relationships or idiosyncratic perceptions at zero acquaintance are not very stable. Thus, first impressions are lasting impressions only when they are consensual.

It is likely that some relational judgments might be more stable than others. For instance, we have not examined affect, or liking. Previous studies have shown that affect is highly relational. We might expect that first-impression affective relational judgments are more stable than trait judgments. We also think it likely that for perceivers who are judging targets toward whom they have stereotypes, relational stabilities might be much stronger. For instance, in judgments of negatively evaluated

TABLE 6.1. Stability of the Target and Relationship Effect

Study	Trait	Component	Stability
Kenny et al. (1992), Study 2	Extraversion	Target	.89[*]
		Relationship	.23
Kenny et al. (1992), Study 3	Extraversion	Target	.72[*]
		Relationship	.19
Albright et al. (1988), Study 1	Extraversion	Target	.72
		Relationship	.10[a]
	Conscientiousness	Target	.81[*]
		Relationship	.20[a]
	Culture	Target	.71
		Relationship	.25[*][a]

[a] Correlation without error variance removed.
[*] $p < .05$.

outgroup members, it might be reasonable to expect strong stability in relational perceptions.

PROCESS

The findings of consensus, self–other agreement, and target accuracy of first impressions are all quite surprising. The primary way that the researchers have attempted to understand these results has been to use the Brunswik (1956) lens model. In that model, a set of cues are presumed to explain the covariation between the judgment and the criterion. For instance, judges of intelligence use the cue of wearing glasses, which might be a valid cue of actual intelligence.

In the zero-acquaintance literature, a key focus has been on stereotypes as possible cues, given that relatively few target behaviors are observed. Because stereotypes are often consensually held, the finding of consensus at zero acquaintance is hardly surprising. Norman and Goldberg (1966) argued that much of consensus is due to stereotypes. The extent to which there are consensual judgments at zero acquaintance implies that to some extent stereotypes have a kernel of truth (Lee, Jussim, & McCauley, 1995). We should realize that stereotypes may be true not because they are true but rather because people believe them to be true—that is, because of self-fulfilling prophecy. It would seem possible that some stereotypes actually reflect the opposite of reality. For instance, in judging how talkative someone would be in a group, people might use the stereotype that women are more talkative than men. Yet, the data show that when gender-neutral topics are discussed in groups men actually tend to talk much more than women (Dovidio, Brown, Heltman, Ellyson, & Keating, 1988).

We have some concerns about the use of the lens model that we wish to discuss. First, we believe that the process of perception is much more complex than what occurs in the lens model. Perceivers' first impressions are determined by a multitude of pieces of information about the target's appearance and behavior. That information is viewed differently by different perceivers. Consider physical attractiveness, which might be seen as a cue in the lens model. It is a mistake to think there is a universally perceived cue of physical attractiveness that perceivers use in making perceptions. People disagree about physical attractiveness about as much as they agree (Honekopp, 2006). Second, just because a cue seems to be effective in a Brunswik analysis does not necessarily mean that perceivers are actually using that cue. They could be using something very different that is correlated with the cue. For instance, Pizzi, Blair, and Judd (2005) have shown that court judges are biased in giving sentences to defendants not so much by race per se but rather by faces with Afrocentric features.

CONCLUSION

Several topics have been understudied in the zero-acquaintance literature. Although there is extensive literature on the perception of personality, there have been fewer studies on the perception in other domains—for example, emotions. For instance, researchers might study judgments at zero acquaintance of targets' emotions (happiness, sadness, and anger). We also think the literature would benefit by a more controlled and focused study of stereotypes. For instance, researchers could more carefully control the composition of groups and measure traits that are stereotype-relevant.

We have given very little attention to individual differences in perception—in particular, what types of perceivers are more accurate at zero acquaintance. The topic has received attention beginning with Estes (1938) and continuing to Ambady, Hallahan, and Rosenthal (1996). Paunonen (1991) even claimed accuracy at zero-acquaintance is due to a few perceivers being accurate. Our own view, initially articulated in Kenny and Albright (1987), is that individual differences in interpersonal perception are fairly weak. It would seem that at zero acquaintance individual differences might be particularly small, because the process is often automatic and requires little cognitive processing.

Our approach emphasizes a statistical model of interpersonal perception, the SRM. Most other researchers employ relatively simpler statistical methods, for example, correlating means. In part the reluctance to adopt the SRM stems from the requirement of specialized software. However, given the recent advances of multilevel modeling, it is now possible to estimate the SRM using conventional software, such as SAS and Amos. We believe that more researchers will start using the SRM, given this change.

This book is testimony to the scientific importance of first impressions. One can make a case that during the past 20 years, the field of person perception has generated more useful knowledge about the perception of targets during the first few minutes than during the remaining years of acquaintance.

NOTE

1. One could argue that the Marcus and Miller study (2003) is not at zero acquaintance, because perceivers do have sufficient information to judge physi-

cal attractiveness. Nonetheless, we include the study because there are so few studies of metaperception at zero acquaintance.

REFERENCES

Albright, L., Kenny, D. A., & Malloy, T. E. (1988). Consensus in personality judgments at zero acquaintance. *Journal of Personality and Social Psychology, 55,* 387–395.

Albright, L., Malloy, T. E., Dong, Q., Kenny, D. A., Fang, X., Winquist, L., et al. (1997). Cross-cultural consensus in personality judgments. *Journal of Personality and Social Psychology, 72,* 558–569.

Altman, I., & Taylor, D. A. (1973). *Social penetration: The development of interpersonal relationships.* New York: Holt, Rinehart & Winston.

Ambady, N., Bernieri, F., & Richeson, J. A. (2000). Toward a histology of social behavior: Judgmental accuracy from thin slices of the behavioral stream. *Advances in Experimental Social Psychology, 32,* 201–271.

Ambady, N., Hallahan, M., & Conner, B. (1999). Accuracy of judgments of sexual orientation from thin slices of behavior. *Journal of Personality and Social Psychology, 77,* 538–547.

Ambady, N., Hallahan, M., & Rosenthal, R. (1995). On judging and being judged accurately in zero-acquaintance situations. *Journal of Personality and Social Psychology, 69,* 518–529.

Ambady, N., & Rosenthal, R. (1992). Thin slices of expressive behavior as predictors of interpersonal consequences: A meta-analysis. *Psychological Bulletin, 111,* 256–274.

Ambady, N., & Rosenthal, R. (1993). Half a minute: Predicting teacher evaluations from thin slices of nonverbal behavior and physical attractiveness. *Journal of Personality and Social Psychology, 64,* 431–441.

Blackman, M. C., & Funder, D. C. (1998). The effect of information on consensus and accuracy in personality judgment. *Journal of Experimental Social Psychology, 34,* 164–181.

Borkenau, P., & Liebler, A. (1992). Trait inferences: Sources validity at zero acquaintance. *Journal of Personality and Social Psychology, 62,* 645–657.

Brunswik, E. (1956). *Perception and the representative design of psychological experiments.* Berkeley: University of California Press.

Chaplin, W. F., Phillips, J. B., Brown, J. D., Clanton, N. R., & Stein, J. L. (2000). Handshaking, gender, personality, and first impressions. *Journal of Personality and Social Psychology, 79,* 110–117.

DiPilato, M., West, S. G., & Chartier, G. M. (1988). Person perception of type As and type Bs: A round robin analysis. *Journal of Social and Personal Relationships, 5,* 263–266.

Dovidio, J. F., Brown, C. E., Heltman, K., Ellyson, S. L., & Keating, C. F. (1988). Power displays between women and men in discussions of gender-linked tasks: A multichannel study. *Journal of Personality and Social Psychology, 55,* 580–587.

Estes, S. G. (1938). Judging personality from expressive behavior. *Journal of Abnormal and Social Behavior, 33*, 217–236.

Funder, D. C. (1987). Errors and mistakes: Evaluating the accuracy of social judgment. *Psychological Bulletin, 101*, 75–90.

Funder, D. C., & Colvin, R. C. (1988). Friends and strangers: Acquaintanceship, agreement, and the accuracy of personality judgment. *Journal of Personality and Social Psychology, 55*, 149–158.

Gosling, S. D., Ko, S. J., Mannarelli, T., & Morris, M. E. (2002). A room with a cue: Judgments of personality based on offices and bedrooms. *Journal of Personality and Social Psychology, 82*, 379–398.

Honekopp, J. (2006). Once more: Is beauty in the eye of the beholder? Relative contributions of private and shared taste to judgments of facial attractiveness. *Journal of Experimental Psychology: Human Perception and Performance, 32*, 199–209.

John, O. P., & Srivastava, S. (1999). The big five trait taxonomy: History, measurement, and theoretical perspectives. In L. A. Pervin & O. P. John (Eds.), *Handbook of personality: Theory and research* (pp. 102–138). New York: Guilford Press.

Jung, T. J. (2006). *Perceptions at zero acquaintance* [raw data].

Kenny, D. A. (1988). Interpersonal perception: A social relations analysis. *Journal of Social and Personal Relationships, 5*, 247–261.

Kenny, D. A. (1994). *Interpersonal perception: A social relations analysis.* New York: Guilford Press.

Kenny, D. A., & Albright, L. (1987). Accuracy in interpersonal perception: A social relations analysis. *Psychological Bulletin, 102*, 390–402.

Kenny, D. A., Albright, L., Malloy, T. E., & Kashy, D. A. (1994). Consensus in interpersonal perception: Acquaintance and the big five. *Psychological Bulletin, 116*, 245–258.

Kenny, D. A., Horner, C., Kashy, D. A., & Chu, L. (1992). Consensus at zero acquaintance: Replication, behavioral cues, and stability. *Journal of Personality and Social Psychology, 62*, 88–97.

Kenny, D. A., & DePaulo, B. M. (1993). Do people know how others view them? An empirical and theoretical account. *Psychological Bulletin, 114*, 145–161.

Kenny, D. A., & La Voie, L. (1984). The social relations model. In L. Berkowitz (Ed.), *Advances in experimental social psychology* (Vol. 18, pp. 142–182). Orlando, FL: Academic Press.

Kenny, D. A., & West, T. V. (2007). Self-perception as interpersonal perception. In J. V. Wood, A. Tesser, & J. G. Holmes (Eds.), *Close relationships and the self* (pp. 119–137). New York: Psychological Press.

Kenrick, D. T., & Funder, D. C. (1988). Profiting from controversy: Lessons from the person–situation debate. *American Psychologist, 43*, 23–34.

Laing, R. D., Phillipson, H., & Lee, A. R. (1966). *Interpersonal perception: A theory and a method of research.* New York: Springer-Verlag.

Lee, Y. T., Jussim, L., & McCauley, C. (1995). *Stereotype accuracy: Toward appreciating group differences.* Washington, DC: American Psychological Association.

Levesque, M. J., & Kenny, D. A. (1993). Accuracy of behavioral predictions at zero acquaintance: A social relations analysis. *Journal of Personality and Social Psychology, 65,* 1178–1187.

Marcus, D., K., & Miller, R. S. (2003). Sex differences in judgments of physical attractiveness: A social relations model. *Personality and Social Psychology Bulletin, 29,* 325–335.

Norman, W. T., & Goldberg, L. R. (1966). Raters, ratees, and randomness in personality structure. *Journal of Personality and Social Psychology, 4,* 681–691.

Passini, F. T., & Norman, W. T. (1966). A universal conception of personality structure. *Journal of Personality and Social Psychology, 4,* 44–49.

Paunonen, S. V. (1991). On the accuracy of ratings of personality by strangers. *Journal of Personality and Social Psychology, 61,* 471–477.

Pizzi, W. T., Blair, I. V., & Judd, C. M. (2005). Discrimination in sentencing on the basis of Afrocentric features. *Michigan Journal of Race and Law, 10,* 327–355.

Rentfrow, P. J., & Gosling, S. D. (2006). Message in a ballad: The role of music preferences in interpersonal perception. *Psychological Science, 17,* 236–242.

Shrout, P. E., & Fleiss, J. L. (1979). Intraclass correlations: Uses in assessing rater reliability. *Psychological Bulletin, 86,* 420–428.

Zebrowitz, L. A., & Collins, M. A. (1997). Accurate social perception at zero acquaintance: The affordances of a Gibsonian approach. *Personality and Social Psychology Review, 1,* 204–223.

CHAPTER 7

You Never Get a Second Chance to Make a First Impression

Behavioral Consequences of First Impressions

MONICA J. HARRIS
CHRISTOPHER P. GARRIS

I need a good quote or anecdote to start this chapter. Everybody knows that. A good opening is critical—something that will grab readers and put them in a good frame of mind while reading and keep those pages turning. But what kind of opening? Maybe a quote from Shakespeare . . . "Your face, my thane, is a book where men read very strange matters." Or what about this William Hazlitt quote: "First impressions are often the truest. . . . A man's look is the work of years; it is stamped on his countenance by the events of his whole life, nay, more, by the hand of nature, and it is not to be got rid of easily." Naw, too stuffy and perhaps perceived as overly pretentious. Maybe something more down-to-earth. I could tell about the time my friend taught the first day of an intro psych class and didn't discover until 10 minutes into it that the *back of her dress was tucked into her pantyhose (true story!). On the other hand, maybe not. It's a cute story but perhaps too flippant. I'd better just stick with the tried-and-true "start with a global statement about the importance of the topic" strategy.*

Literally every interaction we have with a new person entails a first impression. The impressions these others form of us will determine in large part whether they become our friends or lovers; whether they hire us for the job of our dreams; how smoothly or awkwardly our later interactions with them will proceed; whether they keep reading our chapter; and, indeed, whether they have anything at all to do with us in the future. An enormous research literature exists on the factors that determine a first impression. However, what is less known, and what will be the topic of this chapter, are the cognitive and behavioral processes that occur as a result of the first impression that has been formed. In this chapter, we review the empirical literature looking at behavioral consequences of first impressions, with an emphasis on (1) the employment interview, (2) impressions based on physical appearance (with respect to both attractiveness and stigma), and (3) the role of self-fulfilling prophecies in these situations. We focus in particular on the potentially damaging consequences of inaccurate first impressions and the dangers of relying on first impressions in such cases.

THE IMPRESSION THAT MAKES OR BREAKS YOUR CAREER: FIRST IMPRESSIONS AND THE JOB INTERVIEW

Few domains are fraught with as much peril as the job interview, and first impressions play a pivotal role in determining whether a job interview ends successfully (with an offer or a callback) or in dismal failure (with continued unemployment). Reams of scholarly and lay books have been written on self-presentation in the job interview (see Posthuma, Morgeson, & Campion, 2002, for a review). Most job applicants today have a solid understanding of how they should dress and act during an interview: remove the facial piercings; cover up the tattoos; don't chew gum; shake hands; make eye contact; exude confidence; be polite.

However, to focus only on the appearance and behavior of the applicant would be to ignore half of the job interview equation: the cognitions and behavior of the interviewer. Our emphasis in this chapter is on this neglected part of the interview process; in particular, we review the literature on how initial impressions formed by an interviewer (usually as a result of reading a resume or other form of paper credentials) affect the way the interview is carried out and the subsequent decisions made by the interviewer.

Early research in the field of management indicated the exceptionally strong effects of first impressions in employment interviews. In an often cited study Springbett (1958) concluded, "The appearance of the applicant and his application form provide information in the first two or three minutes of the interview which decisively affects final outcome in 85% of the cases" (p. 22). The conclusion that interviewers arrive at snap decisions quickly became an entrenched part of management lore (Buckley & Eder, 1988), despite significant limitations in the methodology of the Springbett (1958) study (interviewers were asked merely to place Xs on a piece of paper during an interview indicating when they had made a decision).

Subsequent studies examining this question yielded smaller, although still very strong, correlations (about $r = .50$) between first impressions and interview outcomes (Buckley & Eder, 1988; see reviews by Macan & Dipboye, 1990, p. 746, and Posthuma et al., 2002). A prototypical example of this literature is a study by Macan and Dipboye (1990), who administered questionnaires to recruiters before and after they interviewed applicants at a university placement office and also collected the impressions of the applicants following the interview. Analyses revealed that recruiters' preinterview impressions of the applicants were correlated ($r = .53$) with their postinterview impressions, indicating strong carryover of the initial impressions. This relationship held even after controlling for recruiters' general impressions of typical students at that university. Recruiters also felt that applicants for whom they had positive preinterview impressions performed better during the interview. Contrary to their hypotheses, however, preinterview impressions were not related to recruiters' estimates of how long the interview lasted or applicants' estimates of how much time was spent gathering information and recruiting. Interestingly, Macan and Dipboye (1990) found that recruiters whose preinterview impressions were negative were more likely to change their opinion of the applicant than those whose preinterview impressions were positive.

One limitation of the Macan and Dipboye (1990) study is that their measures were all self-report in nature, so they did not have any direct measures of process variables that might explain the effect of first impressions on how the interview was carried out. This limitation was corrected in a subsequent study conducted by Dougherty, Turban, and Callendar (1994), one that provides an excellent model for conducting field research on the effects of interviewers' first impressions. Their data set consisted of audiotapes of 79 interviews conducted for a large energy corporation, along with preinterview ratings made by the interviewer of the application forms (containing information about work history and educational background), and the test scores of the applicant. The interviews were subsequently coded by three independent judges for a host of process variables tapping into the degree of positive regard exhibited by the interviewer; the focus of interview questions; time spent during the interview; information-gathering strategies; and the applicant's behavior. Analyses revealed that the more favorable the interviewers' first impressions were, the more positively they treated the applicant, the more they seemed oriented toward extending an offer, and the more positive their vocal style appeared to be. Contrary to the findings of the Macan and Dipboye (1990) study, interviewers who had positive first impressions of the applicant also engaged in more active recruiting of the applicant, that is, attempting to "sell" the company and the job to a greater extent and providing more information about the company. Consistent with this finding, interviewers with positive impressions were also *less* likely to ask questions of the applicant.

Interviewer behavior in turn was related to applicant communication style in the predicted manner: the greater the positive regard of the interviewer, the more positive the applicant behavior. An earlier study using the same data set further documented that interviewers' first impressions were significantly related to final candidate evaluations (Dougherty, Ebert, & Callender, 1986). In sum, these two studies taken together show that interviewers' first impressions alter the way they conduct the interview, and how interviewers conduct the interview is subsequently related to how applicants appear to objective raters and their final evaluation by the interviewer. One limitation of the Dougherty et al. (1994) study, however, is that the analyses were strictly correlational in nature; thus, it is not possible to determine whether interviewer behavior mediated the relations between the first impressions and applicant behavior and interviewer outcomes. However, the Dougherty studies remain impressive for documenting differences in interviewer behavior in actual job interviews as a function of first impressions.

Considerable research has focused on one mechanism in particular by which interviewers' first impressions can have behavioral consequences, and that is the tendency for interviewers to engage in hypothesis-confirming strategies in formulating questions to ask (Dougherty & Turban, 1999). This tendency was first documented in a study by Snyder and Swann (1978) showing that, when individuals were given a profile describing a target as extraverted or introverted, they would select questions from a list that were leading in nature, for example, asking "What would you do to liven up a party?" if the target were presumed to be extraverted. Hypothesis-confirming biases have since been replicated on numerous occasions (Dougherty & Turban, 1999; Leyens, Dardenne, & Fiske, 1998), and because job candidates on interviews are reluctant to either interrupt or challenge the assumptions inherent in an interviewer's question, they may have particularly pernicious effects in the employment context.

Methods for Decreasing Reliance on First Impressions in Job Interviews

With so much at stake in a hiring decision, it is not surprising that considerable research has been invested in studying the interviewing process and attempting to reduce various forms of interviewer bias. The area that has received perhaps the greatest amount of attention is the comparison between structured and unstructured interviews. Advocates of structured interviews argue that the primary consequence of first impressions is to lead an interviewer to ask very different questions of applicants, depending on the favorability of the initial impression. To the extent that different applicants experience different interviews, the argument goes, it makes it harder to evaluate applicants fairly. Although the format of structured interviews varies considerably, in most cases an interview guide is created in advance, and interviewers adhere strictly to it rather than generating questions on the basis of applicants' previous responses.

In theory, structured interviews should minimize bias due to inaccurate first impressions and result in more valid interview decisions. A review comparing the two types of interviews confirms this view, with validity coefficients for unstructured interviews typically ranging between .14 and .33, whereas validity coefficients for structured interviews are substantially higher, .35 to .62 (Campion, Palmer, & Campion, 1997). The downside of structured interviews, though, is that they can be perceived negatively by both applicants and interviewers, who may resent the rigid format.

Other methods have been investigated for reducing interviewer bias. Note taking on the part of interviewers has been shown to reduce the impact of erroneous interviewer expectancies (Biesanz, Neuberg, Judice, & Smith, 1999). Instructing interviewers to form accurate impressions also helps to reduce bias in a laboratory context (Neuberg, 1989), an encouraging finding considering that most employment interviewers care deeply about making accurate impressions. Conducting a situational interview, where candidates are presented with realistic scenarios they are likely to encounter on the job and then report how they would handle them, also results in higher validity coefficients than more standard job-related interviews (McDaniel, Whetzel, Schmidt, & Maurer, 1994).

Is It So Bad for Interviewers to Rely on First Impressions?

The literature reviewed above shares a certain assumption, namely, the idea that job interviewers who form impressions rapidly and then rely on those impressions are somehow treating job applicants unfairly or arriving at less than optimal decisions. Indeed, the literature on methods to decrease interviewers' reliance on first impressions rests on the assumption, usually unstated, that interviewers' decisions will be better if they engage in long, thoughtful face-to-face interviews and delay making a decision until the conclusion of those interviews. However, we can play devil's advocate and point out that the literature on clinical versus actuarial decision making (Dawes, Faust, & Meehl, 1989) would arrive at a quite different conclusion, namely, that hiring decisions might be most optimally achieved through an impartial weighting of paper credentials and that face-to-face interviews impede, rather than facilitate, good hiring decisions.

The problem with traditional job interviews, this literature would argue, is that interviewers will be swayed by irrelevant details or predictors with less validity, or that certain predictors, such as physical appearance, will be given disproportionate weight. Decades of research on intuitive judgments confirm that people are not rational when reaching decisions about other people or events. Instead, we are swayed by biases such as the representative heuristic, where we assume that somebody who *looks* like a good computer programmer, administrative assistant, or fry cook will *be* a good programmer, assistant, or fry cook (Gilovich, Griffin, & Kahneman, 2002; Tversky & Kahneman, 1974).

At this point, readers may be tempted to conclude that it is somewhat perplexing and rather self-contradictory for us to suggest that interviewers might make better personnel selection decisions without the benefit of face-to-face interviews in the context of a chapter warning of the dangers and behavioral consequences of first impressions. However, we believe that there is an important distinction between the selection process and the other domains we describe where first impressions can have damaging consequences. "First impressions" in the interviewing context are almost always operationalized as a resume or job application form that an interviewer examines prior to meeting the applicant. These forms generally contain a large amount of detail directly relevant to the decision at hand: recent job experience, education, training, skills, letters of recommendation, screening test scores, and so forth. Most, if not all, of these factors have demonstrated validity in terms of predicting job performance. Contrast those sources of information with the type of information that can be gleaned in the job interview: Outside of summarizing the relevant job experience, skills, etc., *which have already been conveyed in the application or resume*, the interview will likely primarily communicate aspects of physical appearance, personality, and self-presentation that may, or may not be, relevant to the applicant's ability to perform the job duties.

In short, as Macan and Dipboye (1990) have argued, "The primary effects of preinterview impressions may be in limiting the ability of the interview to contribute unique information to the final decision" (p. 62). The question then becomes what the *incremental validity* of the face-to-face interview really is, and the evidence in this regard is not impressive (Posthuma et al., 2002). One of the obstacles preventing interviews from contributing incremental validity is that they usually take place in a context quite removed from the actual job setting and requirements for which the candidate is being interviewed; yet, we have ample evidence that first impressions are most accurate when the behavior is observed in context, as, for example, observing a teacher in the classroom (Ambady, Bernieri, & Richeson, 2000). To give another example, the standard job talk or sample lecture often given in interviews for academic jobs is probably more predictive of a candidate's potential than the individual meetings with faculty members that tend to make up the greater proportion of the interview process.

BEHAVIORAL CONSEQUENCES OF FIRST IMPRESSIONS BASED ON PHYSICAL APPEARANCE AND STIGMA: BEAUTY AND THE BEAST

As noted above, in the job interview context, first impressions are usually based on a written job application or resume. In almost every other interpersonal context, first impressions stem largely, if not exclusively, from the target's physical appearance. In this section, we offer an overview of the literature on behavioral consequences of first impressions based on distinctively positive or negative physical appearance.

Miller (1970) revealed perhaps the first detailed report of expectations held of attractive individuals, showing that they were considered to be more curious, complex, perceptive, happy, active, amiable, humorous, pleasure-seeking, outspoken, and flexible than unattractive individuals. Patzer (1985) nicely summarized decades of physical attractiveness research: generally, the more physically attractive an individual is, the more positively the person is perceived, the more favorably the person is responded to, and the more successful is the person's personal and professional life. While a layperson could probably guess that the effects of being physically attractive would be positive, the magnitude of these effects on such major life outcomes may seem surprising. After all, how could one's professional outcomes be at the mercy of one's appearance—

a variable that is, for the most part, out of one's control and usually unrelated to the task demands involved in the career? Despite many additional findings consistent with these (see Feingold, 1992, for a meta-analysis), it appears that people do not like to admit that physical attractiveness factors into their impression formation process, suggesting that it is a largely unconscious process. Research with children showing a similar advantage for attractive children in interactions with their peers suggests further that this bias is internalized early in life (Smith, 1985).

More relevant to the current chapter is the question of how impressions based on physical appearance affect the subsequent behavior of the perceiver and target. Research across a wide variety of domains has documented that physically attractive people receive better treatment than unattractive people. For example, people are less likely to help physically unattractive individuals, even when the predicament is not within their control (Shaw, 1972; Dovidio, Piliavin, Schroeder, & Penner, 2006). Research in psychology and law has shown that physically attractive individuals, as defendants, receive less harsh punishments, with one meta-analysis finding that the effect size associated with the attractiveness advantage was considerable ($d = 0.19$; Mazella & Feingold, 1994).

Perhaps even more disturbing than preferential treatment given to attractive defendants is the bias toward attractive students shown by teachers, because it affects a larger proportion of people. More attractive students perform better in school and are more positively regarded by their teachers than their less attractive peers (Murphy, Nelson, & Cheap, 1981; Ritts, Patterson, & Tubbs, 1992). The Feingold meta-analysis (1992) similarly found that attractive people are perceived to be more intelligent (mean $d = 0.32$); the actual correlation between attractiveness and intelligence, however, is low (mean $r = .00$ for intelligence). As has been well documented (and will be discussed in more detail later), positive expectations can result in a self-fulfilling prophecy in that people construct the environment in such a way as to foster their initial expectations. In the educational context, teachers exhibit more warmth toward and devote more attention toward the students they expect to perform well (Harris & Rosenthal, 1985)—in this case, attractive students. Thus, even though physical attractiveness may not bear any direct causal relation to intelligence, attractive students may still end up with greater achievement levels simply because of the teachers' increased positivity and attention toward them.

In sum, a large literature exists documenting the positive treatment received by attractive individuals. An equally large literature exists demonstrating the converse effect: individuals who possess a visible stigma and/or are physically ugly or disfigured often receive negative interpersonal treatment, primarily in the form of rejection or avoidance (Klein &

Snyder, 2003). A visible stigma or one that is made known to a perceiver creates a negative first impression that is often difficult for targets to overcome.

Two explanations exist for the negative social interactions that occur between stigmatized and nonstigmatized individuals, and these explanations point to the various reactions of the perceiver and target as the primary factors. The first explanation is that nonstigmatized perceivers, when confronted with a visibly stigmatized target, experience negative affect, threat, and a motivation to flee the situation (Blascovich, Mendes, Hunter, & Lickel, 2000), resulting in subsequent discrimination. The second explanation focuses on the impact of "stigma consciousness" (Pinel, 1999) on the targets and emphasizes the anxiety and identity threat felt by targets as they anticipate negative treatment by perceivers (see Major & O'Brien, 2005, for a review).

Considerable empirical evidence exists confirming that both of these processes are at work in interactions involving stigmatized persons. Looking first at the reactions of the perceiver, Blascovich and colleagues (Blascovich, Mendes, Hunter, Lickel, & Kowai-Bell, 2001) have collected intriguing data showing that perceivers interacting with a confederate who was wearing facial makeup to give the appearance of a large port-wine birthmark exhibited the cardiovascular markers of threat (i.e., increases in cardiac activity and vascular tone). One admirable feature of this study is that confederates were kept uninformed as to whether they were wearing the birthmark versus translucent makeup, so their own behavior could not have contributed to the perceivers' reactions.

The threat reaction presumably underlies more overtly negative behaviors directed by perceivers toward stigmatized individuals. Robert Kleck has a long and influential program of research showing that physically disabled people are treated more negatively in interactions. In one early demonstration of this effect, participants interacting displayed greater physiological arousal, more behavioral inhibition, and terminated the conversation sooner when interacting with a confederate who was sitting in a wheelchair as compared to a regular chair (Kleck, Ono, & Hastorf, 1966). These results are robust and have been replicated numerous times in subsequent decades (see Hebl & Kleck, 2000, and Hebl, Tickle, & Heatherton, 2000, for reviews). A more recent analysis offers a theoretical refinement, suggesting that nonstigmatized perceivers will adopt an *avoidant style* when interacting with a stigmatized target in a getting-acquainted context, whereas they will adopt a *dominant style* when interacting in a task-oriented context (Klein & Snyder, 2003).

It is important to note that much of the negative behavior displayed toward stigmatized targets often contradicts the self-reported feelings of perceivers about the targets. In one study, male participants who were interacting with a conversation partner they believed to be either gay or straight reported no differences in attitudes toward the confederates in the two conditions, but they sat farther away when discussing a threatening topic with the allegedly gay confederate (Bromgard & Stephan, 2006). In short, verbal behavior directed toward or about the stigmatized target tends to be positive, either due to social desirability or egalitarian values, but this positive behavior may be contradicted by nonverbal avoidance cues that are largely outside the conscious awareness and control of the perceiver (Hebl et al., 2000).

Thus, it seems clear that perceivers approach interactions with stigmatized individuals more negatively. However, a second piece of the puzzle is just as crucial to understanding the negative consequences of stigma-related first impressions, and that involves the reactions of the targets themselves as they enter an interaction knowing that they possess a stigma. Pinel (1999) coined the expression "stigma consciousness" to denote the evaluation apprehension and anxiety that a target possessing a stigma feels when anticipating an interaction with a nonstigmatized individual. Ample experimental data exist showing that targets in such situations react with sufficient anxiety and negative affect that the interactions are adversely affected. Some of the important early work on this effect was done by Farina and colleagues; for example, Farina, Gliha, Boudreau, Allen, and Sherman (1971) found that psychiatric patients who were led to believe that a conversation partner had been informed of their diagnosis performed less well and were rated as more anxious than patients who interacted with somebody they believed did not know about their diagnosis.

These findings were confirmed in an influential study by Kleck and Strenta (1980), who led targets to believe that the confederate they were interacting with believed they either had epilepsy, an unattractive facial scar, or allergies (the control condition). Confederates were, in actuality, blind to the condition of the target. Ratings of the videotaped interaction revealed that targets who believed themselves to be stigmatized appeared more tense and patronizing, and self-reports of the targets showed that they liked the confederate less. Ratings of the confederates, moreover, showed no differences in behavior toward the target that could account for their negative reaction. Research by Blascovich et al. (2000) further confirms that stigmatized targets experience greater physiological arousal.

Hebl et al. (2000) argue that the greater anxiety felt by stigmatized targets stems from several sources: fear of rejection; a feeling of evaluation apprehension and of being "on stage"; self-dislike; and misattributing perceivers' behaviors as reflecting discrimination. Targets will also pick up on the discrepancy between perceiver verbal and nonverbal behavior noted above, and they will be inclined to attribute the negative behavior to antipathy on the part of the perceiver rather than to possible anxiety or discomfort felt by the perceiver, which may in fact be the most likely cause (Hebl et al., 2000).

Overall, these results paint a glum picture for unattractive or stigmatized individuals looking to make a positive first impression. Being attractive carries an array of positive associations and expectations and will likely result in a positive first impression. Furthermore, perceivers have been shown to behave in ways that benefit attractive individuals in arenas that range from the trivial to the extremely important. Moreover, as we discuss next, an unfortunate tendency exists for targets to confirm the negative expectations of the perceiver.

THE SELF-FULFILLING NATURE OF FIRST IMPRESSIONS: RESEARCH ON INTERPERSONAL EXPECTANCY EFFECTS

The interactional "problem" with first impressions is not that we form them but that they can be incorrect. And when our first impressions are wrong—but they influence our behavior toward the target nonetheless—the stage is set for adverse consequences. The interactional consequences of erroneous first impressions is at the heart of research on self-fulfilling prophecies (also variously termed "interpersonal expectancy effects" or "behavioral confirmation"). As originally defined by Merton (1948), a self-fulfilling prophecy is an originally *false* definition of the situation that evokes behaviors making the false conception come true. Empirical research on interpersonal self-fulfilling prophecies had its start with Robert Rosenthal's enormously influential program of research on the biasing effects of experimenters' expectations on their participants' responses. He and his colleagues later branched out to other interpersonal domains, most notably the classroom with the publication of the well-known and controversial *Pygmalion in the Classroom* (Rosenthal & Jacobson, 1968).

Although the idea that experimenters' and teachers' expectations could create self-fulfilling prophecies was initially met with considerable resistance, eventually enough replications were published to quell even the most vocal critics. Meta-analyses of the literature on expectancy effects have subsequently shown that these effects are statistically significant and accompanied by a mean effect size that is moderate in magnitude (Rosenthal & Rubin, 1978; Rosenthal, 1994).

While any expectation could be considered a type of "first impression," for the purposes of this chapter the behavioral confirmation studies with greatest relevance are those that looked at the effects of interpersonal expectancies in everyday interaction. The classic example of this, of course, is the study by Snyder, Tanke, and Berscheid (1977) looking at the effects of manipulated expectations of physical attractiveness on men's interactions with unacquainted women. In the study, female and male participants were led to believe that they would be getting to know an opposite-sex participant during a telephone conversation. Prior to the conversation, male participants were given a description sheet of the female with whom they would be speaking and a photograph of either an attractive or unattractive woman believed to be their conversation partner. Females were told nothing about their partner, nor were they aware of the information their participants received prior to the conversation. Not surprisingly, after seeing the photograph but before conversing, men expected attractive women to embody more positive traits. After conversing, men's impressions remained consistent with their initial expectations: women believed to be attractive were rated more positively, whereas women believed to be unattractive were rated more negatively.

While these results were not particularly surprising and replicate the well-known "what is beautiful is good effect" (Patzer, 1985), more noteworthy are the results found for the ratings of blind coders, which were consistent with the male participants' ratings: those women who had been paired with the attractive photos were rated more positively by the coders. Analysis of the audiotapes revealed the process by which this occurred. Male participants acted upon their expectations of what they believed to be unattractive telephone partners by treating them in a less warm or sociable manner, hence eliciting a more negative reaction from these women. Snyder and his colleagues (1977) concluded that the expectations of the male participant, even over a brief telephone conversation, created a self-fulfilling prophecy that resulted in female participants' behaving in ways consistent with their male partners' initial appearance-based expectations.

Similar results have been found in other behavioral confirmation studies that have manipulated impressions or expectancies regarding a variety of target traits, including personality (Harris & Rosenthal, 1986; Harris, 1989; Stukas & Snyder, 2002), race (Chen & Bargh, 1997; Word, Zanna, & Cooper, 1974), gender (Skrypnek & Snyder, 1982), hyperactivity (Harris, Milich, Corbitt, Hoover, & Brady, 1992), and mental illness (Sibicky & Dovidio, 1986).

Most studies of expectancy effects in a first-impression context have focused on the effects of expectations or impressions formed by a perceiver about a target. As our discussion of stigma showed above, however, we should not neglect the self-fulfilling processes that occur within targets. Knowing that one possesses a distinctive characteristic that creates a negative impression in others may itself be a source of anxiety or threat and lead targets to behave in ways that elicit the behavior they expect to receive from perceivers (Crocker & Garcia, 2006; Klein & Snyder, 2003).

Theoretical Models of Expectancy Effects

In 1980, Darley and Fazio introduced a model, the Social Interaction Sequence, that remains today a useful framework for understanding the processes underlying expectancy effects. In the first step, an impression is formed. Specifically, the perceiver forms an expectation based upon observable traits and the traits the perceiver believes to be associated with them. These expectations can be based upon, but are not limited to, group membership and reputations. Stage 2 involves the way in which the perceiver acts, based upon the evaluations made in stage 1. Darley and Fazio (1980) predict that if the perceiver's expectation is negative the interaction will likely be terminated. This simply means that the perceiver will avoid future interactions and/or exit the current interaction as soon as possible. This step is of vital relevance to targets seeking to change the impression another has formed about them. Obviously, if a perceiver avoids future contact with an individual, his or her impression about this individual is unlikely to change. Therefore, not only are first impressions difficult to change even when given the chance to interact with the perceiver, but also the challenge to the target is to ensure that subsequent interaction will even occur.

If the perceiver does not terminate the sequence, Darley and Fazio state that impressions may still be unlikely to change, because the perceiver may carry out future interactions in ways consistent with the original impression. In stage 3, targets interpret the actions of the perceiver. This stage is important in showing that impression formation is a dynamic process. Targets can attribute the perceiver's behavior dispositionally or recognize that the impression he or she has formed is somehow influencing the perceiver's behavior. The target responds in stage 4, which can be an attempt either to challenge the impressions formed or to mirror them. Reciprocating the behaviors of the perceivers, of course, helps confirm the initial impression.

For those seeking to change the impression another has formed of them, this stage is the key opportunity to do so. First of all, targets must be vigilant to detect whether the perceiver's behavior portrays a positive or negative impression. If positive, targets can continue to present themselves in the same manner; however, if negative, they should be cautious not to reciprocate the perceiver's behavior and may want to behave differently in an attempt to adjust the perceiver's impression. This leads to stage 5, where the perceiver interprets the target's response. Darley and Fazio point out that the perceivers are not well equipped at realizing the extent of their influence on the target's behavior and that the behavior will often be attributed to dispositional traits. This step is important in confirming or challenging the original set of expectancies. The individual being perceived also observes his or her own behavior—stage 6—as being either situationally produced or revealing of the self.

Mediation of Interpersonal Expectancy Effects

The second stage of Darley and Fazio's (1980) model addresses how the perceiver behaves toward the target as a function of the initial impression or expectancy. In many ways, this is the most important step of the model, as it is the perceiver's differential behavior toward the target that provokes the self-fulfilling prophecy. The specific behaviors mediating a perceiver's expectancy will, of course, vary depending on the situation and nature of the expectancy (Harris, 1993); in other words, the behaviors that mediate positive teacher expectancies (e.g., teaching more difficult material, offering more praise after correct answers) will not necessarily be the same as the behaviors that mediate expectancies in other contexts. However, Harris and Rosenthal (1985) argued that mediating behaviors could be classified into one of four broad categories (feedback, input, output, climate), and this model was later refined by Rosenthal (1989, 1994) and renamed the affect–effort theory of expectancy mediation. According to this theory, expectancies affect perceivers' behavior toward targets along the two broad dimensions of *affect*, which reflects largely nonverbal behaviors associated with liking and disliking, and *effort*, which reflects such variables as the amount of time and attention devoted to the target.

In general, perceivers who hold positive impressions of a target will behave more warmly toward the target, smiling more, standing closer, touching the target more often, engaging in more frequent eye contact, and using a warmer tone of voice. These perceivers will also spend more time in the target's company, engaging in more conversation and asking more questions. The perceiver will also be more persistent in interactions with the positive-expectancy target, for example, offering more chances to rectify a mistake or to display appropriate behavior (Harris & Rosenthal, 1985; Rosenthal, 1989). It is not surprising that a target who is the recipient of positive affect and increased effort on the part of the perceiver may therefore reciprocate these behaviors, resulting in behavioral confirmation of the positive expectancy. Nor is it surprising when the recipient of neglectful or hostile behaviors responds in a similarly cold manner. And, of course, in the case of the terminated sequences identified by Darley and Fazio (1980), a target would never even have the opportunity to disconfirm a negative expectancy.

OVERCOMING A NEGATIVE FIRST IMPRESSION: WHAT CAN A TARGET DO?

This latter point raises a pressing question: What can you do when an interaction gets off on the wrong foot? The literature reviewed above posits that the processes underlying impression formation occur extremely quickly and are often automatic and unconscious, an assertion that has been confirmed by the "thin slices of behavior" literature (Ambady & Rosenthal, 1992; Ambady et al., 2000). Furthermore, these original evaluations are often lasting and influential (Fiske, Lin, & Neuberg, 1999). The classic study by Ross, Lepper, and Hubbard (1975) was an early demonstration of this conclusion, showing that even when participants were explicitly subsequently told that information about an individual was false, they persisted in believing it. Ross et al. (1975) explained that participants use an attributional bias to maintain an impression, which makes even disconfirming information seem consistent with one's initial impression.

In short, our discussion to date would probably seem discouraging to targets who flub up in the first seconds of an interaction, as it stresses the rapidity with which impressions are formed and the self-fulfilling nature of negative impressions. However, it would be erroneous to assume that all first impressions are necessarily self-fulfilling or that one can never overcome a negative impression.

Some of the prominent theories of impression formation provide clues for how a negative impression can be overcome. For example, one early theory (Anderson's 1981 information integration model) posits that the perceiver uses cognitive algebra to combine the many components of social information available and then integrates them into an impression. This means that a person can perhaps outweigh a negative first impression with a subsequent showing of positive traits. For example, a waiter may bring the wrong drinks for a customer but avoid an overall negative impression (and lower tip!) by displaying politeness, courtesy, gratitude, and helpfulness. While some variables may be more positive or negative, depending on their valence and presentation, the waiter should be able to cancel out an initial negative impression with a strong showing of positive traits. However, it is difficult to predict just how many positive traits are necessary to balance out a negative trait, and vice versa, due to the subjective nature of weighting involved in cognitive algebra equation.

The continuum model of impression formation (Fiske et al., 1999) also addresses the issue of when and how impressions can be changed. The continuum model proposes that, first, a perceiver immediately categorizes a target based upon the traits available to him or her. Next, depending on whether or not the perceiver feels motivated or interested to think further about this individual, the initial categorization will be evaluated. If the perceiver decides that the initial category was appropriate, no further processing is necessary. However, if it is decided that the initial category is inappropriate, the individual will be recategorized into a category believed to better fit the information available. Lastly, if the perceiver cannot categorize the individual into a category he or she believes to be appropriate, piecemeal processing will take place.

According to the continuum model, the original categorization is the most important step and is powerful and resistant to change. It is predicted that most processing stops after this first step (Fiske et al., 1999). Furthermore, if processing does continue, the initial categorization influences the way information is processed in subsequent steps. For example, if a student is initially categorized as a "slacker" because he or she is continually late to class, it is difficult to change that label. And when information arises that leads the perceiver to reevaluate that categorization—for example, the student makes a brilliant comment in class—the initial label influences the evaluation. Perhaps the student is "an underachiever"—but certainly not "a brilliant student."

However, the continuum model offers some hope for the target who wishes to change a negative impression, and that is in the idea that perceivers will engage in individuating processing when they are especially motivated to form an accurate impression and have the cognitive resources to do so. With respect to accuracy motivation, as we described in the job interviewing section, the more motivated the perceiver is to make an accurate impression of an individual, the more accurate the impression is likely to be (Neuberg, 1989). While accuracy motivation will naturally be high in some contexts (e.g., job interviews, graduate admissions), a target can perhaps also increase perceivers' accuracy motivation by pointing out any mutual outcome dependency. One of the prime ways to increase the interest of a perceiver is to make him or her personally relevant or involved. Studies have shown that participants made personally responsible for the accuracy of their impressions devote more effort to forming them, leading to more individuating impressions (Fiske et al., 1999), especially when the target's behavior did not match the initial expectancy or stereotype (Madon, Guyll, Hilbert, Kyriakatos, & Vogel, 2006).

With respect to the issue of cognitive resources, the literature on dual-process models shows that when perceivers are cognitively busy (stressed, multitasking, etc.) their impressions are likely to be made very quickly—perhaps unconsciously—using biases and stereotypes, and consistent with impressions formed of similar individuals. This has been shown in a number of contexts; for example, Gilbert's work on dispositional versus situational attributions finds that observers will make an automatic dispositional inference but will fail to take the second step of correcting their impressions for situational influences if they are cognitively busy (Gilbert & Malone, 1995). In one empirical demonstration, Gilbert, Pelham, and Krull (1988) showed that participants watching a nervous-looking woman on videotape appropriately attributed her nervousness to the situation (subtitles informed them that the woman was talking about her sexual fantasies) when they were not under cognitive load; however, when participants were made cognitively busy by rehearsing word strings, they were unable to make the situational correction.

Applying this reasoning to the specific context of expectancy effects, Harris and Perkins (1995) found that, when perceivers were made cognitively busy by rehearsing an 8-digit number while interacting with a target, more behavioral confirmation was obtained than when the perceiver was not cognitively busy. Presumably, being under cognitive load prevents perceivers from noticing or attending to expectancy-discrepant behavior on the part of the target and therefore being less likely to revise their expectancies or impressions of the target. Thus, perceivers would continue to act in accordance with their expectancies, which would over time lead targets to reciprocate and thus confirm the expectancy.

Other research shows that the double whammy of low-accuracy motivation and cognitive resources can be especially damaging to perceivers' tendency to make individuating impressions. Moreno and Bodenhausen (1999) manipulated both accuracy motivation and cognitive resources and found that the greatest level of stereotyping occurred for perceivers who had low motivation and less attentional capacity.

The implications for a target hoping to correct a negative impression or to ensure a positive impression in the first place would be to structure the interaction, as much as possible, to ensure that the perceiver has few distractions and to increase as much as possible the perceiver's motivation to reach an accurate perception. Perhaps a comment as casual as "we're going to be working a lot together" (to a new coworker) or "be around each other a lot" (to a new roommate or neighbor), "so let's try to get to know each other well" could be effective in inducing perceivers to engage in more effortful processing.

Highlighting one's unique characteristics or otherwise making oneself appear novel or salient is another possible strategy targets could adopt. Familiar traits—ones that the perceiver has previously experienced when forming impressions—or impressions that have been formed previously are stronger and thus more resistant to change than novel impressions (Stewart, Doan, Gingrich, & Smith, 1998). This makes sense, especially according to the continuum model, where well-established categorizations are less likely to be challenged or reevaluated (Fiske et al., 1999). Thus, targets may have a better opportunity to change the perceiver's impression if the targets' characteristics are novel and/or distinctive in some way. The disadvantage of this approach, of course, is that too much novelty could be perceived especially negatively.

CLOSING THOUGHTS

The literature reviewed above drives home the important point that the impression formation process sometimes begins long before meeting an individual in the flesh. Indeed, the canvas on which we draw our impressions is by no means blank. Reputations, rumors, job or school applications, or offhand comments made by friends all provide perceivers with a rich set of descriptive information—information that may or may not accurately describe the target's personality. Indeed, individuals looking to make a good first impression would be wise to understand that others' impressions will not wait until they are ready to present their attributes; often, impressions will not wait until they have even said a word.

It is thus difficult to write a chapter on the behavioral consequences of first impressions without ending up feeling somewhat pessimistic and cynical about human nature. In the literature reviewed in this chapter, we have seen that people arrive at first impressions incredibly quickly. As we have seen in the other chapters in this volume, much of the time these impressions are accurate and highly diagnostic of the target's behavior and personality. However, sometimes these impressions are not— yet, the perceiver's subsequent behavior toward the target nonetheless reflects the first impressions so hastily drawn. Perceiver behavior can then constrain the target's options and responses, creating a self-fulfilling prophecy, which ironically only serves to cement the perceiver's conclusion that he or she was "right all along" about the target. Sadder yet, targets' awareness and anxiety that this is going on can also contribute to the self-fulfilling nature of negative first impressions.

How many potentially excellent employees have gone unhired because they were, say, obese? How many graduate students have we turned down for our programs because they reminded us of a former student who dropped out after a year? How many of us have missed out on a lifelong, deeply rewarding romantic relationship because the person in question had the "wrong" color of hair or taste in music, or a laugh that was just a little bit too loud? Such scenarios are the fodder of countless date movies, but part of the appeal of those movies is the perceived universality of the experience. Perhaps the real tragedy of the behavioral consequences of first impressions is that we rarely discover when our impressions have led us awry.

ACKNOWLEDGMENTS

We thank Richard Milich for his comments on portions of this draft.

REFERENCES

Ambady, N., Bernieri, F., & Richeson, J. A. (2000). Towards a histology of social behavior: Judgmental accuracy from thin slices of the behavioral stream. *Advances in Experimental Social Psychology, 32*, 201–272.

Ambady, N., & Rosenthal, R. (1992). Thin slices of expressive behavior as predictors of interpersonal consequences: A meta-analysis. *Psychological Bulletin, 111*, 256–274.

Anderson, N. H. (1981). *Foundations of information integration theory.* New York: Academic Press.

Biesanz, J. C., Neuberg, S. L., Judice, T. N., & Smith, D. M. (1999). When interviewers desire accurate impressions: The effects of notetaking on the influence of expectations. *Journal of Applied Social Psychology, 29*(12), 2529–2549.

Blascovich, J., Mendes, W. B., Hunter, S. B., & Lickel, B. (2000). Stigma, threat, and social interactions. In T. F. Heatherton, R. E. Kleck, M. R. Hebl, & J. G. Hull (Eds.), *The social psychology of stigma* (pp. 307–333). New York: Guilford Press.

Blascovich, J., Mendes, W. B., Hunter, S. B., Lickel, B., & Kowai-Bell, N. (2001). Perceiver threat in interactions with stigmatized others. *Journal of Personality and Social Psychology, 80*, 253–267.

Bromgard, G., & Stephan, W. G. (2006). Responses to the stigmatized: Disjunctions in affect, cognitions, and behavior. *Journal of Applied Social Psychology, 36*, 2436–2448.

Buckley, M. R., & Eder, R. W. (1988). B. M. Springbett and the notion of the "snap decision" in the interview. *Journal of Management, 14*(1), 59–67.

Campion, M. A., Palmer, D. K., & Campion, J. E. (1997). A review of structure in the selection interview. *Personnel Psychology, 50*, 655–702.

Chen, M., & Bargh, J. (1997). Nonconscious behavioral confirmation processes: The self-fulfilling consequences of automatic stereotype activation. *Journal of Experimental Social Psychology, 33*, 541–560.

Crocker, J., & Garcia, J. A. (2006). Stigma and the social basis of the self: A synthesis. In S. Levin & C. van Laar (Eds.), *Stigma and group inequality: Social psychological perspectives* (pp. 287–308). Mahwah, NJ: Erlbaum.

Darley, J. M., & Fazio, R. (1980). Expectancy confirmation processes arising in the social interaction sequence. *American Psychologist, 35,* 867–881.

Dawes, R. M., Faust, D., & Meehl, P. E. (1989). Clinical versus actuarial judgment. *Science, 243,* 1668–1674.

Dougherty, T. W., Ebert, R. J., & Callender, J. C. (1986). Policy capturing in the employment interview. *Journal of Applied Psychology, 71,* 9–15.

Dougherty, T. W., & Turban, D. B. (1999). Behavioral confirmation of interviewer expectancies. In R. W. Eder & M. M. Harris (Eds.), *The employment interview handbook* (pp. 259–278). Thousand Oaks, CA: Sage.

Dougherty, T. W., Turban, D. B., & Callender, J. C. (1994). Confirming first impressions in the employment interview: A field study of interviewer behavior. *Journal of Applied Psychology, 79*(5), 659–665.

Dovidio, J. F., Piliavin, J. A., Schroeder, D. A., & Penner, L. (2006). *The social psychology of prosocial behavior.* Mahwah, NJ: Erlbaum.

Farina, A., Gliha, D., Boudreau, L. A., Allen, J. G., & Sherman, M. (1971). Mental illness and the impact of believing others know about it. *Journal of Abnormal Psychology, 77,* 1–5.

Feingold, A. (1992). Good-looking people are not what we think. *Psychological Bulletin, 111,* 304–341.

Fiske, S. T., Lin, M., & Neuberg, S. (1999). The Continuum Model: Ten years later. In S. Chaiken & Y. Trope (Eds.), *Dual-process models in social psychology* (pp. 231–254). New York: Guilford Press.

Gilbert, D. T., & Malone, P. S. (1995). The correspondence bias. *Psychological Bulletin, 117,* 21–38.

Gilbert, D. T., Pelham, B. W., & Krull, D. S. (1988). On cognitive busyness: When person perceivers meet persons perceived. *Journal of Personality and Social Psychology, 54,* 733–740.

Gilovich, T., Griffin, D., & Kahneman, D. (Eds.). (2002). *Heuristics and biases: The psychology of intuitive judgment.* New York: Cambridge University Press.

Harris, M. J. (1989). Personality moderators of expectancy effects: Replication of Harris and Rosenthal (1986). *Journal of Research in Personality, 23,* 381–387.

Harris, M. J. (1993). Issues in studying the mediation of expectancy effects: A taxonomy of expectancy situations. In P. D. Blanck (Ed.), *Interpersonal expectations: Theory, research, and applications* (pp. 350–378). New York: Cambridge University Press.

Harris, M. J., Milich, R., Corbitt, E., Hoover, D., & Brady, M. (1992). Self-fulfilling effects of stigmatizing information on children's social interactions. *Journal of Personality and Social Psychology, 63,* 41–50.

Harris, M. J., & Perkins, R. (1995). Effects of distraction on interpersonal expectancy effects: A social interaction test of the cognitive busyness hypothesis. *Social Cognition, 13,* 163–182.

Harris, M. J., & Rosenthal, R. (1985). Mediation of interpersonal expectancy effects: 31 meta-analyses. *Psychological Bulletin, 97,* 363–386.

Harris, M. J., & Rosenthal, R. (1986). Counselor and client personality as determinants of counselor expectancy effects. *Journal of Personality and Social Psychology, 50,* 362–369.

Hebl, M. R., & Kleck, R. E. (2000). The social consequences of physical disability.

In T. F. Heatherton, R. E. Kleck, M. R. Hebl, & J. G. Hull (Eds.), *The social psychology of stigma* (pp. 419–439). New York: Guilford Press.

Hebl, M. R., Tickler, J., & Heatherton, T. F. (2000). Awkward moments in interactions between nonstigmatized and stigmatized individuals. In T. F. Heatherton, R. E. Kleck, M. R. Hebl, & J. G. Hull (Eds.), *The social psychology of stigma* (pp. 275–306). New York: Guilford Press.

Kleck, R., Ono, H., & Hastorf, A. H. (1966). The effects of physical deviance upon face-to-face interaction. *Human Relations, 19,* 425–436.

Kleck, R., & Strenta, A. (1980). Perceptions of the impact of negatively valued physical characteristics on social interactions. *Journal of Personality and Social Psychology, 39,* 861–873.

Klein, O., & Snyder, M. (2003). Stereotypes and behavioral confirmation: From interpersonal to intergroup perspectives. *Advances in Experimental Social Psychology, 35,* 153–234.

Leyens, J.-P., Dardenne, B., & Fiske, S. T. (1998). Why and under what circumstances is a hypothesis-consistent testing strategy preferred in interviews? *British Journal of Social Psychology, 37,* 259–274.

Macan, T. H., & Dipboye, R. L. (1990). The relationship of interviewers' preinterview impressions to selection and recruitment outcomes. *Personnel Psychology, 43,* 745–768.

Madon, S., Guyll, M., Hilbert, S. J., Kyriakatos, E., & Vogel, D. L. (2006). Stereotyping the stereotypic: When individuals match social stereotypes. *Journal of Applied Social Psychology, 36,* 178–205.

Major, B., & O'Brien, L. T. (2005). The social psychology of stigma. *Annual Review of Psychology, 56,* 393–421.

Mazzella, R., & Feingold, A. (1994). The effects of physical attractiveness, race, socioeconomic status, and gender of defendants and victims on judgments of mock jurors: A meta-analysis. *Journal of Applied Social Psychology, 24,* 1315–1344.

McDaniel, M. A., Whetzel, D. L., Schmidt, F. L., & Maurer, S. D. (1994). The validity of employment interviews: A comprehensive review and meta-analysis. *Journal of Applied Psychology, 79,* 599–616.

Merton, R. K. (1948). The self-fulfilling prophecy. *Antioch Review, 8,* 193–210.

Miller, A. G. (1970). Role of physical attractiveness in impression formation. *Psychonomic Science, 19,* 241–243.

Moreno, K. N., & Bodenhausen, G. V. (1999). Resisting stereotype change: The role of motivation and attentional capacity in defending social beliefs. *Group Processes and Intergroup Relations, 2,* 5–16.

Murphy, M. J., Nelson, D. A., & Cheap, T. L. (1981). Rated and actual performance of high school students as a function of sex and attractiveness. *Psychological Reports, 48,* 103–106.

Neuberg, S. L. (1989). The goal of forming accurate impressions during social interactions: Attenuating the impact of negative expectancies. *Journal of Personality and Social Psychology, 56,* 374–386.

Patzer, G. L. (1985). *The physical attractiveness phenomena.* New York: Plenum Press.

Pinel, E. C. (1999). Stigma consciousness: The psychological legacy of social stereotypes. *Journal of Personality and Social Psychology, 76,* 114–128.

Posthuma, R. A., Morgeson, F. P., & Campion, M. A. (2002). Beyond employment
interview validity: A comprehensive narrative review of recent research and
trends over time. *Personnel Psychology, 55,* 1–81.

Ritts, V., Patterson, M. L., & Tubbs, M. E. (1992). Expectations, impressions, and
judgments of physically attractive students: A review. *Review of Educational
Research, 62,* 413–426.

Rosenthal, R. (1989). *Experimenter expectancy, covert communication, and
meta-analytic methods.* Invited address at the annual meeting of the American Psychological Association, New Orleans.

Rosenthal, R. (1994). Interpersonal expectancy effects: A 30-year perspective.
Current Directions in Psychological Science, 3, 176–179.

Rosenthal, R., & Jacobson, L. (1968). *Pygmalion in the classroom.* New York:
Holt, Rinehart, & Winston.

Rosenthal, R., & Rubin, D. B. (1978). Interpersonal expectancy effects: The first
345 studies. *Behavioral and Brain Sciences, 3,* 377–386.

Ross, L., Lepper, M., & Hubbard, M. (1975). Perseverance in self-perception and
social perception: Biased attributional processes in the debriefing paradigm.
Journal of Personality and Social Psychology, 32, 880–892.

Shaw, J. (1972). Reaction to victims and defendants of varying degrees of attractiveness. *Psychonomic Science, 27,* 229–330.

Sibicky, M., & Dovidio, J. (1986). Stigma of psychological therapy: Stereotypes,
interpersonal reactions, and the self-fulfilling prophecy. *Journal of Counseling Psychology, 33,* 148–154.

Skrypnek, B. J., & Snyder, M. (1982). On the self-perpetuating nature of stereotypes about women and men. *Journal of Experimental Social Psychology, 18,*
277–291.

Smith, G. J. (1985). Facial and full-length ratings of attractiveness related to the social interactions of young children. *Sex Roles, 12,* 287–293.

Snyder, M., & Swann, W. B., Jr. (1978). Hypothesis-testing processes in social interaction. *Journal of Personality and Social Psychology, 36,* 1202–1212.

Snyder, M., Tanke, E. D., & Berscheid, E. (1977). Social perception and interpersonal behavior: On the self-fulfilling nature of social stereotypes. *Journal of
Personality and Social Psychology, 35,* 656–666.

Springbett, B. M. (1958). Factors affecting the final decision in the employment interview. *Canadian Journal of Psychology, 12,* 13–22.

Stewart, T. L., Doan, K. A., Gingrich, B. E., & Smith, E. R. (1998). The actor as
context for social judgments: Effects of prior impressions and stereotypes.
Journal of Personality and Social Psychology, 75, 1132–1154.

Stukas, A. A., & Snyder, M. (2002). Targets' awareness of expectations and behavioral confirmation in ongoing interactions. *Journal of Experimental Social
Psychology, 38,* 31–40.

Tversky, A., & Kahneman, D. (1974). Judgment under uncertainty: Heuristics and
biases. *Science, 185,* 1124–1131.

Word, C. O., Zanna, M. P., & Cooper, J. (1974). The nonverbal mediation of self-
fulfilling prophecies in interracial interaction. *Journal of Experimental Social
Psychology, 11,* 583–591.

PART III

FACIAL CUES

CHAPTER 8

First Impressions from Facial Appearance Cues

LESLIE A. ZEBROWITZ
JOANN M. MONTEPARE

Cultural wisdom enjoins us not to "judge a book by its cover," an admonition suggesting that our natural proclivity is in fact to judge people by their appearance. Considerable social psychological research has shown that this is so. Not only do we make judgments about people from their faces, but also there is a remarkable consensus in our judgments. This consensus encompasses impressions of psychological traits from a wide variety of domains, including social power, social warmth, honesty, physical fitness, and intellectual competence (Zebrowitz & Collins, 1997). Moreover, these consensual judgments are robust across diverse perceivers and targets. For example, young children form impressions that agree with those made by adults (Keating & Bai, 1986; Montepare & Zebrowitz-McArthur, 1989), and perceivers from different ethnic backgrounds form similar impressions whether they are judging faces from their own or different groups (Dion, 2002; Zebrowitz, Montepare, & Lee, 1993). The question remains as to why faces are so compelling and what facial cues give rise to consensual impressions. The present chapter addresses this question by describing (1) methods for identifying facial cues; (2) a guiding conceptual framework that predicts judgments from facial appearance; (3) existing research that documents impressions consistent with that framework; and (4) future research that is needed to answer the question more fully. Although our emphasis is on subjective first impressions from facial cues, some attention is given to the objective accuracy of these impressions to assess the viability of the conceptual framework used to predict them. It should also be noted that both the conceptual framework and many of the methods we discuss are equally applicable to first impressions derived from other nonverbal cues, including gait, gesture, and voice.

METHODS FOR IDENTIFYING FACIAL CUES

A variety of methods have been used to study face perception. Some of these have been used to identify the facial cues that influence first impressions, whereas others have been used only to identify the cues that influence identity, emotion, or social category recognition. We provide a brief description of all of these methods, because it is useful to consider how the latter methods may inform the study of impressions.

Brunswik's lens model (Brunswik, 1956) was one of the earliest methods used to identify the particular physical qualities that influence impressions. Within this model, one would sample facial cues that naturally co-occur in a representative group of faces with the aim of identifying relationships that reveal both the *ecological validity* of cues (e.g., correlations with *actual* age, emotions, traits) and also perceivers' *utilization* of cues (e.g., correlations with *perceiver impressions* of age, emotions, traits). Together, these data can be used to determine what cues contribute to accurate or inaccurate impressions.

The measurement of facial cues within Brunswik's model, as well as in research that has simply examined correlations between facial cues and perceived impressions, has relied on perceivers' subjective ratings or on objective measurements generated manually using rulers (Berry & McArthur, 1985; Cunningham, 1986) or, more recently, by computer software that calculates distances between points marked on a face (Grammer & Thornhill, 1994). Although objective measures may seem preferable, it is difficult to physically measure certain facial qualities (e.g., masculinity, facial averageness). Moreover, some evidence suggests that perceivers' ratings have more predictive validity than objective measures even when the facial cues and the impressions are rated by different perceivers, as they should be to minimize carryover effects (Rhodes, 2006).

A more sophisticated method for assessing facial cues is connectionist modeling. Connectionist models are powerful nonlinear statistical modeling tools that have the property of similarity-based generalization. The process is analogous to regression analysis—the connectionist network learns which facial measurements to use in predicting the category membership of faces. For example, connectionist networks can be trained to distinguish between baby and adult faces. After the two categories are differentiated, generalization effects are examined by providing the network with facial measurements from novel faces, and the network reacts to these faces according to their similarity to babies versus adults. Connectionist models can be trained on facial metrics, face image pixels, or both. Although connectionist modeling can be used to test alternative cognitive or neural models of face processing, it has been used in a more restricted way in research on first impressions from facial cues, namely as a mathematical technique for generating an objective index of the structural similarity of a face to a particular category of faces. The index can then be used to predict first impressions. Although this method can narrow the set of facial inputs required for discrimination, it is difficult to determine how they are combined by the model or to provide meaningful labels for the cues that are influencing discrimination and impressions.

Principal components analysis of faces (PCA) is a type of factor analysis performed on the information provided by face image pixels. In PCA, the features that distinguish a set of faces are described as a set of orthogonal basis images (components). These and other faces then can be represented in PCA space as a list of weights on each of the components, with each face described as a point in the multidimensional PCA space. Research has used PCA to identify facial components involved in recognizing identity (Hancock, Bruce, & Burton, 1998), emotion (Calder, Burton, & Miller, 2001), sex (Valentin, Abdi, & Edelman, 1997), and race (O'Toole, Abdi, Deffenbacher, & Bartlett, 1991). For example, one component may predict the sex of the face, while another predicts an emotion expression. To apply PCA to trait impressions requires determining which components predict particular trait impressions. Given that the particular components that emerge depend upon the set of faces subjected to PCA, it may be necessary to include faces that vary significantly in the impressions they elicit—for example, faces perceived as high and low in dominance. Given the success of identifying components that represent each of several emotions represented in a single PCA, it may also be possible to identify components that represent each of several trait impressions. However, a shortcoming of this method is that it is difficult to understand how the PCA components function and to generate a concise verbal description of them.

Other methods include eye tracking, which has been used to determine where perceivers focus on a face. It also could be used to investigate where perceivers look first or longest when judging particular psychological traits as an index of what facial cues are treated as most informative for different traits. The bubbles technique (Smith, Cottrell, Gosselin, & Schyns, 2005) also can specify the *diagnostic* stimulus information that is effective in influencing the perceivers' judgments. The bubbles technique automatically adjusts a number of small Gaussian windows ("bubbles") revealing parts of the face so that 75% correct categorization is achieved. All sets of bubbles that yield criterion performance are summed to determine the stimulus information for that categorization task. This research has shown that diagnostic information is not perfectly correlated with the information available in the entire face, thereby underscoring the shortcomings of PCA, or connectionist, modeling research that has not integrated statistically differentiable properties of faces with those that guide perception. The bubbles technique also provides a more concrete description of the facial information that conveys various attributes to perceivers. For example, when categorizing faces based on sex, perceivers use information around the eyes and the central upper part of the mouth. When categorizing faces varying in emotion, perceivers use information in different regions to recognize different emotions. When recognizing the identity of faces, perceivers use the entire constellation of facial features together with the jaw line (Smith et al., 2005). The bubbles technique could also be used to examine what information perceivers use when judging faces on various traits.

Whereas the bubbles technique manipulates the *quantity* of facial information available to perceivers, other research has experimentally manipulated the *quality* of the information in order to identify the cues that yield particular impressions. These methods include the manipulation of features within schematic faces (McArthur & Apatow, 1983), computerized morphing techniques that change the appearance of real faces, and face inversion (Bruce & Young, 1998). Whereas the first two methods have been used to study impressions from facial cues, face inversion has not. Research demonstrating that it is more difficult to recognize identity and emotion expressions in inverted than upright faces has been taken as evidence for the holistic processing of these attributes (Bruce & Young, 1998; McKelvie, 1995). It would be interesting to determine whether information about various traits is also processed holistically, yielding less consensual and/or less accurate impressions from inverted than upright faces.

Many theorists have proposed that facial identity is coded relative to an average face, which lies at the center of a computational face space (Clifford & Rhodes, 2005). Within this conceptual framework, both multidimensional scaling (MDS) methods and visual aftereffects have been used to study cues that inform face perception. For example, MDS data from perceiver judgments of the similarity of faces map onto a face space representing spatial relations among different faces that can explain differences in ease of recognizing those that are caricatured (morphed to decrease similarity to an average face), anticaricatured (morphed to increase similarity to an average face), and veridical (Lee, Byatt, & Rhodes, 2000). MDS also has interesting potential for the study of impression formation. For example, perceiver judgments of how similar faces are in dominance could be mapped onto a dominance face space, and investigators could then try to identify the facial dimensions that describe the dominance similarity relationships. Answering this question requires that the faces be independently rated or measured on a set of potential dimensions (e.g., eye size, eyebrow thickness, lip thickness; face shape) and that statistical analyses be performed to locate dimensions in the face space that define the relative positions of the faces

Research using visual aftereffects has demonstrated that identification of a face (e.g., Jim) is facilitated by adapting perceivers to the opposite identity (a face morphed away from Jim through the prototype to the opposite side of the stimulus space to become an anti-Jim—a face with structure and features *opposite* to those of Jim), but not to some other face (anti-Fred—a face with structure and features *different* from those of Jim). This effect holds true even when opposite and nonopposite adapt-test pairs are matched on perceived dissimilarity (Leopold, O'Toole, Vetter, & Blanz, 2001; Rhodes & Jeffery, 2006). The process of adapting to the anti-Jim face shifts the norm or average toward that face so that the original face, Jim, now deviates more from the norm than it did before, becoming easier to identify. Interesting variants on this method have revealed that aftereffects do not generalize across sex categories, suggesting that male and female faces are coded with respect to different average faces (Rhodes et al., 2004). This method also has interesting potential for the study of impression formation. For example, it would be interesting to determine whether adapting to faces that are perceived as highly dominant would shift the norm toward dominant-looking faces, with the result that faces that were average in perceived dominance are now perceived as submissive. If so, this would suggest that facial dominance is coded relative to a face at the center of a computational face space that creates the impression of average dominance.

A CONCEPTUAL FRAMEWORK

Early work on first impressions from facial cues documented some interesting phenomena. Studies by Paul Secord and associates revealed correlations between ratings of varied facial qualities and personality trait impressions (Secord, Dukes, & Bevan, 1954; Secord & Muthard, 1955). Rated facial cues and trait impressions also showed cross-cultural congruence (Secord & Bevan, 1956), and trait impressions from facial cues were sufficiently robust to persist regardless of the occupational label attached to the face (Secord, Bevan, & Dukes, 1953). While these findings are intriguing, a conceptual framework is needed to make sense of the many face–trait correlations as well as to ensure that meaningful correlations are not overlooked as researchers exploit various methods for identifying the facial cues that guide first impressions.

The ecological approach to social perception, grounded in Gibson's theory of object perception (Gibson, 1979), provides a useful conceptual framework for explaining consensual first impressions by means of its overgeneralization hypotheses (Zebrowitz, 1996, 1997; Zebrowitz & Montepare, 2006).[1] Gibson argued that "perceiving is for doing," and he emphasized the co-evolution of perceptual systems and ecological niches. Consistent with these tenets, the ecological approach proposes that innate or well-developed attunements to stimulus information that serve adaptive functions can yield *overgeneralized* perceptions. Specifically, the psychological traits that are accurately revealed by the facial cues that mark low fitness, babies, emotion, and identity are perceived in people whose facial appearance resembles the unfit, babies, a particular emotion, or a particular identity. According to ecological theory, the errors yielded by such overgeneralizations occur because they are less maladaptive than those that might result from failing to respond appropriately to unfit individuals, babies, those in an emotional state, or those with a particular identity. As seen in the following sections, such overgeneralizations have implications for understanding a variety of impressions created by particular facial cues.

IMPRESSIONS CREATED BY FACIAL ATTRACTIVENESS AND ITS COMPONENTS

Attractiveness is the facial quality that has received the most sustained attention in research on first impressions from faces. More attractive faces are judged more positively on a variety of dimensions, an effect dubbed the "attractiveness halo." People with more attractive faces are perceived as more likable, outgoing, and socially competent as well as higher in sexual responsiveness, social power, intelligence, and health (Eagly, Ashmore, Makhijani, & Longo, 1991; Feingold, 1992; Langlois et al., 2000; Zebrowitz, Hall, Murphy, & Rhodes, 2002; Zebrowitz & Rhodes, 2004).

For many years there was no conceptual framework to explain the positive effects of attractiveness on impressions other than the assumption that they reflected cultural teachings. Although that may be true, this explanation begs the question of where those teachings originate. The anomalous face overgeneralization hypothesis suggested by the ecological approach to social perception holds that the adaptive value of recognizing individuals with disease or bad genes has produced a strong preparedness to respond to facial qualities that can mark low fitness (Zebrowitz, Fellous, Mignault, & Andreoletti, 2003; Zebrowitz & Rhodes, 2004). These prepared responses are then overgeneralized to normal individuals whose faces resemble those who are unfit. Evidence for cross-cultural agreement in perceptions of facial attractiveness (Cunningham, Roberts, Barbee, & Druen, 1995; Dion, 2002), together with reactions to variations in facial attractiveness by infants and young children (Kramer, Zebrowitz, San Giovanni, & Sherak, 1995; Ramsey, Langlois, Hoss, Rubenstein, & Griffin, 2004), is consistent with the argument that impressions of faces that vary in attractiveness reflect a prepared response.

Consistent with the anomalous face overgeneralization hypothesis, research investigating qualities that make a face attractive has been guided by the assumption that they will be linked to fitness. These qualities include facial averageness (a facial configuration close to the population mean), symmetry, sexual dimorphism, and youthfulness.[2] The first two are putative signals of developmental stability, or the ability to develop according to design despite environmental stressors (Scheib, Gangestad, & Thornhill, 1999). Additionally, facial averageness might signal genetic diversity, or heterozygosity (Thornhill & Gangestad, 1999), which is associated with a strong immune system (Penn, Damjanovich, & Potts, 2002). High masculinity in male faces is a putative sign of fitness, because it demonstrates sufficient immunocompetence to withstand the stress that testosterone places on the immune system (Folstad & Karter, 1992). High femininity in female faces may signal fitness by virtue of the association of certain feminine features with sexual maturity and fertility, and youthfulness is related to fitness inasmuch as aging often carries declines in cognitive and physical functioning. Implicit in attractiveness research is the assumption of a *linear* relationship between attractiveness and fitness, with emphasis on the greater fitness of highly attractive individuals (Buss, 1989). In contrast, the anomalous face overgeneralization hypothesis argues that appearance provides an accurate index only of low genetic fitness rather than a continuous index of genetic quality and that the attractiveness halo effect is a perceptual by-product of an adaptive attunement to low fitness.[3] Evidence for such an attunement is provided by the finding that the attractiveness halo effect is driven more by the perception that "ugly is bad" than by the perception that "beautiful is good" (Griffin & Langlois, 2006).

Whereas facial attractiveness has been assessed by perceiver ratings, its components have been investigated with a variety of methods (for reviews, see Rhodes, 2006; Zebrowitz & Rhodes, 2002). Faces closer to the population average are more attractive both when natural variations in averageness are assessed by perceiver ratings[4] and when averageness is manipulated experimentally by creating a composite face from several faces. More symmetrical faces are more attractive both when natural variations in symmetry are assessed by perceiver ratings and when symmetry is varied experimentally, so long as the manipulation does not produce structural abnormalities, as is the case for chimeras (mirror image faces created from two right halves or two left halves). More feminine female faces are more attractive when natural variations in femininity are assessed by perceiver ratings, facial measurements, or when facial femininity is experimentally manipulated by creating morphs that exaggerate feminine features. The features that make a face more feminine include a smaller chin, fuller lips, and higher cheekbones. More masculine male faces are more attractive when normal variations in masculinity are assessed by perceiver ratings, and the features that make a face more masculine include a larger chin. On the other hand, facial masculinity that has been manipulated by morphing composite male and female faces is not more attractive. This may reflect the fact that masculine facial qualities like coarse skin and large jaws are lost in composite faces. Younger faces are more attractive, as shown by an age-related linear decline in the judged attractiveness of the same individuals who were photographed from childhood to the late 50s, an effect that was equal for male and female faces (Zebrowitz, Olson, & Hoffman, 1993).

Insofar as more average, symmetrical, sexually dimorphic, and youthful faces are more attractive, it is likely that faces with one or more of these qualities would elicit the same positive impressions as faces higher in overall rated attractiveness. Or, to frame the effects within the anomalous face overgeneralization hypothesis, it is likely that faces lacking these particular qualities would create more negative impressions. However, it is also possible that some of the individual components of attractiveness are linked to unique trait impressions or are even unrelated to trait impressions. We have only a partial answer to this question, as research has not systematically investigated the impressions associated with individual components of attractiveness.

Paralleling impressions of less attractive faces, faces lower in rated or manipulated symmetry are perceived as less intelligent and healthy (Rhodes, Zebrowitz, et al., 2001; Zebrowitz et al., 2002; Zebrowitz & Rhodes, 2004) as well as less honest, even with attractiveness controlled

(Zebrowitz, Voinescu, & Collins, 1996). Faces lower in averageness, either as rated by perceivers or as manipulated by compositing faces, also are perceived as less intelligent and healthy (Rhodes, Zebrowitz, et al., 2001; Zebrowitz et al., 2002; Zebrowitz & Rhodes, 2004). Other research has assessed facial averageness and symmetry by ascertaining the extent to which normal faces activate a neural network trained to identify anomalous faces that are both nonaverage and asymmetrical. The results show less intelligence and health attributed to faces that are more similar to anomalous ones as well as less strength, sociability, and warmth, albeit no less social power (Zebrowitz et al., 2003). Additional research using other methods is needed to determine whether impressions of low sociability and warmth reflect asymmetry or nonaverageness or both. Women's impressions of less masculine-looking men as less healthy and dominant parallel impressions of less attractive faces (Luevano & Zebrowitz, 2007), as do men's impressions of women who lack feminine high cheekbones as less bright, healthy, and sociable (Cunningham, 1986). Impressions of older faces also parallel impressions of less attractive faces, with older faces often perceived as less healthy, cognitively competent, socially powerful, sociable, and warm than younger ones (Montepare & Zebrowitz, 2002; Zebrowitz et al., 2003). Although there are many possible explanations for negative impressions of old faces, anomalous face overgeneralization explains some of the variance. Not only do faces look older when they are morphed away from an average face (O'Toole, Price, Vetter, Bartlett, & Blanz, 1999), but also older faces are more structurally similar to anomalous faces, and the differential impressions of old and young faces are partially mediated by that structural similarity (Zebrowitz et al., 2003).

In evaluating the anomalous face overgeneralization explanation, it is important to consider the question of accuracy. Indeed, attractive people are more healthy, intelligent, and sociable than unattractive people (Feingold, 1992; Langlois et al., 2000; Rhodes, 2006; Zebrowitz et al., 2002). This suggests that the differing first impressions of people who vary in attractiveness may simply reflect some prepared or learned attunement to their actual traits rather than an overgeneralization of reactions to anomalous faces. However, there are two shortcomings in this explanation.

First, attractiveness and actual intelligence or health are significantly correlated for faces in the lower half of the attractiveness distribution but not for faces in the upper half, although attractiveness was positively related to their *perceived* intelligence and health. These results are consistent with the fact that subtle negative deviations from average attractiveness can signal low fitness in a representative population of faces, as manifested in the lower intelligence and maladaptive social traits shown by individuals with minor facial anomalies (Paulhus & Martin, 1986) or facial characteristics associated with fetal alcohol syndrome (Streissguth, Herman, & Smith, 1978). Thus, the level of attractiveness provides a valid cue to low, but not high, intelligence or health. Although people correctly use this cue when it is valid, they also overgeneralize and use it in the upper half of the distribution of facial attractiveness where it is not valid.

A second problem with attributing impressions of faces that vary in attractiveness simply to accurate trait perceptions is that this explanation begs the question of the origin of those traits. As suggested above, one possibility is that unattractive facial qualities are associated with congenital risk factors for certain negative traits even within a relatively normal population. However, there are other possible developmental routes to a relationship between low attractiveness and negative traits. These include self-fulfilling prophecy effects that could be fueled by expectations about less attractive people or by negative evaluative reactions to them that derive from the overgeneralization of reactions to individuals with anomalous faces (Zebrowitz, 1997).

In summary, although additional research is needed to establish relationships between some of the components of facial attractiveness and particular first impressions, the existing research clearly demonstrates that variations in attractiveness and its components have significant influences on first impressions that are consistent with the anomalous face overgeneralization hypothesis. Faces that are rated as less attractive than their peers; that are less symmetrical, less average, and less prototypical for their sex; that are older[5]; or that show greater structural resemblance to anomalous faces, as assessed by connectionist modeling, create impressions of lower social competence, social power, sexual responsiveness, intelligence, and/or poorer health. Moreover, research has shown that these effects hold true across faces and raters from many demographic groups. These results are consistent with the anomalous face overgeneralization hypothesis, and the evidence for accurate impressions at the low but not the high end of the attractiveness continuum suggests that more negative impressions of medium than high attractive faces may reflect an overgeneralization of reactions not only to strikingly anomalous faces but also to faces in the normal population that are marked by minor anomalies.

IMPRESSIONS CREATED BY BABYFACENESS AND ITS COMPONENTS

Babyfaceness, like attractiveness, elicits systematic impressions of people's traits. In particular, more babyfaced individuals are perceived to have more childlike traits—that is, to be more naive, submissive, physically weak, warm, and honest. Whereas research on impressions of attractive faces initially overlooked the stimulus information underlying attractiveness, research on impressions created by babyfaceness has been driven by assumptions about cues that differentiate babies from adults. Drawing on ethological evidence that key stimuli elicit favorable responses to babies, coupled with the evolutionary importance of responding appropriately to such stimuli, the ecological approach to social perception posits a babyface overgeneralization effect whereby strong prepared responses to infantile facial cues may be overgeneralized to nonbabies (Montepare & Zebrowitz, 1998). Evidence for cross-cultural agreement in perceptions of babyfaceness (Zebrowitz et al., 1993), together with reactions to variations in babyfaceness by infants and young children (Keating & Bai, 1986; Kramer et al., 1995; Montepare & Zebrowitz-McArthur, 1989), is consistent with the argument that impressions of faces that vary in babyfaceness reflect a prepared response.

Research testing the babyface overgeneralization hypothesis has utilized manipulations, objective facial measurements, and ratings of features in representative samples of faces to show that the same facial features that differentiate real babies from adults constitute the cues that make nonbabies look babyfaced and elicit impressions suggestive of childlike traits (Keating, 2002; Montepare & Zebrowitz, 1998; Zebrowitz, 1997). These features include larger eyes, higher eyebrows, smaller nose bridges, rounder and less angular faces, and lower vertical placement of features, which creates a higher forehead and a shorter chin. Manipulations of features in schematic drawings of faces revealed that faces with large eyes, low vertical placement of features, and short features were perceived as more babyfaced as well as physically, socially, and intellectually weaker than faces with more mature features. Similarly, decreases in eye size along with reductions in lip size in schematic faces or in computer manipulations of real faces increased their perceived maturity and dominance and decreased their perceived warmth. Ratings and measurements of naturally occurring variations in facial features also have demonstrated that larger eyes, smaller chins, and rounder faces elicit impressions of higher babyfaceness as well as greater warmth, kindness, naivete, physical weakness, and honesty. Other research has assessed babyfaceness by ascertaining the extent to which adult faces activate a neural network trained to identify faces of babies. The results revealed that adult faces that a neural network finds more structurally similar to babies were perceived as more babyfaced, warm, physically weak, naive, and submissive (Zebrowitz et al., 2003).

In comparison to individual facial cues, facial feature composites determined by combining ratings or measurements of individual cues often account for greater variance in trait impressions, suggesting that configural qualities play a role in impressions of babyfaces. However, configural qualities may reflect something more than a mere constellation of features. Indeed, one limitation noted by researchers who have modified individual facial features to ascertain their impact on impressions is that such manipulations can alter the spatial relationships among features, which may inadvertently also influence impressions (Keating & Doyle, 2002). Thus, in exploring impressions created by babyfaceness, it is important to consider configural cues not only as combinations or arrangements of facial features but also as unique spatial facial qualities. Computer modeling techniques have provided information about one such configural, spatial quality. Specifically, Todd, Mark, Shaw, and Pittenger (1980) modeled age-related changes in head shape using a growth-simulating mathematical transformation called cardioidal strain. Impressions of faces subjected to this transformation are consistent with responses to babyfaces. Trait ratings of individual randomly presented profiles representing varying levels of cardioidal strain revealed that more immature profiles were perceived as less reliable, intelligent, strong, and threatening, as well as more lovable, than more mature profiles (Berry & McArthur, 1986).

In evaluating whether the overgeneralization of accurate impressions of babies provides a reasonable explanation for impressions of same-age faces that vary in babyfaceness, it is important to consider the accuracy of those impressions. There is only limited research addressing this question, and it has yielded mixed results. For example, some research suggests that more babyfaced college students are warmer (Berry & Landry, 1997) and less aggressive (Berry, 1990a, 1991a). However, other research investigating a representative sample of individuals across their lifespan found that only for women in later adulthood was there a positive relationship between babyfaceness and the extent to which a profile of personality traits matched stereotypical impressions of babyfaced individuals (Zebrowitz, Collins, & Dutta, 1998). In contrast to the accuracy of the babyface stereotype for older women, the stereotype was inaccurate for boys. Compared with mature-faced boys, those who were more babyfaced showed more negativity in childhood and puberty, more quarrelsomeness and lying in puberty, and more assertiveness and hostility in adolescence, all of which contradict impressions of babyfaced individuals. In addition, more babyfaced young men were more likely to earn military awards, contradicting impressions of the submissiveness and physical weakness that are elicited by babyfaced cues (Collins & Zebrowitz, 1995). Moreover, within a sample of young men at high risk for delinquency, babyfaceness was positively related to the likelihood of being delinquent and, if delinquent, to the number of offenses (Zebrowitz & Lee, 1999).

The mixed results regarding the accuracy of impressions of babyfaced individuals highlights the necessity of considering the origins of actual relationships between babyfaceness and traits, just as is true for attractiveness. The finding that trait impressions of babyfaced boys and young men are opposite to their actual traits may reflect a self-defeating prophecy effect, whereby babyfaced males react against the expectation that they will exhibit childlike warmth and weakness in the physical, social, and intellectual domains by behaving contrary to these undesirable expectations (Zebrowitz et al., 1998). The failure of more babyfaced girls to show behavior contrary to the babyface stereotype and for older babyfaced women to confirm the stereotype may be explained by the fact that the traits expected from babyfaced individuals are consistent with stereotypes of femininity. Thus, babyfaced young girls may not attempt to refute expectations, and babyfaced women may ultimately confirm expectations in a self-fulfilling prophecy effect. Sample differences may also contribute to inconsistencies in the traits shown by more babyfaced individuals. For example, babyfaced adolescents who react against impressions of their physical and social weakness by showing antisocial behavior may not be found in the college samples that revealed lower aggressiveness in babyfaced individuals.

In summary, the existing research clearly demonstrates that variations in babyfaceness and its components have significant influences on first impressions that are consistent with the babyface overgeneralization hypothesis. Faces that are rated as more babyfaced than their peers, that are characterized by greater roundness and one or more additional features including larger eyes, smaller nose bridge, thinner eyebrows, fuller lips, and smaller chin, or that show greater structural resemblance to faces of actual babies, as assessed by connectionist modeling, are perceived to have more childlike traits. Moreover, these effects hold true across faces and raters from many demographic groups. While these results support a babyface overgeneralization effect, the evidence for accurate or inaccurate impressions may be explained by self-fulfilling and self-defeating prophecy effects instigated by social expectancies that derive from babyface overgeneralization.

IMPRESSIONS CREATED BY FACIAL EXPRESSIONS

Drawing on Darwin's (1872) evolutionary view of the adaptive value of emotion expressions for social communication, some nonverbal theorists suggest that, in addition to providing valid information about people's affective states, facial expressions of emotion may also reveal information about people's behavioral intentions (Ekman, 1997; Frijda, 1995). In particular, displays of emotion may signal approach, attack, or avoidance, which conveys to perceivers the likely affiliativeness or dominance of a person's behavior in addition to how happy, angry, or afraid a person feels. For example, happiness may be viewed as an approach expression that conveys to perceivers not only a target's positive affective state but also a person's likelihood of acting in a friendly, confident, and assertive way. On the other hand, anger may be viewed as an attack expression that conveys a person's likelihood of acting in a domineering, hostile, and unfriendly manner. A related perspective argues that facial expressions of emotion give rise to stable trait impressions via the process of *temporal extension*, whereby "the perceiver regards a momentary characteristic of the person as if it were an enduring attribute" (Secord, 1958). Thus, an angry person may be viewed not only as likely to act momentarily in an unaffiliative or dominant way but also as possessing enduring low affiliative or high dominant traits (e.g., being unsociable, unfriendly, unsympathetic, cold, forceful).

Consistent with the foregoing ideas, happy expressions yield impressions of traits associated with high affiliation and high dominance (Hess, Blairy, & Kleck, 2000; Knutson, 1996; Montepare & Dobish, 2003), and infants with positive facial expressions (e.g., happy, excited, cheerful) are seen as sociable, easy to care for, and active (Karraker & Stern, 1990). Research on smiles, the primary component of a happy expression, has shown that they also elicit impressions of greater sincerity (Reis et al., 1990). However, smiles have also been shown to elicit impressions of lower rather than the higher dominance that has been associated with happy expressions (Keating, Mazur, & Segall, 1981; Reis et al., 1990). These divergent results may reflect differences in definitions of dominance and/or the manner in which the facial cues were manipulated (e.g., posed vs. induced emotion expressions). They may also reflect subtle differences in the types of smiles that can convey diverse social messages (LaFrance & Hecht, 1995). Additional research is needed to identify the trait impressions elicited by the distinctive facial cues that communicate happiness.

Whereas impressions of dominance from happy expressions are variable, angry expressions consistently elicit impressions of high dominance as well as low affiliation. Similarly, lower eyebrows alone, a hallmark of the expression of anger, also elicit impressions of higher dominance, at least in Western cultures (Keating et al., 1981). Clever research that examined primitive masks from diverse cultures has revealed more abstract configural qualities that contribute to the perception of anger and threat as well as associated trait impressions, and similar results have been obtained in research using abstract patterns as stimuli. More specifically, diagonality and angularity communicated messages about anger and threat, and angular patterns evoked more negative, potent, and active impressions than did more curvilinear ones (Aronoff, Woike, & Hyman, 1992).

Expressions of sadness and fear elicit impressions of traits associated with low dominance and moderate affiliation (Hess et al., 2000; Knutson, 1996; Montepare & Dobish, 2003). Interestingly, although fear expressions are judged as unpleasant, they facilitate approach behaviors in perceivers (Marsh, Ambady, & Kleck, 2005). One interpretation is that, although fear expressions look unsociable, they invite help and assistance. Such differences show that the relationship between trait impressions and subsequent behavioral actions warrants further consideration.

The foregoing research documents trait impressions from facial expression cues that are consistent with Darwinian speculations about the information value of emotion expression and Secord's concept of temporal extension. However, these frameworks do not address the question of why particular emotion expressions look the way they do. One answer to that question is that particular facial expressions alter certain physiological states via muscle actions that prepare individuals for adaptive behavioral actions, as an extension of the vascular theory of emotional efference (Zajonc, Murphy, & Inglehart, 1989). Another answer to that question that also has implications for the associated trait impressions was proposed by Marsh, Ambady, and Kleck (2005), who suggested that both the morphology of emotion expressions and the impressions they elicit derive from the adaptive utility of their mimicking variations in facial maturity. More specifically, they argued that fear and anger expressions evolved to mimic babies' faces and mature faces, respectively. The rationale for this prediction was that it is adaptive for those experiencing fear to elicit reactions paralleling those elicited by helpless babies and for those experiencing anger to elicit reactions paralleling those elicited by powerful adults. The prediction that impressions of emotion expressions derive from their differential resemblance to babies is a variant of the babyface overgeneralization hypothesis.

Consistent with their reasoning, Marsh et al. (2005) found that faces expressing anger were judged as more mature-faced than those expressing fear. Anger and fear expressions were also judged to differ in facial qualities that differentiate the faces of babies and adults, with anger expressions judged to have thinner lips, lower brows, more angular features, and smaller eyes. Finally, anger and fear expressions were judged to differ in traits previously associated with variations in babyfaceness, such as dominance, strength, shrewdness, and warmth. Another study

(Zebrowitz, Kikuchi, & Fellous, 2007) used connectionist models to provide objective evidence of physical resemblance between the facial structure of emotion expressions and faces varying in maturity. They showed that differences among emotions in their structural similarity to babies, as determined by a connectionist model, partially mediated differential impressions of the dominance and affiliation of people posing surprise and anger expressions. Since surprise expressions are often precursors to fear expressions and also structurally resemble them (Calder et al., 2001; de Bonis, 2003; Posamentier & Abdi, 2003), these results lend support to the Marsh et al. (2005) hypothesis. Zebrowitz, Kikuchi, and Fellous (2007) also found that impressions of happy faces were not mediated by a resemblance to babies. Rather, it was the greater attractiveness of happy faces that partially mediated impressions of their more affiliative traits. The fact that babyfaceness did not mediate impressions of happy expressions also supports the Marsh et al. (2005) hypothesis, since their evolutionary argument for impressions of fear and anger would be undercut had babyfaceness also mediated impressions of happy people, for whom there is no obvious adaptive value in mimicking helpless babies or powerful adults.

Marsh et al. (2005, Study 3) found that manipulations of expressions in the eye region alone influenced the perceived maturity of fearful versus angry faces more than manipulations using the entire face, and Zebrowitz, Kikuchi, and Fellous (2007) found that surprise expressions resembled babies in eye region metrics but not in full facial metrics. Moreover, the impression of lower dominance and higher affiliation in surprise than neutral faces was mediated by their differential resemblance to babies' faces only in the eye region. The importance of the eye region is consistent with the fact that large eyes mark surprise and fear expressions as well as babies' faces, the latter due to relatively less growth of the eyes than other facial features from birth to maturity (Enlow, 1990). It is also consistent with other research that has documented the primacy of the eye region in emotion perception (Adolphs et al., 2005; Tipples, Atkinson, & Young, 2002). Whereas resemblance to babies in the eye region characterized surprise expressions, the eye region was less central to identifying anger expressions, which were characterized by low resemblance to babies in full facial metrics.

In addition to the influence of people's transient emotion expressions on perceptions of their traits, the resemblance of their permanent facial structure to an emotion expression also influences trait impressions. This effect was identified by Zebrowitz as *emotion overgeneralization* (Zebrowitz, 1996, 1997). According to ecological theory (Zebrowitz & Montepare, 2006), the adaptive value of responding appropriately to emotional expressions, such as avoiding an angry person and approaching a happy one, has produced a strong preparedness to respond to the facial qualities that communicate emotion that is overgeneralized to individuals whose facial structure resembles a particular emotional expression.

Consistent with the emotion overgeneralization hypothesis, Montepare and Dobish (2003) found that some neutral expression faces create perceptions of an angry demeanor and elicit impressions of low affiliative traits; others create perceptions of a happy demeanor and elicit impressions of high affiliative traits. Given the evidence that trait impressions from emotion expressions can be partially explained by an emotion's resemblance to babies or the emotion's attractiveness, it is possible that the trait impressions of neutral expression faces were mediated by their structural babyfaceness or attractiveness. However, the influence on trait impressions of neutral faces' resemblance to emotion expressions held up when babyfaceness and attractiveness were statistically controlled. Thus, there is an emotion overgeneralization effect in impressions of neutral expression faces that derives from a structural resemblance to emotion expressions that is independent of these other facial qualities.

The accuracy of trait impressions from emotion expressions and emotion overgeneralizations has received little attention. However, one study that examined the accuracy of trait impressions elicited by emotion cues suggests that neutral faces whose structural properties resemble an emotion expression may provide accurate trait information, at least in older adults. In particular, Malatesta, Fiore, and Messina (1987) found a positive relationship between ratings of the emotional facial demeanor of older adult women posing neutral expressions and their scores on trait scales of emotional dispositions. For example, women whose neutral faces looked angry actually scored higher on a hostile personality dimension. Whether such effects reflect the remodeling of the face over time as a function of recurrent emotion expressions or some other process remains to be determined, as does the generality of such accuracy when judging young adult faces.

In summary, facial expressions are rich and complex vehicles for social communication. In addition to providing perceivers with information about a person's affective state, they also give rise to impressions about a person's immediate behavioral tendencies and enduring traits. Evolved sensitivities to affective cues, temporal extensions, babyfaceness, and the overgeneralization of reactions to emotion expressions are some of the processes that appear to drive impressions related to facial expressions. Although the perception of emotion from facial expressions has cross-cultural and cross-age generality (Ekman, 1994; Izard, 1994), there is also greater attunement to the information provided by expressions from one's own social group (Elfenbein & Ambady, 2003; Malatesta, Izard, Culver, & Nicholich, 1987). Future research is needed to determine whether facial expressions create consensual trait impressions across perceivers from different cultural groups and of different ages.

IMPRESSIONS CREATED BY FACIAL FAMILIARITY

Almost 40 years ago, research demonstrated more positive reactions to stimuli that had been previously seen, including faces (Zajonc, 1968). More recently, Zebrowitz proposed the familiar face overgeneralization (FFO) hypothesis, which holds that *perceived* familiarity as well as actual familiarity can influence impressions of faces.[6] Grounded in the ecological theory of social perception, the FFO hypothesis argues that the utility of differentiating known individuals from strangers has produced a tendency for responses to strangers to vary as a function of their resemblance to known individuals (Zebrowitz, 1996, 1997).

Consistent with the FFO hypothesis, reactions to people do depend on their facial resemblance to known others. For example, peers appeared more trustworthy when their photos were morphed so that they resembled the perceiver (DeBruine, 2002). In addition, people expressed a preference for the job candidate whose face more closely resembled someone who had just treated them kindly, and they avoided a stranger whose face more closely resembled someone who had just treated them irritably (Lewicki, 1985). People also expected greater fairness from a professor whose face more closely resembled the prototypical face of a set of professors known to be fair than that of a set known to be unfair, even though they had no conscious awareness of the dimension on which the faces varied (Hill, Lewicki, Czyzewska, & Schuller, 1990). Such effects exemplify what has been called *episodic* familiarity (Peskin & Newell, 2004).

In addition to the idiosyncratic effects of FFO associated with "episodic" familiarity, a broader consequence is that prejudiced responses to strangers of another race may vary with the familiarity of their appearance. Such effects exemplify what has been called *general* familiarity (Peskin & Newell, 2004). This type of familiarity is illustrated by the finding that faces closer to the population average are rated as more familiar even when they have never been seen before (Roggman, Langlois, Hubbs-Tait, & Rieser-Danner, 1994) and that 6-month-old infants attended to a stranger's face that was an averaged prototype of known faces as if it were familiar (Rubenstein, Kalakanis, & Langlois, 1999).

There are several reasons to expect FFO to contribute to racial prejudice. First, prototypical facial structure varies across racial groups.[7] Second, communities are often racially segregated. Consequently, strangers from one's own racial group should appear more familiar than strangers from a different racial group because they are more similar to a known facial prototype. Coupled with evidence that people prefer faces that have become familiar through repeated exposure, the greater familiarity of faces of strangers from one's own racial group should yield a preference for those faces. Consistent with this argument, the enhanced liking of known faces that results from exposure can generalize to similar-looking strangers (Rhodes, Halberstadt, & Brajkovich, 2001). More pertinent to race-related impressions, 3-month-old infants showed a visual preference for own-race faces only if they were living in a racially segregated environment (Bar-Haim, Ziv, Lamy, & Hodes, 2006). Moreover, variations in the average familiarity of faces across raters of a given race made a significant contribution to in-group favoritism and race stereotypes (Zebrowitz, Bronstad, & Lee, 2007). In particular, the lower familiarity of own- than other-race faces mediated the in-group favoritism of Koreans, White Americans, and Black Americans as shown in ratings of the likability of faces. Face familiarity also contributed to the strength of culturally based race stereotypes. Negative stereotypes were partially mediated by the unfamiliarity of other-race faces, showing a significant reduction when familiarity was controlled. Positive stereotypes were partially suppressed by the unfamiliarity of other race faces, showing a significant increase when familiarity was controlled. These results suggest that the unfamiliarity of other-race faces contributes not only to likability—the standard effect of familiarity in mere exposure research—but also to a dual process stereotyping in which both cultural beliefs and negative affective reactions to unfamiliarity each make a contribution.

The contribution of an unfamiliar appearance to racial prejudice and stereotypes is consistent with recent evidence that more prototypical Black faces or Afrocentric-looking faces of either race elicit more negative reactions from White perceivers (Blair, Judd, Sadler, & Jenkins, 2002; Eberhardt, Goff, Purdie, & Davies, 2004; Livingston & Brewer, 2002; Maddox, 2004). Additional research is needed to ascertain what qualities of other race faces contribute to their unfamiliarity with its attendant negative effects on likability and impressions and how to ameliorate those effects. Research examining other facial cues to familiarity, including idiosyncratic ones, would also be worthwhile.

IMPRESSIONS CREATED BY OTHER FACIAL QUALITIES

Most of the research reviewed in the previous sections has examined responses to structural variations in gray-scale facial images, with little attention to dynamic or textural facial qualities. However, evidence indicates that impressions also vary as a function of facial dynamics, which includes rigid motion, such as a head nod or a head cant, and nonrigid motion, such as the raising of an eyebrow or the flaring of a nostril. Impressions are also influenced by variations in facial texture, which includes skin quality, color, and luminance (Fink, Grammer, & Matts, 2006; Russell, 2003). The face overgeneralization hypotheses provide explanations for impressions elicited by dynamic and textural facial cues, just as they do for impressions elicited by structural ones. Given the lack of relevant research, the accuracy of impressions created by these other facial cues must await a future discussion. However, it is worth noting that the fact that dynamic cues are sometimes voluntary provides reason to expect a stronger link between impressions and actual traits than is found for structural cues over which people have little control. In addition, dynamic cues become available in actual social interactions that, according to the ecological approach, are often required for affordances to be accurately revealed (see McArthur & Baron, 1983).

Dynamic Facial Qualities

Research examining dynamic qualities has used methodologies that isolate their effects from those of structural ones. Some researchers have used the point-light technique (Johansson, 1973), in which the pattern of facial movements is represented as small luminous dots moving across a black background. Others have used motion capture, in which the pattern of facial movements of different types of faces is superimposed on a common model (Hill & Johnston, 2001). The little research that is available suggests that dynamic cues may be an important source of influence on first impressions. For one thing, research supporting a dual process model of face perception has demonstrated functional and neurological divisions in the processing of identity information in static faces versus the processing of emotion and other dynamic information, like eye gaze (Bruce & Young, 1986; Haxby, Hoffman, & Gobbini, 2002). In addition, biological motion activates a distinctive network of brain areas (Grossman & Blake, 2005). Moreover, dynamic cues contribute to many facets of face perception that could be related to impression formation, including emotion, fitness, sex, age, and identity.

Evidence for the contribution of dynamic facial information to the perception of emotions has been provided by research comparing impressions of moving and static faces as well as research using point-light displays of facial movement (Bassili, 1978) and computer-simulated animations (Sato & Yoshikawa, 2004; Wehrle, Kaiser, Schmidt, & Scherer, 2000). The significance of dynamic cues is underscored by the finding that recognition of subtle emotion expressions is better from moving than static faces (Ambadar, Schooler, & Cohen, 2005). Just as trait impressions are linked to particular structural cues to emotion, so may they be linked to the facial movements that distinguish particular emotions. In addition to temporal extensions from dynamic emotion cues to trait impressions, there also may be an emotion overgeneralization effect in which nonemotional facial movements that resemble some emotion elicit related trait impressions.

Facial movement can be a cue to low fitness, and it influences judgments of attractiveness. For example, the facial masking of Parkinsonian patients yields low expressivity (Pentland, Pitcairn, Gray, & Riddle, 1987), and both depressed and schizophrenic patients show reduced facial activity in the upper part of their face as compared with normals during social interactions (Schneider, Heimann, Himer, & Huss, 1990). Thus, anomalous face overgeneralization may yield negative trait impressions of normal individuals with low facial activity. Indeed, greater facial expressiveness in normal individuals increases impressions of attractiveness and associated positive traits (DePaulo, Blank, & Swaim, 1992; Riggio & Friedman, 1986). Moreover, judgments of the attractiveness of dynamic faces are only weakly correlated with judgments of the same faces presented in static displays, with perceived emotion more influential for dynamic faces (Rubenstein, 2005). This finding underscores the importance of considering dynamic information when predicting impressions from facial cues.

Dynamic facial information also contributes to sex identification. Perceivers achieved sex recognition at greater than chance levels merely from facial movements depicted in point-light displays (Berry, 1991b) or using motion capture techniques to animate an average head with the movements of men or women (Hill & Johnston, 2001). The latter study further revealed that nonrigid motion cues were more useful than rigid head movements. Dynamic cues also facilitate better recognition of sexual orientation, although dynamic facial cues have not been separated from other dynamic cues (Ambady, Hallahan, & Conner, 1999). These findings suggest that facial movement may be a sexually dimorphic cue that contributes to attractiveness judgments and associated trait impressions.

Perceivers also can discern relative age from the facial movements of children, middle-aged adults, and elderly adults depicted in point-light displays. Moreover, the movement patterns in children's faces elicited impressions of lower power than those in adult faces even with perceived age controlled (Berry, 1990b). It would be interesting to determine whether there is a babyface overgeneralization effect shown in impressions of adults with more childlike facial dynamics, paralleling impressions of young adults with more elderly gaits (Montepare & Zebrowitz-McArthur, 1988).

Like emotion, fitness, gender, and age, identity also can be revealed in facial movements. This was shown in judgments of point-light displays (Bruce, Valentine, Gruneberg, Morris, & Sykes, 1988) and using motion capture techniques, which revealed that rigid head movements were the more useful cue (Bruce et al., 1988; Hill & Johnston, 2001). Thus facial movement might also contribute to familiar face overgeneralization effects, either idiosyncratic or related to a perceiver's in-group, if there are differences in facial dynamics across social groups. This is an interesting question that has received little attention (Manstead, 1991).

Textural Qualities

To study textural cues, researchers have compared perceptions of 3D images that show the shape of faces without any texture cues to perceptions of 2D arrays that show skin quality, color, and luminance without any 3D shape (Hill, Bruce, & Akamatsu, 1995). They have also examined relationships between naturally occurring or manipulated textural qualities and impressions. Evidence that textural qualities should not be ignored is provided by the finding that eyebrows make a greater contribution to accurate face recognition than even the eyes do (Sadr, Jarudi, & Sinha, 2003) and that beards also make significant contribution to accurate face recognition (Terry, 1994).[8] Like dynamic cues, textural cues contribute to many facets of face perception that could be related to impression formation, including fitness, sex, age, emotion, and identity.

Skin texture provides cues to fitness, with a more homogeneous skin surface judged more attractive and healthier, which is consistent with the fact that skin anomalies are a common sign of disease (Fink, Grammer, & Thornhill, 2001). Additional research would be useful to determine whether a homogenous skin surface contributes to other components of the attractiveness halo effect. Skin quality also contributes to the recognition of face sex as evidenced by the finding that perceivers made more accurate sex judgments from photographs of faces in which texture and color were visible than they did from 3D representations of faces obtained by laser scanning in which these cues were absent (Bruce, Burton, Hanna, & Healey, 1993). Because the men were clean-shaven and all faces were masked to obscure the hair, the texture cues were limited to skin quality and eyebrows. Because women have smoother, lighter skin and thinner eyebrows than men, one or more of these texture cues may contribute to sex recognition (Frost, 1988; Yamaguchi, Hirukawa, & Kanazawa, 1995).

The finding that skin quality is involved in sex recognition suggests it may be among the sexually dimorphic cues that contribute to impressions of attractiveness and associated traits. Indeed, a preference for lighter skin is most pronounced in judgments of female faces (Maddox & Chase, 2004; van den Berghe & Frost, 1986). Lighter skin may be more preferred in women not only because it has a sexually dimorphic quality but also because it signals youthfulness and fertility. The diagnosticity of skin color for fertility comes from the fact that skin darkens during pregnancy, infertile phases of the menstrual cycle, and at menopause (van den Berghe & Frost, 1986; Wong & Ellis, 1989). Another possible explanation is that the preference is an overgeneralization of positive responses to infants, who, as noted below, are lighter-skinned than adults (Fink et al., 2001; Frost, 1988). Research that systematically investigates whether lighter skin elicits trait impressions that match the attractiveness halo effect or those that match the babyface overgeneralization effect may provide insight as to the origins of the preference for lighter-skinned women.

Babies differ from adults not only in facial structure but also in their smoother and lighter skin, rosier cheeks, redder lips, and lighter eyebrows (Frost, 1988; Zebrowitz, 1997). Overgeneralization effects may result in the attribution of more childlike traits to adults who manifest one or more of these qualities. Textural cues also contribute to impressions of emotions that are marked by distinctive eyebrows and skin color, with faces reddening in anger or embarrassment and paling in fear. These cues may contribute to emotion overgeneralization effects in which people with naturally ruddy or pale complexions may be perceived to have the traits associated with the emotions they signal.

Textural cues also seem likely to contribute to impressions of face familiarity and associated traits. Insofar as eyebrows make a highly significant contribution to accurate face recognition (Sadr et al., 2003), they may also contribute to variations in face familiarity and associated impressions. Skin color is a more certain candidate for influences on familiar face overgeneralization, since people report that it is the primary cue used to judge whether another person is African, Caucasian, or Hispanic, and that it is second only to eyes when judging whether another person is Asian (Brown, Dane, & Durham, 1998). Thus, skin color may have been a primary cue used by perceivers who were asked to rate how "prototypically Black" or "Afrocentric" a face looked, accounting in large part for the effects of this variable on impressions discussed in the section on familiar face overgeneralization.

SUMMARY AND FUTURE DIRECTIONS

Research on impression formation has a long and distinguished history in social psychology. However, most of this research has taken a social cognitive approach, focusing on the cognitive processes involved in forming impressions from verbal descriptions of people's traits rather than the facial or other nonverbal cues that produce the impressions in the first place. At least two developments have advanced research on facial cues in recent years. One is a conceptual framework—the ecological approach to person perception—that can predict what facial cues create particular impressions and why they do so. The other development is advances in methods to study facial cues. Although much more can be done to exploit innovative methods like connectionist modeling, principal components analysis, eye tracking, the bubbles technique, multidimensional scaling, and visual aftereffects, the research reviewed in this chapter reveals that much has been learned about the facial cues that influence first impressions. Specifically, facial cues related to fitness, age, emotion, and familiarity exert effects on first impressions that are predicted by the face overgeneralization hypotheses.

With a guiding theory and diverse tools in hand, researchers are poised to explore several questions that have received insufficient attention. First, there is a need to investigate further both the dynamic cues as well as the textural cues, including hair[8], that are associated with fitness, age, emotion, or familiarity, as well as the impressions, either accurate or overgeneralized, that these cues elicit. Second, there is a need to investigate the relative contribution of structural, textural, and dynamic facial cues to impressions as well as the relative impact of these cues versus vocal and body ones. It would also be instructive to determine the relative contributions to first impressions of attractiveness, babyfaceness, resemblance to an emotion, and familiarity, which may depend on the impression of interest. More generally, greater attention to the *function* of judgments based on facial appearance cues is needed to advance our understanding. This entails examining the behavioral affordances communicated by facial cues—that is, the opportunities for social interaction that they signal—because impressions are not an end in themselves but a guide to behavior (Gibson, 1979; McArthur & Baron, 1983). A functional approach also requires investigating perceiver attunements that influence attention to facial cues, because perceiver goals will likely influence their use of particular cues. Research on behavioral affordances and perceiver attunements will shed further light on the accuracy of impressions from facial cues, and, when accuracy is discovered, research will be needed to ascertain the developmental pathways that give rise to relationships between facial appearance and actual psychological attributes (see Zebrowitz, 1997; Zebrowitz & Collins, 1997). Although the overgeneralization hypotheses call more attention to biases than to accuracy, the ecological approach to person perception from which they were derived provides a useful foundation for a broader functional analysis of judgments from facial appearance cues (see Zebrowitz & Montepare, 2006).

ACKNOWLEDGMENT

This work was supported by National Institute of Health Grant Nos. MH066836 and K02MH72603 to Leslie A. Zebrowitz.

NOTES

1. The ecological approach to social perception and the overgeneralization hypotheses do not constitute a hypothetico-deductive theory from which specific inferences and falsifiable hypotheses follow, but rather provide a general conceptual model that can integrate existing research findings and highlight significant research questions.
2. Although faces with more positive expressions, whether naturally occurring or posed, are also more attractive than those with less positive expressions, this research will be discussed in the subsequent section of this chapter titled "Impressions Created by Facial Expressions."
3. It should be noted that reactions to anomalous unattractive faces may be cast more generally as by-products of preferences for prototypes, be they faces or other stimuli, perhaps generated by their greater familiarity (Halberstadt & Rhodes, 2000). However, this hypothesis cannot readily explain the finding that impressions are accurate for faces that deviate from the average "prototypic" face in one direction, but not for those that deviate in another direction, as discussed below.
4. Averageness is assessed through ratings of its converse, distinctiveness—how easy it would be to pick the face out in a crowd.
5. As discussed above, negative impressions of older faces are partially mediated by their greater resemblance to anomalous faces.
6. This hypothesis has sometimes been labeled "identity overgeneralization."
7. Although anthropologists and biologists question the validity of race as a scientific concept, race is a widely accepted concept in folk psychology. While recognizing that clear decisions on category membership are problematic, we nevertheless use the "fuzzy" category system of racial groups.
8. Scalp hair also makes a strong contribution to impressions, although it has been ignored or even hidden in much of the research examining facial cues. The attractiveness of people's scalp hair has a strong influence on overall attractiveness ratings, after mouth and eyes (Terry, 1977), suggesting that hair qualities may be among cues that contribute to impressions associated with the attractiveness halo effect, particularly via their sexual dimorphism and age-related variations. Hair qualities may also contribute to face familiarity, since they vary across time and culture, as do impressions of people who vary in hair color and texture (see McArthur, 1982).

REFERENCES

Adolphs, R., Gosselin, F., Buchanan, T. W., Tranel, D., Schyns, P., & Damasio, A. R. (2005). A mechanism for impaired fear recognition after amygdala damage. *Nature, 433,* 68–72.

Ambadar, Z., Schooler, J. W., & Cohen, J. F. (2005). Deciphering the enigmatic face: The importance of facial dynamics in interpreting subtle facial expressions. *Psychological Science, 16,* 403–410.

Ambady, N., Hallahan, M., & Conner, B. (1999). Accuracy of judgments of sexual orientation from thin slices of behavior. *Journal of Personality and Social Psychology, 77,* 538–547.

Aronoff, J., Woike, B. A., & Hyman, L. M. (1992). Which are the stimuli in facial displays of anger and happiness? Configurational bases of emotion recognition. *Journal of Personality and Social Psychology, 62,* 1050–1066.

Bar-Haim, Y., Ziv, T., Lamy, D., & Hodes, R. M. (2006). Nature and nurture in own-race face processing. *Psychological Science, 17,* 159–163.

Bassili, J. N. (1978). Facial motion in the perception of faces and of emotional expression. *Journal of Experimental Psychology: Human Perception and Performance, 4,* 373–379.

Berry, D. S. (1990a). Taking people at face value: Evidence for the kernel of truth hypothesis. *Social Cognition, 8,* 343–361.

Berry, D. S. (1990b). What can a moving face tell us? *Journal of Personality and Social Psychology, 58,* 1004–1014.

Berry, D. S. (1991a). Accuracy in social perception: Contribution of facial and vocal information. *Journal of Personality and Social Psychology, 61,* 298–307.

Berry, D. S. (1991b). Child and adult sensitivity to gender information in patterns of facial motion. *Ecological Psychology, 3,* 349–366.

Berry, D. S., & Landry, J. C. (1997). Facial maturity and daily social interaction. *Journal of Personality and Social Psychology, 72,* 570–580.

Berry, D. S., & McArthur, L. A. (1985). Some components and consequences of a babyface. *Journal of Personality and Social Psychology, 48,* 312–323.

Berry, D. S., & McArthur, L. A. (1986). Perceiving character in faces: The impact of age-related craniofacial changes on social perception. *Psychological Bulletin, 100,* 3–18.

Blair, I. V., Judd, C. M., Sadler, M. S., & Jenkins, C. (2002). The role of Afrocentric features in person perception: Judging by features and categories. *Journal of Personality and Social Psychology, 83,* 5–25.

Brown, T. D., Jr., Dane, F. C., & Durham, M. D. (1998). Perception of race and ethnicity. *Journal of Social Behavior and Personality, 13,* 295–306.

Bruce, V., Burton, A. M., Hanna, E., & Healey, P. (1993). Sex discrimination: How do we tell the difference between male and female faces? *Perception, 22,* 131–152.

Bruce, V., Valentine, T., Gruneberg, M. M., Morris, P. E., & Sykes, R. N. (1988). When a nod's as good as a wink: The role of dynamic information in facial recognition. In M. M. Gruneberg, P. E. Morris, & R. N. Sykes (Eds.), *Practical aspects of memory: Current research and issues: Vol. 1. Memory in everyday life* (pp. 169–174). New York: Wiley.

Bruce, V., & Young, A. (1986). Understanding face recognition. *British Journal of Psychology, 77,* 305–327.

Bruce, V., & Young, A. (1998). *In the eye of the beholder: The science of face perception.* New York: Oxford University Press.

Brunswik, E. (1956). *Perception and the representative design of psychological experiments.* Berkeley, CA: University of California Press.

Buss, D. M. (1989). Sex differences in human mate preferences: Evolutionary hypotheses tested in 37 cultures. *Behavioral and Brain Sciences, 12,* 1–49.

Calder, A. J., Burton, A. M., & Miller, P. (2001). A principal component analysis of facial expressions. *Vision Research, 41,* 1179–1208.

Clifford, C. W. G. E., & Rhodes, G. E. (2005). *Fitting the mind to the world: Adaptation and after-effects in high-level vision.* Oxford, UK: Oxford University Press.

Collins, M. A., & Zebrowitz, L. A. (1995). The contributions of appearance to occupational outcomes in civilian and military settings. *Journal of Applied Social Psychology, 25,* 129–163.

Cunningham, M. R. (1986). Measuring the physical in physical attractiveness: Quasi-experiments on the sociobiology of female facial beauty. *Journal of Personality and Social Psychology, 50,* 925–935.

Cunningham, M. R., Roberts, A. R., Barbee, A. P., & Druen, P. B. (1995). "Their ideas of beauty are, on the whole, the same as ours": Consistency and variability in the cross-cultural perception of female physical attractiveness. *Journal of Personality and Social Psychology, 68,* 261–279.

Darwin, C. (1872). *The expression of emotion in man and animals.* London: John Murray.

de Bonis, M. (2003). Causes and reasons in failures to perceive fearful faces. In M. Katsikitis (Ed.), *Human face: Measurement and meaning* (pp. 149–167). Dordrecht, Netherlands: Kluwer Academic Publishers.

DeBruine, L. (2002). Facial resemblance enhances trust. *Proceedings of the Royal Society of London, Series B: Biological Sciences, 269,* 1307–1312.

DePaulo, B. M., Blank, A. L., & Swaim, G. W. (1992). Expressiveness and expressive control. *Personality and Social Psychology Bulletin, 18,* 276–285.

Dion, K. K. (2002). Cultural perspectives on facial attractiveness. In C. Rhodes & L. A. Zebrowitz (Eds.), *Facial attractiveness: Evolutionary, cognitive, and social perspectives* (pp. 239–259). Westport, CT: Ablex.

Eagly, A. H., Ashmore, R. D., Makhijani, M. G., & Longo, L. C. (1991). What is beautiful is good, but: A meta-analytic review of research on the physical attractiveness stereotype. *Psychological Bulletin, 110,* 109–128.

Eberhardt, J. L., Goff, P. A., Purdie, V. J., & Davies, P. G. (2004). Seeing black: Race, crime, and visual processing. *Journal of Personality and Social Psychology, 87,* 876–893.

Ekman, P. (1994). Strong evidence for universals in facial expressions: A reply to Russell's mistaken critique. *Psychological Bulletin, 115,* 268–287.

Ekman, P. (1997). Should we call it expression or communication? *Innovations in Social Science Research, 10,* 333–344.

Elfenbein, H. A., & Ambady, N. (2003). When familiarity breeds accuracy: Cultural exposure and facial emotion recognition. *Journal of Personality and Social Psychology, 85,* 276–290.

Enlow, D. H. (1990). *Facial growth* (3rd ed.). Philadelphia: Harcourt Brace.

Feingold, A. (1992). Good-looking people are not what we think. *Psychological Bulletin, 111,* 304–341.

Fink, B., Grammer, K., & Matts, P. J. (2006). Visible skin color distribution plays a role in the perception of age, attractiveness, and health in female faces. *Evolution and Human Behavior, 27,* 433–442.

Fink, B., Grammer, K., & Thornhill, R. (2001). Human (Homo sapiens) facial attractiveness in relation to skin texture and color. *Journal of Comparative Psychology, 115,* 92–99.

Folstad, I., & Karter, A. J. (1992). Parasites, bright males and the immunocompetence handicap. *American Naturalist, 139,* 603–622.

Frijda, N. H. (1995). Expression, emotion, neither, or both? *Cognition and Emotion, 9,* 617–663.

Frost, P. (1988). Human skin color: A possible relationship between its sexual dimorphism and its social perception. *Perspectives in Biology and Medicine, 32,* 38–58.

Gibson, J. J. (1979). *The ecological approach to visual perception.* Boston: Houghton Mifflin.

Grammer, K., & Thornhill, R. (1994). Human (Homo sapiens) facial attractiveness and sexual selection: The role of symmetry and averageness. *Journal of Comparative Psychology, 108,* 233–242.

Griffin, A. M., & Langlois, J. H. (2006). Stereotype directionality and attractiveness stereotyping: Is beauty good or is ugly bad? *Social Cognition, 24,* 187–206.

Grossman, E. D., & Blake, R. (2005). Brain areas active during visual perception of biological motion. In J. T. Cacioppo, & G. G. Berntson (Eds.), *Social neuroscience: Key readings.* (pp. 101–114). New York: Psychology Press.

Halberstadt, J., & Rhodes, G. (2000). The attractiveness of nonface averages: Implications for an evolutionary explanation of the attractiveness of average faces. *Psychological Science, 11,* 285–289.

Hancock, P. J. B., Bruce, V., & Burton, M. A. (1998). A comparison of two computer-based face identification systems with human perceptions of faces. *Vision Research, 38,* 2277–2288.

Haxby, J. V., Hoffman, E. A., & Gobbini, M. I. (2002). Human neural systems for face recognition and social communication. *Biological Psychiatry, 51,* 59–67.

Hess, U., Blairy, S., & Kleck, R. E. (2000). The influence of facial emotion displays, gender, and ethnicity on judgments of dominance and affiliation. *Journal of Nonverbal Behavior, 24,* 265–283.

Hill, H., Bruce, V., & Akamatsu, S. (1995). Perceiving the sex and race of faces: The role of shape and colour. *Proceedings of the Royal Society of London, Series B: Biological Sciences, 261,* 367–373.

Hill, H., & Johnston, A. (2001). Categorizing sex and identity from the biological motion of faces. *Current Biology, 11,* 880–885.

Hill, T., Lewicki, P., Czyzewska, M., & Schuller, G. (1990). The role of learned inferential encoding rules in the perception of faces: Effects of non-conscious self-perpetuation of a bias. *Journal of Experimental Social Psychology, 26,* 350–371.

Izard, C. E. (1994). Innate and universal facial expressions: Evidence from developmental and cross-cultural research. *Psychological Bulletin, 15,* 288–299.

Johansson, G. (1973). Visual perception of biological motion and a model for its analysis. *Perception and Psychophysics, 14,* 201–211.

Karraker, K. H., & Stern, M. (1990). Infant physical attractiveness and facial expression: Effects on adult perceptions. *Basic and Applied Social Psychology, 11,* 371–385.

Keating, C. F. (2002). Charismatic faces: Social status cues put face appeal in context. In G. Rhodes & L. A. Zebrowitz (Eds.), *Facial attractiveness: Evolutionary, cognitive, and social perspectives* (pp. 153–192). Westport, CT: Ablex.

Keating, C. F., & Bai, D. L. (1986). Children's attributions of social dominance from facial cues. *Child Development, 57,* 1269–1276.

Keating, C. F., & Doyle, J. (2002). The faces of desirable mates and dates contain mixed social status cues. *Journal of Experimental Social Psychology, 38,* 414–424.

Keating, C. F., Mazur, A., & Segall, M. H. (1981). A cross-cultural exploration of physiognomic traits of dominance and happiness. *Ethology and Sociobiology, 2,* 41–48.

Knutson, B. (1996). Facial expressions of emotion influence interpersonal trait inferences. *Journal of Nonverbal Behavior, 20,* 165–182.

Kramer, S., Zebrowitz, L. A., San Giovanni, J. P., & Sherak, B. (1995). Infants' preferences for attractiveness and babyfaceness. In B. G. Bardy, R. J. Bootsma, & Y. Guiard (Eds.), *Studies in perception and action III* (pp. 389–392). Mahwah, NJ: Erlbaum.

LaFrance, M., & Hecht, M. A. (1995). Why smiles generate leniency. *Personality and Social Psychology Bulletin, 21,* 207–214.

Langlois, J. H., Kalakanis, L., Rubenstein, A. J., Larson, A., Hallam, M., & Smoot, M. (2000). Maxims or myths of beauty? A meta-analytic and theoretical review. *Psychological Bulletin, 126,* 390–423.

Lee, K. J., Byatt, G., & Rhodes, G. (2000). Caricature effects, distinctiveness, and identification: Testing the face-space framework. *Psychological Science, 11,* 379–385.

Leopold, D. A., O'Toole, A. J., Vetter, T., & Blanz, V. (2001). Prototype-referenced shape encoding revealed by high-level aftereffects. *Nature Neuroscience, 4,* 89–94.

Lewicki, P. (1985). Nonconscious biasing effects of single instances on subsequent judgments. *Journal of Personality and Social Psychology, 48,* 563–574.

Livingston, R. W., & Brewer, M. B. (2002). What are we really priming? Cue-based versus category-based processing of facial stimuli. *Journal of Personality and Social Psychology, 82,* 5–18.

Luevano, V. X., & Zebrowitz, L. A. (2007). Do impressions of health, dominance, and warmth explain why masculine faces are preferred more in a short-term mate? *Evolutionary Psychology, 5,* 15–27.

Maddox, K. B. (2004). Perspectives on racial phenotypicality bias. *Personality and Social Psychology Review, 8,* 383–401.

Maddox, K. B., & Chase, S. G. (2004). Manipulating subcategory salience: Exploring the link between skin tone and social perception of Blacks. *European Journal of Social Psychology, 34*, 533–546.

Malatesta, C., Fiore, M., & Messina, J. (1987). Affect, personality and expressive characteristics of older people. *Psychology and Aging, 2*, 64–69.

Malatesta, C., Izard, C. E., Culver, C., & Nicholich, M. (1987). Emotion communication skills in young, middle-aged, and older women. *Psychology and Aging, 2*, 193–203.

Manstead, A. S. R. (1991). Expressiveness as an individual difference. In A. S. R. Manstead, R. S. Feldman, & B. Rimé (Eds.), *Fundamentals of nonverbal behavior* (pp. 285–328). Cambridge, UK: Cambridge University Press.

Marsh, A. A., Ambady, N., & Kleck, R. E. (2005). The effects of fear and anger facial expressions on approach and avoidance related behaviors. *Emotion, 5*, 119–124.

McArthur, L. Z. (1982). Judging a book by its cover: A cognitive analysis of the relationship between physical appearance and stereotyping. In A. Hastorf & A. Isen (Eds.), *Cognitive social psychology*. New York: Elsevier North Holland, Inc.

McArthur, L. Z., & Apatow, K. (1983). Impressions of baby-faced adults. *Social Cognition, 2*, 315–342.

McArthur, L. Z., & Baron, R. A. (1983). An ecological approach to social perception. *Psychological Review, 90*, 215–238.

McKelvie, S. J. (1995). Emotional expression in upside-down faces: Evidence for configurational and componential processing. *British Journal of Social Psychology, 34*, 325–334.

Montepare, J. M., & Dobish, H. (2003). The contribution of emotion perceptions and their overgeneralizations to trait impressions. *Journal of Nonverbal Behavior, 27*, 237–254.

Montepare, J. M., & Zebrowitz, L. A. (1998). "Person perception comes of age": The salience and significance of age in social judgments. In M. Zanna (Ed.), *Advances in experimental social psychology* (Vol. 30, pp. 93–163). San Diego, CA: Academic Press.

Montepare, J. M., & Zebrowitz, L. A. (2002). A social–developmental view of ageism. In T. D. Nelson (Ed.), *Ageism: Stereotyping and prejudice against older persons* (pp. 77–125). Cambridge, MA: MIT Press.

Montepare, J. M., & Zebrowitz-McArthur, L. (1988). Impressions of people created by age-related qualities of their gaits. *Journal of Personality and Social Psychology, 55*, 547–556.

Montepare, J. M., & Zebrowitz-McArthur, L. (1989). Children's perceptions of babyfaced adults. *Perceptual and Motor Skills, 69*, 467–472.

O'Toole, A. J., Abdi, H., Deffenbacher, K. A., & Bartlett, J. C. (1991). Classifying faces by race and sex using an auto-associative memory trained for recognition. In K. J. Hammond & D. Gentner (Eds.), *Proceedings of the 13th Annual Conference of the Cognitive Sciences Society*. Mahwah, NJ: Erlbaum.

O'Toole, A. J., Price, T., Vetter, T., Bartlett, J. C., & Blanz, V. (1999). 3D shape and 2D surface textures of human faces: The role of "averages" in attractiveness and age. *Image and Vision Computing, 18*, 9–19.

Paulhus, D. L., & Martin, C. L. (1986). Predicting adult temperament from minor physical anomalies. *Journal of Personality and Social Psychology, 50*, 1235–1239.

Penn, D. J., Damjanovich, K., & Potts, W. K. (2002). MHC heterozygosity confers a selective advantage against multiple-strain infections. *Proceedings of the National Academy of Sciences of the United States of America, 99*, 11260–11264.

Pentland, B., Pitcairn, T. K., Gray, J. M., & Riddle, W. J. R. (1987). The effects of reduced expression in Parkinson's disease on impression formation by health professionals. *Clinical Rehabilitation, 1*, 307–313.

Peskin, M., & Newell, F. N. (2004). Familiarity breeds attraction: Effect of exposure on the attractiveness of typical and distinctive faces. *Perception, 33*, 147–157.

Posamentier, M. T., & Abdi, H. (2003). Processing faces and facial expressions. *Neuropsychology Review, 13*, 113–143.

Ramsey, J. L., Langlois, J. H., Hoss, R. A., Rubenstein, A. J., & Griffin, A. M. (2004). Origins of a stereotype: Categorization of facial attractiveness by 6-month-old infants. *Developmental Science, 7*, 201–211.

Reis, H. T., Wilson, I. M., Monestere, C., Bernstein, S., Clark, K., Seidl, E., et al. (1990). What is smiling is beautiful and good. *European Journal of Social Psychology, 20*, 259–267.

Rhodes, G. (2006). The evolutionary psychology of facial beauty. *Annual Review of Psychology, 57*, 199–226.

Rhodes, G., Halberstadt, J., & Brajkovich, G. (2001). Generalization of mere exposure effects to averaged composite faces. *Social Cognition, 19*, 57–70.

Rhodes, G., & Jeffery, L. (2006). Adaptive norm-based coding of facial identity. *Vision Research, 46*, 2977–2987.

Rhodes, G., Jeffery, L., Watson, T. L., Jaquet, E., Winkler, C., & Clifford, C. W. G. (2004). Orientation-contingent face aftereffects and implications for face-coding mechanisms. *Current Biology, 14*, 2119–2123.

Rhodes, G., Zebrowitz, L. A., Clark, A., Kalick, S. M., Hightower, A., & McKay, R. (2001). Do facial averageness and symmetry signal health? *Evolution and Human Behavior, 22*, 31–46.

Riggio, R. E., & Friedman, H. (1986). Impression formation: The role of expressive behavior. *Journal of Personality and Social Psychology, 50*, 421–427.

Roggman, L. A., Langlois, J. H., Hubbs-Tait, L., & Rieser-Danner, L. A. (1994). Infant day-care, attachment, and the "file drawer problem." *Child Development, 65*, 1429–1443.

Rubenstein, A. J. (2005). Variation in perceived attractiveness: Differences between dynamic and static faces. *Psychological Science, 16*, 759–762.

Rubenstein, A. J., Kalakanis, L., & Langlois, J. H. (1999). Infant preferences for attractive faces: A cognitive explanation. *Developmental Psychology, 15*, 848–855.

Russell, R. (2003). Sex, beauty, and the relative luminance of facial features. *Perception, 32*, 1093–1107.

Sadr, J., Jarudi, I., & Sinha, P. (2003). The role of eyebrows in face recognition. *Perception, 32*, 285–293.

Sato, W., & Yoshikawa, S. (2004). The dynamic aspects of emotional facial expressions. *Cognition and Emotion, 18*, 701–710.

Scheib, J. E., Gangestad, S. W., & Thornhill, R. (1999). Facial attractiveness, symmetry, and cues to good genes. *Proceedings of the Royal Society of London, Series B: Biological Sciences, 266*, 1913–1917.

Schneider, F., Heimann, H., Himer, W., & Huss, D. (1990). Computer-based analysis of facial action in schizophrenic and depressed patients. *European Archives of Psychiatry and Clinical Neuroscience, 240*, 67–76.

Secord, P. (1958). Facial features and inference processes in interpersonal perception. In R. Tagiuri & L. Petrullo (Eds.), *Person perception and interpersonal behavior* (pp. 300–315). Stanford, CA: Stanford University Press.

Secord, P. F., & Bevan, W. (1956). Personalities in faces: III. A cross-cultural comparison of impressions of physiognomy and personality in faces. *Journal of Social Psychology, 43*, 283–288.

Secord, P. F., Bevan, W., Jr., & Dukes, W. F. (1953). Occupational and physiognomic stereotypes in the perception of photographs. *Journal of Social Psychology, 37*, 261–270.

Secord, P. F., Dukes, W. F., & Bevan, W. (1954). Personalities in faces: I. An experiment in social perceiving. *Genetic Psychology Monographs, 49*, 231–270.

Secord, P. F., & Muthard, J. E. (1955). Personalities in faces: IV. A descriptive analysis of the perception of women's faces and the identificaiton of some physiognomic determinants. *Journal of Psychology: Interdisciplinary and Applied, 39*, 269–278.

Smith, M. L., Cottrell, G. W., Gosselin, F., & Schyns, P. G. (2005). Transmitting and decoding facial expressions. *Psychological Science, 16*, 184–189.

Streissguth, A. P., Herman, C. S., & Smith, D. W. (1978). Intelligence, behavior, and dysmorphogenesis in the fetal alcohol syndrome: A report on 20 patients. *The Journal of Pediatrics, 92*, 363–367.

Terry, R. L. (1994). Effects of facial transformations on accuracy of recognition. *Journal of Social Psychology, 134*, 483–492.

Terry, R. L. (1977). Further evidence on components of facial attractiveness. *Perceptual and Motor Skills, 45*, 130.

Thornhill, R., & Gangestad, S. W. (1999). Facial attractiveness. *Trends in Cognitive Sciences, 3*, 452–460.

Tipples, J., Atkinson, A. P., & Young, A. W. (2002). The eyebrow: A salient social signal. *Emotion, 2*, 288–296.

Todd, J. T., Mark, L. S., Shaw, R. E., & Pittenger, J. B. (1980). The perception of human growth. *Scientific American, 24*, 106–114.

Valentin, D., Abdi, H., & Edelman, B. (1997). What represents a face?: A computational approach for the integration of physiological and psychological data. *Perception, 26*, 1271–1288.

van den Berghe, P. L., & Frost, P. (1986). Skin color preference, sexual dimporphism, and sexual selection: A case of gene–culture co-evolution? *Ethnic Racial Studies, 9*, 87–113.

Wehrle, T., Kaiser, S., Schmidt, S., & Scherer, K. R. (2000). Studying the dynamics of emotional expression using synthesized facial muscle movements. *Journal of Personality and Social Psychology, 78*, 105–119.

Wong, R. C., & Ellis, C. N. (1989). Physiologic skin changes in pregnancy. *Seminars in Dermatology, 8,* 7–11.

Yamaguchi, M. K., Hirukawa, T., & Kanazawa, S. (1995). Judgment of gender through facial parts. *Perception, 24,* 563–575.

Zajonc, R. B. (1968). Attitudinal effects of mere exposure. *Journal of Personality and Social Psychology, 9*(2, Part 2), 1–27.

Zajonc, R. B., Murphy, S. T., & Inglehart, M. (1989). Feeling and facial efference: Implications of the vascular theory of emotion. *Psychological Review, 96,* 395–416.

Zebrowitz, L. A. (1996). Physical appearance as a basis for stereotyping. In M. H. N. McRae & C. Stangor (Eds.), *Foundation of stereotypes and stereotyping* (pp. 79–120). New York: Guilford Press.

Zebrowitz, L. A. (1997). *Reading faces: Window to the soul?* Boulder, CO: Westview Press.

Zebrowitz, L. A., Bronstad, P. M., & Lee, H. K. (2007). The contribution of face familiarity to ingroup favoritism and stereotyping. *Social Cognition, 25,* 306–338.

Zebrowitz, L. A., & Collins, M. A. (1997). Accurate social perception at zero acquaintance: The affordances of a Gibsonian approach. *Personality and Social Psychology Review, 1,* 204–223.

Zebrowitz, L. A., Collins, M. A., & Dutta, R. (1998). The relationship between appearance and personality across the life span. *Personality and Social Psychology Bulletin, 24,* 736–749.

Zebrowitz, L. A., Fellous, J. M., Mignault, A., & Andreoletti, C. (2003). Trait impressions as overgeneralized responses to adaptively significant facial qualities: Evidence from connectionist modeling. *Personality and Social Psychology Review, 7,* 194–215.

Zebrowitz, L. A., Hall, J. A., Murphy, N. A., & Rhodes, G. (2002). Looking smart and looking good: Facial cues to intelligence and their origins. *Personality and Social Psychology Bulletin, 28,* 238–249.

Zebrowitz, L. A., Kikuchi, M., & Fellous, J. M. (2007). Are effects of emotion expression on trait impressions mediated by babyfaceness? Evidence from connectionist modeling *Personality and Social Psychology Bulletin, 33,* 648–662.

Zebrowitz, L. A., & Lee, S. Y. (1999). Appearance, stereotype incongruent behavior, and social relationships. *Personality and Social Psychology Bulletin, 25,* 569–584.

Zebrowitz, L. A., & Montepare, J. M. (2006). The ecological approach to person perception: Evolutionary roots and contemporary offshoots. In M. Schaller, J. A. Simpson, & D. T. Kenrick (Eds.), *Evolution and social psychology* (pp. 81–113). New York: Psychology Press.

Zebrowitz, L. A., Montepare, J. M., & Lee, H. K. (1993). They don't all look alike: Individual impressions of other racial groups. *Journal of Personality and Social Psychology, 65,* 85–101.

Zebrowitz, L. A., Olson, K., & Hoffman, K. (1993). Stability of babyfaceness and attractiveness across the lifespan. *Journal of Personality and Social Psychology, 64*(3), 453–466.

Zebrowitz, L. A., & Rhodes, G. (2002). Nature let a hundred flowers bloom: The multiple ways and wherefores of attractiveness. In G. Rhodes & L. A. Zebrowitz (Eds.), *Facial attractiveness: Evolutionary, cognitive, and social perspectives. Advances in visual cognition* (Vol. 1, pp. 261–293). Westport, CT: Ablex.

Zebrowitz, L. A., & Rhodes, G. (2004). Sensitivity to "bad genes" and the anomalous face overgeneralization effect: Cue validity, cue utilization, and accuracy in judging intelligence and health. *Journal of Nonverbal Behavior, 28,* 167–185.

Zebrowitz, L. A., Voinescu, L., & Collins, M. A. (1996). "Wide-eyed" and "crooked-faced": Determinants of perceived and real honesty across the life span. *Personality and Social Psychology Bulletin, 22,* 1258–1269.

CHAPTER 9

Social Categorization and Beyond

How Facial Features Impact Social Judgment

KEITH B. MADDOX
KRISTIN N. DUKES

The human face conveys information to help determine a person's identity, category membership, personality, emotional or mood state, what he or she might be thinking about or looking at, and the veracity of his or her verbal behavior (Bodenhausen & Macrae, 2006; Mason, Cloutier, & Macrae, 2006). The face tells us so much about others that is potentially relevant to social thought and action. Yet, aside from a few notable research programs, this important area of research remains understudied in social psychology (Bodenhausen & Macrae, 2006; Zebrowitz, 2006). In contrast, and perhaps understandably, researchers have focused on more explicit aspects of behavior and their implications for social judgment and interaction; particularly in the realm of social categorization and its consequences for stereotyping, prejudice, and discrimination. In this chapter, we argue that the disproportionate attention given to behavior from social psychological researchers has resulted in theories that, while extremely useful, are missing important pieces of the social perception puzzle. A case in point: many models of social perception recognize that perceivers are sensitive to within-group variability in behavior and that this sensitivity has implications for social categorization and its consequences. However, in their focus on behavior, these models neglect perceivers' sensitivity to within-group variation in facial appearance and the potential implications of this sensitivity for intergroup judgment and behavior.

That trend is rapidly changing. This chapter focuses on a particular piece of that puzzle: stereotyping, prejudice, and discrimination guided by facial cues. In particular, we seek to outline several recent investigations that must give pause to those who endorse traditional models of category representation and judgment. On balance, these studies reveal that within-category variation in facial features provides more information in the service of social judgment than previous theories and investigations have assumed. That is, contrary to the assumptions and assertions of many traditional models, perceivers are sensitive to within-category variation in features of the face in the service of social categorization and the activation of associated stereotypes and prejudices. Individuals who more closely resemble category prototypes are more likely to be viewed through the lens of category stereotypes. In this chapter, we review several recent theoretical accounts based on evidence suggesting that this process may occur through two routes: indirectly through categorization processes or directly through processes independent of categorization.

FACIAL FEATURES AND IMPRESSION FORMATION: EXPLORING A THEORETICAL LACUNA

There are multiple social psychological models that seek to describe the implications of a particular mental representation for judgments about social targets. Many of these (e.g., Bodenhausen & Macrae, 1998; Kunda & Thagard, 1996) have their bases in two extremely influential models of impression formation. These two models and their implications for the role of facial features in social perception are described below.

Brewer's Dual-Process Model

The dual-process model of impression formation (Brewer, 1988; Brewer & Feinstein, 1999) states that social targets are initially classified through an identification process. This is a preconscious categorization of the target "along well-established stimulus dimensions such as gender, age, and skin color" (Brewer, 1988, p. 6). If the stimulus is determined to be relevant to the perceiver's current goals, a crucial decision point is reached. Here, the model posits two distinct modes of impression formation, depending on whether the stimulus or situation elicits the self-involvement of the perceiver. If self-involvement is high, person-based impression formation (personalization) takes place. This is a bottom-up process in which inferences and judgments are based on the piecemeal integration of a social target's attributes. If self-involvement is low, category-based impression formation takes place. This is a top-down process where preexisting knowledge about social category membership influences inferences and judgments about a target.

In this model, categories take the form of prototypes: amalgams of features that have been abstracted from individual exemplars previously encountered. With a new instance (target), impression formation processes are determined by the degree of fit between the target and the category representation it activates. In addition, Brewer assumes that the pattern-matching process is constrained by this initial activation—it is less likely that the process will reinitiate with a different category. Thus, if the fit between the initial category and the instance is poor, the target will be compared to subtypes of the initial category rather than restarting with a new category. If adequate fit cannot be established between the social target and the category subtypes, individuation takes place in which the target attributes are integrated in a piecemeal fashion.

Fiske and Neuberg's Continuum Model

The continuum model (Fiske, Lin, & Neuberg, 1999; Fiske & Neuberg, 1990) posits that social impression formation processes vary on a single continuum ranging from category-based to piecemeal integration of a target's features. The location on the continuum depends jointly on the information available about the target and the perceiver's level of motivation. The process begins with an initial categorization of the individual based on salient features, such as physical characteristics. Moreover, Fiske and her colleagues argue that "certain social categories— such as gender, ethnicity, and age—are 'privileged' in that they can be easily applied to most people one encounters" (Fiske et al., 1999, pp. 233–234).

Initial categorization is followed by an assessment of whether the perceiver is motivated to process the target in greater detail. If so, attentional resources are allotted to the task of confirming the initial categorization, with a bias toward preserving that categorization. If the perceived fit between the target's attributes and the category representation is poor, recategorization takes place. This includes a comparison of the target to relevant subcategories, exemplars, and other representations. If recategorization fails, the perceiver attempts piecemeal integration of the target's attributes, with the goal of forming a coherent impression. The model concludes with the public or private expression of the impression through affective, cognitive, or behavioral channels.

WHAT ROLE FOR FACIAL FEATURES?

As with other models of category representation, both the dual-process and continuum models of impression formation have been compared, contrasted, and extensively tested in the literature (Brewer & Feinstein, 1999; Fiske et al., 1999). Both provide a great deal of explanatory power for the range of studies examining person perception. In the realm of stereotyping, prejudice, and discrimination, the implications of behavior for the activation of stereotypic personality traits and stereotype change are well documented (Fiske, 1998; Rothbart & John, 1985). However, a focus on the interaction between category membership and behavior has led to a theoretical void with regard to facial features. Applications of each model have been limited to considering facial features as merely a conduit to category activation (Maddox, 2004). That is, facial features may help perceivers to place a target into a relevant social category, but their role ends at that point. These traditional social psychological perspectives have either not considered or dismissed the possibility that within-category variation in facial appearance has implications for the interpersonal and societal outcomes of others (Maddox, 2004). Consider two individuals who might be consensually categorized as Black and yet possess different degrees of facial prototypicality (to aid this exercise, picture Tiger Woods and Michael Jordan). Holding behavior constant, traditional models assume that, as Blacks, these individuals would be equally likely to be viewed through the lens of category stereotypes, to elicit similar degrees of prejudice, and to be treated in the same manner.

There is some social psychological evidence to support this perspective (Atkinson et al., 1996; Secord, 1959; Secord, Bevan, & Katz, 1956). However, there is also evidence that perceivers are sensitive to within-category variation in facial appearance. One well-documented phenomenon concerns stereotyping based on phenotypic facial characteristics related to perceived age (for a review see Berry & McArthur, 1986). Researchers have also explored the "babyish overgeneralization effect" for other potentially stereotypic attributions such as gender, height, weight, nationality, and criminality (Zebrowitz, 1996). Other studies have explored the impact of facial characteristics on stereotyping, such as judgments of the elderly (Brewer, Dull, & Lui, 1981; Brewer & Lui, 1984) and Blacks (Maddox & Gray, 2002). These studies and others will be described in greater detail below. Our point here is simply to point out that many existing models of impression formation cannot easily accommodate the within-category findings.

FACIAL CUES: INDIRECT AND DIRECT INFLUENCES ON SOCIAL REPRESENTATION AND JUDGMENT

Research has suggested that facial cues can lead to stereotyping, prejudice, and discrimination through two routes. The first is an indirect route by which features contribute to the determination of category membership, similar to that posited in traditional models of impression formation. The second reflects a direct route by which features influence judgments above and beyond the influence of category information.

Facial Cues and Categorical Bias

As suggested by traditional models of impression formation, features can help one to determine membership in a particular category, potentially subjecting the target to available stereotypes. While these models recognize that behavioral typicality—the extent to which behavior reflects cultural stereotypes about a target's group—may impact judgments, most have been somewhat rigid in their consideration of the influence of facial typicality—the extent to which facial features reflect cultural stereotypes about a target's group (Maddox, 2004). This view might be characterized as an "all-or-nothing" perspective when considering the influence of variation in facial cues. Regardless of within-group variability in facial typicality, all targets are stereotyped similarly once categorized as a member of particular category. For example, in the presence of certain defining characteristics such as light or dark skin color, a target may be categorized by race (e.g., Allport, 1954; Rothbart & John, 1985). However, skin color may vary greatly within a racial group. From an "all-or-nothing" perspective, this variation is irrelevant to the stereotyping of category members.

Early social psychological demonstration that within-group variation in facial features does in fact influence social judgments was provided by Brewer, Dull, and Lui (1981), who conducted a study concerning young persons' perceptions of the elderly. They tested the hypothesis that young people have differentiated category representations of the elderly, consisting of various subtypes. Unknown to the participants, these researchers had identified three potential subtypes of elderly people as the focus of the study: grandmothers, elder statesmen, and senior citizens. Ten photographs represented each subtype. In one task, participants were presented with all of the photographs and asked to sort them into piles, or categories, as they thought appropriate. Using cluster analysis, the researchers compared the pattern obtained from their participants to the predicted pattern of sorting (clustering the photos into three distinct subtypes) and found that participants sorted the photographs in a manner consistent with the *a priori* subcategories. This finding was used as partial evidence that representations of others can be described as consisting of distinct subtypes. A similar pattern of data was obtained among a sample of elderly participants (Brewer & Lui, 1984). This seminal evidence for the existence of meaningful social subtypes was gathered through investigations that focused on perceptions of faces (not behavior). Thus, we find it somewhat ironic that traditional social psychological models of category representation have undervalued the contribution of within-category variations in behavior.

Subsequent investigations have noted this distinction and investigated the role of facial feature variations among members of other social categories. Maddox and Gray (2002, Study 1) used this evidence of age-related subtypes as a rationale to explore the existence of racial subtypes as a function of skin tone among Blacks. The study used the category confusion paradigm developed by Taylor and colleagues (Taylor, Fiske, Etcoff, & Ruderman, 1978). Black and White participants viewed simulated interactions in which the skin tone of the Black male discussants was varied through digital manipulation. Following this task, participants were unexpectedly asked to match each statement with the discussant who had made it. Inferences about category representation can be drawn when examining the pattern of errors made on this task. *Within-category* errors occurred when participants confused the correct discussant with a person from within the *same* skin tone category (confusion among light-skinned or among dark-skinned discussants). *Between-category* errors occurred when participants confused the correct discussant with someone from the *opposite* skin tone category (confusion between light-skinned *and* dark-skinned discussants). The results revealed that participants made more within-category than between-category errors, suggesting that they attended to, encoded, and used the skin tone of the discussants in making their statement assignments.

Evidence also suggests that the salience of skin tone is malleable. Contextual factors may operate to make skin tone more or less salient. Guided by the model of social category salience proposed by Blanz (1999) that considers both person and contextual factors, Maddox and

Chase (2004) used the category confusion paradigm to investigate contextual influences on the salience of skin tone-based subcategories. Two experiments demonstrated that a manipulation of issue relevance during a group discussion among light- and dark-skinned Blacks enhanced the category salience of skin tone, revealed in the pattern of within- and between-category errors. Discussion topics relevant to the racial politics of skin tone (race relations in the United States) led to increased skin tone salience as compared to neutral topics (potential leisure activities or environmental issues). Group membership seemed to make little difference. Across both the Maddox investigations, the pattern of skin tone category salience occurred for both Black and White participants, suggesting that skin tone cued meaningful subcategories in these perceivers. The same was true of age-related subtypes for both young (Brewer et al., 1981) and elderly (Brewer & Lui, 1984) perceivers. Thus, sensitivity to subtypes of a category may be similar for perceivers regardless of their own membership in the category.

How Face-Related Subcategory Membership Affects Stereotyping and Prejudice

Research suggesting that within-group facial feature variation may be associated with meaningful subcategory is complemented by evidence that this subcategory membership affects stereotyping and prejudice. Brewer et al. (1981) used a paradigm in which participants made trait associations for photographs representing two types of subsets of elderly people. *Meaningful* subsets consisted of photographs of individuals from one of the proposed subtypes: grandmothers, elder statesmen, or senior citizens. *Nonmeaningful* subsets consisted of photographs of members taken from each subtype, representing the superordinate category. Participants were shown six sets of photographs independently in a random order. Each set consisted of three photos. In the meaningful condition, subjects saw two sets consisting of photographs from each subtype, totaling six sets. In the nonmeaningful condition, participants saw six sets, each consisting of one photograph from each subtype (thereby representing the superordinate category). Participants were also presented with a checklist of 44 trait adjectives taken from previous research on stereotypes of the elderly and asked to indicate those personality traits on the checklist that the three people pictured had in common. Comparison of the number of traits checked off for each subset as well as the content of those traits indicated that (1) more traits were checked off for meaningful versus nonmeaningful subsets and (2) that trait content agreement was greater *within* meaningful subsets than *between* meaningful subsets.

In other words, participants checked off the same traits for similar sub-types and different traits for dissimilar subtypes. In addition, many of the characteristics associated with different subtypes were distinct from those associated with the superordinate category. These findings were presented as evidence that the richest trait associations are found at the subtype level (grandmothers, elder statesmen, and senior citizens) and not the superordinate level (elderly people).

Since that demonstration, others studies have interpreted these find-ings as the result of facial cues activating subcategory membership and associated stereotypes. For instance, Dixon and Maddox (2005) used a digital manipulation of skin tone and race among a multiple-race sample of participants. They varied the race and skin tone of an alleged perpe-trator in a crime story. Participants were exposed to a crime story briefly featuring optionally, a White, light-skinned Black, medium-skinned Black, or dark-skinned Black perpetrator. Dixon and Maddox assessed whether exposure to these stories could influence various story-related judgments among viewers. There were no differences in impression judg-ments as a function of skin tone. However, among heavy news viewers, they did find that the brief exposure to a photo of a dark-skinned Black perpetrator during a crime story led to more emotional discomfort about the story than exposure to a White perpetrator associated with the same story. No differences surfaced when comparing dark-skinned Black and light-skinned Black perpetrators or when comparing light-Black and White perpetrators. The authors suggested that, compared to the light-skinned Black perpetrator, the dark-skinned Black perpetrator achieved a certain threshold to activate category stereotypes associating Blacks and criminality. It appeared that dark-skinned Blacks represented a dis-tinct subcategory of Blacks (those more associated with criminality) from light-skinned Blacks. Facial feature subcategory associations also exist on an implicit level. Using an implicit association test (IAT) that paired high and low prototypic Hispanic faces with positive and nega-tive attributes, Uhlmann, Dasgupta, Elgueta, Greenwald, and Swanson (2002) found implicit preference for less typical Hispanic faces over more typical Hispanic faces among both light-skinned and dark-skinned Hispanic participants. These authors also interpreted their findings as reflecting meaningful subcategories of individuals of Hispanic descent.

Theses studies suggest that facial features measured implicitly or explicitly may exert an influence over the categorization and judgment of individuals who belong to the same superordinate category. Spe-cifically, facial features may activate meaningful subcategories with rich trait and affective associations. This perspective stands in contrast to the assumptions of traditional models of impression formation that fail to recognize a role for facial feature-related subtypes. In the next section, we consider another role of facial features that traditional models fail to capture, a role that is entirely independent of categorization processes.

Facial Cues and "Feature Bias"

Blair and colleagues (Blair, 2006; Blair, Chapleau, & Judd, 2005; Blair, Judd, & Chapleau, 2004; Blair, Judd, & Fallman, 2004; Blair, Judd, Sadler, & Jenkins, 2002) have examined the role of racial phenotypic features and racial category membership in stereotyping of Black and White men depicted in photographs. In a seminal series of studies (Blair et al., 2002), White participants were asked to rate the faces of Black and White males for their degree of fit with descriptive scenarios. These faces varied in the extent to which the individuals exhibited features that were considered Afrocentric (e.g., dark brown skin, broad nose, full lips, and coarse hair). The scenarios described behaviors that were stereotypical or counterstereotypical of Black or White Americans. Not surprisingly, the researchers found strong evidence for traditional racial category-based stereotyping. However, they also observed a phenomenon they termed "feature bias"—stereotyping and prejudice based on Afrocentric features even when controlling for the influence of racial category membership—on judgments of both Black *and* White males. In other words, regardless of the race of the person pictured, faces with more Afrocentric features we stereotyped more than those with less Afrocentric features. This suggests that White perceivers are using elements of the Black American stereotype to make judgments of White males who exhibit Afrocentric features. As such, these findings represent evidence that contradicts the predictions of more traditional models of impression formation that have assumed that stereotype use is mediated by categorization.

The influence of racial feature variation has also been demonstrated in tasks designed to measure indirect and direct implicit evaluations (Livingston, 2001; Livingston & Brewer, 2002; Uhlmann et al., 2002). Livingston (2001, Study 3) explored the role of individual differences in the information value of Afrocentric facial features on implicit evaluative priming. Livingston hypothesized that individual differences in the belief that external physical characteristics are related to internal personality characteristics would predict the use of physical (facial) cues in social judgments. In this experiment, participants identified as high or low in this reliance on perceptual cues were supraliminally primed with several faces of males and females, each of whom was either Black or

White. As the manipulation of facial appearance, the last block of faces contained either high prototypic or low prototypic Blacks. The researchers examined the influence of this manipulation on the interpretation of a Donald paragraph (Srull & Wyer, 1979) that described a race-unspecified target who performs a series of ambiguously aggressive behaviors (relevant to the stereotype of Blacks). While the results of a recognition task demonstrated that all participants were sensitive to variations in physical prototypicality, only participants who were high in their reliance on perceptual cues were influenced by the priming manipulation. These participants made more stereotypic evaluations of the ambiguous target presented in the paragraph after being primed with high prototypic compared to low prototypic faces. Participants low on this index of perceptual cue reliance showed no differentiation in response to high and low prototypic primes. In addition to demonstrating an indirect implicit influence of racial feature variation on evaluation, these results suggest that individuals may exhibit different degrees of sensitivity to this variation.

Providing more direct evidence of the implicit influence of racial feature variation on evaluation, Livingston and Brewer (2002) found that highly prototypic Black faces were associated with more negative implicit evaluations than less prototypic Black faces. They used a sequential priming paradigm (Fazio, Jackson, Dunton, & Williams, 1995) that measured affective reactions to Black faces that were high and low in racial prototypicality. In two experiments, automatic evaluative responses indicated negative evaluations of Black faces that were high in racial prototypicality as compared to those that were low in racial prototypicality (Experiments 1 and 5). Evidence from another experiment suggests that facial characteristics elicit preconscious cue-based processing prior to, or in lieu of, category-based processing (Experiment 3). In this experiment, participants completed a conceptual judgment task involving stereotype-relevant words instead of the evaluative task used in other experiments. Responses to these words were not affected by manipulations of racial prototypicality, a finding that suggests a limited influence of category knowledge.

It should be noted that, while the Livingston investigations described here focused mainly on implicit evaluations, the research by Blair and her colleagues described above provides evidence for the influence of facial features on explicit semantic and evaluative judgments. More importantly, each of these lines of research strongly suggests a role for facial features that is not mediated by categorization processes. That is, they point to a direct association between facial cues and category-relevant thoughts and feelings that is independent of the categorization of the target. These findings represent a significant deviation from the assumptions of traditional models of impression formation. We now turn to some interesting lines of research that extend our understanding of the boundaries of facial feature influences.

Exploring the Complexities of Facial Cue-Based Social Judgments

Not content to "simply" demonstrate the influence of facial feature variation on social thought and evaluation, researchers have begun to explore the implications of facial feature variation for more nuanced aspects of intergroup perception. Blair et al. (2005) examined the interaction between Afrocentric features and diagnostic information on stereotypic judgments. Previous research has focused on the extent to which a target's racial category membership and behavior may influence stereotypic judgments of him or her. That research has demonstrated that, under certain conditions, diagnostic behavioral information can override the influence of a category stereotype (e.g., Locksley, Borgida, Brekke, & Hepburn, 1980). These researchers wondered whether the same was true with respect to the influence of feature-based stereotypes. A majority White sample of participants was presented with several photographs of Blacks who varied in perceived Afrocentricity. Each photograph was paired with descriptions of four situations in which the person was reported to have behaved aggressively (stereotype-consistent) or nonaggressively (stereotype-inconsistent). Participants' task was to estimate the likelihood that each target would behave aggressively or nonaggressively in a fifth situation. Results showed that participants relied heavily on the behavioral information when making a prediction about aggression in the fifth scenario. However, the presence of Afrocentric features was also a significant, albeit weaker, influence.

These findings fall outside the scope of the predictive lens provided by traditional theoretical models. As such, feature-based stereotyping and prejudice may pose additional problems for those interested in counteracting their influence. Sczesny, Spreemann, and Stahlberg (2006) explored the role of gender stereotypical physical appearance on perceptions of competence. Across two experiments, participants viewed a description and photograph of a man or woman who had either stereotypically masculine or feminine facial characteristics. Using direct (Experiment 1) and indirect (Experiment 2) measures of leadership competence, participants viewed stereotypically masculine targets as more competent than stereotypically feminine targets. However, the results of the direct measure reflected more favorable ratings toward women, while the indirect measure revealed a bias in favor of men. But why the divergence in the direction of sex stereotyping using direct and indirect measures? The authors posited that, while the direct measure was subject to control by participants who may not want to display sex biases in responding, the indirect measure was not.

Indeed, research has demonstrated that, while category-based stereotyping may be controlled or mitigated, feature-based stereotyping is a highly efficient process that may operate unabated. Researchers have used a variety of methods to attempt to disrupt feature-based stereotyping, with little success. For example, Blair (2006) used the face inversion technique to explore the efficiency of Afrocentric features in stereotyping. Research on the face inversion effect (Valentine, 1991) reveals that inverted faces are less easily recognized compared to upright faces, a finding that is attributed to the disruption of holistic processing of a face. In her research, Blair (2006) presented Black faces of varying degrees of Afrocentricity and asked participants to rate the degree to which stereotype-relevant paragraphs described each face. Half of the participants saw upright faces while conducting this task, while the others saw inverted faces. The results revealed that faces with a greater degree of Afrocentric appearance were stereotyped more, both positively and negatively, than faces with a less Afrocentric appearance. Supporting the argument that facial feature stereotyping is highly efficient, face inversion did not affect the degree of stereotyping based on Afrocentric features.

Similar evidence on the efficiency of feature-based stereotyping was provided by Sczesny and Kühnen (2004), who examined the role of perceived gender stereotypical physical appearance on perceptions of leadership competence. Participants reviewed the application materials for a potential job candidate accompanied by a photograph of a man or woman who was stereotypically masculine or feminine in facial appearance (operationalized as short vs. long hair, large vs. small nose, and strong vs. fine features). While reporting their impression of the candidates, participants were also placed under conditions of low or high cognitive capacity. Results revealed that the use of the sex category was influenced by the capacity manipulation but the use of physical features was not. Specifically, women were rated as more competent than men when cognitive capacity was high, but the reverse was true when capacity was low. Targets with masculine features were rated as more competent that those with feminine features independent of capacity. Thus, cognitive capacity seemed to impair stereotyping based on the sex of the targets but not the gender typicality of their features.

These results parallel evidence provided by Blair, Judd, and Fallman (2004), who used a dual-task manipulation to explore the efficiency of stereotyping on the basis of race and Afrocentric features. Their results showed that cognitive load did not affect the degree of stereotyping based on Afrocentric features. Regardless of cognitive load, targets with more Afrocentric features were stereotyped to a greater degree than those with less Afrocentric features. In a second experiment, participants completed the task either with instructions to suppress their stereotypes about the targets or without such instructions. Participants with suppression instructions were successful in mitigating race-based stereotyping compared to those without. However, the suppression manipulation had no influence on stereotyping based on Afrocentric features, even when the experimenters identified the specific features that participants should be aware of (Blair, Judd, & Fallman, 2004; Experiments 3 and 4). Sczesny and Kühnen (2004) documented a similar effect in a pilot study. Their results showed that, while people are quite aware of the potential influence of biological sex on stereotypes about leadership ability, they are less aware of the potential influence of physical appearance. The conclusion drawn from these studies is that feature-based stereotyping is highly efficient, even more efficient than category-based stereotyping. This efficiency may bypass peoples' attempts to control their stereotyping, perhaps because perceivers are unaware of how features affect judgments.

The failure of attempts at suppression is disheartening, as feature-based stereotyping yields undesirable societal consequences. In addition to disparities based on educational, socioeconomic, and occupational opportunities and other interpersonal outcomes (for reviews see Herring, Keith, & Horton, 2004; Maddox, 2004), feature-based stereotyping has been demonstrated to influence outcomes in the criminal justice system. Blair, Judd, and Chapleau (2004) explored the role of Afrocentricity in criminal sentencing. Photographs and criminal histories for Black and White inmates were sampled from a criminal database maintained by the State of Florida Department of Corrections. Photographs were coded for the presence of Afrocentric features, while criminal histories were coded for several variables, including severity of crime and length of sentence. The results revealed little influence of race on sentencing; Blacks and Whites received sentences of similar length when controlling for crime-relevant factors such as the severity of the crime. However, using the same controls, the presence of Afrocentric features was a significant predictor of longer sentences regardless of the race of the inmate. Because judges are responsible for sentencing offenders in Florida, these archival data strongly imply among judges an ability to adjust for the influence of racial category membership in their sentencing but an inability to do so for Afrocentric features (Blair, 2006). Similar results come from a study by Eberhardt, Davies, Purdie-Vaughns, and Johnson (2006). They asked a (majority White) sample of undergraduates to rate the stereotypicality of faces of 44 Black men who had been convicted of murder in Philadelphia, Pennsylvania, from 1979 to 1999.

When examining the actual sentencing in those cases, they found that stereotypically Black criminal offenders were more likely to have received the death penalty compared to less stereotypically Black offenders. Interestingly, this pattern only held in cases where the victim was White. Nonetheless, these results suggest that the influence of feature-based stereotyping can be quite severe.

Summary

It should be clear that the findings reviewed in this section fall outside the predictive lens of "traditional" theoretical models of impression formation briefly outlined above. Contrary to those perspectives, they suggest (1) sensitivity to within-category feature variation in the determination of subcategory membership and (2) stereotyping and prejudice based on facial features that is independent of categorization or category membership. Furthermore, sensitivity to facial features can lead to novel outcomes such as the reduced impact of diagnostic behavioral information in the use of stereotypes. In addition, they also demonstrate that feature-based stereotyping is a highly efficient process, with potentially severe consequences for its targets. These findings lead us to conclude that a consideration of the face and the information it provides may contribute to a more comprehensive view of social perception, including its antecedents and consequences. This goal may be achieved through revisions to existing models of impression formation that reflect the perceiver's sensitivity to within-category facial feature variation and account for the independent influence of facial features apart from categorization processes.

THE ANTECEDENTS AND CONSEQUENCES
OF FACIAL FEATURE-BASED CATEGORIZATION

Investigations examining the role of facial features in stereotyping, prejudice, and discrimination have contributed to increased attention to the interplay between category knowledge and facial features. When at one time the two went hand in hand, researchers are now beginning to realize that category knowledge and facial features may have independent effects on social judgment. As evidence suggesting that perceivers are sensitive to within-category variation in facial characteristics continues to mount, investigators are increasing their focus on the precursors and implications of facial feature variation for social representations. Some investigations are concerned with the implications of feature variation for categorization, while others have focused on how categorization influences perception of and memory for facial features. We now consider these lines of research.

Category Selection from Facial Cues

Social psychologists have long acknowledged that, because facial features lie on a vast continuum representing a complex array of information, humans may cope with this complexity through categorization by age, race, and sex (Allport, 1954; Fiske, 1998; Fiske & Taylor, 1991). Categorization effectively minimizes the significance of within-category variation, thus making the information provided by features more manageable. There is some question, however, about which features perceivers use to create these categories. Most researchers rely on lay conceptions that specify the features that will lead us to categorize a face as old or young, Black or White, male or female. Very few researchers have sought to verify these lay conceptions empirically. Brown, Dane, and Durham (1998) asked a multiple-race sample of participants to rate the importance of several dimensions of nine facial features (eyes, nose, hair, cheeks, forehead, mouth, skin color, ears, and eyebrows) when deciding whether another person belonged to a racial group. Except for skin color, participants rated the importance of the color, shape, placement on the face, and size of each feature. The researchers manipulated the presumed race/ethnicity of the target of judgment. Participants were asked to rank the features that would be important toward determining whether a person was African, Asian, Caucasian, Hispanic, and a fifth condition where the racial/ethnic group was left unspecified. In the unspecified condition, participants were asked to rank the importance of the features in determining a person's race in general. Overall, participants emphasized skin color among other aspects of phenotypic appearance in determining racial group membership, followed by hair, eyes, nose, mouth, cheeks, eyebrows, forehead, and ears. While the initial analyses examined each racial category in isolation, subsequent analyses used the race-unspecified target as a basis of comparison for each racial category. While skin color remained an important feature overall, the importance of other features varied as a function of the racial category. For Africans, hair, nose, and mouth were rated as more important, while eyes were rated as less important. For Asians, eyes were the distinctive feature. For Hispanics, eyebrows were the distinctive feature. Caucasian targets were rated equally to the race-unspecified target, suggesting that failure to specify race leads to the assumption that the target is White. These data suggest that skin color is the most distinguishing feature for racial categories, but specific racial groups have characteristics that set them apart from others.

Additional evidence suggests that the relative importance of features may depend on the race of the respondent. Deregowski, Ellis, and Shepherd (1975) used a slightly different methodology to investigate attention to facial features. These researchers examined in-group and out-group descriptions of Black and White faces. Black (Kenyan) and White (British) teens were asked to give a verbal description of faces of Black and White males and females. Once coded, these descriptions revealed that neither Blacks nor Whites were likely to mention skin color, although Whites were more likely to mention race when looking at Black faces. Blacks were more likely to mention the outline of the face, hair position, eye size, eyebrows, chin, and ears, while Whites focused on hair texture, hair color, and eye color. There were no significant differences in mentioning features as a function of the race or gender of the face.

These data are largely consistent with many lay conceptions of the relationship among various facial features and racial category membership. However, it is not necessarily the case that lay theories about the features that determine category membership map onto the actual features that people use. To our knowledge, only one study has attempted to delineate the importance of phenotypic facial features for social categorization, independent of lay conceptions. Brown and Perrett (1993) explored the facial features that are used to determine gender. Through morphing, they created prototypic images of male and female faces without hair. In the first part of the study, individual features and pairs of features from these prototypes were presented in isolation to a sample of participants for the purpose of sex categorization. They found that, based on categorization tendencies, the brows and eyes—in combination and each alone—carried the most gender information. These were followed by the jaw, chin, nose and mouth, and mouth. In the second part of the study, participants viewed whole prototypic faces that had been substituted with parts of faces from the other gender prototype. An examination of these feature substitutions on categorization revealed that the effect of feature substitutions were fairly uniform for male and female faces. The categorization of male faces was disrupted most when a female chin, brows and eyes, or jaw was included in the images. Categorization of female faces was disrupted when the substitution was a male jaw or brows and eyes. The sex of the participant played a role in these data as well. Male participants were much more restrictive in their criterion to classify a face as male than female participants. Males required a greater degree of masculinity to categorize a face as male as compared to females.

Neuroimaging techniques have also provided opportunities for researchers to study the antecedents of categorization. Studies of this nature have demonstrated that people are sensitive to information about race and gender within 150 milliseconds of being presented with a face, well before category information is thought to be activated (Ito & Urland, 2003). However, as outlined above, very little research has explored exactly which facial features are used to make categorization judgments. One approach has been to examine how perceivers process faces with ambiguous features. Willadsen-Jensen and Ito (2006) demonstrated that racially ambiguous faces elicited a distinct pattern of event-related potential (ERP) activity as compared to racially distinct faces. White participants viewed faces of Whites and Asians (Experiment 1) or Whites and Blacks (Experiment 2) intermixed with faces that were morphed to appear racially ambiguous. Their task was to categorize each face according to race during ERP recording. Results revealed that, early on, racially ambiguous faces were distinguished from Asian or Black faces but not from White ones. Later judgments do show differentiation of ambiguous faces from other racial groups, though still showing the most similarity to Whites.

Another approach is to attempt to isolate a single feature thought to be important in the categorization of faces. Ronquillo and colleagues (2007) explored the role of skin tone variation in amygdala responses to Black and White faces. White participants were presented with faces of Black and White males whose skin tone had been digitally manipulated to be either light or dark. Results replicated previous research showing greater amygdala activation to out-group faces relative to in-group faces (for reviews, see Eberhardt, 2005, and Phelps & Thomas, 2003). In a novel finding, the data reflected greater activation to dark-skinned faces relative to light-skinned faces. However, while this pattern held for both Black and White faces, it was only statistically reliable for White faces. Follow-up analyses revealed that the dark White, light Black, and dark Black faces led to similar levels of amygdala activation, and each was greater than that elicited by light White faces. To our knowledge, this is the first demonstration of sensitivity to skin tone, or any single phenotypic feature, at the neural level.

It is clear that there is a great deal of work that could be done to explore the role that facial features play in categorization. Through their focus on the relative importance of individual facial features, the work by Brown and colleagues (1998) as well as Deregowski and colleagues (1975) provide some clues to the lay conceptions governing the relationship between facial features and category membership. Unlike the previous studies, the investigation by Brown and Perrett (1993) does not tell us the specific nature of the individual features that are associated with male and female faces. Rather, it provides information about the regions of the face that are most used by participants in determining gender. It is unclear as to whether these regions map onto what participants would report if given the opportunity. The imaging work described here suggests at least some convergence, but some divergence, between lay conceptions of the relationship between facial features and category membership. Rather than dismissing lay perspectives entirely, it may be important to understand them and how they may deviate from the actual processes underlying categorization judgments. Much like previous researchers who pointed out the failure of introspection with respect to understanding the influences on behavior (Nisbett & Wilson, 1977), accurate knowledge of the features that influence our judgments of category membership, or knowledge of how features may affect our judgments directly, could be useful in helping to counteract any undesirable influences. However, we have seen that knowing is only half the battle. It is not clear that even explicit knowledge of the potential of features to influence judgments can mitigate their impact (e.g., Blair, Judd, & Fallman, 2004). More explicit understanding of the processes by which features impact judgments may lead to more successful interventions.

Facial Features and Category Ambiguity: Distortions in Perception and Memory

Rather than exploring facial features as antecedents to categorization, several researchers have explored the relationship between features and categories through investigations of the role that categorization may play in the subsequent recollection of facial features. For example, Corneille, Huart, Becquart, and Brédart (2004) examined the impact of categorization on the recognition of ethnically ambiguous faces. White participants studied a morphed target face that reflected 30%, 50%, or 70% of a particular ethnicity on the Caucasian–North African or the Caucasian–Asian continuum. Category information was introduced through an ethnically distinctive name and stereotypic behavioral profile immediately after studying the target face (Experiment 1) or through a category label associated with the target face during the study phase (Experiment 2). After a distracter task, participants were asked to identify the correct face presented earlier from among the targets and a series of foils, also morphs, representing 10% and 20% deviations from the target in each direction on the continuum. Results revealed that participants selected foils that were consistent with their initial categorizations.

Results from a second identification task conducted 1 week after the original session also showed a pattern of assimilation. However, assimilation to the experimenter-provided categorization did not occur for the most racially ambiguous faces (50% morphs). The authors suggest that this may have occurred because, in general, the category information associated with the highly ambiguous faces did not reflect participants' spontaneous categorizations of the faces.

This overall pattern was partially supported in another set of experiments examining moderately and highly ambiguous faces. Huart, Corneille, and Becquart (2005) used a similar methodology to examine gender ambiguity and found that the recollection of moderately ambiguous faces was distorted toward the typical category member. However, contrary to the finding with ethnicity, recognition of highly gender ambiguous faces that were presented along with categorization cues (first names) was biased toward the category suggested by the cue (Experiment 2). In a third experiment, they determined that this effect took place during encoding of the face: when the names were presented after the initial presentation of the face (during the recognition task), the gender of the name did not influence the choice of distracters. These studies demonstrate that perceiver's knowledge of the features associated with categories can result in the distortion of ambiguous faces in memory, particularly when category information is activated while a face is encoded.

As we have seen in other areas of facial feature processing, individuals may differ in their susceptibility to feature distortions in memory. Eberhardt, Dasgupta, and Banaszynski (2003) demonstrated that category knowledge, paired with individual differences in implicit theories (Levy & Dweck, 1998), can influence memory for faces and facial features. In two studies, White participants were presented with faces morphed from Black and White males. Some versions of each face (the targets) were racially ambiguous, while other versions (the foils) were decidedly either Black or White. Participants studied the ambiguous target photographs, then some demographic information about each person pictured. Embedded in this information was a manipulation of the photographs' apparent race (Black or White) introduced through a category label. Participants were also assigned to conditions according to whether they had been previously identified as an entity theorist or an incremental theorist. Following a second look at the face and a distracter task, participants were presented with two foils, one Black and one White, selected from the same continuum as the target face. The participants' task was to determine which face had been presented. In fact, neither face had been presented. Results from both studies revealed that entity theorists chose foils that were phenotypically more similar to the label that had been associated with the ambiguous target face, while incremental theorists chose faces that were phenotypically dissimilar to the label. In other words, entity theorists showed a pattern of assimilation to the racial category label, while incremental theorists showed a pattern of contrast from the racial category label. In Study 2, participants were presented with the target face again, after the recognition task, and instructed to draw the face as accurately as possible. Judges blind to the experimental conditions rated these faces for racial category membership and found the same pattern of assimilation and contrast for entity and incremental theorists, respectively. This bias in perception occurred despite the fact that the target face was visible to participants for the duration of the drawing task.

In contrast to studies exploring the role that category activation may play in the processing of facial features, Eberhardt, Goff, Purdie, and Davies (2004, Study 4) explored the role of stereotype activation on attention to and memory for faces. The faces used in the study had been sampled from a criminal offender database in Florida and tested for perceived racial stereotypicality of facial features (skin tone, lips, nose, and hair). Participants were a majority White sample of police officers who were primed with crime- or noncrime-related words during a vigilance task, reflecting a manipulation of Black stereotype activation. Next, participants were given a dot-probe task where one Black and one White face were presented side by side for a short duration, followed by a dot probe in the location of one of the two photographs. Their task was to report the location of the dot (left or right) by using the appropriate response key. Next, in a surprise recognition task, they were presented with one lineup of Black faces and another of White faces. In each lineup, only one face (target) had been presented during the dot-probe task. It was accompanied by four distracters: two faces that were more stereotypical and two that were less stereotypical. The results revealed that participants' choices of Black faces during the recognition task varied as a function of exposure to the primes. Those exposed to the crime-related primes were more likely to choose stereotypically Black distracters as compared to those exposed to the primes unrelated to crime. Further supporting the role of stereotype activation on judgments of faces, Eberhardt and colleagues demonstrated that a separate sample of police officers from the same population reported that high stereotypic Black faces looked more like criminals as compared to low stereotypic Black faces (2004, Experiment 5).

Similarly, Oliver, Jackson, Moses, and Dangerfield (2004) found that White participants' memory for the race-related facial characteristics of a photograph that had been presented with a news story was influenced by the stereotypicality of the story. Participants were presented with several news stories, including one story embedded with a composite photograph of a Black male. Four versions of that story varied with respect to its stereotypic association with Blacks and whether or not it described a crime. Participants were asked to read the stories and later completed a memory task. Among these was a face reconstruction task, in which participants used a computer program to reproduce the face of the Black male that had been presented with the story of interest. Based on pretest ratings, that photograph had been constructed with features (noses, mouths, and skin tone) that hovered around the midpoint of the continuum between Afrocentric and Eurocentric features. The memory task revealed a bias in participants' memory of that face. Participants who read stories about violent and nonviolent crime constructed faces that were more Afrocentric than the original face, while participants reading about noncrime-related stories did not, regardless of their stereotypicality.

In addition to the activation of category knowledge, single stereotypic features of a face can affect memory for other stereotype-relevant features of the face. For example, MacLin and Malpass (2001, 2003) identified hairstyle as a feature that can help participants to disambiguate the race of a face. They presented participants with ambiguous race faces—hairless faces with features that overlapped perceived Hispanic and Black racial categories (dark eyes, broad nose, and full lips). By varying the type of hairstyle on these faces, they not only changed the perceived racial category of these faces but also influenced perceptions of other characteristics. Faces presented with a stereotypically Black hairstyle were perceived as having a darker complexion, deeper eyes, a narrower face, and a wider mouth than faces presented with a stereotypically Hispanic hairstyle.

Similarly, the context in which a face is presented can affect the perception of stereotypic features. Levin and Banaji (2006) found evidence for distortions in the perceived lightness and darkness of Black and White faces driven by conceptual knowledge among participants. Across three experiments, a majority White sample of participants was required to match the brightness (skin tone) of a target face to that of a Black or White comparison face. The perceived race of the target face was varied through the presentation of phenotypically Black and White faces (Experiment 1) or line drawings (Experiment 3) or phenotypically ambiguous faces labeled as Black or White (Experiment 2). Using a technique where participants could adjust the brightness of a face or designated sample by using key presses, participants were more likely to match Black faces to darker comparisons than White faces.

These findings suggest that distortions in the perceived skin tone and other facial features may reflect a top-down process. Changes in the perceived category membership of a face appeared to activate associations with typical members of that category and created distortions toward stereotypical values on category-relevant dimensions. These studies demonstrate that category information can be activated through the introduction of a category label, a single category-defining feature, the presence of multiple stereotypical facial features, or (to a lesser extent) a judgment context that reflects a stereotypic trait. Furthermore, they provide some evidence that implicit theories may play a role in determining "objective" perception. The results also converge with research suggesting that other aspects of conceptual knowledge such as perceived facial affect and implicit racial prejudice (Hugenberg & Bodenhausen, 2004) and explicit racial prejudice (Blascovich, Wyer, Swart, & Kibler, 1997) play a role in the categorization of racially ambiguous faces. However, this conclusion should be regarded as tentative. In some investigations, an individual's prejudice level does not contribute to biased perceptions of facial features (Levin & Banaji, 2006; Eberhardt et al., 2003).

Summary

These studies suggest a reciprocal relationship between facial features and social categories. Facial features contribute to the determination of category membership, and category information can distort the perception and recollection of facial features. In addition, these processes are influenced by several factors including the category membership of the perceiver, implicit theories, and (perhaps) prejudice level. More to the point of this chapter, many of these findings reflect questions that might not have been asked from the strict perspective of traditional models of category representation and impression formation; models that neglect the role of facial features in social perception. We now describe a model that attempts to accommodate the findings considered to this point.

EXPLAINING FACIAL FEATURE BIASES

Despite the shortcomings of mainstream models of impression formation that underemphasize the information that can be gained from facial features, we have maintained that these frameworks simply require "tweaking" to begin to address the influence of facial characteristics on social judgments (Maddox, 2004; Maddox & Gray, 2002; Maddox & Chase, 2004). Maddox (2004) outlined a model of racial phenotypicality bias in an effort to align more traditional findings accounted

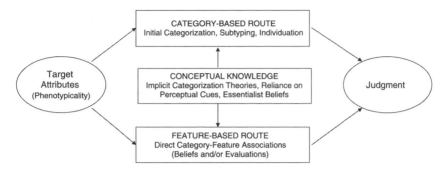

FIGURE 9.1. A model of racial phenotypicality bias. From Maddox (2004). Copyright 2004 by Sage Publications. Reprinted by permission.

for by models of impression formation with evidence that perceivers are sensitive to within-category variations in facial phenotypic appearance (see Figure 9.1). While that discussion focused on race, this model is easily expanded to include any basis of category membership that is informed by facial features (e.g., ethnicity, gender, age, sexual orientation). The model, described briefly here, incorporates suggested revisions to traditional models of person perception (Blair et al., 2002; Maddox & Gray, 2002; Zebrowitz, 1996). Processing begins with the identification of a person's physical attributes that act as cues to salient category dimensions such as age, sex, and race. At this stage, the nature of feature processing diverges into two routes of information processing that operate simultaneously and largely independently.

The Category-Based Route

The first is a category-based route, as proposed by Maddox and Gray (2002), based on traditional approaches to social representation and judgment (Brewer, 1988; Fiske & Neuberg, 1990). Through this route, processing of the target's phenotypic features results in racial categorization. This categorization can be based on either a single salient feature (e.g., skin tone) or a global assessment of multiple features (e.g., Afrocentricity). At this point, the individual may be placed into a relevant subcategory as a function of racial phenotypicality (e.g., light-skinned or dark-skinned), depending on the perceiver's conceptual framework. Only salient subcategory representations may guide the process of categorization. Subcategory use is more or less likely, depending on person characteristics or contextual cues present in the judgment context (Maddox & Chase, 2004). Once a fit between the target and the (sub)category membership is established, associated stereotypes or prejudices (Maddox & Gray, 2002) may be used in interpersonal judgments.

The Feature-Based Route

The second route is feature-based, influencing social perception apart from the traditional range of category-based processing. This route employs direct associations between phenotypic features and stereotypic traits (Blair et al., 2002) or prejudiced affect (Livingston & Brewer, 2002). These associations may be learned over time or may reflect innate knowledge of social information that may be overgeneralized to other individuals with similar features (Zebrowitz, 1996). An important aspect of this route is that phenotype continues to influence target judgments in situations even when racial categorization overrides within-race variations through the category-based route (Blair et al., 2002). Furthermore, the information that features convey will be applied regardless of the target's racial category membership (Blair et al., 2002; Secord, 1958; Zebrowitz, 1996) and is less subject to conscious control (Blair et al., 2005).

The Role of Conceptual Knowledge

The model also recognizes varieties of conceptual knowledge that may guide the processing of target attributes through both the category-based route and the feature-based route. Possibilities include metaphorical associations with various colors (Secord, 1958), early childhood experiences with lightness and darkness (Williams, Boswell, & Best, 1975), essentialist beliefs (Haslam, Rothschild, & Ernst, 2002), implicit causal theories (Medin & Ortony, 1989), cultural standards of physical attractiveness (Breland, 1998), and beliefs about the relationship between physical features and personality (Livingston, 2001). Each of these and other factors may contribute to category-based and/or feature-based judgments.

CONCLUSION

Our goal in this chapter is not to suggest that category-based accounts of stereotyping and prejudice developed through studies focused on behavioral variability among social targets are uninformative. To the contrary, categorization may very well override the significance of within-category facial variability in many, perhaps even most, situations. Instead, we maintain that these views are unable to deal with the complex nature of social perception and particularly the indirect and direct contribution of facial features to social stereotyping, prejudice, and discrimination. The model we concluded with here represents an attempt at integrating recent research examining facial features with traditional approaches focused on behavior in the realm of racial stereotyping and prejudice. As our review highlights, the landscape of face prejudice research is dominated by investigations of race. However, similar attempts at integration may focus on any other basis of categorization that is informed by facial cues. Hopefully, the work described here will represent the beginning of a sustained empirical emphasis on the face and all of the social information that it affords.

REFERENCES

Allport, G. W. (1954). *The nature of prejudice*. Cambridge, MA: Addison-Wesley.

Atkinson, D. R., Brown, M. T., Parham, T. A., Matthews, L. G., Landrum-Brown, J., & Kim, A. U. (1996). African American client skin tone and clinical judgments of African American and European American psychologists. *Professional Psychology: Research and Practice, 27,* 500–505.

Berry, D. S., & McArthur, L. Z. (1986). Perceiving character in faces: The impact of age-related craniofacial changes on social perception. *Psychological Bulletin, 100,* 3–18.

Blair, I. V. (2006). The efficient use of race and Afrocentric features in inverted faces. *Social Cognition, 24,* 563–579.

Blair, I. V., Chapleau, K. M., & Judd, C. M. (2005). The use of Afrocentric features as cues for judgment in the presence of diagnostic information. *European Journal of Social Psychology, 35,* 59–68.

Blair, I. V., Judd, C. M., & Chapleau, K. M. (2004). The influence of Afrocentric facial features in criminal sentencing. *Psychological Science, 15,* 674–679.

Blair, I. V., Judd, C. M., & Fallman, J. L. (2004). The automaticity of race and Afrocentric facial features in social judgments. *Journal of Personality and Social Psychology, 87,* 763–778.

Blair, I. V., Judd, C. M., Sadler, M. S., & Jenkins, C. (2002). The role of Afrocentric features in person perception: Judging by features and categories. *Journal of Personality and Social Psychology, 83,* 5–25.

Blanz, M. (1999). Accessibility and fit as determinants of the salience of social categorizations. *European Journal of Social Psychology, 29,* 43–74.

Blascovich, J., Wyer, N. A., Swart, L. A., & Kibler, J. L. (1997). Racism and racial categorization. *Journal of Personality and Social Psychology, 72,* 1364–1372.

Bodenhausen, G. V., & Macrae, C. N. (1998). Stereotype activation and inhibition. In R. S. Wyer Jr. (Ed.), *Advances in social cognition* (Vol. 11, pp. 1–52). Mahwah, NJ: Erlbaum.

Bodenhausen, G. V., & Macrae, C. (2006). Putting a face on person perception. *Social Cognition, 24,* 511–515.

Breland, A. M. (1998). A model for differential perceptions of competence based on skin tone among African Americans. *Journal of Multicultural Counseling and Development, 26,* 294–311.

Brewer, M. B. (1988). A dual-process model of impression formation. In T. K. Srull & R. S. Wyer (Eds.), *Advances in social cognition: A dual process model of impression formation* (pp. 1–36). Hillsdale, NJ: Erlbaum.

Brewer, M. B., Dull, V., & Lui, L. (1981). Perceptions of the elderly: Stereotypes as prototypes. *Journal of Personality and Social Psychology, 41,* 656–670.

Brewer, M. B., & Feinstein, A. S. H. (1999). Dual processes in the cognitive representation of persons and social categories. In S. Chaiken & Y. Trope (Eds.), *Dual-process theories in social psychology* (pp. 255–270). New York: Guilford Press.

Brewer, M. B., & Lui, L. (1984). Categorization of the elderly by the elderly: Effects of perceiver's category membership. *Personality and Social Psychology Bulletin, 10,* 585–595.

Brown, E., & Perrett, D. I. (1993). What gives a face its gender? *Perception, 22,* 829–840.

Brown, T. D., Dane, F. C., & Durham, M. D. (1998). Perception of race and ethnicity. *Journal of Social Behavior and Personality, 13,* 295–306.

Corneille, O., Huart, J., Becquart, E., & Brédart, S. (2004). When memory shifts toward more typical category exemplars: Accentuation effects in the recollection of ethnically ambiguous faces. *Journal of Personality and Social Psychology, 86,* 236–250.

Deregowski, J. B., Ellis, H. D., & Shepherd, J. W. (1975). Descriptions of White and Black faces by White and Black subjects. *International Journal of Psychology, 10,* 119–123.

Dixon, T. L., & Maddox, K. B. (2005). Skin tone, crime news, and social reality judgments: Priming the schema of the dark and dangerous Black criminal. *Journal of Applied Social Psychology, 35,* 1555–1570.

Eberhardt, J. L. (2005). Imaging race. *American Psychologist, 60,* 181–190.

Eberhardt, J. L., Dasgupta, N., & Banaszynski, T. L. (2003). Believing is seeing: The effects of racial labels and implicit beliefs on face perception. *Personality and Social Psychology Bulletin, 29,* 360–370.

Eberhardt, J. L., Davies, P. G., Purdie-Vaughns, V. J., & Johnson, S. L. (2006). Looking deathworthy: Perceived stereotypicality of Black defendants predicts capital-sentencing outcomes. *Psychological Science, 17,* 383–386.

Eberhardt, J. L., Goff, P. A., Purdie, V. J., & Davies, P. G. (2004). Seeing Black: Race, crime, and visual processing. *Journal of Personality and Social Psychology, 87,* 876–893.

Fazio, R. H., Jackson, J. R., Dunton, B. C., & Williams, C. J. (1995). Variability in automatic activation as an unobstrusive measure of racial attitudes: A bona fide pipeline? *Journal of Personality and Social Psychology, 69,* 1013–1027.

Fiske, S. T. (1998). Stereotyping, prejudice, and discrimination. In D. T. Gilbert, S. T. Fiske, & G. Lindzey (Eds.), *The handbook of social psychology* (4th ed., Vol. 2, pp. 357–411). New York: McGraw-Hill.

Fiske, S. T., Lin, M., & Neuberg, S. L. (1999). The continuum model: Ten years later. In S. Chaiken & Y. Trope (Eds.), *Dual-process theories in social psychology* (pp. 231–254). New York: Guilford Press.

Fiske, S. T., & Neuberg, S. L. (1990). A continuum of impression formation, from category-based to individuating processes: Influences of information and motivation on attention and interpretation. In M. P. Zanna (Ed.), *Advances in experimental social psychology* (Vol. 23, pp. 1–74). San Diego, CA: Academic Press.

Fiske, S. T., & Taylor, S. E. (1991). *Social cognition* (2nd ed.). New York: McGraw-Hill.

Haslam, N., Rothschild, L., & Ernst, D. (2002). Are essentialist beliefs associated with prejudice? *British Journal of Social Psychology, 41,* 87–100.

Herring, C., Keith, V. M., & Horton, D. H. (Eds.). (2004). *Skin deep: How race and complexion matter in the "color-blind" era.* Chicago: University of Illinois Press.

Huart, J., Corneille, O., & Becquart, E. (2005). Face-based categorization, context-based categorization, and distortions in the recollection of gender ambiguous faces. *Journal of Experimental Social Psychology, 41,* 598–608.

Hugenberg, K., & Bodenhausen, G. V. (2004). Ambiguity in social categorization: The role of prejudice and facial affect in race categorization. *Psychological Science, 15,* 342–345.

Ito, T. A., & Urland, G. R. (2003). Race and gender on the brain: Electrocortical measures of attention to the race and gender of multiply categorizable individuals. *Journal of Personality and Social Psychology, 85,* 616–626.

Kunda, Z., & Thagard, P. (1996). Forming impressions from stereotypes, traits, and behaviors: A parallel-constraint-satisfaction theory. *Psychological Review, 103,* 284–308.

Levin, D. T., & Banaji, M. R. (2006). Distortions in the perceived lightness of faces: The role of race categories. *Journal of Experimental Psychology: General, 135,* 501–512.

Levy, S. R., & Dweck, C. S. (1998). Trait- versus process-focused social judgment. *Social Cognition, 16,* 151–172.

Livingston, R. W. (2001). What you see is what you get: Systematic variability in perceptual-based social judgment. *Personality and Social Psychology Bulletin, 27,* 1086–1096.

Livingston, R. W., & Brewer, M. B. (2002). What are we really priming? Cue-based versus category-based processing of facial stimuli. *Journal of Personality and Social Psychology, 82,* 5–18.

Locksley, A., Borgida, E., Brekke, N., & Hepburn, C. (1980). Sex stereotypes and social judgment. *Journal of Personality and Social Psychology, 39,* 821–831.

MacLin, O. H., & Malpass, R. S. (2001). Racial categorization of faces: The ambiguous race face effect. *Psychology, Public Policy, and Law, 7,* 98–118.

MacLin, O. H., & Malpass, R. S. (2003). The ambiguous-race face illusion. *Perception, 32,* 249–252.

Maddox, K. B. (2004). Perspectives on racial phenotypicality bias. *Personality and Social Psychology Review, 8,* 383–401.

Maddox, K. B., & Chase, S. G. (2004). Manipulating category salience: Further evidence for skin tone-based representations of Black Americans. *European Journal of Social Psychology, 34,* 533–546.

Maddox, K. B., & Gray, S. A. (2002). Cognitive representations of Black Americans: Reexploring the role of skin tone. *Personality and Social Psychology Bulletin, 28,* 250–259.

Mason, M. F., Cloutier, J., & Macrae, C. (2006). On construing others: Category and stereotype activation from facial cues. *Social Cognition, 24,* 540–562.

Medin, D. L., & Ortony, A. (1989). Psychological essentialism. In S. Vosniadou & A. Ortony (Eds.), *Similarity and analogical reasoning* (pp. 179–195).

Nisbett, R. E., & Wilson, T. D. (1977). Telling more than we can know: Verbal reports on mental processes. *Psychological Review, 84,* 231–259.

Oliver, M. B., Jackson, R. L., II, Moses, N. N., & Dangerfield, C. L. (2004). The face of crime: Viewers' memory of race-related facial features of individuals pictured in the news. *Journal of Communication, 54,* 88–104.

Phelps, E. A., & Thomas, L. A. (2003). Race, behavior, and the brain: The role of neuroimaging in understanding complex social behaviors. *Political Psychology, 24,* 747–758.

Ronquillo, J., Denson, T. F., Lickel, B., Lu, Z.-L., Nandy, A., & Maddox, K. B. (2007). The effects of skin tone on race-related amygdala activity: An fMRI investigation. *Social Cognitive and Affective Neuroscience, 12,* 39–44.

Rothbart, M., & John, O. P. (1985). Social categorization and behavioral episodes: A cognitive analysis of effects of intergroup contact. *Journal of Social Issues, 41,* 81–104.

Sczesny, S., & Kühnen, U. (2004). Meta-cognition about biological sex and gender-stereotypic physical appearance: Consequences for the assessment of leadership competence. *Personality and Social Psychology Bulletin, 30,* 13–21.

Sczesny, S., Spreemann, S., & Stahlberg, D. (2006). Masculine = competent? Physical appearance and sex as sources of gender-stereotypic attributions. *Swiss Journal of Psychology—Schweizerische Zeitschrift fur Psychologie—Revue Suisse de Psychologie, 65,* 15–23.

Secord, P. F. (1958). Facial features and inference processes in interpersonal perception. In R. Tagiuri & L. Petrullo (Eds.), *Person perception and interpersonal behavior* (pp. 300–315). Stanford, CA: Stanford, University Press.

Secord, P. F. (1959). Stereotyping and favorableness in the perception of Negro faces. *Journal of Abnormal and Social Psychology, 59,* 309–314.

Secord, P. F., Bevan, W., & Katz, B. (1956). The negro stereotype and perceptual accentuation. *Journal of Abnormal and Social Psychology, 53,* 78–83.

Srull, T. K., & Wyer, R. S. (1979). The role of category accessibility in the interpretation of information about persons: Some determinants and implications. *Journal of Personality and Social Psychology, 37,* 1660–1672.

Taylor, S. E., Fiske, S. T., Etcoff, N. L., & Ruderman, A. J. (1978). Categorical and contextual bases of person memory and stereotyping. *Journal of Personality and Social Psychology, 36,* 778–793.

Uhlmann, E., Dasgupta, N., Elgueta, A., Greenwald, A. G., & Swanson, J. (2002). Subgroup prejudice based on skin color among Hispanics in the United States and Latin America. *Social Cognition, 20,* 198–226.

Valentine, T. (1991). A unified account of the effects of distinctiveness, inversion, and race in face recognition. *The Quarterly Journal of Experimental Psychology A: Human Experimental Psychology, 43A*, 161–204.

Willadsen-Jensen, E. C., & Ito, T. A. (2006). Ambiguity and the timecourse of racial perception. *Social Cognition, 24*, 580–606.

Williams, J. E., Boswell, D. A., & Best, D. L. (1975). Evaluative responses of preschool children to the colors White and Black. *Child Development, 46*, 501–508.

Zebrowitz, L. (1996). Physical appearance as a basis of stereotyping. In C. N. Macrae, C. Stangor, & M. Hewstone (Eds.), *Stereotypes and stereotyping* (pp. 79–120). New York: Guilford Press.

Zebrowitz, L. A. (2006). Finally, faces find favor. *Social Cognition, 24*, 657–701.

CHAPTER 10

The Role of Facial Expression in Person Perception

URSULA HESS
REGINALD B. ADAMS, JR.
ROBERT E. KLECK

T he role of emotional displays in how we perceive and react to others has long been a question posed by students of human behavior. Aristotle, for example, noted that "those who do not get angry at things at which it is right to be angry are considered foolish, and so are those who do not get angry in the right manner, at the right time, and with the right people. It is thought that they do not feel or resent an injury, and that if a man is never angry he will not stand up for himself; and it is considered servile to put up with an insult to oneself or suffer one's friends to be insulted" (Nicomachean Ethics IV.5).

This quote suggests that not only can we accurately perceive felt anger when expressed by others but also that as perceivers of that anger we are likely to draw important inferences regarding the expresser's character. Although the assertion that emotional expressions convey more than just information concerning the emotional state of another has appeared in the writings of many, an empirical examination of this idea has until recently largely been absent from the person perception literature (for some exceptions see Hess, Blairy, & Kleck, 2000; Knutson, 1996).

If one goes back a little over a hundred years to Darwin's seminal work on facial expression (1872/1965), one would find that most of the subsequent research on the perception of emotion has focused on the perceiver's ability to "get" the emotional message. Much effort has been devoted to how such factors as the sex (e.g., Hall, 1990), cultural background (e.g., Matsumoto et. al., 2002), psychiatric status (e.g., Mendlewicz, Linkowski, Bazelmans, & Philippot, 2005), or the perceiver's own arousal (e.g., Niedenthal, Halberstadt, Margolin, & Innes-Ker, 2000) might impact this accuracy. In this process, relatively little attention has been devoted to the issue of the further person perception inferences that a perceiver might draw from the knowledge that a given expresser has displayed a given emotion within a particular social context. Put another way, the perceiver has largely been treated as an emotion expression decoding machine who perceives a given expression independent of the specific expresser or the context in which it is shown. In effect, the investigation into the decoding process generally stops once an emotion label is affixed to the expression. What the perceiver brings to the task by way of social stereotypes or expectations, and what inferences that perceiver makes beyond simply labeling the emotion, has received relatively little attention.

The accuracy perspective is congruent with the neo-Darwinian view that has largely dominated the field since Ekman's (1972) seminal book on facial expression. It essentially sees emotion expressions as strong innate signals generated in response to stimuli that act as unconditioned elicitors (Öhman, 1999). In this view, facial displays result from automatic processes that leave little room for variation. Given the motive to demonstrate the universality of emotional communication via specific facial behavior, individual differences on either the encoding or decoding side have been treated as error variance rather than as variables that might importantly modulate what is perceived in a given expression. This is not to say that the neo-Darwinian perspective has gone unchalleged, but much of this challenge has focused on attempts to undermine the universality assertion rather than on identifying the specific contextual and individual differences that play a role in the encoding and decoding processes (e.g., Russell, 1994).

Yet, it should also be noted that for much of the 20th century Darwin's thesis of universality was rejected out of hand by anthropologists and psychologists committed to a learning approach or to an emphasis on the importance of cultural context in shaping what is displayed on the face (e.g., Birdwhistell, 1970; Kleinberg, 1938). When Ekman and his colleagues (Ekman, Sorenson, & Friesen, 1969) and Izard (1971) independently offered evidence of similar cross-cultural interpretations of prototypical facial displays of specific emotions, those favoring a universality argument and those favoring a position of cultural relativism got into a lively debate. As Niedenthal, Krauth-Gruber, and Ric (2006) note in their recent book, most contemporary psychologists now favor an "interactionist perspective" in which both innate and cultural factors are seen to play some role. A meta-analysis of emotion judgment studies by Elfenbein and Ambady (2002) confirms the reasonableness of such a stance.

As noted earlier, it is our view that the debate concerning decoding accuracy and its implications for a universalist or culturally relative position is partially responsible for the lack of an analysis regarding how affective cues provided by the face may interact with or modulate the nature of the trait inferences and first impressions gained on the basis of facial appearance and emotional displays. This neglect is particularly surprising in that the very channel that transmits the emotion signal, the face, also transmits information about the social context, the social characteristics of the expresser, as well as his or her behavioral intentions. If such information is literally embodied in the expressive display, separating out the information carried by the expression itself from that information carried by all of those cues that co-occur with the expression is admittedly difficult. At the very least one would expect there to be important and complex interactions between information provided by the facial expression and that provided by these co-occuring cues (e.g., whether the expressor is male or female, young or old, an in-group or out-group member, etc.). As we will argue later in this chapter, the Brunswick lens model may be particularly helpful in the task of sorting out some of this complexity.

A set of recent studies by Adams and his colleagues (Adams & Kleck, 2003, 2005; Adams, Gordon, Baird, Ambady, & Kleck, 2003; Hess, Adams, & Kleck, 2007; see also Ganel, Goshen-Gottstein, & Goodale, 2005; Graham & LaBar, 2007; Sander, Granjean, Kaiser, Wehrle, & Scherer, 2007) serves to illustrate just how focused most of the research on facial expression has been on the facial display, independent of other cues that can co-occur within the face. Their specific interest was in the role gaze direction might play in the inferences perceivers draw from given expressions of emotion. Gaze direction is something not usually thought to be part of the emotional expression itself (e.g., Ellsworth & Ross, 1975; Fehr & Exline, 1987). Indeed, the faces employed in nearly all expression decoding studies have used stimuli where the expresser's gaze is directed at the perceiver. The general argument made concerning the effect of direct gaze is that it plays an important role in the perception of the intensity of the emotion but not in the perception of its quality (e.g., Argyle & Cook, 1976; Kleinke, 1986; Webbink, 1986). An obvious reason this might be the case is that direct gaze signals that the perceiver is the object of whatever emotion is being displayed by the expresser and thus captivates attentional resources (Cary, 1978; Ellsworth & Ross, 1975; Grumet, 1999; Macrae, Hood, Milne, Rowe, & Mason, 2002). The several studies published by Adams and his colleagues support the *shared signal hypothesis,* demonstrating that the gaze direction of the expresser can affect the efficiency with which a given display is processed as well as determine the quality of the emotion that will be perceived in a blended or ambiguous expression. They argue that when different facial cues such as the specific expression and the direction of gaze share the same signal value (e.g., approach or avoidance) the shared signal facilitates overall processing efficiency. Others have reported evidence supporting perceptual integration in the processing of these cues. These studies also demonstrate that when gaze and emotion are not of relatively equal discriminability, direct gaze effects do occur (e.g., Graham & LaBar, 2007). Thus, gaze direction appears not only to influence emotion perception but also to do so through the competing processes of direct perceptual integration and indirect attention capture.

If the social and nonsocial information inherent in the face that displays an emotion are important, so also are factors inherent to the perceiver. For example, the stereotypes he or she holds with regard to members of different groups may include presumptions concerning their emotional lives. Two examples of these presumptions are the finding that women are generally thought to be more emotionally expressive of all emotions except anger (Fischer, 1993) and that in most countries individuals from the northern part of a given country are thought to be less emotional than those from the southern part of the country (Pennebaker, Rimé, & Blankenship, 1996). Given the pervasive influence of stereotype knowledge on judgment processes, it is likely that both emotional and trait inferences are influenced by such presumptions. Consistent with this argument, racial stereotypes have recently been demonstrated by Hugenberg and Bodenhausen (2003) to affect emotion processing. Specifically, they found that individuals high in implicit prejudice toward African Americans demonstrated greater readiness to perceive anger in Black faces than in White faces.

In what follows we will review evidence showing that emotion perception processes are impacted by the apparent social group membership of the expresser. We will further show that emotion expressions impact first impressions of the behavioral intentions and personality characteristics of the expresser. The recent call by Bodenhausen and Macrae (2006) to put "a face on social perception" emphasizes the fact that "the face has far more to offer than affective signals alone." Zebrowitz and her colleagues have, of course, been making this argument for many years in regard to neutral facial appearance (see Chapter 8 in this volume). Here we will focus on the complex interactions that exist between facial expressions and other important socially relevant information carried by the face. Further, some attention will be given to the emotional stereotypes the perceiver brings to the situation and how these stereotypes affect what is perceived in any given affective signal. Perceiving others is truly an interactive process to which both the encoder and decoder contribute.

The present work focuses on the human face and the information that both facial morphology and facial expression can provide. However, the voice also transmits information regarding both personality (e.g., Scherer, 1978) and emotion (e.g., Scherer, 2003), as does posture (e.g., Henley, 1977, 1995; Pitterman & Nowicki, 2004). It is likely, therefore, that similar processes to those described below apply to these sources of emotional information as well.

EMOTION PERCEPTION IN A SOCIAL CONTEXT

There are two principal strategies for decoding emotion displays (Kirouac & Hess, 1999). First, in the absence of any contextual information, the sender's expressions can be used to draw inferences regarding his or her presumed emotional state, using a pattern-matching approach (Buck, 1984). This is the strategy tested in most studies of emotion-decoding ability, where participants typically rate the emotions from faces of unknown others. The second strategy depends upon the knowledge that the perceiver possesses regarding both the sender and the social situation in which the interaction is taking place. This information permits the perceiver to take the perspective of the encoder and helps him or her to correctly infer the emotional state that the sender is most likely experiencing.

It is important to note that in everyday life full-blown facial expressions are by far the exception. Rather, what are observed in natural settings are most often weak and transient facial movements. Furthermore, facial expressions are not necessarily expressed in the canonic form established by emotion researchers (e.g., Ekman et al., 1969). Indeed, facial expressions can be expressed partially, or they can be the result of blends that convey different emotions at the same time (Ekman & O'Sullivan, 1991). Thus, in real life, facial expressions rarely occur in the form of clear, prototypical signals, even though such stimuli are the ones most often used in emotion expression research. More commonly, the facial expressions we encounter are weak, elusive, or blended, resulting in a signal that often is ambiguous. This ambiguity itself suggests that significant interpretive work is needed. Particularly in the context of first impressions, this interpretative work will of necessity be partially based on stereotype knowledge about social groups rather than detailed personal knowledge about an individual's emotionality.

The social group context can impact all the sources of information on which decoding strategies depend. Specifically, certain factors that covary with group membership, such as facial appearance, may lead perceivers to interpret the same facial expressive movements quite differently, depending upon the specific nature of the face on which they are displayed. Thus, facial morphological differences between men and women or members of different racial groups may enhance or obscure some expressive elements and hence bias pattern matching. The facial morphology of women and younger individuals, for example, appears to enhance the cues associated with happiness, whereas those of men and older individuals enhance the cues associated with anger (Hess et al., 2007). The facial morphology differences across racial groups may have a similar impact on the clarity of cues associated with specific emotions (Beaupré & Hess, 2005). Further, independent of the cues actually present on the face of another, the perceptions of these are obviously going to be filtered through the goals, concerns, motivations, and stereotypes that individuals bring to an interaction. These factors may attract attention away from or toward the cues specifically linked to particular emotions.

THE ACTIVE PERCEIVER

This view of the decoding process is well described by an adaptation of Brunswick's lens model by Scherer (1978, 2003). According to this model (see Figure 10.1) an emotional state may be externalized via distal indicator cues. This process is influenced by the situational context, the relationship between the encoder and decoder, and the cultural context. Thus, a specific emotional state may be expressed differently or not at all, depending on context variables. Individuals may, for example, express their anger more freely in the presence of understanding friends than in the presence of the boss who caused the anger. The decoder in turn has access not to the distal indicator cues but rather to proximal percepts. This implies that the decoder may not perceive all of the cues that were signaled, perhaps because they were too weak or because the decoder did not pay sufficient attention to note all relevant cues.

Conversely, the decoder may use percepts that are not in fact actual cues regarding the emotional state of the encoder. Malatesta and colleagues (Malatesta, Fiore, & Messina, 1987; Malatesta, Izard, Culver, &

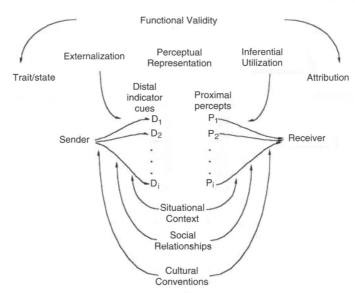

FIGURE 10.1. Modified Brunswik lens model. Adapted with permission from Scherer (1978). Copyright 1978 by Wiley.

Nicolich, 1987), for example, found some evidence that older people are often perceived as sad based on facial morphological cues that are simply due to old age, such as the sagging corners of the eyes and mouth. In this case the perceiver mistakes stable morphological features for expressive cues. Importantly, the interpretation of the proximal percepts is subject to the same social context influences as is the externalization of the distal indicator cues.

INFERRING BEHAVIORAL INTENTIONS AND DISPOSITIONS FROM EMOTION EXPRESSIONS

What happens once an individual has "decoded" an emotion expression? From the perspective of research on decoding ability, the task is done as soon as an emotional label has been affixed to the expression. Yet, as noted earlier, emotion expressions are not just a signal of emotional states. Rather, in many cases, they provide social information to the perceiver. In particular, they provide information regarding the sender's understanding of the situation as well as the sender's behavioral intentions (Hess, Banse, & Kappas, 1995).

In this vein, Frijda, Kuipers, and ter Shure (1989) define emotions as states of action readiness—that is, "the individual's readiness or unreadiness to engage in interaction with the environment" (p. 213). These states have been operationalized with statements such as "I wanted to oppose, to assault; hurt or insult" and "I did not want to oppose, I wanted to yield to someone else's wishes" (p. 213). Thus, states of action readiness describe the behavioral intentions of individuals who experience an emotional state. A person who shows anger also signals an intention to (aggressively) approach the offending other, whereas a person who in the same situation shows sadness, signals impuissance and withdrawal. Consistent with this, research has found that participants detect the apparent approach of angry faces faster than the apparent withdrawal of the same faces (Adams, Ambady, Macrae, & Kleck, 2006).

This view of emotions implies that observers should be able to reverse-engineer an expresser's perception of an emotion-eliciting event. For example, the person showing anger should be perceived as being more dominant because the person sees him- or herself as able to address the situation at hand and attack or resist the opposition. In contrast, the person showing sadness should be perceived as submitting to the situation because they do not see how it is possible to oppose. In short, emotional expressions tell us something about the appraisals being made by the encoder. In turn, these appraisals provide information on the person's dispositions and enduring traits and modulate the first impressions that are formed of him or her. An individual who reacts with anger to failure also signals their belief that they have the power and competence to redress the situation (Lewis, 2000), whereas the person who reacts with sadness tells us that they are at their limit for coping with the failure. This information in turn leads to attributions of personality and ability. Hence, in the context of first impressions, just observing one emotional episode can—as suggested by Aristotle—lead to rather global inferences about the expresser. Thus, knowing how a person reacts emotionally to a specific situation may tell us a lot about the person in general, particularly when encountering him or her for the first time.

Yet, one might wonder whether the same emotional expressions shown by different individuals are perceived in the same way. As noted above, the social context and in particular the social group membership of the expresser impact our perception of emotion expressions. In what follows we will focus on one example of this phenomenon, the perception of anger and happiness in men and women.

SAUCE FOR THE GOOSE IS NOT SAUCE FOR THE GANDER: THE PERCEPTION OF EMOTIONS AS A FUNCTION OF THE GENDER OF THE EXPRESSER

One of the best-documented gender stereotypes regards male and female emotionality. Thus, women report smiling more and are considered by others to smile more than are men. In turn, men's displays of anger have been reported to be both more pervasive and are generally perceived as more acceptable than are women's displays of this emotion (Brody & Hall, 2000; Fischer, 1993; Hall, Carney, & Murphy, 2002). These observed differences in emotional expressivity between men and women are accompanied by strong stereotypical expectations that individuals hold regarding sex differences in emotionality. These expectations are socialized early and can have dramatic consequences for the perception of emotion in others. For example, not only adults but even children as young as 5 years old tend to consider a crying baby as "mad" when the baby is assumed to be a boy but not when the same baby is assumed to be a girl (Condry & Condry, 1976; Haugh, Hoffman, & Cowan, 1980).

These generalized expectations regarding men and women's emotion displays are not without consequences for human emotion communication. Specifically, they seem to influence how men and women's facial expressions are perceived. For example, Gaelick, Bodenhausen, and Wyer (1985) found that husbands tend to interpret the simple absence of smiling during a marital dispute as a sign of hostility on the part of their wives, whereas wives tend to interpret the simple absence of hostility displays by their husbands in such disputes as a sign of love. Further, Hess, Blairy, and Kleck (1997) found that facial expressions of happiness and sadness are better recognized and rated as more intense when shown by a woman, whereas anger expressions are better recognized and rated as more intense when shown by a man. Given that the expressions used in this study were taken from a standardized set with careful control of the expressions, it is unlikely that the actual expressions were different across the sexes. However, there is an element in the stimuli used by Hess et al. that differed between men and women—the degree of social dominance communicated by the faces. Male faces are generally rated as showing more dominance than are female faces, and this difference tends to be quite large. In the study by Hess, Blairy, and Kleck (2000), men who displayed anger or happiness were rated about three times more dominant than women showing the same expressions.

These considerations offer an alternative—albeit related—explanation for the findings by Hess et al. (1997). Specifically, the stereotype bias in emotion perception they reported may not be directly related to the sex of the sender per se but could be mediated by the perceived dominance of the sender. The perception of dominance is strongly confounded with the sex of a stimulus person, in part because the morphological cues associated with perceived high dominance such as a square jaw, thick eyebrows, and receding hairlines (Keating, 1985; Senior, Phillips, Barnes, & David, 1999) are generally more typical for men than for women.

Hess et al. (2007) proposed the notion that some aspects of facial expressive behavior and morphological cues to dominance and affiliation are equivalent in both their appearance and their effects on emotional attributions. This notion is partially based on Darwin's (1872/ 1965) suggestion of an equivalence between certain emotional behaviors in animals and more enduring morphological appearance characteristics. Importantly in the present context, he proposed that piloerection and the utterance of harsh sounds by "angry" animals are "voluntarily" enacted to make the animal appear larger and hence a more threatening adversary (see, e.g., pp. 95 and 104). Recent work using connectionist modeling provides evidence for a perceptual overlap between the physical cues and the meanings derived from them along the dominance and affiliation continua (Zebrowitz, Kikuchi, & Fellous, 2007; see also Calder & Young, 2005, for a review of related work using principal components analyses).

The notion of a functional equivalence between morphology and expression also implies that there are important interactions between facial expressions and facial morphology in the decoding of expressions of emotion. Specifically, persons with dominant-appearing faces may not only be perceived as particularly capable of anger but also when anger is expressed on such a face it should be seen as quite intense. Likewise, a more affiliative-appearing face displaying happiness may be seen as happier than would a less affiliative face displaying the identical facial movement.

We initially tested the functional equivalence hypothesis by examining differences in the attribution of emotions to men and women (Hess, Adams, & Kleck, 2004, 2005).[1] In general, individuals attribute higher levels of emotional expressivity to women than to men with the exception of anger, which is seen as more frequent in men (see, e.g., Fischer, 1993). This pattern is also found when participants are presented with vignettes describing a specific emotion-eliciting event (Hess, Senécal, et al., 2000). These stereotypical expectations regarding men and women's emotionality seem to be strongly normative (Hess et al., 2005).

In a correlational design, Hess et al. (2005) showed that the differences in perceived dominance and affiliation, as a function of facial appearance differences between men and women, mediate the perception of emotionality. To test this expectation experimentally, men's and women's faces were equated with regard to the level of dominance and affiliation they convey. Specifically, the interior of the face contains markers of dominance and affiliation (i.e., square jaw, heavy eyebrows), whereas hairstyle is a very potent marker of sex but not of social motives. Thus, by combining androgynous interior faces with male and female hairstyles, apparent men and women with identical facial appearance can be created. For both neutral faces and posed emotion displays

(Adams, Hess, & Kleck, 2007, Study 4; Hess et al., 2004, Study 2) parallel findings obtained such that for ratings of anger and happiness a pattern opposite to the gender stereotypical pattern was found. That is, when equated for facial appearance, apparent women were seen as more likely to show anger and less likely to show happiness than were apparent men. Similarly, expressions of anger by apparent women were rated as more intense and their expressions of happiness as less intense than when the identical expressions appeared on the faces of apparent men.

This reversal demands an explanation, as it suggests that intrinsically, facial appearance being equal, women are perceived as more anger-prone and less likely to be happy than are men. We propose that this reversal is due to the equivalence between morphological and expressive cues of dominance and affiliation, which leads to an interaction between these two sets of cues. That is, anger expressions emphasize some of the features that make a face appear dominant (e.g., the mouth region often appears especially square, and frowning reduces the distance between eyebrows and eyes). Conversely, smiling enhances the appearance of roundness of the face that is associated with perceived affiliation motivation and babyishness. Due to the manner in which the present stimuli were constructed, the expressive cues for anger and happiness were not "compensated for" by gender-typical appearance (the faces were chosen specifically because they were androgynous and were credible as either male or female). In some ways one could say that by depriving the interior of the face of clear gender cues we actually amplified the expressive cues to anger in women and happiness in men, which are normally "obscured" or reduced by the gender-typical facial appearance.

To reiterate, we are arguing that facial morphology and certain emotional expressions are parallel messaging systems with regard to the emotion inferences they generate. However, to the degree that both morphology and expression have to use the same "canvas" to communicate, there is a possibility of perceptual interference. Specifically, some of the same facial features that signal dominance and affiliation are used in expressive behavior and hence change appearance. In this process the facial appearance cues can either enhance or attenuate the perceived intensity of the expression. The implications of these findings for more general person perception processes should be obvious. Hess et al. (2007) also report the results of an experiment designed to assess the relative contributions of gender, the gender role stereotype, and facial appearance on men and women's perceived emotionality. The findings suggest that while both of the latter do influence these perceptions, gender per se does not. This implies that knowledge about gender roles and the perceptual effects of facial morphology combine to make men appear more anger-prone and their expressions more angry, whereas women are seen as more likely to smile and their smiles to be indicative of greater happiness.

The research by Hess et al. (2004, 2005, 2007) serves to highlight the influence of facial morphology on the perception and interpretation of emotional facial expressions. In a similar vein, Marsh, Adams, and Kleck (2005) found evidence for functional equivalence between mature versus babyfacedness, on the one hand, and the signal value of angry versus fear faces, on the other. Yet, it is clear that not all traits that may be attributed to a person on the basis of facial appearance have a functional equivalence in expressive displays. There is no evidence, for example, that facial expressions lead to such trait attributions as trustworthiness or conscientiousness even though these are also traits of great relevance to a social species.

In sum, emotional facial expressions, via their shared signal value with morphological trait cues, signal behavioral intentions to perceivers. In turn, the morphological cues contained in the face tend to bias the decoding of emotion expressions in a manner consistent with those cues. Thus, men's anger and women's smiles are stronger signals for these specific affects because they are supported by an underlying facial morphology consistent with each of those expressions. Conversely, women's anger and men's smiles are partially veiled by the morphological context in which they are shown.

ANGRY PEOPLE ARE TOUGHER

As mentioned earlier, emotional expressions have signal value not only because of their functional equivalence to morphological cues but also because they inform us about the expresser's appraisals of the social situation. These include the motivational goals and resources that the expresser is perceived to bring to the situation.

Appraisal theories of emotion (see, e.g., Ellsworth & Scherer, 2003) lead to clear predictions regarding the personality inferences that observers will likely draw from facial expressive displays alone. Although appraisal theories vary with regard to both the number of appraisal categories they include and the exact definition of these categories, there is substantial overlap. Thus, a simplified model of the emotion-eliciting process as conceived of by appraisal theories starts with the perception of a change in the environment by the organism (novelty). This change is evaluated by the person according to its likely degree of pleasantness or benefit for him or her. Put another way, the change is responded to in accordance with whether it is either consistent with the motivational state of the individual or obstructs the individual's goals. The individuals also evaluate their ability to cope with or adjust to the change. Yet a further set of evaluations is made in regard to the correspondence with relevant social and personal norms.

Importantly, appraisals relate to the subjective perception of the stimulus and not its objective characteristics. That is, different people may appraise the same situation differently, and different situations may lead to the same appraisals in different people. To cite an example, if I am walking through the woods and encounter a bear, my perception of the bear's presence would be one of very high goal obstruction, and I would be most uncertain regarding my coping potential in that instance. However, if my neighbor is bear hunting and encounters the same bear, he will evaluate the bear's presence as goal-conducive and his coping potential as high. I would probably experience panic, whereas he is likely to experience elation. It therefore follows that, when someone sees my expression of panic in the above situation, they can deduce my lack of felt competence to deal with the situation even if this is the first time they have seen me in such a context.

Following this logic, we can predict that expressions of anger and happiness (which both presume power to be high) should be perceived as reflecting social dominance. It should be noted that this prediction for happiness, which is signaled by smiling behavior, differs from views that focus upon the appeasement function of smiles (e.g., Henley, 1977, 1995; LaFrance & Henley, 1994). In contrast, expressions of sadness and fear presume low power and should be perceived as signaling low dominance. With regard to disgust, appraisal theories do not specify a level of power; yet, as part of the contempt—anger—disgust triad (Rozin, Lowery, Imada, & Haidt, 1999), it should be perceived similarly to anger. Based on an appraisal of controllability and power, anger should further signal competence, whereas sadness or fear should signal incompetence with regard to the emotion-eliciting object at hand. Also, because anger is elicited by goal obstruction, it should signal the presence of some sort of undesirable event.

Appraisal theories of emotion, however, do not allow us directly to predict attributions of affiliation. Yet, smiling is generally a sign of affiliation (see, e.g., Hess, Beaupré, & Cheung, 2002). Fear has also been argued to elicit affiliative reactions in conspecifics (Bauer & Gariépy, 2001; Marsh et al., 2005). Anger directed at the perceiver, in contrast, signals danger and should be perceived as low in affiliative intent (e.g., Aronoff, Woike, & Hyman, 1992). Also, sadness, which signals a greater tendency to withdraw (see, e.g., Argyle & Cook, 1976; Fehr & Exline, 1987), should be perceived as less affiliative.

In recent years, a limited number of studies have largely supported these predictions. Knutson (1996), for example, showed still photos with facial expressions of anger, fear, disgust, sadness, and happiness to participants and asked them to provide their assessment of the targets' dominance and affiliation. As predicted above, angry and disgust expressions lead to high attributions of dominance and low attributions of affiliation. Individuals who showed happiness expressions were perceived as high in both dominance and affiliation. In contrast, individuals who showed sadness or fear were rated as low in dominance. However, they were not rated as high in affiliative intent. Hess, Blairy, and Kleck (2000) essentially replicated these effects but were able to show that these attributions were moderated by the gender and ethnicity of the expresser and varied with the intensity of the expression. Thus, weak smiles were already perceived as signaling affiliation, whereas only strong frowns signaled dominance.

The issue of whether emotion expressions can provide information concerning an individual's competence was addressed in studies by Lewis (2000) and Tiedens (2001). Tiedens conducted a series of studies showing that more status is conferred on an individual who shows anger rather than sadness and that this effect is mediated by the perceived competence of the expresser. Lewis (2000) also found that a manager who showed anger in response to bad news was perceived as more competent than a manager who showed sadness, but only when the manager was a man. Women were perceived as equally low in competence regardless of which emotion they showed, but as high in competence when they reacted with a neutral expression. It is possible that the generally negative view of emotional women in the workplace mediates this specific effect, showing again the impact of the social context on the perception and interpretation of emotions and on person attributions.

Finally, Hareli et al. (2007) found that individuals who displayed anger when presenting a complaint were judged to be more subjectively credible—that is, were judged to feel harmed—but only when the complaint was of an ambiguous nature. In this case, given the ambiguity of the objective situation, the display of anger emphasized the goal obstruction perceived by the complainant and thereby rendered the complainant more credible.

In sum, the above research shows that facial expressions of emotion express more than just emotion. Rather, they are informative about an individual's behavioral intentions and of the goals and resources that an individual is perceived to bring to the situation. These perceptions in turn allow us to extrapolate from the specific context to the trait and dispositional nature of the person. Such extrapolations may play a particularly important role in the formation of first impressions.

BE CAREFUL WHEN SHARING YOUR ANNOYANCE:
THE INFLUENCE OF TALKING ABOUT
AN ANGER EVENT ON LIKABILITY

In the preceding section we have demonstrated that when people are shown pictures, short videos, or vignettes of angry people they rate these individuals as particularly high in dominance and toughness but also to some degree as unlikable. Yet, all of these are very "thin behavioral slices" (Ambady, Bernieri, & Richeson, 2000), in which only very limited information is transmitted. What happens if people interact with a person for a longer period and have a variety of occasions to see that person behave? In this case will anger still drive attributions of personality characteristics? We investigated this question as part of a larger study. In this study 144 participants were paired in 72 male–female dyads. Psychophysiological measures were taken, and participants saw each other during electrode preparation. They then played a game together for about 10 minutes during which they habituated to the electrodes. Following this, a status manipulation was conducted. Participants were then randomly assigned to one of two conditions: either they had to tell their interaction partner about a happiness-eliciting event in their life or about an anger-eliciting event. At the end of the experiment participants were separated and asked, among other questions, to give their impression of their interaction partner, using a series of adjectives. The adjective pairs (sociable vs. not sociable, friendly vs. unfriendly, likable vs. not likable, interested vs. uninterested, tender vs. hard, and good vs. bad) were combined into one likability scale (a = .86). A marginally significant emotion effect was found, $F(1, 130)$ = 2.75, p = .099 as well as a significant Emotion × Status interaction, $F(2, 130)$ = 5.55, p = .005, which was qualified by an Emotion × Status × Sex interaction, $F(2, 130)$ = 7.58, p = .001. Overall, as expected, individuals who were randomly assigned to talk about an anger-eliciting event they had experienced were perceived as less likable than were individuals who were assigned to talk about something that made them happy. There were two exceptions though. First, women rated men of equal status as more likable when they related an anger story than when they related a happiness story. Second, men rated higher-status women as least likable regardless of the emotional tone of their story.

These data highlight the two central issues we have discussed in this chapter. First, they show that emotion expressions can have an important impact on first impressions. What is noteworthy in this regard is that participants were in one another's presence for more than 1.5 hours by the time they made their judgments. Of this time, less than

10 minutes were devoted to the actual telling of the story. In addition, they saw their interaction partner interact with the experimenters during set-up, they interacted themselves with the partner during the initial game playing session, and the partner also listened to their story. Thus, they had a variety of sources of information to draw from when making their judgments. In addition, participants were aware that the partner had not chosen the topic but that the topic had been assigned by the experimenter. Nonetheless, the emotional tone of the story impacted on their impressions of the interaction partner's likability and traits.

Second, the data also show that emotion expressions are not interpreted in a social vacuum. The social context, in this case the gender and status of the interaction partner, moderated the judgments. It is noteworthy that for women with superior status the emotional tone of the story did not make a difference: they were rated as less likable. This parallels the findings by Hess, Adams, and Kleck (2005), who found that for women who are described as high in dominance the expression of anger is perceived as normatively appropriate, yet at the same time they are rated as less likable than are men expressing the same emotion. Fischer (2002) has called this effect the "bitch" factor.

CONCLUSION

As Aristotle already knew, what we express emotionally and the circumstances in which we express these affects reveals a great deal to others about what we are like as persons. Hence, when we see someone for the first time, his or her emotional reactions to the situation or elements of it have considerable informative value regarding the nature of the person. Emotions are not expressed in a social vacuum. In fact, the very medium that transmits emotional information, the face, also transmits information about important social characteristics of an individual. This information, especially when we first meet someone and do not have individuating information at hand, will moderate not only our perception of the emotions expressed but also our perceptions of the individual expressing them. In our view, research on emotion perception has greatly underestimated the complexity of these processes and the important social information that can be derived from where and when and by whom these expressions are displayed. In addition, the perceiver is not a passive processor of these expressions but filters the available cues through, among other things, the lenses of social stereotypes and the nature of their social relationship with the expresser.

ACKNOWLEDGMENT

Preparation of this chapter was supported by a National Science Foundation Grant (No. 0544533) to Robert E. Kleck, Ursula Hess, and Reginald B. Adams, Jr., and a grant from the Social Sciences and Humanities Research Council to Ursula Hess.

NOTE

1. Note that the *functional equivalence hypothesis* differs from the previously mentioned *shared signal hypothesis* in that the latter refers only to shared meaning among facial cues whereas the former refers to shared meaning derived via the resemblance of one cue to another, a notion building on Darwin's observation that expression can mimic stable appearance in the service of eliciting similar responses.

REFERENCES

Adams, R. B., Jr., Ambady, N., Macrae, C. N., & Kleck, R. E. (2006). Emotional expressions forecast approach–avoidance behavior. *Motivation and Emotion, 30*, 177–186.

Adams, R. B., Jr., Hess, U., & Kleck, R. E. (2007). *Emotion in the neutral face: The influence of gender-emotion stereotypes and gender-related facial appearance*. Manuscript submitted for publication.

Adams, R. B., Jr., Gordon, H. L., Baird, A. A., Ambady, N., & Kleck, R. E. (2003). Effects of gaze on amygdala sensitivity to anger and fear faces. *Science, 300*, 1536.

Adams, R. B., Jr., & Kleck, R. E. (2003). Perceived gaze direction and the processing of facial displays of emotion. *Psychological Science, 14*, 644–647.

Adams, R. B., Jr., & Kleck, R. E. (2005). The effects of direct and averted gaze on the perception of facially communicated emotion. *Emotion, 5*, 3–11.

Ambady, N., Bernieri, F., & Richeson, J. (2000). Towards a histology of social behavior: Judgmental accuracy from thin slices of behavior. In M. P. Zanna (Ed.), *Advances in experimental social psychology* (Vol. 32, pp. 201–272). New York: Academic Press.

Argyle, M., & Cook, M. (1976). *Gaze and mutual gaze*. Oxford, NY: Cambridge University Press.

Aronoff, J., Woike, B. A., & Hyman, L. M. (1992). Which are the stimuli in facial displays of anger and happiness? Configurational bases of emotion recognition. *Journal of Personality and Social Psychology, 62*, 1050–1066.

Bauer, D. J., & Gariépy, J. L. (2001). The functions of freezing in the social interactions of juvenile high- and low-aggressive mice. *Aggressive Behavior, 27*, 463–475.

Beaupré, M. G., & Hess, U. (2005). Cross-cultural emotion recognition among

Canadian ethnic groups. *Journal of Cross-Cultural Psychology, 36,* 355–370.

Birdwhistell, R. L. (1970). *Kinesics and context: Essays on body motion communication.* Oxford, UK: University of Pennsylvania Press.

Bodenhausen, G. V., & Macrae, C. N. (2006). Putting a face on person perception. *Social Cognition, 5,* 511–515.

Brody, L. R., & Hall, J. A. (2000). Gender, emotion, and expression. In M. Lewis & J. M. Haviland (Eds.), *Handbook of emotions* (2nd ed., pp. 447–460). New York: Guilford Press.

Buck, R. (1984). Nonverbal receiving ability. In R. Buck (Ed.), *The communication of emotion* (pp. 209–242). New York: Guilford Press.

Calder, A. J., & Young, A. W. (2005). Understanding the recognition of facial identity and facial expression. *Nature Reviews Neuroscience, 6,* 641–651.

Cary, M. S. (1978). The role of gaze in the initiation of conversation. *Social Psychology Quarterly, 41,* 269–271.

Condry, J., & Condry, S. (1976). Sex differences: A study in the eye of the beholder, *Child Development, 47,* 817.

Darwin, C. (1965). *The expression of the emotions in man and animals.* Chicago: University of Chicago Press. (Originally published 1872)

Ekman, P. (1972). *Emotion in the human face.* New York: Pergamon Press.

Ekman, P., & O'Sullivan, M. (1991). Facial expression: Methods, means, and moues. In R. S. Feldman & B. Rimé (Eds.), *Fundamentals of nonverbal behavior* (pp. 163–199). Cambridge, UK: Cambridge University Press.

Ekman, P., Sorenson, E. R., & Friesen, W. V. (1969). Pan-cultural elements in facial displays of emotion. *Science, 164* (3875), 86–88.

Elfenbein, H. A., & Ambady, N. (2002). Is there an in-group advantage in emotion recognition? *Psychological Bulletin, 128,* 243–249.

Ellsworth, P. C., & Ross, L. (1975). Intimacy responses to direct gaze. *Journal of Experimental Social Psychology, 11,* 592–613.

Ellsworth, P. C., & Scherer, K. R. (2003). Appraisal processes in emotion. In R. J. Davidson, H. Goldsmith, & K. R. Scherer (Eds.), *Handbook of affective sciences.* New York and Oxford, UK: Oxford University Press.

Fehr, B. J., & Exline, R. V. (1987). Social visual interaction: A conceptual and literature review. In A. W. Siegman & S. Feldstein (Eds.), *Nonverbal behavior and communication* (pp. 225–325). Hillsdale, NJ: Erlbaum.

Fischer, A. H. (1993). Sex differences in emotionality: Fact or stereotype? *Feminism & Psychology, 3,* 303–318.

Fischer, A. H. (2002, July 20–24). Anger politics: *Why women are (seen as) bitches.* Paper presented at the 12th conference of the International Society for Research on Emotion, Cuenca, Spain.

Frijda, N. H., Kuipers, P., & ter Shure, E. (1989). Relations between emotion appraisal and emotional action readiness. *Journal of Personality and Social Psychology, 57,* 212–228.

Gaelick, L., Bodenhausen, G. V., & Wyer, R. S. (1985). Emotional communication in close relationships. *Journal of Personality and Social Psychology, 49,* 1246–1265.

Ganel, T., Goshen-Gottstein, Y., & Goodale, M. (2005). Interactions between the processing gaze direction and facial expression. *Vision Research, 49,* 1911–1200.

Graham, R., & LaBar, K. S. (2007). The Garner selective attention paradigm reveals dependencies between emotional expression and gaze direction in face perception. *Emotion, 7,* 296–313.

Grumet, G. W. (1999). Kinesic cues: The body, eyes, and face. In L. K. Guerrero & J. A. DeVito (Eds.), *The nonverbal communication reader: Classic and contemporary readings* (pp. 48–89). Prospect Heights, IL: Waveland Press.

Hall, J. A. (1990). *Nonverbal sex differences: Accuracy of communication and expressive style.* Baltimore, MD: Johns Hopkins University Press.

Hall, J. A., Carney, D. R., & Murphy, N. A. (2002). Gender differences in smiling. In M. H. Abel (Ed.), *An empirical reflection on the smile* (pp. 155–185). New York: Edwin Mellen Press.

Hareli, S., Harush, R., Suleiman, R., Cosette, M., Bergeron, S., Lavoie, V., et al. (2007). *When scowling may be a good thing: The influence of anger expressions on credibility.* Manuscript submitted for publication.

Haugh, S. S., Hoffman, C. D., & Cowan, G. (1980). The eye of the very young beholder: Sex typing of infants by young children. *Child Development, 51,* 598–600.

Henley, N. M. (1977). *Body politics: Power, sex and nonverbal communication.* Englewood Cliffs, NJ: Prentice Hall.

Henley, N. M. (1995). Body politics revisited: What do we know today? In P. J. Kalbfleisch & M. J. Cody (Eds.), *Gender, power, and communication in human relationships* (pp. 27–61). Hillsdale, NJ: Erlbaum.

Hess, U., Adams, R. B., Jr., & Kleck, R. E. (2004). Facial appearance, gender, and emotion expression. *Emotion, 4,* 378–388.

Hess, U., Adams, R. B., Jr., & Kleck, R. E. (2005). Who may frown and who should smile? Dominance, affiliation, and the display of happiness and anger. *Cognition and Emotion, 19,* 515–536.

Hess, U., Adams, R. B., Jr., & Kleck, R. E. (2007). When two do the same it might not mean the same: The perception of emotional expressions shown by men and women. In U. Hess & P. Philippot (Eds.), *Group dynamics and emotional expression.* New York: Cambridge University Press.

Hess, U., Banse, R., & Kappas, A. (1995). The intensity of facial expression is determined by underlying affective state and social situation. *Journal of Personality and Social Psychology, 69,* 280–288.

Hess, U., Beaupré, M. G., & Cheung, N. (2002). Who to whom and why—cultural differences and similarities in the function of smiles. In M. Abel & C. H. Ceia (Eds.), *An empirical reflection on the smile* (pp. 187–216). New York: Edwin Mellen Press.

Hess, U., Blairy, S., & Kleck, R. E. (1997). The intensity of emotional facial expressions and decoding accuracy. *Journal of Nonverbal Behavior, 21,* 241–257.

Hess, U., Blairy, S., & Kleck, R. E. (2000). The influence of expression intensity, gender, and ethnicity on judgments of dominance and affiliation. *Journal of Nonverbal Behavior, 24,* 265–283.

Hess, U., Senécal, S., Kirouac, G., Herrera, P., Philippot, P., & Kleck, R. E. (2000).

Emotional expressivity in men and women: Stereotypes and self-perceptions. *Cognition and Emotion, 14,* 609–642.

Hugenberg, K., & Bodenhausen, G. V. (2003). Facing prejudice: Implicit prejudice and the perception of facial threat. *Psychological Science, 14,* 640–643.

Izard, C. E. (1971). *The face of emotion.* East Norwalk, CT: Appleton-Century-Crofts.

Keating, C. F. (1985). Human dominance signals: The primate in us. In S. L. Ellyson & J. F. Dovidio (Eds.), *Power, dominance, and nonverbal communication* (pp. 89–108). New York: Springer Verlag.

Kirouac, G., & Hess, U. (1999). Group membership and the decoding of nonverbal behavior. In P. Philippot, R. Feldman, & E. Coats (Eds.), *The social context of nonverbal behavior* (pp. 182–210). New York: Cambridge University Press.

Kleinke, C. L. (1986). Gaze and eye contact: A research review. *Psychological Bulletin, 100,* 78–100.

Kleinberg, O. (1938). Emotional expression in Chinese literature. *Journal of Abnormal and Social Psychology, 33,* 517–520.

Knutson, B. (1996). Facial expressions of emotion influence interpersonal trait inferences. *Journal of Nonverbal Behavior, 20,* 165–182.

LaFrance, M., & Henley, N. M. (1994). On oppressing hypotheses: Or differences in nonverbal sensitivity revisited. In H. L. Radtke & H. J. Stam (Eds.), *Power/gender: Social relations in theory and practice. Inquiries in social construction* (pp. 287–311). London: Sage.

Lewis, K. M. (2000). When leaders display emotion: How followers respond to negative emotional expression of male and female leaders. *Journal of Organizational Behavior, 21,* 221–234.

Macrae, C. N., Hood, B. M., Milne, A. B., Rowe, A. C., & Mason, M. F. (2002). Are you looking at me? Gaze and person perception. *Psychological Science, 13,* 460–464.

Malatesta, C. Z., Fiore, M. J., & Messina, J. J. (1987). Affect, personality, and facial expressive characteristics of older people. *Psychology and Aging, 2,* 64–69.

Malatesta, C. Z., Izard, C. E., Culver, C., & Nicolich, M. (1987). Emotion communication skills in young, middle-aged, and older women. *Psychology and Aging, 2,* 193–203.

Marsh, A. A., Adams, R. B., Jr., & Kleck, R. E. (2005). Why do fear and anger look the way they do? Form and social function in facial expressions. *Personality and Social Psychological Bulletin, 31,* 73–86.

Matsumoto, D., Consolacion, T., Yamada, H., Suzuki, R., Franklin, B., Paul, S., et al. (2002). American-Japanese cultural differences in judgments of emotional expressions of different intensities. *Cognition and Emotion, 16,* 721–747.

Mendlewicz, L., Linkowski, P., Bazelmans, C., & Philippot, P. (2005). Decoding emotional facial expressions in depressed and anorexic patients. *Journal of Affective Disorders, 89,* 195–199.

Niedenthal, P. M., Halberstadt, J. B., Margolin, J., & Innes-Ker, A. H. (2000). Emotional state and the detection of change in facial expression of emotion. *European Journal of Social Psychology, 30,* 211–222.

Neidenthal, P. M., Krauth-Gruber, S., & Ric, F. (2006). *Psychology of emotion: Interpersonal, experiential, and cognitive approaches*. New York: Psychology Press.

Öhman, A. (1999). Distinguishing unconscious from conscious emotional processes: Methodological consideration and theoretical implications. In T. Dalgleish & M. J. Power (Eds.), *Handbook of cognition and emotion* (pp. 765–782). Chichester, UK: Wiley.

Pennebaker, J. W., Rimé, B., & Blankenship, V. E. (1996). Stereotypes of emotional expressiveness of northerners and southerners: A cross-cultural test of Montesquieu's hypothesis. *Journal of Personality and Social Psychology, 70*, 372–380.

Pitterman, H., & Nowicki, S., Jr. (2004). A test of the ability to identify emotion in human standing and sitting postures: The diagnostic analysis of nonverbal accuracy-2 Posture test (DANVA2-POS). *Genetic, Social and General Psychology Monographs, 130*, 146–162.

Rozin, P., Lowery, L., Imada, S., & Haidt, J. (1999). The CAD triad hypothesis: A mapping between three moral emotions (contempt, anger, disgust) and three moral codes (community, autonomy, divinity). *Journal of Personality and Social Psychology, 76*, 574–586.

Russell, J. A. (1994). Is there universal recognition of emotion from facial expression? A review of cross-cultural studies. *Psychological Bulletin, 115*, 102–141.

Sander, D., Grandjean, D., Kaiser, S., Wehrle, T., & Scherer, K. R. (2007). Interaction effects of perceived gaze direction and dynamic facial expression: Evidence for appraisal theories of emotion. *European Journal of Cognitive Psychology, 19*, 470–480.

Scherer, K. R. (1978). Personality inference from voice quality: The loud voice of extroversion. *European Journal of Social Psychology, 8*, 467–487.

Scherer, K. R. (2003). Vocal communication of emotion: A review of research paradigms. *Speech Communication, 40*, 227–256.

Senior, C., Phillips, M. L., Barnes, J., & David, A. S. (1999). An investigation into the perception of dominance from schematic faces: A study using the worldwide web. *Behavior Research Methods, Instruments and Computers, 31*, 341–346.

Tiedens, L. Z. (2001). Anger and advancement versus sadness and subjugation: The effect of negative emotion expressions on social status conferral. *Journal of Personality and Social Psychology, 80*, 86–94.

Webbink, P. (1986). *The power of the eyes*. New York: Springer.

Zebrowitz, L. A., Kikuchi, M., & Fellous, J. M. (2007). Are effects of emotion expression on trait impressions mediated by babyfaceness? Evidence from connectionist modeling. *Personality and Social Psychology Bulletin, 33*, 296–313.

CHAPTER 11

Putting Facial Expressions Back in Context

HILLEL AVIEZER
RAN R. HASSIN
SHLOMO BENTIN
YAACOV TROPE

Imagine yourself walking alone down a dark alley after midnight. Suddenly, you freeze. The man seen in Figure 11.1 is standing straight ahead of you. In a split second, you recognize the anger so strongly evident by the expression on his face and by his tightly clenched fist. Terrified, you turn around, running for your life. Two long minutes later, you are safe in the main street.

Admittedly, this scenario might seem to be taken from yet another rejected Hollywood script, and such an event would certainly prove quite rare in our everyday life. Nevertheless, it captures an essential but seemingly forgotten truth, namely, that facial expressions are typically perceived in a rich context (Russell, 2003; Trope, 1986). In our everyday experiences, angry faces might be accompanied by clenched fists, sad faces are more frequent at funerals than at weddings, and disgusted faces seem to be paired with that unidentified lump of mold growing at the back of our refrigerator. From an evolutionary standpoint, it seems safe to assume that our ancestors had no exposure to isolated facial expres-

FIGURE 11.1. A basic facial expression from Ekman and Friesen (1976). All images of facial expressions in this chapter are reproduced with permission from the Paul Ekman Group.

sions. It is thus implausible that our ability to recognize facial expressions and map them into emotion categories evolved in complete isolation from our ability to recognize the context in which the faces are embedded. It is very surprising, therefore, that while literally hundreds of studies have examined the perception of isolated facial expressions, only a handful have asked how the perception of the expressions on faces might be influenced by their natural surroundings. In fact, with a few exceptions (e.g., Meeren, van Heijnsbergen, & de Gelder, 2005), most contemporary accounts of the perception of facial expressions ignore the role of context altogether.

On the other hand, the neglect of context in studies of face perception might be justified. After all, certain facial configurations tend to be highly reliable (though not infallible) indicators of the internal emotional state, and there is a strong tendency for these configurations to be similar across human cultures (e.g., Ekman, 1993; Keltner, Ekman, Gonzaga, & Beer, 2003). According to this logic, basic emotional facial expressions directly reflect the emotional state of the person expressing them (Buck, 1994). In fact, in some cases (e.g., threat-related expressions) it might even prove advantageous to ignore irrelevant or distracting contextual information and extract the signal directly from the face. According to this line of thought, our ability to recognize prototypical basic facial expressions accurately would surely be maintained regardless of the context in which they appear. Or . . . would it?

Let us revisit the threatening foe depicted in Figure 11.1, undeniably, not the person we would hope to encounter in a dark alley (or probably any other location). Now, take a close look at his face, and try to ignore his waving clenched fist. How would you describe the facial expression? Is it sad? Is it surprised? Perhaps you see the expression as happy, disgusted, or fearful? If you were anything like the participants in our studies, you would have described his facial expression as angry. It might then seem surprising to discover that his facial expression is actually one carefully posed to signal the prototypical and universal muscular movements of disgust (Ekman & Friesen, 1976). Nevertheless, when the expression is viewed in a context suggesting aggression, the disgusted quality of the expression seems to be lost, and the face appears angry.

This fact is particularly surprising given that anger and disgust are actually very different basic emotions at almost every possible level of analysis (Rozin, Haidt, & McCauley, 2000; Panksepp, 1998). Anger has been described as an innate emotional reaction to an actual or perceived threat (Panksepp, 1998). In contrast, disgust is, at its core, a defense against the incorporation of contaminated foods, and as this emotion develops, the revulsion extends as far as to include immoral acts (Haidt, McCauley, & Rozin, 1994; Rozin & Fallon, 1987).

How, then, is it possible that prototypical disgust faces seen in an anger-inducing context (such as the one in Figure 11.1) become nearly indistinguishable from angry faces in an anger context? As we will later show, such effects occur over a wide range of facial expressions placed in a wide range of contexts. Thus, in contrast to the prevailing view of facial expressions, discrete facial configurations do not exhibit a one-to-one mapping with specific emotion categories.

CHAPTER OUTLINE

We start this chapter by briefly reviewing past work on context and facial expressions.[1] As we will see, most studies did not directly address the question of how context might influence the perception of facial expressions themselves.

We next review three diverging views with regard to the most basic, irreducible, emotional information that is assumed to be read-out from the facial configuration in a context-immune manner. We will show that one's stance regarding the atoms of emotion perception bears directly on one's expectations regarding face–context interactions.

Finally, we present a model and empirical studies showing that context changes the perception of facial expressions in a systematic manner. Specifically, dramatic context effects can be predicted from the physical and perceptual similarity that is shared between the configurations of different facial expressions.

RESEARCH ON FACIAL EXPRESSIONS: HISTORICAL NOTES

The eminent naturalist Charles Darwin is frequently cited as the father of current research on facial expressions. Yet, Darwin himself acknowledged that much important work on the topic had been done prior to the publication of his *The Expression of Emotions in Man and Animals* 1965/1872). For example, Bell (1806) described in detail the physiology and anatomy related to facial expressions. Similarly, Duchenne (1862) conducted extensive research on the physiology and classification of facial muscles by electrically stimulating the facial muscles of his models. Both Bell and Duchenne shared a very clear creationist view of the nature of facial expressions. Naturally, they viewed these expressions as a special God-given gift. Consequently, facial expressions were considered at that time uniquely human (Fridlund, 1994).

It was in this context that Darwin's goal in *The Expression of Emotions in Man and Animals* should be understood (Fridlund, 1994). In his treatise, Darwin passionately challenged the notion that facial expressions were uniquely human by demonstrating similarities between expressions in man and animals. In addition, even if his methodology lacked scientific rigor, Darwin was the first to conduct several cross-cultural studies seeking evidence for the universality of human facial expressions (Ekman, 1999).

Darwin concluded that facial expressions are universal, and by doing so he laid the foundations for decades of research to come. The notion of universality implied that emotional facial configurations served as stable, predictable, and accurate signals. After all, a signal that would change its meaning every time it appears would hardly qualify as a universal indicator of any specific emotion (Carroll & Russell, 1996). Interestingly, despite the popularity and importance of Darwin's book, it would take nearly a century for his ideas on facial expressions to influence the scientific community.

EXPRESSIONS IN CONTEXT: EARLY RESEARCH

Between the years 1914 to 1940, many psychologists were preoccupied with the basic question of whether accurate judgments of emotion from facial expressions were at all possible (reviewed by Ekman, Friesen, & Ellsworth, 1972). Experimenting with expressions in context became a popular tool for answering this fundamental question. Notably, although these researchers experimented with facial expressions in context, their motivation was not to understand the complex interactions between these two sources of emotion information. Rather, they attempted to prove or disprove the popular notion that facial expressions were clear emotional signals.

In an influential study, Landis (1924) photographed facial expressions while the "actors" were engaged in various emotion-evoking situations (e.g., smelling ammonia, being shocked, looking at pornographic pictures, decapitating a rat, etc). He then presented the images of the evoked expressions to a new group of participants and asked them to describe the photographed person's emotion. Landis's findings were striking: the observers' judgments were not consistently related to the actual emotions supposedly elicited by the emotional situations. He concluded that "it is practically impossible to name accurately the 'emotion' being experienced by a subject when one has only a photograph of the face on which to base the judgment." Face expressions, argued Landis, are amorphous. Take away the information provided by the situational context, and the expressions lose their ability to convey information about an individual's internal emotional state.

Other studies did not yield such extreme conclusions. Nevertheless, they demonstrated an important role for contextual information. Within this research framework, Goodenough and Tinker (1931) developed a technique that would later dominate the field. In their paradigm, a facial expression was presented with a short story serving as context. For example, Goodenough and Tinker presented their participants with a facial expression (e.g., a smiling face) and a short verbal vignette (e.g., just heard his best friend died) and asked observers to judge what emotion was felt by that person. Their results showed that both facial expressions and their context were important in the attribution of emotion to others. In the same vein, Munn (1940) presented participants with candid pictures from magazines such as *Life*. In his study, he presented expressive faces in isolation (e.g., a fearful face) versus expressive faces in a full visual scene (a fearful face displayed by a woman fleeing an attacker). His results confirmed that for many emotions the additional contextual information was crucial in the process of attributing emotion to others. Note that, like Goodenough and Tinker, Munn was interested in emotion attribution, not emotion perception, asking his participants "What emotion is being experienced by this person?," not "What is the facial expression displayed by this person?" These and other studies were reviewed by Bruner and Tagiuiri (1954) and Tagiuri (1969), the former concluding, "All in all, one wonders about the significance of studies of the recognition of 'facial expressions of emotions,' in isolation of context" (1954, p. 638).

For the sake of our discussion, it is important to stress again that the motivation for these studies was based on the more general debate of whether facial expressions are, indeed, universal and accurate signatures of emotion. In addition, these studies focused on the more general phenomenon of emotion attribution and consequently did not explore the possibility that the perception of the facial expression itself could be altered by context. Nevertheless, the consensus from these studies downplayed the importance of faces, independent of context, as cues to an actor's emotional state.

As we describe in the following section, research on processing isolated facial expressions was about to enjoy a renaissance in a series of studies stressing the face as a signal that can stand on its own, independent of context.

FACIAL EXPRESSIONS AS DISCRETE EMOTIONAL CATEGORIES

The pendulum began swinging back with the pioneering works of Sylvan Tomkins (1962–1963), an enthusiast of Darwin's ideas on the value of facial expressions. Tomkins was well aware of the fact that Darwin's "proof" for the universality of facial expressions was based on inadequate methodology. In his attempt to reinvestigate the universality question, Tomkins independently advised Ekman (1972) and Izard (1971) to carry out cross-cultural research and sent them out to gather data from various isolated literate and preliterate cultures. Their results demonstrated a high degree of cross-cultural agreement on the display of certain expressions as indicators of emotions and on the extent to which these same expressions are recognized to be indicators of those emotions (Ekman, 1972; Izard, 1971). Ultimately, the findings led to the formulation of the influential neurocultural theory of emotion (e.g., Ekman, 1972, 1993, 2003; Keltner et al., 2003; Tompkins, 1962–1963). Briefly, this theory argues for the existence of a limited number of basic emotions that are expressed distinctively by the configuration of one's face (among other correlates). These expressions are viewed as genetically determined (Erickson & Schulkin, 2003; Galati, Scherer, & Ricci-Bitti, 1997), universal (Ekman, 1993, 1999), and perceptually discrete (Young et al., 1997). In addition, Ekman and Friesen (1976) helped organize the research in the field by providing other scientists with a standardized, anatomically based, and theory-driven picture set of emotional faces (Ekman & Friesen, 1976; Matsumoto & Ekman, 1988). This tool became the gold standard for most research on facial expressions.

The impact and importance of Ekman's work cannot be overestimated, and his theories still lead mainstream conceptualization in facial expression research. Arguably, the hallmark of his tradition was that specific emotional categories could be directly "read out" in a bottom-up manner from the configuration of the face musculature (e.g., Buck, 1994; Nakamura, Buck, & Kenny, 1990; Tomkins, 1962–1963). According to this view, all of the necessary information for the recognition of basic facial expressions is embedded in their distinctive *physical configurations*.

REVISITING EXPRESSIONS IN CONTEXT: EKMAN'S CRITIQUE

The renaissance of facial expressions as accurate signatures of emotion was on its way, but it was not yet complete. A lingering question was still unanswered: Why did past research demonstrate such a major role for context in the process of emotion attribution? Ekman et al. (1972) addressed this problem in an influential review by meticulously criticizing previous studies for using faces that were vague and ambiguous in comparison to the contexts. If one wished to reach meaningful - conclusions about the relative dominance of the expression of the face versus the emotion induced by the context in which they appear, then both sources would need to be equally strong (Ekman et al., 1972).

Following Ekman et al.'s recommendation, several replications of past experiments were performed. In nearly all of these, variants of the Goodenough and Tinker (1931) paradigm (pairing facial expressions with verbal context) were the methodology of choice (e.g., Watson, 1972; Knudsen & Muzeraki, 1983; Wallbott, 1988; Nakamura et al., 1990). By and large, the results showed that when the face and context were equally clear and strong, the attribution of emotion was determined by the facial expression. However, it is crucial to stress once again that these researchers were not interested in the question of how the context might change the *perception* of the face. Instead, they asked how participants choose from among these different sources of information and reach a decision concerning the emotion of the person they are judging. For this reason, participants in these studies were not asked to categorize the expression of the face itself.

DISCRETE EMOTIONS AS THE "ATOMS" OF EXPRESSION

As previously mentioned, discrete theories contest that specific emotional categories can be directly read out in a bottom-up manner from the configuration of the facial expression (e.g., Buck 1994; Nakamura et al., 1990; Tomkins, 1962–1963). According to this view, the *atoms* in expressive faces are discrete face configurations that represent basic emotions (e.g., anger, fear, disgust). Each basic (expressive) face configuration is a unique facial atom that is immediately recognized by normal, healthy perceivers as belonging to a specific emotion category.

In support of this view, it has been shown that computerized network models can categorically differentiate basic expressions based purely on their structural characteristics (Calder, Burton, Miller, Young, & Akamatsu, 2001; Daily, Cottrell, Padgett, & Adolphs, 2002; Etcoff & Magee, 1992; Smith, Cottrell, Gosselin, & Schyns, 2005; Susskind, Littlewort, Bartlett, Movellan, & Anderson, 2007). For example, Susskind et al. (2007) have shown that a computational model that has no concept of emotion categories can categorize facial expressions based solely on pure data-driven similarity between image pixels. This notion—that all the necessary information for the categorization facial expressions is embedded in the face itself—resonates with McArthur and Baron's (1983) concept of "direct perception" (cf. Gibson, 1950) in social stimuli. According to their theory the raw sensory input (i.e., the configuration of the face) is sufficient for directly perceiving various emotional signals (the atoms) without need for more complex "top-down" processes.

Although the discrete view of facial expressions proved to be very productive in enhancing our understanding of isolated expression perception, it came with an unfortunate price. Specifically, the role of context in the processing of facial expressions was minimized, if not completely forgotten (Calder & Young, 2005; Ekman & O'Sullivan, 1988; Smith et al., 2005).

As we describe next, the notion of facial expressions as discrete entities that signal specific emotions has its opponents in the dimensional theories of emotion. As we shall see, these theories emphasize the more basic underlying affective dimensions of valence and arousal that are read out from the face in a context-immune manner.

DIMENSIONAL–CONTEXTUAL MODELS OF EMOTION PERCEPTION

The view that basic facial expressions of emotion are distinct and context-resilient entities has not gone unchallenged. According to the circumplex model of emotion (Russell, 1980, 2003), all of the emotions can be characterized by a conjunction of values along two underlying factors that consist of bipolar dimensions. As can be seen in Figure 11.2, these bipolar dimensions include valence (pleasant vs. unpleasant face) and arousal (activated or deactivated face). Importantly, these broad dimensional values, but not specific emotion categories, are considered to be expressed in the face.

Based on research pioneered by Woodworth and Schlosberg (1954), the circumplex model considers emotional facial expressions to be systematically related to one another by their degree of arousal and valence. Thus, expressions can be located next to or distant from one another in a two dimensional circular arrangement. Some expressions that share similar degrees of arousal and valence will be located adjacently (e.g., anger and disgust), while other faces (e.g., those expressing sadness and fear) that encompass different levels of valence or arousal will be positioned in nonadjacent locations on the circumplex (Russell, 2003; Russell & Bullock, 1985; Woodworth & Schlosberg, 1954).

Direct evidence for the psychological perceptual reality of this model was obtained by Russell and Bullock (1985). In their study, a group of preschoolers and adults was asked to group together facial expressions of people who appear to feel alike. When the results were analyzed, a clear bipolar representation, with the factors of valence and

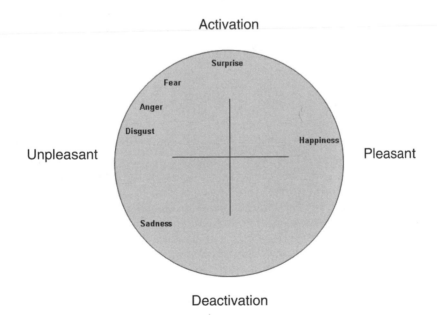

FIGURE 11.2. A schematic representation of the location of basic emotions on the circumplex model. Every basic emotion has been placed roughly in its appropriate location as predicted by dimensional theories (e.g., see Russell, 1997). The location of each emotion reflects the combination of the two bipolar dimensions of arousal (activation) and valence (pleasantness).

arousal, emerged for both groups. Importantly, the fact that preschoolers are not conceptually and linguistically proficient with specific emotion categories (such as anger, fear, disgust, etc.) did not affect the overall representational structure that they ascribed to the faces.

EMOTIONAL DIMENSIONS AS THE "ATOMS" OF EXPRESSION

According to the dimensional account of facial expressions, the "atoms" of facial expression perception consist of valence and arousal.[2] As atoms, the values of the dimensions are considered to be read out directly from the face and thus to be immune to contextual influence. For example, faces with negative valence should be perceived as negative regardless of the context in which they appear.

Based on the circumplex model, Russell and Bullock (1985) and Russell (1997) have tentatively suggested a two-stage model for recognizing emotional facial expressions. At the first stage, the basic dimensions of valence and arousal are directly "read out" from the face rapidly and effortlessly. This stage is assumed to be immune to contextual influence (Russell, 1997). However, the end product perceived in this first stage (e.g. high arousal, negative valence) is considered to be highly amorphous with regard to the specific emotional category that can be inferred from the configuration of the face. Referring back to Figure 11.2, a face conveying high levels of displeasure and high levels of arousal should be compatible with a range of specific emotions (e.g., anger, fear, disgust) occupying the quadrant from about "9–12 o'clock" in the circumplex (Russell, 1997, p. 311).

How, then, do people perceive specific emotion categories in their mundane experience? This matter is resolved at the second stage of the model, in which a specific emotion category is attributed to the face in a more laborious and effortful top-down process. In contrast to the first stage, this second "disambiguation stage" is assumed to depend heavily on contextual information and "top-down" processing (Larsen & Diener, 1992; Russell, 1997, 2003). Thus, dimensional models recognize the role that context has on mapping facial expressions into emotion categories, albeit not in the perception of valence and arousal from the face (Carroll & Russell, 1996; Posner, Russell, & Peterson, 2005; Russell, 1980, 1997, 2003; Russell & Bullock, 1985, 1986; Barrett, 2006).

The latter assumption was tested by Carroll and Russell (1996) in yet another study utilizing the Goodenough–Tinker paradigm (i.e., pairing facial expressions with short contextual stories). In their study, they paired emotional faces with emotionally incongruent contexts that nevertheless shared similar emotional dimensions (i.e., similar degrees of arousal and valence). For example, a fearful face was paired with an anger-inducing context (but not a happiness-inducing context). After seeing the facial expression and hearing its paired contextual vignette, participants were asked to decide which emotion the person might be feeling. As the researchers predicted, the majority of participants chose the emotion suggested by the context.

All the same, these data say little about contextual influence on the *perception* of facial expression. As previously noted, the traditional use of the Goodenough and Tinker paradigm implicated emotion *attribution*, not emotion *perception*. Similarly, in Carroll and Russell's (1996) study, participants were asked, "What emotion is the person feeling?," not "What is the facial expression displayed by this person?" As such, these studies focused on the more general phenomenon of emotion attribution but not on the specific process of perceiving the expression of the face. Therefore, it is unclear if the perception of the facial expressions in that study were at all influenced by context.

A TWO-STAGE MODEL OF ATTRIBUTION

It is interesting that a formal model describing the relation between the perception of facial expression and context was not put forward initially by emotion theorists or psychologists focused on face perception, but by social psychologists studying attributions. Researchers studying attributions have pondered over the process by which ordinary people figure out the causes of other people's behavior (Gilbert, 1998). Early attribution theorists (e.g., Kelley, 1967, 1972; Jones & Davis, 1965) have shown that people view behaviors as the combined result of situational context and enduring predispositions. According to these classical accounts, if someone's behavior would be sufficiently explained by the situation, people would have no logical reason to infer anything about the enduring character of that person.

For example, if John is just about to plunge to his first bungee jump, we might not attribute his fearful face to an enduring fearful disposition but to the situation. If, however, John displays the same face while sitting at home on his couch, we might just consider him a very anxious fellow. Hence, according to Kelley (1972), the attribution of a personal disposition is inversely related to the strength of the situational context. Other researchers have noticed, however, that people have a surprising tendency to downplay situational demands and evaluate the behavior of others in terms of enduring character despite logical expectations (Ichheiser, 1949; Jones & Harris, 1967; Ross, 1977). This tendency to downplay situational context has been termed the *"fundamental attribution bias"* (Ross, 1977).

The common theme to these theories was that they all dealt extensively with the rather late stages of attribution, occurring after the behavior (i.e., the fearful face) was already identified. In contrast, they completely ignored the initial stages in which the behavior itself was perceptually processed. It was in this context that Trope (1986) asked: How is the face recognized as fearful in the first place?

AMBIGUITY AND EXPRESSION PERCEPTION

In order to answer this question, Trope (1986) suggested a model in which the attribution process was broken down into two stages. The first stage (on which we will focus here) consisted of identification, and the second consisted of dispositional inferences. At the initial identification stage, situational cues (e.g., upcoming bungee jump), behavioral cues (e.g., fearful face), and cues concerning prior knowledge about the perceived person (e.g., that person is usually scared of his own shadow) all have the potential of interacting to influence our attribution of emotion. Consequently, Trope argued, in order to predict the outcomes of the identification process, we must take into consideration the ambiguity of both the context and the behavior. According to this line of thought, ambiguous facial expressions are equally and highly associated with more than one emotion category[3] (e.g., a facial expression that has an equal chance of being categorized as happy or angry). Unambiguous facial expressions, in contrast, are strongly associated with only one category (e.g., a face that is only categorized as angry). Of course, just as a facial expression can be ambiguous or unambiguous, so can the context in which it appears. For example, the death of a friend after years of suffering from cancer might equally be considered as relieving as well as saddening.

Importantly, Trope (1986) posited that the effect of context on behavior identification should increase with the ambiguity of the facial expression and decrease with the ambiguity of the context. For example, imagine that we see an ambiguous facial expression that equally signals anger and fear. Now, if we were to know that a bungee jump was the context in which that face appeared, the contextual expectation of fear would affect the categorization of the ambiguous face, and it would be identified as fearful. Thus, the model allows for behavioral cues, such as facial expressions, to be directly influenced by various contextual cues.

In this model, context has the potential power of drastically shifting the classification of ambiguous cues from one category to the other. However, basic prototypical universal expressions, which are fairly unambiguous, should prove to be contextually immune.

The two-stage model was experimentally tested by pairing faces with contextual verbal descriptions. Yet, in contrast to previous studies, Trope (1986) had his participants categorize the *facial expression itself*. Critically, some of the expressions were ambiguous, and some were unambiguous. All faces were paired with a short situational description. For example, an ambiguous happy-angry face was paired with an angry situation and with a happy situation. Similarly, unambiguous angry and happy faces were paired with both angry and happy contexts. As hypothesized, dramatic contextual effects were found only when the facial expressions were ambiguous.

WHEN ARE CONTEXTUAL EFFECTS EXPECTED? A SUMMARY

Theorists that consider facial expressions as discrete categories have usually ignored the role of context in expression perception (e.g., Ekman et al., 1972; Ekman & O'Sullivan, 1988). Prototypical basic facial expressions were viewed as signals that conveyed unambiguous emotional meanings. As such, the role of context in that process was minimized. Thus, theories of discrete expressions predict that specific emotional categories (e.g. anger, fear, disgust) should be directly read out from the face configuration regardless of the context in which it appears (Ekman & O'Sullivan, 1988).

In contrast, dimensional models permit contextual effects, albeit to a limited degree. Context might strongly shift the categorization of expressions *within* given values of valence and arousal, for example, within a given quadrant of the circumplex. However, contextual information would not be expected to shift the values of the fundamental dimensions that are perceived in the face (Carroll & Russell, 1996; Russell, 1997). Hence, contextual information would not be expected to cause shifts between facial expressions that are positioned in different quadrants of the circumplex.

Finally, Trope's (1986) model predicts contextual effects as a function of empirical ambiguity, with no *a priori* differentiation between any kind of facial expression or dimension. Furthermore, the model assumes that the lowest degree of ambiguity matches those facial expressions identified as "basic" by Ekman and Friesen (1976). Hence, it clearly follows that those basic facial expressions will be least prone to context effects.

REVISING THE TWO-STAGE MODEL:
CONTEXT EFFECTS AND PHYSICAL SIMILARITY

Past research has usually presented faces and contexts from different modalities (e.g., Carroll & Russell, 1996). However, this practice has its limits. Most notably, it has been demonstrated that emotions are more accessible from pictures of faces than from verbal descriptions of situations (Fernandez-Dols & Carroll, 1997). We intended to embark on a program of research that can bypass this inequality. Our initial concern involved finding a reliable tool in which various prototypical facial expressions could be presented while embedded in different naturalistic contexts. Specifically, we aimed for the face and context both to be visual and to be experienced together as an integrated and unitary scene. To this end, we decided to investigate visual context effects by utilizing the fact that body behavior, gestures, and scenes might serve as natural and rich contexts in which to interpret the emotion cues conveyed by the face (e.g., Wallbott, 1998; Meeren et al., 2005; Van den Stock, Righart, & deGelder, 2007; for a review see de Gelder et al., 2006).

In the preparation of the stimuli (e.g., Figure 11.1), we carefully merged pictures of models engaged in various emotion-evoking situations (e.g., holding dirty diapers, waving angry fists, etc.) with images of facial expressions (for similar methodology see Meeren et al., 2005). For the faces we used "gold standard" facial expressions from the standardized sets of Ekman and Friesen (1976) and Matsumoto and Ekman (1988), thus ensuring that the expressions conveyed by the isolated faces were clear and unambiguous. Indeed, our pilot studies with Israeli and Canadian populations of undergraduate students confirmed that the expressions of the isolated faces are recognized with a satisfactory degree of accuracy, replicating the data of Ekman and Friesen (1976).

In an initial pilot study, we presented basic expressions with a range of affective contexts. For example, we "planted" an anger face on an athlete running a hurdle race (Figure 11.3), a disgust face on a person who was waving an angry fist (Figure 11.1) and a disgust face on a person displaying confusion by shrugging his shoulders (Figure 11.4). Participants were shown the images with no time limit and were instructed to choose the option that best described the facial expression in the picture. In addition to the options describing the basic emotions, we also included options that corresponded to the contexts.

Remarkably, in all of our face–context combinations the recognition of the "original" basic expression was practically lost. Instead, facial expressions were categorized in accordance with the context in which they appeared. Consider the hurdle-race runner in Figure 11.3.

FIGURE 11.3. A basic facial expression of anger in the context of determination (facial expression from Matsumoto & Ekman, 1988). Reproduced with permission from the Paul Ekman Group.

When his facial expression is presented in isolation, it serves as a highly unambiguous signature of anger (categorized by 91% as anger in the published norms by Matsumoto & Ekman, 1988). Yet, when the face was presented in a context suggesting "determination," not even one of our 24 participants chose anger as the emotion portrayed by the face, and the dominant response was "determination." Figure 11.4 presents yet another example of the powerful effect context may exert on unambiguous facial expressions. Although the face in isolation was recognized as disgust by nearly 90% of the viewers (Matsumoto & Ekman, 1988), that recognition level was reduced to 0% when the face was presented in a context suggesting confusion.

These examples make it clear that context can induce a radical shift in the categorization of unambiguous expressions portrayed by faces. Critically, and in contrast to most previous studies, our participants were specifically attempting to categorize the *facial expression* rather than to attribute an emotion to the target. Our next step was to look for the rules that govern these contextual effects. Specifically, we wished to un-

FIGURE 11.4. Basic expression of disgust in the context of confusion (facial expression from Matsumoto & Ekman, 1988). Reproduced with permission from the Paul Ekman Group.

derstand when contextual effects would prevail and when they would diminish.

PHYSICAL SIMILARITY AND "EMOTION SEEDS"

One way of understanding the effects of context on expression perception is by considering the inherent but only latent physical similarity that resides within basic facial expressions. Each expression includes physical features (i.e., face muscular movements) that are associated, to varying degrees, with faces that express different emotions. For example, whereas certain features in disgust faces might be relatively unique to disgust, such as the wrinkled nose, other features, such as the furrowed brows, are shared with other expressions (Smith & Scott, 1997). As a result, a given facial expression X may share many features with emotion Y but few features with emotion Z. Each facial expression, then, is confounded to varying degrees with other facial expressions with which it shares physical information.

To the above end, we introduce the term "emotion seeds" to describe this shared physical information. This term underscores the fact that, when viewed in isolation, the *shared* physical input has very little impact, and the seeds remain inert. However, when faces are perceived in context, these seeds may become highly relevant and "grow" significantly, influencing the perception of the facial expression. We next elaborate on these concepts and describe how emotion seeds are defined as well as how they might alter the perception of the facial expressions.

Emotion seeds in faces are at least partly a function of similarity between expressions, and hence they can be assessed using computational models that calculate this similarity (Dailey et al., 2002; Susskind et al., 2007). For example, Susskind et al. (2007) used an algorithm that was designed to make seven-way forced-choice categorizations of basic expressions. The process was purely data-driven from the similarities in the pixels of the expression images, and the model does not have any *a priori* concept of emotion. The results showed that different facial expressions could be assigned to distinct groups based purely on their physical properties. Critically, good agreement was found between the model and the judgments of human participants who rated the faces with respect to to six basic emotions (anger, happiness, surprise, sadness, fear, and disgust) on a scale from 1 to 7 (1 = not at all; 7 = very much). Hence, it seems likely that the patterns of human emotion categorization could be driven by the low-level physical similarities among expressions.

Figure 11.5 illustrates the network classifications for the six basic facial expressions. Each cluster represents a different facial expression

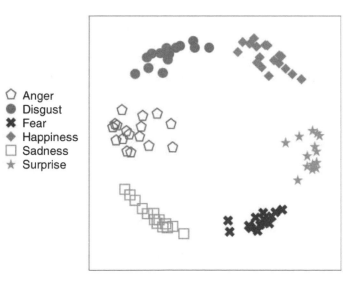

FIGURE 11.5. Computer-based categorization of facial expressions based on the physical similarity between the different facial configurations. Emotion categories placed next to each other are more physically similar. Adapted from Susskind, Littlewort, Bartlett, Movellan, and Anderson (2007).

category, and the location of each cluster represents the relative physical similarity between the different expressions. For example, the expressions of disgust were classified as most similar to those of anger, less similar to sad faces, and even less similar to fear faces. Thus, one can think of disgust expressions as sharing many emotion seeds with anger faces, some emotion seeds with sad faces, and very few emotion seeds with fear faces.

Corroborating evidence comes from analyzing the errors of facial expression categorizations in the norms provided by Ekman and Friesen (1976). For example, as we noted, the computational model shows that disgust faces hold declining degrees of emotion seeds with the expressions of anger, sadness, and fear, respectively. This finding is mirrored in the Ekman and Friesen (1976) error analysis, as evident in the declining average confusability between the expressions of disgust and anger (6%), disgust and sadness (3%), and disgust and fear (1%).

In short, both the computerized analysis of physical similarity between facial expressions and human errors strongly suggest that facial expressions are ambiguous to varying degrees with other facial expressions with which they share physical features. Under the typical experimental design in which faces are shown devoid of any context, the emotion seeds remain latent. Indeed, the average rate of confusability between isolated facial expressions is negligible. Yet, it seems that these seeds grow and exert powerful effects when the faces are placed in context. When is it, then, that the emotion seeds sprout?

CONTEXTUAL EFFECTS AND "EMOTION SEEDS"

How do the physical similarities among various expressions relate to contextual effects? As we have previously claimed, each facial expression is ambiguous to varying degrees with others, depending on the amount of shared physical features. Independently, contexts differ in the extent to which they can activate one or more emotions. Context effects on faces depend, we argue, on the emotion seeds shared by the target expression (i.e., the actual face being judged) and by the facial expression that would typically be associated with the emotional context.

This notion of ambiguity differs from previous accounts that emphasized the ambiguity of facial expressions as a property of the expression (Trope, 1986). In contrast, the current conceptualization argues that facial expressions should not be thought of as simply ambiguous *or* as unambiguous. For instance, due to the physical similarity between the two facial configurations, sad faces encompass seeds of disgust. Yet, the disgust concealed in sad faces will not be evident unless activated by the appropriate context. This ambiguity would probably remain latent if the sad face were presented in the context of a person celebrating his birthday party with his close friends. This is the case because surprise birthday parties do not strongly activate the notion of disgust, and, consequently, the seed remains dormant. In contrast, consider the same sad face appearing in the context of a person holding a soiled pair of underwear. Since this context can strongly activate the emotion seed of disgust, it would result in the sad face being perceived as disgusted.

Thus, a given facial expression may be *highly ambiguous* with respect to some physically similar expressions yet *highly unambiguous* with respect to other physically dissimilar expressions. The specific combination of facial expression and context, we argue, would ultimately determine the occurrence and magnitude of context effects.

"EMOTION SEEDS" IN CONTEXT: ILLUSTRATIVE RESEARCH

In our first study, we examined the relationship between the magnitude of context effect and the physical similarity between the actual facial expression and the expression typically associated with the context. Specifically we assumed that the magnitude of the context effect would positively correlate with the degree of similarity (and, ex hypothesis, the amount of shared seeds; Aviezer et al., in press).

To achieve this goal we presented faces that expressed disgust in the contexts of bodies gesturing disgust, anger, sadness, and fear. Crucially, the facial expressions associated with these contexts were less and less similar (and hence shared fewer emotion seeds) with the original disgust expression (see Susskind et al., 2007). In other words, each of these contexts suggests a facial expression that is physically more distant from disgust, as determined by the computational model (Figure 11.5). Consequently, disgust expressions were predicted to be highly influenced by the anger context, moderately influenced by the sad context, and only slightly influenced by the fear context.

Our design could also tackle a nagging concern from our pilot results, namely, that participants might have simply been ignoring the faces in the presented images. Although our instructions were explicit, participants might have rather relied on the perhaps more salient context than on the face. If participants were merely ignoring the face, then contextual effects in the current design should manifest equally regardless of the unique face–context combination. If our results would show differential context effects, however, then we could safely conclude that the faces are not being ignored.

We used the same experimental procedure as described in the pilot study. Ten prototypical facial expressions of disgust from the database, each from a different model (5 female, 5 male), were used to ensure a wide representation of the facial expression (Ekman & Friesen, 1976). Participants were required to categorize the expressions of the faces with no time limit, and the face in each trial remained in full view until a response was made. In a control condition, participants were also required to categorize the same facial expressions in isolation and the contextual scenes with the faces blanked out.

CROSS-CATEGORY CONTEXT EFFECTS

We defined accurate responses as those in which the face was categorized as belonging to the anatomically-based category of disgust (Ekman & Friesen, 1976). The average accuracy for the isolated disgust faces was 65.6% (chance level = 16.7%). Although somewhat lower than expected from the average published norms, such performance is within the range of normal performance (Young et al., 2002). The faceless context images were recognized with a much higher agreement, ranging from 92% to 96%, with *no significant differences between the various* contexts (Aviezer et al., 2007). Hence, any differences in the perception of the disgust faces placed in context could not be readily attributed only to differences in context strength.

The average recognition accuracy of the disgust faces was measured in each context in which they were embedded. Our results showed the dramatic effect of context. The mean accuracy for the disgust faces was 91% when placed in a disgust context, 59% when placed in the fear context, 35% when placed in the sadness context, and 11% when placed in the anger context. Critically, the categorization accuracy of the facial expressions declined linearly as a function of the physical similarity between the actual face and the facial expressions suggested by the context. Consistent with our theorizing, then, the anger context yielded the most powerful context effect. We believe it did so because the disgust and anger faces are physically similar and hence share a great deal of emotion seeds. Consequently, participants were at chance level at their recognition of the disgusted faces when presented in an anger context. In contrast, the fear context exerted a relatively modest influence on the recognition of the facial expression. We believe that the influence of this context was modest because disgust faces and fear faces share little physical similarity; hence, few seeds of "fear" are present in the "disgust" expression.

We next examined if the facial expressions of disgust were categorized, indeed, as belonging to the context categories or, alternatively, if the perception of disgust was hampered by incongruent context with no systematic bias toward the context. A bias toward the context could corroborate our view that the degree of these categorizations depended on seed ambiguity induced by the physical similarity between the expressions. Remarkably, the probability of categorizing disgust faces in a disgust context as disgusted (91%) did not differ significantly from the probability of categorizing the same disgust faces as expressing anger when placed in an anger context (87%). Furthermore, disgust faces in a sad context were nearly equally likely to be placed into the sad (29%) or disgust (35%) categories (Aviezer et al., in press). However, when the disgust faces were presented in the fear context, participants were far less likely to categorize the face as fear (13%) than they were to categorize it as disgust (59%).

Together, these results confirm that the participants were not ignoring the face and choosing the label suggested by context nor was their categorization merely interfered with by an incongruent context (cf. Meeren et al., 2005). On the contrary, it seems that the respondents were paying close attention to the context as well as to the face (which, indeed, was their task). Most importantly, the emotional information provided by the context and the expression of the face seemed to *interact* in a highly predictable manner. Further experimentation in our lab has confirmed that these effects apply to a wide range of facial expressions, including fear, anger, and sadness, as well as disgust. In addition, we have shown that the results are not an artifact of the response format available to participants. For example, we allowed participants to choose more than one correct answer as well as to choose none of the options by selecting a "none of the above" response. These variations in the experimental task did not result in any significant changes to the results.

It is interesting to compare our results with those obtained by Meeren et al. (2005), who conducted a conceptually similar study that examined the influence of body language (expressing fear and anger) on the rapid categorization of facial expressions (fear and anger). In their study, faces and contexts were presented in both congruent (e.g., fear on fear) and incongruent (e.g., fear on anger) combinations. Their results indicated Stroop-like interference effects (e.g., lower accuracy and higher RTs for incongruent pairs) but *no contextually induced categorical shifts* (Meeren et al., 2005). Hence, notwithstanding the interference, the majority of facial expression categorizations corresponded to the original expression conveyed by the faces, regardless of whether they appeared with congruent or incongruent body language. In light of our theory and results, the lack of cross-categorical context effects in the Meeren et al. (2005) study might be explained by the fact that they limited their investigation to facial expressions of fear and anger that are in fact quite dissimilar at the physical level (Susskind et al., 2007). Consequently, anger and fear share few emotion seeds, and context effects do not prevail.

CROSS-DIMENSIONAL CONTEXT EFFECTS

As we argued earlier, dimensional models, such as the circumplex, consider the dimensions of arousal and valence to be the basic atoms of affect perception (Russell, 1997; Russell & Bullock, 1986). These values are considered contextually invariable since they can be unequivocally "read out" from the facial configuration. For example, a consistent finding in dimensional models (e.g. Russell & Bullock, 1985; Russell, 1997) is that facial expressions of sadness and fear are very distant from each other, occupying separate quadrants of the circumplex (see Figure 11.2). This stems from the obvious fact that the two expressions differ greatly in their degree of arousal. Interestingly however, when the physical similarity between sadness and fear is examined, it becomes apparent that the two share substantial degrees of physical similarity (Susskind et al., 2007; see Figure 11.5). Thus, diverging predictions can be made with regard to the viability of achieving context effects that aim at crossing the border of dimensional arousal.

On the one hand, the circumplex model views this as highly unlikely due to the very different levels of arousal and valence accompanying the emotions of sadness and fear. Because, ex hypothesis, these dimensions are directly and unambiguously read out from the facial configuration, they should not be altered by context. Therefore, dimensional models would predict that, regardless of the context, low-arousal sad expressions should not be perceived as conveying high arousal. On the other hand, the emotion seed approach does not restrict contextual effects to cases that share dimensional values but to cases that share physically based similarity. Thus, we do not consider the values of the facial dimensions of arousal and valence as contextually immune. For example, given their physical similarity, sadness and fear might indeed be potential candidates for contextual cross-category shifts.

In an attempt to examine if the perception of arousal might shift due to context, we presented different faces expressing sadness in a highly arousing fear context (see the example in Figure 11.6) or in a congruent low-arousal sad context (Aviezer et al., in press). Participants were required to rate the valence and arousal of the faces without referring to a specific emotional category. We used a computerized version of the 9 × 9 "affect grid," which represents valence and arousal in its bipolar axes (Russell, Weiss, & Mendelsohn, 1989). Using this tool, emo-

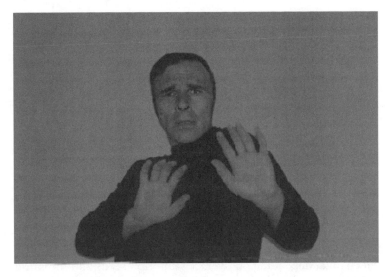

FIGURE 11.6. Example of a basic facial expression of sadness (low arousal) in fear context (high arousal). Facial expression from Ekman and Friesen (1976). Reproduced with permission from the Paul Ekman Group.

tional stimuli can be simultaneously rated for arousal and valence on a 1–9 scale. Importantly, both the arousal and valence scales are bipolar (positive to negative, high-arousal to low-arousal), with a neutral midpoint assigned the value of 5, represented by a central gray square in the grid.

As predicted by the "emotion seeds" approach, the results showed that the fearful context resulted in a categorical shift in the perception of arousal. Whereas sad faces in a sad context were rated as portraying low arousal (4.4 out of 9), sad faces in a fear context were rated as portraying high arousal (6.7 out of 9). It seems, then, that at least under certain conditions the perception of arousal may not be immune to contextual influence. In a subsequent stage, participants also categorized the specific emotions of the same facial expressions.[4] Replicating previous results, the context also induced a complete categorical shift in the categorization of the faces (Aviezer et al., in press). For example, the face in Figure 11.6 was categorized as fearful by nearly 60% of the participants, whereas only 17% categorized it as sad (which is in fact the intended emotion). In conclusion, it appears that physically based emotion seeds can be used as a useful conceptualization of when context effects on dimension and emotion perception will occur.

Although the notion of emotion seeds brings us closer to understanding the rules and constraints of context effects on processing facial expressions, it is clearly not enough. The fact that certain physically based "seeds" of emotion lay latent in each facial expression is in itself insufficient in explaining the *mechanism* by which the seed can grow. In the following section we sketch a tentative model in which we describe how trace levels of emotion seeds might be contextually magnified, resulting in striking effects on facial expression perception. The model suggests an attentional mechanism that may explain the changes that facial expressions undergo when placed in different contexts.

AN ATTENTIONAL BIAS MODEL

The basic premise of the attentional bias model is that context can influence the perception of facial expressions by guiding the viewer's attention to various facial regions that correspond to the emotion suggested by the context (e.g., Bar, 2004). This attentional bias can result in a perceptual change, depending on the face's emotion seeds and the emotional category associated with the context. If attention is diverted by the context to the facial feature of the emotion seeds, then, metaphorically speaking, the seed is watered by attention, a process that allows it to exert its influence of emotion perception.

Facial expressions include features that convey both unambiguous and ambiguous information (Smith & Scott, 1997; Smith et al., 2005). For example, certain features in disgust faces might be relatively unique to disgust (e.g., the wrinkled nose), while other features are shared with other expressions (e.g., the furrowed eyebrows). Facial expression recognition takes place by viewers extracting as much information as possible from specific areas of the face (Smith et al., 2005). Indeed, ample evidence from behavioral studies and eye-movement recording shows that when we categorize different expressions we focus visual attention on different regions of the face (Calder, Young, Keane, & Dean, 2000; Smith et al., 2005, Sullivan & Kirkpatrick, 1996; Wong, Cronin-Golomb, & Neargarder, 2005).

When facial expressions are perceived in context, the contextual cues invoke an associated category, which then serves as a source of expectations concerning the categorization of the facial expressions (Bar, 2004; Trope, 1986). Under these conditions, we hypothesize that attention is diverted *away* from the components that are diagnostic of the original expression and *toward* the emotion seeds. Consequently, very small degrees of emotion seeds that would otherwise be ignored become disproportionably magnified by attention.

In sum, context effects will depend on both the emotion seeds of the target facial expression and the extent to which the context activates one of the latent seeds that resides in the face. One interesting prediction that may be deduced from the attentional bias model is that the attentional processing of facial expressions will differ depending on the contexts in which the faces appear. We next describe some preliminary evidence for this hypothesis from eye-movement tracking.

EYE SCANNING AND ATTENTIONAL BIAS

The attentional model posits that facial expression recognition takes place by viewers extracting as much information as possible from the diagnostic areas of the face (Smith et al., 2005). Indeed, converging evidence has accumulated demonstrating that different regions of the face are crucial for the accurate recognition of specific facial expressions. For example, Calder et al. (2000) had viewers categorize facial expressions while being presented with only the top half or bottom half segments of the face. Their result indicated that some expressions (e.g. anger) were more recognizable from the top half whereas others (e.g. disgust) were better recognized from the bottom half.

Similar results were obtained by studies that examined the critical regions for expression recognition with *bubbles* (Gosselin & Schyns, 2001). In that technique, participants are presented with various bubbles that consist of windows to the facial expression, each composed from different spatial frequency bandwidths and Gaussian filters. By examining the bubbles that are crucial for correct categorization, the diagnostic regions for the recognition of each expression can be determined. The results from that study have shown that distinct locations in the face are utilized when decoding different facial expressions (Smith et al., 2005). Specifically, the regions critical for disgust perception included the lower mouth region; however, the eye region was critical for anger recognition. This finding has also been replicated in eye tracking studies. For example, Wong et al. (2005) had participants passively view facial expressions without any categorization task. Their results have shown that, while viewing anger faces, scanning (the number and duration of fixations) was much more pronounced on the eye region than on the mouth region. In contrast, when viewing disgust faces, a more symmetrical scanning pattern existed between the eyes and mouth (Wong et al., 2005).

Given the well-established segregation between the eye region and mouth region for the recognition of disgust and anger expressions, we were motivated to examine if context would induce changes in the characteristic scanning of these facial expressions. According to the attentional bias model, we conjectured that the scanning of the face should be influenced by the context rather than by the configuration of the face alone. We hypothesized that the number and duration of fixations to the different facial features will differ as a function of the context in which faces appears. Therefore, disgust expressions in the context of anger were expected to be scanned as congruent anger expressions, with more scanning to the upper eye regions. Conversely, anger expressions in the context of disgust were expected to be scanned as congruent disgust expressions, with a more symmetrical scanning pattern between the mouth and eye regions.

We compared the scanning of anger and disgust facial expressions, each occurring in a congruent (e.g., anger face–anger context) or incongruent (e.g. anger face–disgust context) condition (Aviezer et al., in press). Ten different prototypical expression exemplars appeared in each condition. Eye path scanning was measured with EyeLink II, a 500 Hz infrared pupil-centered eye tracker. All stimuli were randomly presented while participants viewed and categorized the faces.

The results indicated that visual scanning of expressive faces changed systematically as a function of the context in which the faces appeared. When anger faces appeared in a congruent anger context, more fixations were made to the eye (5.1) than to the mouth (3) regions. However, when the same faces appeared in a disgust context, a symmetrical pattern of fixations was observed between the eyes and mouth (3.4, and 3.3, respectively). Conversely, when disgust faces appeared in a disgust context, the number of fixations to the mouth (3.4) and eye (3.2) regions was symmetrical. Yet, when the same faces appeared in an anger context, more fixations were made to the eye regions (5) than to the mouth region (3.6). Interestingly, this striking influence of context was evident from the very first gaze to the face, suggesting that the attentional bias reflects a rapid initial stage rather than a late influence of semantic processing (Aviezer et al., in press).

Thus, facial expressions of disgust and anger are distinctly scanned when placed in neutral context. However, when incongruent combinations are formed between anger and disgust faces and contexts, the categorization and characteristic eye-scanning patterns are reversed, reflecting the expression context. This pattern of eye scanning is consistent with the attentional bias model. However, more research is necessary to determine the causal relationship between the behavioral context effect and the eye-scanning pattern.

SUMMARY AND CONCLUSION

In this chapter, we challenged the two major views of facial expression perception. Discrete theories contest the view that facial expressions convey specific emotional categories (e.g., Buck, 1994; Nakamura et al.,

1990; Tompkins, 1962–1963). In contrast, dimensional theories hold that emotional faces convey the broad affective dimensions of valence and arousal (Russell, 1997; Russell & Bullock, 1986). Both accounts assume that the perception of the basic atoms of facial expressions (discrete categories for the former, affective dimensions for the latter) is immune to contextual influences, since they can be directly and unambiguously read out from the face.

In contrast, we present data that demonstrate that the perception of both types of emotional atoms is highly influenced by context. Furthermore, we suggest that contextual influence on the perception of facial expressions can best be understood by examining the physical properties of the facial expressions. We highlighted the fact that each facial expression includes physical features that are associated, to varying degrees, with faces that express other emotions. We then introduced the notion of *emotion seeds*, reflecting the shared physical and perceptual similarity that resides between different expressions. As we have demonstrated, these seeds may alter the perception of the face when they are activated by context.

According to our conceptualization, a given facial expression may be *highly ambiguous* with respect to some physically similar expressions and yet *highly unambiguous* with respect to other expressions that are more physically dissimilar. The specific combination between facial expression and context would ultimately determine the occurrence and magnitude of context effects.

We then proposed an attentional bias model as a means of understanding the mechanisms that underlie contextual effects. The basic premise of this model is that context can influence the perception of facial expressions by guiding the viewer's attention to features in the face that correspond to the emotion suggested by the context. This attentional bias can result in a perceptual change, depending on the face's emotion seeds and the emotional category suggested by the context. We closed the chapter by presenting eye-scanning data that are consistent with the model's predictions, showing that the scanning of an emotional face may follow the pattern of fixations typical of the emotion suggested by the context rather than by the configuration of the face.

Current models of facial expression perception generally ignore the role of context and consider each facial expression as an isolated entity that is perceived in a void. We suggest that this view should be revised and that there is an important role for context in emotion perception. However, the framework proposed in this chapter does not stop at this general level. Rather, it begins to characterize the very rules and mechanisms that govern face and context interactions.

NOTES

1. Note that although the theories we address in this chapter are essentially theories of *emotion*, we strictly limit ourselves to the aspect of *facial expression* and its *perception*.
2. Note that Russell (1997) also considers "quasi-physical" facial information, such as nose wrinkling, crying, etc., to be directly *read out* from the face. However, we focus on the more central dimensions that are represented in the circumplex.
3. Note that ambiguous stimuli are not vague, as the latter are not strongly associated with any category.
4. This block appeared always second, to prevent contamination from the specific semantic category assigned to the face to the valence or arousal ratings.

REFERENCES

Aviezer, H., Hassin, R. R., Ryan, J., Grady, C., Susskind, J., Anderson, A., et al. (in press). Angry, disgusted or afraid? Studies on the malleability of facial expressions perception. *Psychological Science.*

Bar, M. (2004). Visual objects in context. *Nature Reviews Neuroscience, 5,* 617–629.

Barrett, L. F. (2006). Solving the emotion paradox: Categorization and the experience of emotion. *Personality and Social Psychology Review, 10,* 20–46.

Bell, C. (1806). *Essays on the anatomy of expression in painting.* London: J. Murray.

Bruner, J. S., & Tagiuri, R. (1954). The perception of people. In G. Lindzey (Ed.), *Handbook of social psychology* (Vol. 2, pp. 634–654). Cambridge, MA: Addison-Wesley.

Buck, R. (1994). Social and emotional functions in facial expression and communication: The readout hypothesis. *Biological Psychology, 38,* 95–115.

Calder, A. J., Burton, A. M., Miller, P., Young, A. W., & Akamatsu, S. (2001). A principal component analysis of facial expressions. *Vision Research, 41(9),* 1179–1208.

Calder A. J., & Young, A. W. (2005). Understanding the recognition of facial identity and facial expression. *Nature Reviews Neuroscience, 6,* 641–651.

Calder, A. J., Young, A. W., Keane, J., & Dean, M. (2000). Configural information in facial expression perception. *Journal of Experimental Psychology: Human Perception and Performance, 26,* 527–551.

Carroll, J. M., & Russell, J. A. (1996). Do facial expressions signal specific emotions? Judging emotion from the face in context. *Journal of Personality and Social Psychology, 70,* 205–218.

Dailey, M. N., Cottrell, G. W., Padgett, C., & Adolphs, R. (2002). EMPATH: A neural network that categorizes facial expressions. *Journal of Cognitive Neuroscience, 14,* 1158–1173.

Darwin, C. (1965). *The expression of the emotions in man and animals.* Chicago: University of Chicago Press. (Original work published 1872)

de Gelder, B., Meeren, H. K. M., Righart, R., Van den Stock, J., van de Riet, W. A. C., & Tamietto, M. (2006). Beyond the face: Exploring rapid influences of context on face processing. *Progress in Brain Research, 155*, 37–48.

Duchenne, G. B. (1862). *Mécanisme de la physionomie humaine ou analyse électrophysiologique de l'expression des passions applicable à la pratique des arts plastiques.* Paris: Jules Renouard.

Ekman, P. (1972). Universals and cultural differences in facial expressions of emotion. In J. K. Cole (Ed.), *Nebraska Symposium on Motivation* (Vol. 19, pp. 207–283). Lincoln: University of Nebraska Press.

Ekman, P. (1993). Facial expression of emotion. *American Psychologist. 48*, 384–392.

Ekman P. (1999). Basic emotions. In T. Dalgleish & M. Power (Eds.), *Handbook of cognition and emotion* (pp. 134–157). Sussex, UK: Wiley.

Ekman, P. (2003). Darwin, deception, and facial expression. *Annals of the New York Academy of Sciences, 1000*, 205–221.

Ekman, P., & Friesen, W. V. (1976). *Pictures of facial affect.* Palo Alto, CA: Consulting Psychologists Press.

Ekman, P., Friesen, W. V., & Ellsworth, P. (1972). *Emotion in the human face: Guidelines for research and an integration of findings.* Elmsford, NY: Pergamon Press.

Ekman, P., & O'Sullivan, M. (1988). The role of context in interpreting facial expression: Comment on Russell and Fehr (1987). *Journal of Experimental Psychology, 117*, 86–88.

Erickson, K., & Schulkin, J. (2003). Facial expressions of emotion: A cognitive neuroscience perspective. *Brain and Cognition, 52*, 52–60.

Etcoff, N. L., & Magee, J. J. (1992). Categorical perception of facial expressions. *Cognition, 44*, 227–240.

Fernandez-Dols, J. M., & Carroll, J. M. (1997). Is the meaning perceived in facial expression independent of its context? In J. A. Russell & J. M. Fernandez-Dols (Eds.), *The psychology of facial expressions* (pp. 275–294). New York: Cambridge University Press.

Fridlund, A. J. (1994). *Human facial expression: An evolutionary view.* New York: Academic Press.

Galati, D., Scherer, K. R., & Ricci-Bitti, P. E. (1997). Voluntary facial expression of emotion: Comparing congenitally blind with normally sighted encoders. *Journal of Personality and Social Psychology, 73*, 1363–1379.

Gibson, J. J. (1950). *The perception of the visual world.* Boston: Houghton Mifflin.

Gilbert, D. T. (1998). Ordinary personology. In D. T. Gilbert, S. T. Fiske, & G. Lindzey (Eds.), *The handbook of social psychology* (4th ed., Vol. 2, pp. 89–150). New York: McGraw-Hill.

Goodenough, F. L., & Tinker, M. A. (1931). The relative potency of facial expression verbal description of stimulus in the judgment of emotion. *Comparative Psychology, 12*, 365–370.

Gosselin, F., & Schyns, P. G. (2001). Bubbles: A new technique to reveal the use of visual information in recognition tasks. *Vision Research, 41,* 2261–2271.

Haidt, J., McCauley, C. R., & Rozin, P. (1994). A scale to measure disgust sensitivity. *Personality and Individual Differences, 16,* 701–713.

Ichheiser, G. (1949). *Misunderstandings in human relations: A study in false social perception.* Chicago: University of Chicago Press.

Izard, C. E. (1971). *The face of emotion.* New York: Appleton-Century-Crofts.

Jones, E. E., & Davis, K. E. (1965). From acts to dispositions: The attribution process in social psychology. In L. Berkowitz (Ed.), *Advances in experimental social psychology* (Vol. 2, pp. 219–266). New York: Academic Press.

Jones, E. E., & Harris, V. A. (1967). The attribution of attitudes. *Journal of Experimental Social Psychology, 3,* 1–24.

Kelley, H. H. (1967). Attribution theory in social psychology. In D. Levine (Ed.), *Nebraska Symposium on Motivation* (Vol. 15, pp. 192–238). Lincoln: University of Nebraska Press.

Kelley, H. H. (1972). Attribution in social interaction. In E. E. Jones, D. E. Kanouse, H. H. Kelley, R. E. Nisbett, S. Valins, & B. Weiner (Eds.), *Attribution: Perceiving the causes of behavior* (pp. 1–26). Morristown, NJ: General Learning Press.

Keltner, D., Ekman, P., Gonzaga, G. C., & Beer, J. (2003). Facial expression of emotion. In R. J. Davidson, K. R. Scherer, & H. H. Goldsmith (Eds.), *Handbook of affective sciences* (pp. 415–432). New York: Oxford University Press.

Knudsen, H. R., & Muzeraki, L. H. (1983). The effects of verbal statements of context on facial expressions of emotion. *Journal of Nonverbal Behavior, 7,* 202–212.

Landis, C. (1924). Studies of emotional reactions: II. General behavior and facial expression. *Journal of Comparative Psychology, 4,* 447–509.

Larsen, R. J., & Diener, E. (1992). Promises and problems with the circumplex model of emotion. In M. S. Clark (Ed.), *Review of personality and social psychology: Emotion* (Vol. 13, pp. 25–59). Newbury Park, CA: Sage.

Matsumoto, D., & Ekman, P. (1988). *Japanese and Caucasian facial expressions of emotion (JACFEE).* Unpublished slide set and brochure, Department of Psychology, San Francisco State University, San Francisco.

McArthur, L. Z., & Baron, R. M. (1983). Toward an ecological theory of social perception. *Psychological Review, 90,* 215–238.

Meeren, H. K., van Heijnsbergen, C. C., & de Gelder, B. (2005). Rapid perceptual integration of facial expression and emotional body language. *Proceedings of the National Academy of Sciences USA, 102*(45), 16518–16523.

Munn, N. L. (1940). The effect of knowledge of the situation upon judgment of emotion from facial expressions. *Journal of Abnormal and Social Psychology, 35,* 324–338.

Nakamura, M., Buck, R., & Kenny, D. (1990). Relative contributions of expressive behavior and contextual information to the judgment of the emotional state of another. *Journal of Personality and Social Psychology, 59,* 1032–1039.

Panksepp, J. (1998). *Affective neuroscience: The foundations of human and animal emotions.* New York: Oxford University Press.

Posner, J., Russell, J., & Peterson, B. S. (2005). The circumplex model of affect: An integrative approach to affective neuroscience, cognitive development, and psychopathology. *Development and Psychopathology, 17*, 715–1734.

Ross, L. (1977). The intuitive psychologist and his shortcomings: Distortions in the attribution process. In L. Berkowitz (Ed.), *Advances in experimental social psychology* (Vol. 10, pp. 173–240). Orlando, FL: Academic Press.

Rozin, P., & Fallon, A. E. (1987). A perspective on disgust. *Psychological Review, 94*, 23–41.

Rozin, P., Haidt, J., & McCauley, C. R. (2000). Disgust. In M. Lewis & J. Haviland (Eds.), *Handbook of emotions* (2nd ed., pp. 637–653). New York: Guilford Press.

Russell, J. A. (1980). A circumplex model of affect. *Journal of Personality and Social Psychology, 39*, 1161–1178.

Russell, J. A. (1997). Reading emotions from and into faces: Resurrecting a dimensional–contextual perspective. In J. A. Russell & J. M. Fernandez-Dols (Eds.), *The psychology of facial expressions*. New York: Cambridge University Press.

Russell, J. A. (2003). Core affect and the psychological construction of emotion. *Psychological Review, 110*, 145–72.

Russell, J. A., & Bullock, M. (1985). Multidimensional scaling of emotional expressions: Similarity from preschoolers to adults. *Journal of Personality and Social Psychology, 48*, 1290–1298.

Russell, J. A., & Bullock, M. (1986). Fuzzy concepts and the perception of emotion in facial expressions. *Social Cognition, 4*, 309–341.

Russell, J. A., Weiss, A., & Mendelsohn, G. A. (1989). Affect grid: A single-item scale of pleasure and arousal. *Journal of Personality and Social Psychology, 57*, 493–502.

Smith, C. A., & Scott, H. S. (1997). A componential approach to the meaning of facial expressions. In J. A. Russell & J. M. Fernandez-Dols (Eds.), *The psychology of facial expressions*. New York: Cambridge University Press.

Smith, M. L., Cottrell, G. W., Gosselin, F., & Schyns, P. G. (2005). Transmitting and decoding facial expressions. *Psychological Science, 16*, 184–189.

Sullivan, L. A., & Kirkpatrick S. W. (1996). Facial interpretation and component consistency. *Genetic, Social, and General Psychology Monographs, 122*, 389–404.

Susskind, J. M., Littlewort, G., Bartlett, M. S., Movellan, J., & Anderson, A. K. (2007). Human and computer recognition of facial expressions of emotion. *Neuropsychologia, 45*, 152–162.

Tagiuri, R. (1969). Person perception. In G. Lindsey & E. Aronson (Eds.), *Handbook of social psychology* (Vol. 3, pp. 395–437) London: Addison-Wesley.

Tomkins, S. S. (1962–1963). *Affect, imagery, consciousness* (Vol. 1 2). New York: Springer.

Trope, Y. (1986). Identification and inferential processes in dispositional attribution. *Psychological Review, 93*, 239–257.

Van den Stock, J., Righart, R., & de Gelder, B. (2007). Whole body expressions influence recognition of facial expressions and emotional prosody. *Emotion, 7*, 487–499.

Wallbott, H. G. (1988). In and out of context: Influences of facial expression and context information on emotion attributions. *British Journal of Social Psychology, 27,* 357–369.

Watson, S. G. (1972). Judgment of emotion from facial and contextual cue combinations. *Journal of Personality and Social Psychology, 24,* 334–342.

Wong, B., Cronin-Golomb, A., & Neargarder, S. (2005). Patterns of visual scanning as predictors of emotion identification in normal aging. *Neuropsychology, 19*(6), 739–749.

Woodworth, R. S., & Schlosberg, H. (1954). *Experimental psychology.* New York: Holt, Rinehart & Winston.

Young, A. W., Perrett, D., Calder, A., Sprengelmeyer, R., & Ekman, P. (2002). *Facial expressions of emotions: Stimuli and test (FEEST).* Thurstone, UK: Thames Valley Test Company.

Young, A. W., Rowland, D., Calder, A. J., Etcoff, N. L., Seth, A., & Perrett, D. I. (1997). Facial expression megamix: Tests of dimensional and category accounts of emotion regulation. *Cognition, 63,* 271–313.

PART IV

BEHAVIORAL AND ENVIRONMENTAL CUES

CHAPTER 12

Remnants of the Recent Past

Influences of Priming on First Impressions

MAX WEISBUCH
CHRISTIAN UNKELBACH
KLAUS FIEDLER

Your recent history influences what's on your mind (see Higgins, 1996), what you like or dislike (e.g., Murphy & Zajonc, 1993), what goals you pursue (e.g., Bargh, Gollwitzer, Lee-Chai, Barndollar, & Trotschel, 2001), and what you think of yourself (e.g., Baldwin, Carrell, & Lopez, 1990). It should therefore come as no surprise that your first impressions of other people are also influenced by your recent past. In fact, what you, as a "perceiver," think of a stranger (a "target") may be especially saturated with your recent history.

First impression judgments typically must be made in the absence of at least some pertinent information and therefore require perceivers to "fill in the gaps." These gaps may be filled with whatever is on one's mind (whatever is "accessible") and what is accessible is often a function of one's recent past (see Higgins, 1996). For example, if one's recent environmental history included watching a violent television show, thoughts of aggression may be especially accessible, and a stranger might appear to be especially aggressive. Thus, first impression judgments are likely to reflect one's recent environmental history. This chapter is about the role of *priming* (read: "recent environmental history") in first impression judgments.

The influence of priming on first impressions is far from simple—the aim of this chapter is to sort out some of the complexities in this relationship. Before proceeding, however, we need to make a few preliminary points. First, our discussion will be limited to that of priming influences on *first impressions*—the general phenomenon of priming is beyond the scope of this chapter (for overviews, see Higgins, 1996; Ratcliff & McKoon, 1988; Musch & Klauer, 2003). Our discussion will focus only on those theories most clearly relevant to first impressions and only on those research findings that involve first impressions. As such, interpretation-comparison (e.g., Stapel, Koomen, & Van der Pligt, 1997), inclusion-exclusion (Schwarz & Bless, 1992b), and flexible correction (Wegener & Petty, 1997) models will frame the discussion. Second, the vast majority of research on first impressions and priming has employed written behavioral descriptions as first impression stimuli. This methodological shortcoming will be discussed at the end of this chapter; however, it is important to keep this limitation in mind when forming conclusions about priming and first impressions. Finally, we have chosen to divide this chapter into two types of complexities: complexities associated with the content of an environmental cue and complexities associated with the mind that the environmental cue enters.

ENVIRONMENTAL CUE CONTENT

An investigation into the impact of priming on first impressions should probably start with a short definition of the term "priming"; the dictionary definition of "making ready" or "preparing" comes very close to the scientific meaning. When social psychologists talk about priming, they usually refer to recent or current experiences that passively create an internal readiness (Bargh & Chartrand, 2000): A stimulus is thought to make particular concepts accessible, and these accessible concepts are likely to guide processing and judgment. One classic study illustrating the impact of environmental cues (i.e., primes) on first impressions was conducted by Higgins, Rholes, and Jones (1977). Participants in this experiment were first given the task of solving scrambled sentences; unscrambled, these sentences included positive or negative personality traits (e.g., reckless vs. adventurous). Afterward, participants were given a short description of a person named "Donald." This description was ambiguous, as some of Donald's deeds (e.g., climbing Mt. McKinley) could be construed as either adventurous or reckless. The outcome variable of interest was participants' impression of Donald. As expected, when participants were primed with positive traits (adventurous), they reported a favorable impression of Donald; however, when they were primed with negative traits (reckless), they reported unfavorable impressions of Donald. Clearly, the activation of the negative and positive concepts prepared, or laid the groundwork, for participants' interpretation of Donald's behavior and the resulting first impression.

Recent environmental history can either exert a positive impact, a negative impact, or no impact on first impressions. For example, imagine that prior to meeting George you ran into your intelligent friend Bill. The encounter with Bill may increase, decrease, or not influence your first impression of George's intelligence. *Assimilation* occurs when a first impression changes in the direction of the environmental cue. *Contrast* occurs when a first impression changes in the opposite direction of the environmental cue. *Null effects* occur when a first impression does not change at all following the introduction of an environmental cue. Several related theoretical models have been developed to predict when environmental cues will lead to assimilation, contrast, or null effects. In the following, we present several of these models.

Trait versus Exemplar Primes: Opposing Effects on First Impressions

A variety of cognitive representations may become accessible following exposure to an environmental cue. Assume again that you have run into your intelligent friend Bill prior to encountering George. The abstract idea of intelligence, the more concrete idea of Bill, or even one of Bill's social categories (e.g., White) may become accessible—more confusingly, all three may become accessible. As several scholars have noted (Higgins, 1996; Wyer & Srull, 1989; Stapel & Koomen, 1998), researchers have rarely distinguished among these types of accessible material. That is, trait terms ("intelligent") and exemplars (intelligent individuals) have been used interchangeably to make certain information accessible. This lack of conceptual detail only presents a problem if we assume that abstract representations of intelligence, for example, exert different effects on first impressions than representations of *Bill's* intelligence. The first theoretical model that we will consider details how first impressions can be influenced by concrete exemplars and abstract traits.

The Interpretation–Comparison Model

Stapel and Koomen (1998, 2001a; Stapel, Koomen, & Van der Pligt, 1996, 1997; see also Wyer & Srull, 1989) argue that assimilation is much more likely when abstract traits (e.g., intelligence) are accessible than when exemplar traits (e.g., Bill's intelligence) are accessible. Indeed, many of the early studies utilized abstract traits in priming procedures. For example, Bargh, Lombardi, and Higgins (1988) used the scrambled sentence task described earlier (see Higgins et al., 1977) to prime either "inconsiderate" or "outgoing." Note that this priming procedure should activate abstract traits ("inconsiderate") rather than concrete exemplars ("inconsiderate Frank"). After a distracter task, participants read a paragraph that described a target person as ambiguous with regard to the traits in question. Participants were much more likely to label the target person in accordance with the primed (versus nonprimed) trait. Such assimilation effects were observed in several influential studies (Bargh & Pietromonaco, 1982; Higgins et al., 1977; Srull & Wyer, 1979). However, other studies reported contrast effects (e.g., Herr, 1986) despite utilizing similar paradigms. The important difference between these conflicting studies appears to be *how* the trait cue was presented. When the cue was presented as an abstract trait concept (hostility vs. kindness), assimilation resulted, whereas when the cue was presented as a concrete exemplar (Adolph Hitler and Santa Claus as indicative of hostility and kindness), contrast effects resulted.

Stapel and Koomen (1998, 2001a) argue that abstract trait cues influence subsequent first impression judgments by biasing interpretation of the target during encoding. In contrast, exemplar cues influence subsequent first impression judgments because these exemplars are used as a standard against which to compare the target. The idea is that person exemplar cues activate distinct mental representations with clear object boundaries and can therefore serve as clear anchoring standards. Conversely, abstract representations lack distinctiveness, have no clear object boundaries or anchor points, and are therefore unlikely to be used as comparison standards (Brown, 1953; Helson, 1964). The lack of clear boundaries in abstract traits makes it especially likely that there will be "spillover" from the abstract trait representation to subsequent interpretations. Thus, abstract cues bias encoding of the first impression toward the cue, resulting in assimilation.

According to this *interpretation–comparison* perspective, abstract trait cues only exert an assimilation effect if presented prior to encoding (for a similar perspective, see Trope, 1986). Otherwise, there would be no opportunity for these cues to influence encoding of the target individual. Person exemplar cues, though, exert a contrast effect when presented at any time before the judgment. That is, standards of comparison are utilized at the time of the judgment—thus, the standard only needs to be accessible at the time of judgment. To test these hypotheses, Stapel and colleagues (1997) asked participants to form a first impression of "Donald" from a paragraph that was ambiguous with regard to whether Donald was hostile and unfriendly or assertive and friendly. Environmental cues were either abstract traits ("hostile" or "friendly") or concrete exemplars of those traits ("Hitler" or "Gandhi"). Abstract trait cues only resulted in assimilation when presented prior to the paragraph—when these cues were presented after the paragraph but before judgment, there was no effect. Person exemplar cues resulted in contrast, regardless of when they were introduced. These findings support the idea that abstract traits exert their assimilative influence at the encoding stage, whereas concrete exemplars exert their influence at the judgment stage.

In summary, the influence of environmental cues depends on whether those cues exert an influence at encoding or judgment. According to the interpretation–comparison model, abstract trait cues influence the interpretation of a novel person at encoding; hence, abstract trait cues invite assimilation effects. Exemplar trait cues influence the comparison standard used to judge a novel person; hence, exemplar trait cues invite contrast effects.

The Inclusion–Exclusion Model

Although less detailed than the interpretation–comparison model with regard to stages of processing, the inclusion–exclusion model (Schwarz & Bless, 1992b, 2007) elaborates on the role of mental representation in forming predictions for assimilation or contrast. This model assumes that accessible material is either (1) assimilated into the representation of the target (inclusion) or (2) excluded from the representation of the target and instead used to construct a comparison standard (exclusion). Thus, when abstract trait representations bias interpretation of the target at encoding, the inclusion–exclusion model maintains that the accessible trait has been assimilated into the representation of the target. And where the interpretation–comparison model suggests that person exemplars are used as *the* comparison standard at judgment, the inclusion–exclusion model maintains that exemplars simply alter the representation of the comparison standard. As with the interpretation–comparison model, a critical determinant of inclusion or exclusion is the distinctness of the primed construct—when indistinct, it is likely to bleed into the target. In contrast, when the primed construct is distinct and has clear boundaries (e.g., an exemplar), it is excluded from the target and used to construct a comparison standard.

Inclusion–Exclusion and Applicability. The interpretation–comparison and inclusion–exclusion models make similar predictions with regard to abstract trait versus exemplar-based primes. The inclusion–exclusion model, however, adds predictive power with regard to cue-target applicability. That is, similarity between cue and target should increase the likelihood that one representation bleeds over into the other ("inclusion"). Thus, increased *applicability* of cue to target should increase assimilation effects. Indeed, there is evidence that assimilation effects are only achieved when environmental cues are applicable to the target judgment (Erdley & D'Agostino, 1988; Higgins, 1996; Sedikides, 1990). For example, in one study (Higgins and colleagues, 1977; see above), abstract adventurous/reckless cues, but not abstract obedient/disrespectful cues, influenced first impression adventurous/reckless judgments. In other words, only applicable cues were likely to be "included" in the target representation.

More recent research has refined this rather strict definition of applicability. For example, Stapel and Koomen (2000, 2005) have shown that priming broad concepts (e.g., "good") can lead to general assimilation effects across categories. That is, certain broad traits ("good") were superordinate to other more specific traits ("kind") such that priming the former influenced judgments of the latter. Thus, simply increasing prime breadth increases the likelihood of applicability, especially when prime and target are evaluatively consistent.

The general principle of applicability is also relevant to understanding the role of social category membership in priming first impressions. Banaji, Hardin, and Rothman (1993) have argued that accessible abstract traits will only influence first impression judgments when those traits are associated with the target's social category. For example, Banaji and colleagues found that first impressions of females, but not males, were influenced by an abstract "dependent" cue. The converse was true when the abstract cue was one of "aggressiveness" (see also Stapel & Koomen, 1998). Hence, abstract trait cues only influenced first impressions when the cues were associated with the social category of the target person. This conjecture is further supported by classic work on automatic stereotype activation in first impressions (Devine, 1989; Lepore & Brown, 1997). That is, this research used a male first impression target following an abstract trait cueing procedure. As such, the accessible trait ("hostile," generated from other abstract African American trait cues) would have been applicable to the target, since aggressiveness is associated with males.

In summary, the inclusion–exclusion model (in its most basic form) makes similar predictions as the interpretation–comparison model. Both models predict assimilation with abstract cues and contrast with exemplar cues. The inclusion–exclusion model is especially relevant for modeling the role of applicability. Specifically, applicable primes are those that are similar to the target and thereby likely to be included in the first impression representation, resulting in assimilation. These models have been useful in describing how the content of an environmental cue might alter first impression judgments.

Exemplar-Based Priming: Some Theoretical Misgivings

The story so far has been simple: applicable abstract trait primes lead to assimilative first impressions, and exemplar trait primes lead to contrasting first impressions. The story has been framed within two theoretical perspectives, the inclusion–exclusion model and the interpretation–comparison model. However, any simple and broad scientific story is sure to have a number of qualifications—a problem often described as "the problem of induction" (Hume, 2000/1748). For example, the simple story that "grass is green" has some qualifications. That does not mean that grass is never green nor that the principles that cause grass to be green are somehow incorrect. The qualifications, however, imply that a broader theory may be necessary for describing when grass will be green, when it will be a different color, and why. Likewise, the fact that the inclusion–exclusion model and the interpretation–comparison model enjoy only qualified predictive success does not imply that either of these models is "wrong" or "incorrect." Rather, a broader theory may be necessary to describe when these models are most appropriate.

First, the effects of "moderate" exemplars do not conform well to either approach. *A priori* predictions derived from the inclusion–exclusion model and the interpretation–comparison model both suggest that decreasing the extremity of an exemplar prime (e.g., from "Hitler" to "Alice Cooper") would decrease the size of a contrast effect. For example, because the inclusion–exclusion model suggests that primed examplars are potentially included in representations of the standard, there should be a linear relationship, such that more/less extreme exemplars are associated with stronger/weaker contrast effects. Empirical evidence has been inconsistent with these predictions: moderate exemplars appear to prime assimilative first impressions rather than muted but contrastive first impressions (e.g., Moskowitz & Skurnik, 1999; Stapel et al., 1997).

The inconsistency of these findings with the interpretation–comparison model led Stapel and colleagues (1997) to the hypothesis that person exemplars exhibit a small assimilative effect at encoding. The idea was that the small assimilative effect would be overwhelmed at judgment when the exemplar was sufficiently extreme but not when the exemplar was only "moderate." Indeed, findings supported their hypothesis. However, by adding these post hoc hypotheses, Stapel and colleagues (1997) risked creating an almost unfalsifiable model whose broader principles cannot be tested. As such, it may be more fruitful to explore when the more parsimonious initial model will and will not be predictive.

In any case, the simple story has just become more complicated—exemplar trait primes do not always lead to contrasting first impression judgments. As Herr, Sherman, and Fazio (1983) pointed out, however, inter-exemplar contrast is probably the norm. Thus, the limitations of the inclusion–exclusion and interpretation–contrast models in this domain may be relatively modest.

The second qualification regards the application of exemplar trait primes to first impression targets. The inclusion–exclusion and interpretation–comparison models suggest that exemplar trait priming should yield contrast to the degree that exemplar and target belong to the same social category. That is, similar exemplars are clearly more relevant to the target than are dissimilar exemplars and are therefore more likely to be used as comparison standards. Indeed, person exemplar cues (Hitler, Gandhi) lead to contrast in first impression judgments (hostile, friendly), whereas animal exemplar cues (shark, puppy) do not (Stapel & Koomen, 1996; Stapel et al., 1996, 1997). Similarly, female exemplar cues, but not male exemplar cues, led to a contrast in a subsequent first impression of a *female target* (Stapel & Koomen, 1998). However, neither model can explain, on an *a priori* basis, why inapplicable exemplars (animals, males) have been associated with assimilation effects. Yet, another post hoc alteration to the interpretation–comparison model was prepared to explain these effects (see Stapel & Koomen, 1998), again putting the interpretation–comparison model at risk of being unfalsifiable.

We have reviewed two phenomena that do not appear to be well modeled, *a priori*, by either the inclusion–exclusion model or the interpretation–comparison model. Given the wealth of factors that may bear on the phenomenon of first impression priming, it is likely that there are other factors that also do not fit exactly within these two models. However, these models are quite broad, and many hypotheses may be derived from them—in fact, many of these hypotheses have been supported. As such, it would be inappropriate to label either of these models "incorrect"—both appear to have considerable predictive power. The message from this section is simply that there are several areas of first impression priming in need of more appropriate *a priori* hypotheses derived from a parsimonious larger model.

Environmental Cue Content: Summary

In summary, abstract trait primes generally lead to assimilative first impressions, and exemplar trait primes generally lead to contrasting first impressions—findings that are well modeled by both the inclusion–exclusion model and the interpretation–comparison model. These effects are strongest with applicable abstract trait primes and with applicable exemplar trait primes. Several research findings in this area may be benefited by better *a priori* modeling.

HOW PRIMING FIRST IMPRESSIONS DEPENDS ON THE MIND

Just as first impressions are not made in a vacuum, environmental cues are not processed by empty minds. Human beings are not passive recipients of environmental input but active information processors (e.g., Piaget, 1954; Goldstein, 2002)—people have goals, expectations, and learning histories. Thus, if two people look at the exact same object, they do not necessarily *see* the same thing (e.g., Balcetis & Dunning, 2006). In this section, we will examine how the mind moderates the influence of environmental cues on first impression judgments. We will first review conscious correction processes and then review the impact of goals.

Conscious Correction of Priming

Imagine that you have just met George and have decided that he is quite unintelligent. Upon reflection, however, you realize that George just seems unintelligent because you recently had lunch with your brilliant friend Bill, and, indeed, everyone seems rather stupid in comparison to Bill. Hence, you decide that George is simply average rather than unintelligent. This example illustrates that people can be aware of biases in their judgments (Nelson, 1996; Wegner & Wenzlaff, 1996) and often attempt to correct for these biases (Wilson & Brekke, 1994). First impression judgments should not be an exception to this rule; as such, the influence of environmental cues on first impressions is amenable to correction. This section examines the conditions under which the influence of environmental cues are consciously corrected (or overcorrected).

Imagine again that you just met George and judged him to be quite unintelligent; however, this time you did not make a correction, despite the fact that you passed by your brilliant friend Bill earlier. Why have you failed to make a correction? Perhaps you do not remember seeing Bill. Or perhaps you remember seeing Bill but do not believe that the brief meeting biased your impression of George. Note that the current example included only a brief encounter while the former example included a prolonged encounter (lunch). Indeed, subtle and brief cues are less likely than blatant or prolonged cues to invite conscious corrections. In research on first impression judgments, environmental cues range from the extremely subtle (even subliminal) variety to the "hit 'em over the head" variety. As an example of a subtle cue, Bargh and Pietromonaco (1982) presented hostile or neutral words subliminally. Participants were unable to identify the content of these words; yet, those exposed to hostile words were subsequently more likely than those exposed to the neutral words to form a hostile first impression of an ambiguously hostile target. This assimilative effect of subliminal influences on first impressions has been replicated (e.g., Bargh, Bond, Lombardi, & Tota, 1986).

All else being equal, subtle influences on first impression judgments do appear to be less amenable to conscious correction than more blatant influences. This does not imply, however, that subtle influences are immune to correction. In fact, nonconscious correction processes are common for some perceptual processes. For instance, the human visual system is constantly making corrections. As you approach an object, that object takes up an increasingly large proportion of your retina; yet, you don't perceive that object to be growing larger—your perceptual system has nonconsciously corrected for the influence of retinal proportion on size perception. It is likewise possible that first perceptions incur nonconscious corrections for environmental influences. Obviously, the underlying processes would be different, but the rationale is analogous— correction of subtle or nonconscious influences of environmental history are possible.

Conversely, awareness of an environmental cue is *not* sufficient for correction and does not imply that the cue is "blatant." For example, in many studies (e.g., Higgins et al., 1977; Srull & Wyer, 1979) participants engage in the "scrambled sentence" procedure outlined above. In this paradigm, participants are aware of the environmental cues, yet the primed abstract traits typically elicit assimilation effects, suggesting that correction does not occur. One possibility is that at the time of judgment participants do not consciously recall the priming event. Lombardi, Higgins, and Bargh (1987) provided support for this explanation. Using the scrambled sentence procedure, these researchers found that participants who could recall the primed construct apparently corrected for the influence of the prime; that is, these participants did *not* exhibit assimilation effects in their first impressions of a target. Thus, failure to recall the priming event is one condition that can short-circuit correction attempts.

It is also possible, however, to recall a priming event but not understand that the event could influence a first impression judgment. For instance, in one experiment (Lepore & Brown, 2002), participants were or were not exposed to social category labels likely to make the trait "hostility" accessible (see Devine, 1989). Importantly, in this procedure nearly all participants could recall the primed trait words; however, only some of the participants drew a connection between the priming task and the subsequent first impression task. Those participants who *did* draw a connection between the priming task and the impression formation task were uninfluenced by the priming task. In contrast, those who *did not* draw a connection were influenced by the primed trait words. Here, it seemed that awareness of the influence, rather than awareness or recall of the prime, was the crucial element in producing correction.

In response to the complexities involved with correction, several models have emerged to explain when and how people will correct for environmental influences. Although these models share many assumptions (such as that blatant cues are typically corrected for), we will focus on the flexible correction model (Wegener & Petty, 1995, 1997), as it highlights the role of individual minds. Specifically, the flexible correction model assumes that perceivers have naive theories about the influence of particular types of cues. For example, whereas I might believe (as an author of a chapter on priming) that even an ephemeral experience is likely to influence my first impression judgments, another individual may not have that belief. The introduction of an ephemeral cue into our environments might thus result in correction for me but not others. This consideration of individual minds permits especially fine-grained predictions for corrections.

A second important reason for covering the flexible correction model in detail is that this model (as opposed to earlier models; e.g., Martin, 1986) builds on the idea that both assimilation *and* contrast can result from environmental cues, independent of correction. For example, the immediate effect of intelligent Bill on impressions of George may be contrastive, and the attempted correction may be to remove this contrast—earlier models would have difficulty with this scenario. Thus, the flexible correction model builds more directly on the models we have thus far reviewed and maintains that contrast can arise from rather automatic influences—as such, effortful correction may lead to assimilation rather than contrast.

In some ways, the flexible correction model is quite similar to the mental contamination model of Wilson and Brekke (1994); in this model, contamination is defined as any unwanted influence on thoughts, feelings, judgments, or decisions. Clearly, the impact of priming on first impressions can be seen as mental contamination. According to Wilson and Brekke, to avoid contamination, people must be aware of the unwanted process, they must be motivated to correct it, they need to know the size and direction of the bias, and they need the means to adjust their judgment. The flexible correction model shares these premises but adds that overcorrection is a function of the naive theory of

bias—specifically, overcorrection will occur (given motivation and ability) if an environmental cue is theorized to exert a stronger bias than it
actually does.

The flexible correction model can be applied to a variety of findings. For example, when participants are reminded of the priming episode prior to making first impression judgments, correction usually follows. In one study participants were asked to write down adjectives as
they were presented orally—the adjectives were either synonyms of
"friendly" or "dishonorable." After a distraction task, participants were
either asked to recall these words (reminder) or not (no-reminder). Subsequent ratings of an ambiguously friendly/dishonorable target reflected
assimilation effects when there was no reminder but contrast effects
when there was a reminder (Strack, Schwarz, Bless, Kubler, & Wänke,
1993). According to the flexible correction model, participants overcorrected for the perceived influence of the prime—presumably, their naive
theories suggested that priming of this type could exert a stronger influence than was actually observed. In fact, over- or undercorrection should
not be uncommon—people appear to have quite inaccurate beliefs about
the extent to which various events cloud judgment (Nisbett & Wilson,
1977). Thus, naive theories are often incorrect, leading to frequent over-
or under-correction.

Building on this idea, Stapel, Koomen, and Zeelenberg (1998) asked
participants to indicate whether they thought priming would lead to assimilation or contrast effects—most participants thought that the priming task would lead to assimilation, regardless of whether it was abstract
or exemplar priming. In this same priming study, some participants were
asked to make sure that their ratings were not influenced by the priming
task (correction condition). In general, abstract trait priming led to assimilation, whereas exemplar trait priming led to contrast. However,
among participants in the correction condition, only contrast effects
were observed. In other words, participants' naive theories about the influence of priming (i.e., assimilation) caused them to (over)correct for
their supposed bias, even though this bias was not apparent in the exemplar condition. Thus, naive theories can help to explain why correction
processes sometimes fail.

The timing of conscious correction can also be an important factor
in first impression judgments. Specifically, correction prior to exposure
to the target may result in quite different corrections than those that occur after exposure to the target. Stapel and Koomen (1999) proposed
that it is difficult to reconstruct the exact influence of a prime that has
already occurred and that correction attempts that occur after exposure
to the target are likely to be quite general; corrections prior to exposure
are likely to be specific to the primed trait. Results of at least one study
supported this distinction between pre- and post-encoding correction

(Stapel & Koomen, 1999). Thus, distinctions between pre- and post-encoding corrections may be important to draw when considering the ultimate impact of correction on first impression judgments.

One important distinction generally not drawn in the correction literature—and therefore not addressed by the flexible correction model—is the distinction between conscious correction processes and "unpriming." The concept of *unpriming* is based on the idea that prime influences are generally not eternal—instead, certain processes are responsible for shutting off the influence of a prime. One "shutting-off" process appears to be the use of the prime—that is, similar to emotional catharsis or task completion, the explicit use (influence) of a prime negates its subsequent power (e.g., Sparrow & Wegner, 2006). It is possible to apply this reasoning to studies in which participants "correct" for prime influences after drawing a connection between the prime and the target judgment. That is, drawing an association between the prime and the target task can be considered an influence of the prime—at this point, the influence of the prime may be shut down via "unpriming" rather than via a conscious realization about the likely influence of the prime. By this reasoning, blatant primes or recallable primes are unsuccessful not by virtue of conscious correction but instead by virtue of unpriming. This reasoning does not currently have direct empirical support, as conscious correction has not been compared with unpriming.

In summary, environmental cues can range from subtle to obvious. As they become less and less subtle, people become more and more likely to alter subsequent first impression judgments away from the presumed direction of influence. Correction processes are likely to range from unconscious to completely conscious and are especially likely when people can draw a connection between the priming event and the first impression judgment. The flexible correction model helps to explain when and how much people will correct their first impressions for the presumed influence of environmental cues.

Processing Goals

Imagine again that you are to form a first impression of George after encountering intelligent Bill. You are to negotiate a deal with George, however, and as such it is extremely important that your impression of George's intelligence be accurate. Indeed, when people are especially motivated to be accurate, research (described below) has shown that they are unlikely to be influenced by environmental cues. Although research on goals in first impressions has focused mainly on accuracy goals, there are a variety of goals that may be active as people form first impressions. In this section we review how these goals may moderate the influence of environmental cues on first impressions.

Accuracy Goals

People would prefer to not be biased (Wilson & Brekke, 1994). Most would prefer their impressions of a target individual to be based on that individual's behaviors and characteristics rather than on an irrelevant remnant of recent experience. Indeed, one assumption of the inclusion–exclusion model is that a given piece of information will not be used in judgment if it is perceived as irrelevant to the judgment itself. Likewise, the flexible correction model assumes that people would like to be unbiased in their judgments—otherwise, why would people try to correct for biases? The extent to which people have this motivation, however, varies by person and by situation. For example, when Wilson and Brekke (1994) asked people to consider how much they would be bothered by being biased in various circumstances, people indicated that they would be quite concerned about being biased in a major life decision but not terribly concerned about being biased in preferences for recreational activities. Concern for a lack of bias in first impressions probably falls somewhere in between a major life decision and preferences for recreational activities, but probably closer to the latter. Thus, although accuracy motivation is likely to be somewhat apparent in first impression judgments, it is by no means inevitable.

Increases in accuracy motivation should lead to increasingly accurate first impressions, unbiased by recent environmental cues. That is, accuracy motivation prompts (1) systematic processing and careful consideration of a target's characteristics and behaviors (Chaiken, Giner-Sorolla, & Chen, 1996), (2) consideration of a wide variety of alternative possibilities (Ford & Kruglanski, 1995), and/or (3) constant revising of the impression (Tetlock, 1992). All of these processes may lead to correction processes (Wegener & Petty, 1997) or the consideration of more information (which would dilute the impact of the prime; Schwarz & Bless, 2007).

To examine whether accuracy motivation reduces the influence of environmental cues on first impressions, Ford and Kruglanski (1995) primed participants with positive or negative trait terms and subsequently asked participants to form an impression of an individual who behaved in an ambiguous manner. After the priming task but prior to encoding information about the target, some participants were told that they should form as accurate an impression as they could, since they would be asked to justify their impression to the experimenter. The standard assimilation effect occurred only for participants who were *not* given the accuracy instructions. These findings suggested that first impressions might not be terribly influenced by environmental cues among people with especially strong accuracy motivation (see also Thompson,

Roman, Moskowitz, Chaiken, & Bargh, 1994). However, because accuracy motivation instills correction processes regardless of when such motivation is activated, it remains possible that accuracy motivation produces several different types of correction processes—some that occur before and some that occur after the priming effect.

In summary, although accuracy motivation may produce a variety of effects on judgment in general, as applied to first impressions, it appears to eliminate or reverse the impact of abstract trait primes. It should be noted, however, that accuracy motivation appears to have little if any effect on the impact of exemplar trait primes (see Stapel et al., 1998).

Communication Goals

Often, the reason that people are motivated to be accurate in their judgments is because they will be accountable to others for those judgments. Indeed, accountability manipulations are commonly used in experiments to create accuracy motivation (see Tetlock, 1992). However, knowing that one has to communicate a judgment to others can instigate goals beyond accuracy. For example, with preexisting knowledge of another's attitude on a particular topic, one may alter his views on that topic to coincide with those of this other person (e.g., Heider, 1958). Indeed, recent findings suggest that attitudes and beliefs will change in the direction of actual or anticipated interaction partners (Lowery, Hardin, & Sinclair, 2001; Sinclair, Lowery, Hardin, & Colangelo, 2004). First impression judgments may follow similar rules—specifically, with knowledge of a third party's attitude toward a target, one may alter the first impression of that target in the direction of the third party's attitude. Just as accuracy motives may reduce the influence of some primes via recoding of the impression formed, so may interpersonal communication goals. Sedikides (1990) observed support for this hypothesis. Participants were told that they would be communicating an impression of a target person to a recipient. The recipient was described as either liking or disliking the target (or no information was provided about the recipient). Either prior to or after these instructions, participants were primed, via a scrambled sentence task, with either positive or negative traits about the target. After reading the ambiguous target description, participants described their first impressions of the target. As expected, standard assimilation effects were observed on the primed trait dimensions when no information was given about the recipient. However, there was no priming effect when the attitude of the recipient was known—impressions were positive when the recipient was described as liking the target and negative when the recipient was described as disliking the target. These effects held regardless of whether the communication instructions were provided before priming, after priming, or after description of the target.

This study suggests that participants either encoded or recoded the target representation according to the views of the recipient, overwhelming any effects of the prime on the target representation. Thus, both accuracy goals and communication goals may dilute or eliminate influences of abstract trait priming on first impressions.

Impression Formation Goals

Although we often make first impressions of others because we are trying to do so, at other times we are too busy or simply uninterested in making a conscious impression judgment. When busy or uninterested, though, we may sometimes unintentionally form impressions of others (Bassili, 1989; Uleman & Moskowitz, 1994; Winter & Uleman, 1984; see also Chapter 13 in this volume). Nonetheless, our later judgments of an individual may be different depending on whether or not we intended to form an impression of that individual (Hastie & Park, 1986). In most studies examining the role of environmental cues in first impressions, participants are given instructions to form an impression prior to their judgments—thus, most effects of priming on first impressions have been observed under circumstances in which perceivers have an active impression formation goal. In an effort to clarify the role of impression formation goals in modulating the impact of environmental cues on first impressions, we review here the handful of studies that have manipulated impression formation goals in priming experiments.

One route that researchers have taken is to examine impression formation goals active during *exposure* to environmental cues. Building on research on spontaneous trait inferences, Moskowitz and Roman (1992) used behavioral descriptions as primes. Research on spontaneous trait inferences has shown that people spontaneously infer traits from behavioral description sentences, but only when perceivers are motivated to form an impression will these traits be connected to the target (e.g., Bassili, 1989). Thus, behavioral description sentences should activate abstract traits in the absence of impression formation goals but exemplar-based traits (traits connected to actors) in the presence of impression formation goals. Moskowitz and Roman (1992) instructed some participants (but not others) to form an impression of individuals in behavioral description sentences. All participants then formed an impression of an ambiguous target person. Among those given impression formation instructions, prime-target contrast occurred, presumably because these participants inferred exemplar-based traits. Otherwise prime-target assimilation occurred, presumably because these participants inferred abstract traits from the behavior descriptions (see also Stapel et al., 1996).

Finally—and perhaps unsurprisingly, given the discussion thus far—when perceivers are asked to "interpret" a target's behavior, assimilation effects follow environmental cues, whereas when perceivers are asked to "compare" a target to other people, contrast effects follow environmental cues (Stapel & Koomen, 2001a). Thus, the influence of impression formation goals on the prime-target relationship may depend on the specific form of those impression formation goals.

In general, behaviors encountered by a perceiver just prior to meeting a target person can alter first impressions of that target person. When those preceding behaviors are encountered in the presence of impression formation goals, first impression judgments of a subsequent target are contrasted away from the preceding behaviors. However, if encountered in the absence of impression formation goals, first impression judgments of a target are assimilated to preceding behaviors. Thus, listening to Bill give an intelligent speech may cause a perceiver to think that George is intelligent, unintelligent, or neither, depending on the impression formation goals of the perceiver.

CONCLUSIONS AND FUTURE DIRECTIONS

When we meet someone for the first time, our minds are not empty. They are filled with thoughts and expectations, some of which have been made active by recent cues in the environment. This chapter has focused on the role of one's recent environmental history on first impression judgments. In other words, this chapter examined the role of *priming* in first impression judgments.

The review focused on factors that determine whether a particular environmental cue will have an assimilative, contrasting, or null effect. In general, assimilative effects are likely when subtle abstract cues are encountered prior to a first impression. That is, our first impression of an individual will change toward the recently encountered cue. Contrasting effects are likely when exemplar cues (read: people), and especially extreme exemplar cues, are encountered prior to a first impression. That is, our first impression of an individual will change away from the recently encountered cue. These effects were described in terms of the interpretation–comparison model (e.g., Stapel et al., 1996, 1997) and the inclusion–exclusion model (Schwarz & Bless, 1992b, 2007). Specifically, subtle abstract cues are likely to influence encoding of a novel person and are likely to be melded with the representation of that person. Exemplar cues are more distinct, such that they can be used as standards of comparison (or they can alter the standard representation) in judging the target. Most priming effects in first impression judgments are consistent with these two models, although some studies show contradictory findings (e.g., that concrete exemplars sometimes lead to assimilation).

In addition to properties of the environmental cues themselves, properties of the mind at any particular time can modify the influence of environmental history. For example, the flexible correction model suggests that individuals will use their naive theories of influence and correct (often overcorrect) for the perceived influence of environmental history. As different minds will have different naive theories, it is likely that individuals' first impressions of a target person will be differentially influenced by environmental history. It appears, however, that since naive theories about exemplar cues are typically wrong, the effects of even blatant exemplar cues can go uncorrected (they cause contrast).

Naive theories of influence are but one property of the mind likely to mute, amplify, or reverse the influence of environmental history. In particular, the mind is likely to have goals both while encountering the environmental cue and while forming a first impression. When people are particularly motivated to be accurate, they are indeed unlikely to be influenced by irrelevant environmental cues, though this may not hold true for cues that influence comparison standards (e.g., concrete exemplars). When communication goals dictate the formation of particular judgments, those judgments are generally formed and drown out any effects of the environmental cue. And although abstract and exemplar cues generally lead to assimilation and contrast effects, respectively, interpretation and comparison goals generally foster assimilation and contrast independent of the type of cue.

These general effects, however, should be considered in light of the fact that nearly all of these studies have utilized paradigms in which written behavioral descriptions were used as the "target behavior." Although this *may* be an appropriate operational definition, and although we may often form first impressions of people through hearsay, first impressions are typically formed of people in the flesh. That is, perceivers have plenty of other information (appearance, body language, etc.) to accompany the more obvious behavior typically described in a sentence. Although these differences *may not* alter the influence of environmental cues, this topic should be investigated empirically rather than assumed. Consider, for example, the role of accuracy motivation. With behavioral description studies, accuracy motivation typically leads to more accurate (less biased) first impression judgments, and these effects are thought to occur through an increase in systematic processing (Thompson et al., 1994). In nonverbal first impression studies, however, deliberative processing appears to reduce accuracy (e.g., Ambady & Gray, 2002). These divergent findings highlight the idea that different processes may under-lie first impressions formed from behavioral descriptions and those formed with more complete (though perhaps brief) information about a person. To foster a better and more complete understanding of the role of environmental cues in first impressions, future research should include a variety of first impression exposure, including behavioral de-scriptions (e.g., Srull & Wyer, 1979), nonverbal and verbal thin slices (e.g., Ambady & Rosenthal, 1992), environmental information (Gos-ling, Ko, Mannarelli, & Morris, 2002), and pictorial descriptions (e.g., Fiedler, Schenck, Watling, & Menges, 2005).

Beyond this caveat, there exists a fairly consistent empirical picture of how first impressions depend on the perceiver's recent history. To many, the simple version of this picture is far from revelatory. Most psy-chologists understand that apparently "objective" reality is heavily clouded by the contents of our minds. In that sense it is not surprising that one's recent experience can influence judgments of others. What may be surprising, however, is the complexity of the processes involved in priming first impressions. Recent history does not exert a unidirec-tional influence—both the direction and extent of influence are contin-gent on a variety of factors. In fact, modification of naive theories or cue content or processing goals can eliminate, accentuate, or even reverse priming effects that were otherwise well modeled. The complexity of factors that modify priming influences might be taken as evidence of an active mind attempting to use all available information in an otherwise uncertain temporal-cultural context. That is, some have suggested that the key adaptation of the human mind is its ability to help humans adapt to a historically dynamic environment (Quartz & Sejnowski, 2002). Per-haps future researchers will thereby discover that the mind uses its recent history as an acceptable context with which to evaluate the social world. In this sense, then, it might be said that the mind doesn't *cloud* social reality but rather *constructs* a social reality appropriate to its recent his-tory. By this reasoning, recent history does not so much distort first im-pression judgments as it does situate those judgments.

REFERENCES

Ambady, N., & Gray, H. M. (2002). On being sad and mistaken: Mood effects on the accuracy of thin-slice judgments. *Journal of Personality and Social Psy-chology, 83,* 947–961.

Balcetis, E., & Dunning, D. (2006). See what you want to see: Motivational influ-ences on visual perception. *Journal of Personality and Social Psychology, 91,* 612–625.

Baldwin, M. W., Carrell, S. E., & Lopez, D. F. (1990). Priming relationship schemas: My advisor and the pope are watching me from the back of my mind. *Journal of Experimental Social Psychology, 26,* 435–454.

Banaji, M. R., Hardin, C., & Rothman, A. J. (1993). Implicit stereotyping in person judgment. *Journal of Personality and Social Psychology, 65,* 272–281.

Bargh, J. A., Bond, R. N., Lombardi, W. J., & Tota, M. E. (1986). The additive nature of chronic and temporary sources of construct accessibility. *Journal of Personality and Social Psychology, 50,* 869–878.

Bargh, J. A., & Chartrand, T. L. (2000). The mind in the middle: A practical guide to priming and automaticity research. In H. T. Reis & C. M. Judd (Eds.), *Handbook of research methods in social and personality psychology* (pp. 253–285). Cambridge, UK: Cambridge University Press.

Bargh, J. A., Gollwitzer, P. M., Lee-Chai, A., Barndollar, K., & Trotschel, R. (2001). The automated will: Nonconscious activation and pursuit of behavioral goals. *Journal of Personality and Social Psychology, 81,* 1014–1027.

Bargh, J. A., Lombardi, W., & Higgins, E. T. (1988). Automaticity of chronically accessible constructs in Person × Situation effects on person perception: It's just a matter of time. *Journal of Personality and Social Psychology, 55,* 599–605.

Bargh, J. A., & Pietromonaco, P. (1982). Automatic information processing and social perception: The influence of trait information presented outside of conscious awareness on impression formation. *Journal of Personality and Social Psychology, 49,* 1129–1146.

Baissili, J. N. (1989). Trait encoding in behavior identification and dispositional inference. *Personality and Social Psychology Bulletin, 15,* 285–296.

Brown, D. R. (1953). Stimulus-similarity and the anchoring of subjective scales. *American Journal of Psychology, 66,* 199–214.

Chaiken, S., Giner-Sorolla, R., & Chen, S. (1996). Beyond accuracy: Defense and impression motives in heuristic and systematic information processing. In P. M. Gollwitzer & J. A. Bargh (Eds.), *The psychology of action: Linking motivation and cognition to behavior* (pp. 553–578). New York: Guilford Press.

Devine, P. G. (1989). Stereotypes and prejudice: Their automatic and controlled components. *Journal of Personality and Social Psychology, 56,* 5–18.

Erdley, C. A., & D'Agostino, P. R. (1988). Cognitive and affective components of automatic priming effects. *Journal of Personality and Social Psychology, 54,* 741–747.

Fiedler, K., Schenck, W., Watling, M., & Menges, J. I. (2005). Priming trait inferences through pictures and moving pictures: The impact of open and closed mindsets. *Journal of Personality and Social Psychology, 88,* 229–244.

Ford, T. E., & Kruglanski, A. W. (1995). Effects of epistemic motivations on the use of accessible constructs in social judgment. *Personality and Social Psychology Bulletin, 21,* 950–962.

Goldstein, E. B. (2002). *Sensation and perception.* Pacific Grove, CA: Wadsworth.

Gosling, S. D., Ko, S. J., Mannarelli, T., & Morris, M. E. (2002). A room with a cue: Personality judgments based on offices and bedrooms. *Journal of Personality and Social Psychology, 82,* 379–398.

Hastie, R., & Park, B. (1986). The relationship between memory and judgment depends on whether the judgment task is memory-based or on-line. *Psychological Review, 93,* 258–268.

Heider, F. (1958). *The psychology of interpersonal relations.* New York: Wiley.

Helson, H. (1964). *Adaptation-level theory: An experimental and systematic approach to behavior.* New York: Harper & Row.

Herr, P. M. (1986). Consequences of priming: Judgment and behavior. *Journal of Personality and Social Psychology, 51,* 1106–1115.

Herr, P. M., Sherman, S. J., & Fazio, R. H. (1983). On the consequences of priming: Assimilation and contrast effects. *Journal of Experimental Social Psychology, 19,* 323–340.

Higgins, E. T. (1996). Knowledge activation: Accessibility, applicability, and salience. In E. T. Higgins & A. W. Kruglanski (Eds.), *Social psychology: Handbook of basic principles* (pp. 133–168). New York: Guilford Press.

Higgins, E. T., Rholes, W. S., & Jones, C. R. (1977). Category accessibility and impression formation. *Journal of Experimental Social Psychology, 13,* 141–154.

Hume, D. (2000). *An enquiry concerning human understanding.* New York: Oxford University Press. (Original work published 1748)

Jacobs, R. A., & Fine., I. (1999). Experience-dependent integration of texture and motion cues to depth. *Vision Research, 39,* 4062–4075.

Lepore, L., & Brown, R. (1997). Category and stereotype activation: Is prejudice inevitable? *Journal of Personality and Social Psychology, 72,* 275–287.

Lepore, L., & Brown, R. (2002). The role of awareness: Divergent automatic stereotype activation and implicit judgment correction. *Social Cognition, 20,* 321–351.

Lombardi, W. J., Higgins, E. T., & Bargh, J. A. (1987). The role of consciousness in priming effects of categorization. *Personality and Social Psychology Bulletin, 13,* 411–429.

Lowery, B. S., Hardin, C. D., & Sinclair, S. (2001). Social influence effects on automatic racial prejudice. *Journal of Personality and Social Psychology, 81,* 842–855.

Martin, L. L. (1986). Set/reset: Use and disuse of concepts in impression formation. *Journal of Personality and Social Psychology, 51,* 493–504.

Moskowitz, G. B., & Roman, R. J. (1992). Spontaneous trait inferences as self-generated primes: Implications for conscious social judgment. *Journal of Personality and Social Psychology, 62,* 728–738.

Moskowitz, G. B., & Skurnik, I. W. (1999). Contrast effects as determined by the type of prime: Trait versus exemplar primes initiate processing strategies that differ in how accessible constructs are used. *Journal of Personality and Social Psychology, 76,* 911–927.

Murphy, S. T., & Zajonc, R. B. (1993). Affect, cognition, and awareness: Affective priming with optimal and suboptimal stimulus exposures. *Journal of Personality and Social Psychology, 64,* 723–739.

Musch, J., & Klauer, K. C. (Eds.). (2003). *The psychology of evaluation: Affective processes in cognition and emotion.* Mahwah, NJ: Erlbaum.

Nelson, T. O. (1996). Consciousness and metacognition. *American Psychologist,* *51*(2), 102–116.

Nisbett, R. E., & Wilson, T. D. (1977). Telling more than we can know: Verbal reports on mental processes. *Psychological Review, 84,* 231–259.

Piaget, J. (1954). *The construction of reality in the child.* New York: Free Press.

Quartz, S. R., & Sejnowski, T. J. (2002). *Liars, lovers, and heroes: What the new brain science reveals about how we become who we are.* New York: HarperCollins.

Ratcliff, R., & McKoon, G. (1988). A retrieval theory of priming in memory. *Psychological Review, 95,* 385–408.

Schwarz, N., & Bless, H. (1992a). Scandals and the public's trust in politicians: Assimilation and contrast effects. *Personality and Social Psychology Bulletin, 18,* 574–579.

Schwarz, N., & Bless, H. (1992b). Constructing reality and its alternatives: An inclusion/exclusion model of assimilation and contrast effects in social judgment. In L. L. Martin & A. Tesser (Eds.), *The construction of social judgments* (pp. 217–245). Hillsdale, NJ: Erlbaum.

Schwarz, N., & Bless, H. (2007). Mental construal processes: The inclusion/exclusion model. In D. Stapel & J. Suls (Eds.), *Assimilation and contrast in social psychology* (pp. 119–141). New York: Psychology Press.

Sedikides, C. (1990). Effects of fortuitously activated constructs versus activated communication goals on person impressions. *Journal of Personality and Social Psychology, 58,* 397–408.

Sinclair, S., Lowery, B. S., Hardin, C. D., & Colangelo, A. (2004). Social tuning of automatic racial attitudes: The role of affiliation motivation. *Journal of Personality and Social Psychology, 89,* 583–592.

Sparrow, B., & Wegner, D. M. (2006). Unpriming: The deactivation of thoughts through expression. *Journal of Personality and Social Psychology, 91,* 1009–1019.

Srull, T. K., & Wyer, R. S. (1979). The role of category accessibility in the interpretation of information about persons: Some determinants and implications. *Journal of Personality and Social Psychology, 37,* 1660–1672.

Stapel, D. A., & Koomen, W. (1996). Differential consequences of trait inferences: A direct test of the trait-referent hypothesis. *European Journal of Social Psychology, 26,* 827–838.

Stapel, D. A., & Koomen, W. (1998). When stereotype activation results in (counter) stereotypical judgments: Priming stereotype-relevant traits and exemplars. *Journal of Experimental Social Psychology, 34,* 136–163.

Stapel, D. A., & Koomen, W. (1999). Correction processes in person judgments: The role of timing. *European Journal of Social Psychology, 29,* 131–138.

Stapel, D. A., & Koomen, W. (2000). How far do we go beyond the information given? The impact of knowledge activation on interpretation and inference. *Journal of Personality and Social Psychology, 78,* 19–37.

Stapel, D. A., & Koomen, W. (2001a). The impact of interpretation versus comparison goals on knowledge accessibility effects. *Journal of Experimental Social Psychology, 37,* 134–149.

Stapel, D. A., & Koomen, W. (2001b). When we wonder what it all means: Interpretation goals facilitate accessibility and stereotyping effects. *Personality and Social Psychology Bulletin, 27,* 915–929.

Stapel, D. A., & Koomen, W. (2005). When less is more: The consequences of affective primacy for subliminal priming effects. *Personality and Social Psychology Bulletin, 31,* 1286–1295.

Stapel, D. A., Koomen, W., & Van der Pligt, J. (1996). The referents of trait inferences: The impact of trait concepts versus actor–trait links on subsequent judgments. *Journal of Personality and Social Psychology, 70,* 437–450.

Stapel, D. A., Koomen, W., & Van der Pligt, J. (1997). Categories of category accessibility: The impact of trait versus exemplar priming on person judgments. *Journal of Experimental Social Psychology, 33,* 44–76.

Stapel, D. A., Koomen, W., & Zeelenberg, M. (1998). The impact of accuracy motivation on interpretation, comparison, and correction processes: Accuracy x knowledge accessibility effects. *Journal of Personality and Social Psychology, 74,* 878–893.

Strack, F., Schwarz, N., Bless, H., Kubler, A., & Wanke, M. (1993). Awareness of the influence as a determinant of assimilation versus contrast. *European Journal of Social Psychology, 23,* 53–62.

Tetlock, P. E. (1992). The impact of accountability on judgment and choice. Toward a social contingency model. In M. P. Zanna (Ed.), *Advances in experimental social psychology,* (Vol. 25, pp. 331–376). San Diego, CA: Academic Press.

Thompson, E. P., Roman, R. J., Moskowitz, G. B., Chaiken, S., & Bargh, J. A. (1994). Accuracy motivation attenuates covert priming: The systematic processing of social information. *Journal of Personality and Social Psychology, 66,* 474–489.

Trope, Y. (1986). Identification and inferential processes in dispositional attribution. *Psychological Review, 93,* 239–257.

Uleman, J. S., & Moskowitz, G. B. (1994). Unintended effects of goals on unintended inferences. *Journal of Personality and Social Psychology, 66,* 490–501.

Wegener, D. T., & Petty, R. E. (1995). Flexible correction processes in social judgment: The role of naive theories in corrections for perceived bias. *Journal of Personality and Social Psychology, 68,* 36–51.

Wegener, D. T., & Petty, R. E. (1997). The flexible correction model: The role of naïve theories of bias in bias correction. In M. P. Zanna (Ed.), *Advances in experimental psychology* (Vol. 29, pp. 141–208). New York: Academic Press.

Wegner, D. M., & Wenzlaff, R. M. (1996). Mental control. In E. T. Higgins & A. W. Kruglanski (Eds.), *Social psychology: Handbook of basic principles* (pp. 466–492). New York: Guilford Press.

Wilson, T. D., & Brekke, N. (1994). Mental contamination and mental correction:

Unwanted influences on judgments and evaluations. *Psychological Bulletin, 116*, 117–142.

Winter, L., & Uleman, J. S. (1984). When are social judgments made?: Evidence for the spontaneousness of trait inferences. *Journal of Personality and Social Psychology, 47*, 237–252.

Wyer, R. S., & Srull, T. K. (1989). *Memory and cognition in its social context.* Hillsdale, NJ: Erlbaum.

CHAPTER 13

Spontaneous Impressions Derived from Observations of Behavior

What a Long, Strange Trip It's Been (and It's Not Over Yet)

JOHN J. SKOWRONSKI
DONAL E. CARLSTON
JESSICA HARTNETT

Perceptions of others are relevant to virtually every human endeavor. Hence, it is not surprising that person perception represents one of the oldest (Asch, 1946; Schneider, Hastorf, & Ellsworth, 1979; Tagiuri & Petrullo, 1958) and most central (see Funder, 1999; Wyer & Lambert, 1994) domains in social psychology. By examining judgments made from different kinds and combinations of stimuli, social psychologists have learned much about judgment rules and processes implicated in person perception and how these vary across situations, perceivers, and targets (see Gilbert, 1998). Moreover, the processes and phenomena underlying person perception illuminate broader aspects of cognition that have concerned psychologists since the days of William James (1890).

In one type of person perception experiment, people first learn of others' behaviors and then report feelings or attributions about those others, often by completing trait rating scales. The results of such experiments have been crucial to understanding the judgments that people make about others. The present chapter focuses on whether, when, and how to detect the extent to which such judgments are made spontaneously. Much of the research described in this chapter attempted to assess spontaneous impressions indirectly, without asking people to directly report their impressions of others. While this indirectness avoids one drawback to directly asking people their impressions—namely, that direct assessments may prompt relevant inferences—it raises a host of other interpretive and methodological issues. This chapter reviews these issues and in doing so tells the story of research on spontaneous impressions derived from behavior. It reviews where the area has been, discusses where it is now, and provides some suggestions as to where it should be going.

Although spontaneous impressions are the focus of the present chapter, an underlying assumption is that such judgments are often the causes of people's behaviors. For example, imagine a scenario in which a person's car has broken down on a dark, isolated roadway. A stranger steps out of the darkness and approaches. If the driver perceives the stranger's sudden approach as evidence of his malicious nature, this may lead to self-protective responses (e.g., fight-or-flight). On the other hand, if the driver interprets the stranger's sudden approach as evidence of his good-hearted nature, the driver may react in a friendly manner. The study of how humans subjectively interpret and react to the ambiguous behavior of others has influenced theorizing in a host of areas, including aggression (perception of hostile intent prompts aggressive behavior; Dodge, Price, Bachorowski, & Newman, 1990), child abuse (abusive parents more often interpret a child's behavior as disobedience or rebelliousness; Milner, 2003), and self-perception (the effects of failure depend on whether it is interpreted as reflecting deficiencies in ability; Dweck, 1999). Hence, the principles, ideas, and findings of this chapter can ultimately be quite useful to those interested in aspects of interpersonal behavior.

SPONTANEOUS TRAIT INFERENCES:
THE CONTEXT SET BY ATTRIBUTION THEORIES

However, we are not immediately interested in such applications. Instead, our focus is directly on interpersonal judgments that perceivers make about others. In this regard, one of the issues that occupied early trait researchers' attention concerned the conditions (if any) under which people would make trait inferences spontaneously. That some kinds of inferences were made spontaneously under some conditions was settled quite quickly. For example, Taylor (1982) reported that 95% of a sample of cancer patients made attributions about the causes of their cancer, as did 70% of patients' family members. Similarly, Lau and Russell (1980) examined newspaper reports of sporting events and found that they often contained attributions for victory and (especially) defeat.

Particularly intriguing were data collected by Smith and Miller (1983). Their research team gave subjects trait-implying sentences, each describing a different actor. Each sentence was accompanied by one of eight questions, and the time taken to respond to these was recorded. Among the shortest latencies were answers to questions about the actor's intentions and questions about whether a given trait described the actor. From these data, Smith and Miller concluded that people: (1) make causal inferences while encoding each sentence and (2) store these inferences in memory with representations of the sentences. These inferences are then simply accessed and "read out" in response to inference-related questions, which accounts for the rapid responding to those questions (also see Carlston, 1980; Carlston & Skowronski, 1986). While the Smith and Miller data suggest that people do make inferences spontaneously, their methodology could not demonstrate this unequivocally. It is possible that over the course of the study participants came to realize that only eight questions were involved, one of which asked about actor motives and one about actor traits. One could argue that the Smith and Miller study suggests the spontaneity of inference-making only under conditions where such inferential goals were chronically activated.

Nonetheless, such results were generally interpreted as suggesting that attributions are sometimes made spontaneously but may be more likely under some circumstances than others. As suggested by the cancer patient and newspaper report studies, one such circumstance is when an outcome is unexpected (for converging results, see Hastie, 1984; Kanazawa, 1992; Weiner, 1985). A second condition is when a perceiver expects to interact with the target, an expectation that seemingly increases the importance of understanding this individual (Devine, Sedikides, & Fuhrman, 1989). A third condition, illustrated by the Smith and Miller (1983) study, is when inference goals are chronically activated. In fact, attribution researchers have documented a host of such conditions (see Gilbert, 1998).

These findings and interpretations were sensible, given the theoretical tenor of the time. The flavor of the debate was set by attribution theories of the sort proposed by Jones and Davis (1965) and Kelley (1967). These theories argued for a paradigm grounded in consciousness and rationalism. Specifically, perceivers received information and sifted through it, much as a scientist would, to discern the causes of behavior. Only after causal analysis was completed (and if the behavior was not attributed to the situation) would people make a trait attribution to an actor. In theory, because causal analysis is hard (and people are sometimes cognitively lazy), perceivers need a good reason to engage in a causal analysis—a strong need to understand unexpected events or to understand a person who might be important to one's future. These, then, were the conditions that seemed necessary to foment spontaneous inferences.

INDIRECT ASSESSMENT OF INFERENCES:
A REVELATION AND A REVOLUTION

One implication of the conscious/rationalist conceptions that dominated this era, then, was that though people would sometimes spontaneously engage in trait inference making, they were not inclined to do so in most situations. Admittedly, this was a position that we advocated ourselves (see Carlston & Skowronski, 1986; also see Hastie & Park, 1986). Given this widely held assumption, results reported by Winter and Uleman (1984) caused quite a stir. Winter and Uleman were concerned that the methodologies typically used to explore inference making may have prompted inferential activity, negating their value as tests of the spontaneity of such inference making. Winter and Uleman tried to eliminate this confound by devising a method of assessing spontaneous inference making without directly asking people to report their inferences.

Their method was based on Thomson and Tulving's (1970) encoding specificity principle, which suggests that concepts considered during the encoding of material serve as the best retrieval cues for that material. In Winter and Uleman's (1984) method, participants read sentences (e.g., "the reporter steps on his girlfriend's feet during the foxtrot") that implied different traits (e.g., clumsy) and then completed a cued retrieval test. Winter and Uleman argued that if people inferred traits while reading the stimulus sentences, then the implied traits should serve as superior retrieval cues. In fact, trait cues did produce superior recall to some other kinds of relevant trait cues, and they were actually as effective as cues that conveyed the gist of the original stimulus sentences. Consequently, Winter and Uleman concluded that their data demonstrated spontaneous inference making during the sentence reading task.

Especially important was the implication of the data that people did this routinely, without any special reason to do so. In fact, the cued recall studies suggested that spontaneous inference making was quite robust, even occurring when the sentences were presented to participants as distracters to a supposed "primary task" of solving math problems (Winter, Uleman, & Cunniff, 1985).

Gilbert (1998, p. 112) amusingly characterizes the impact of this study on the area as follows: "The study was inventive, important, and imperfect, thus guaranteeing a slew of dissections, extensions, replications, and rejoinders." One of these "dissections" was the criticism (Bassili, 1989a, 1989b; Higgins & Bargh, 1987) that while people might have inferred traits in the process of encoding the behavior, there was little evidence in the Winter and Uleman paradigm that people were making inferences *about the actor.* To clarify this point, consider the behavior *"the reporter steps on his girlfriend's feet during the foxtrot."* One might activate a trait (clumsy) and use it to characterize the behavior (that was a clumsy thing to do). However, this is different from actually attributing the trait *to* the actor (the reporter was clumsy). This distinction is central to several recent models of attribution (see Gilbert, 1998; Trope & Gaunt, 2000; also see Newman & Uleman, 1993).

Indeed, data from the Winter and Uleman paradigm seemed to validate this criticism. Each of the sentences used by Winter and Uleman had a consistent four-part structure: an actor, a verb, a direct or indirect object, and a prepositional phrase (e.g., the plumber/slips/an extra $50/into his wife's purse). In a series of studies (e.g., Winter & Uleman, 1984; Uleman, Newman, & Winter, 1992; Uleman, Winborne, Winter, & Shechter, 1986; Uleman & Moskowitz, 1994) the Uleman group explored the extent to which trait terms prompted recall of these different sentence components. Results suggested that the trait terms (e.g., "clumsy") strongly cued recall of the verbs (e.g., "steps on") but only weakly (if at all) cued recall of the actors (e.g., "the reporter"). It is reasonable to conclude from such data that perceivers were making inferences about the behaviors they read about; it is less evident that they were making inferences about the actors who performed those behaviors.

A similar critique can be applied to data obtained during the 1980s and 1990s using several other indirect trait inference assessment paradigms. These include the *recognition probe paradigm* (Newman, 1991, 1993; Uleman, Hon, Roman, & Moskowitz, 1996), in which subjects must reject trait words that never appeared in a trait-implying story read by the subjects. This should be a difficult task if trait inferences were made in response to reading those stories, and this difficulty should be reflected in long response latencies and a high error rate. Other paradigms include: (1) *the delayed recognition task*, in which participants are presented with stories that are new but have the same trait implications as stories actually presented earlier, and participants must decide whether these new stories were seen before, a difficult task (as reflected in long latencies and high error rates) if trait inferences were made from the original story (D'Agostino, 1991); (2) *the lexical decision task*, in which subjects read trait-implying stories and then make word/nonword judgments about letter strings, typically responding faster when the string depicts a story-relevant trait (Zarate, Uleman, & Voils, 2001); and (3) *the word stem completion task,* in which subjects read trait-implying stories and then attempt to complete ambiguous word stems, generally by producing words related to the trait implications of stories (Whitney, Waring, & Zingmark, 1992). Because all of these dependent measures were collected independently of the context provided by the actors who performed the behaviors, it is unclear in each case whether the obtained results simply reflect processes involved in interpretation and characterization of the behaviors, or whether they actually reflect processes involved in making trait inferences about the actors.

LET'S HIT THE LINKS!: THE RELEARNING PARADIGM AND SPONTANEOUS TRAIT INFERENCES

One of the authors of this chapter (Don Carlston) raised similar points in discussions that occurred with a second author (John Skowronski) during a long drive from the Midwest to North Carolina for the Duck Conference on Social Cognition. Don's aversion to flying led him to prefer the (relatively unsafe) minivan to the (relatively safe) airplane, and John often (unwisely?) accompanied him on these lengthy sojourns. The drive time was used to discuss and plan research (just imagine how much work can be accomplished when confined in a small space with one's collaborator for about 20 hours). Given the importance of these discussions to the research that we later conducted, it might have been appropriate to award Chrysler coauthorship on the papers that resulted.

Don suggested in these discussions that if an inference was made about an actor, then one consequence should be the formation of an association between the cognitive representation of that actor and that of the inferred trait. Don also noted that a method was available to assess such associations: an updated version of the classic Ebbinghaus relearning method, results from which had been extensively reviewed by MacLeod (1988).

The paradigm that developed from those minivan discussions was straightforward. First, participants were presented with photos of college students accompanied by textual descriptions of behavior, which they were told were transcribed from the photographed "informants" self-descriptions. On critical trials, the behavior implied a trait (e.g., "I was walking down the street one day and a saw a puppy on the sidewalk. I kicked it out of my way" implies the trait "cruel"). Some participants were instructed to form impressions, whereas others were given a nonimpression goal (simply to familiarize themselves with materials to be used later in the study). It was thought that when participants made inferences about the informants from the behavior descriptions, an association would be formed between that trait and the informant.

According to Ebbingahus's relearning principle, people can more readily relearn material that was previously known than they can learn comparable material for the first time. Consequently, the existence of associations between an informant and a trait is evidenced when participants who first read a relevant behavior can "relearn" the pairing of the informant's photo and the implied trait more readily than participants who did not read the behavior can "learn" the same pairing. Participants were shown photo–trait pairs and were asked to learn them so that they would be able to recall the word when prompted with the photo. For some participants, these pairs involved an informant photo paired with the trait implied by that person's previously read behavior; other participants saw the same photo–trait pair but without having first read the trait-implying behavior. As expected, participants were better able to recall the photo–trait pair when they had previously read the relevant behavior than when they had not, suggesting that they were essentially "relearning" something that they already knew (Carlston & Skowronski, 1994; also see D'Agostino & Hawk, 1998). Importantly, this superior recall was evident both for those participants told to form impressions and those given an alternative goal. Subsequent research confirmed that the magnitude of savings was always comparable whether participants were instructed to form impressions or did so spontaneously (Carlston & Skowronski, 1994, Studies 1–4; Carlston, Skowronski, & Sparks, 1995).

Additional analyses suggested that this "savings in relearning" effect was independent of explicit memory. That is, the effect occurred regardless of whether people could accurately recognize the behavior that was described by the informant (Carlston & Skowronski, 1994, Studies 3 and 4), or whether they could explicitly recall the trait when cued by informant photos (Carlston et al., 1995). Moreover, the effect was durable, persisting for at least 7 days after initial exposure to the behavior descriptions (Carlston & Skowronski, 1994, Study 3).

In fact, the effect turned out to be so robust that it conflicted with the prevailing conviction that attributional activity varies depending on circumstances (Carlston & Skowronski, 1986). Although variability in the effect was eventually obtained (Carlston & Skowronski, 2005; Crawford, Skowronski, Stiff, & Scherer, 2007), the seeming invulnerability of initial results to any changes in experimental procedures led to a variety of artifactual explanations. For example, it was suggested that the familiarization instructions left participants without an explicit processing goal, which may have caused them to engage in impression formation as a default strategy. This possibility was addressed by giving participants a plausible alternative to the goal (to memorize the stimuli), which previous attribution research suggested might interfere with attribution processes. However, participants given the memorization goal showed the same magnitude of savings as participants given impression or familiarization instructions (Carlston & Skowronski, 1994, Study 4).

Another proposal was that the extremity of the behavior descriptions used as stimuli led participants to make inferences spontaneously that they might not make at all if presented with more moderate behaviors. This argument is specious, however, as stimuli can always be created that are so weak or ambiguous that they lack clear trait implications, and under those circumstances inferences (spontaneous or otherwise) are unlikely to eventuate. We chose not to pursue the question of how weak stimuli have to be for participants to eschew spontaneous inference making, though we concede that there is undoubtedly a point at which this will occur.

Instead, we opted to explore whether participants had to actually think about the intended trait for a savings effect to occur. Thus, we (Carlston et al., 1995, Study 2) forced participants to record their initial inferences about informants as they read each behavioral description. Then we examined whether savings effects occurred only when this initial inference matched the trait term that participants were asked to learn in the savings task. Relearning effects were, in fact, strongest when there was such a match, but some relearning effect remained even when there was not. Carlston et al. examined whether this residual savings was due to evaluative congruence between participants' recorded inference and the trait to be memorized, but found no evidence to support this (however, more recent research suggests that evaluative factors may contribute to savings when the memorization task is explicitly designed to detect this; Ho, Carlston, & Skowronski, 2008). Regardless of the reason, the results of this experiment suggested that, while most of the obtained savings effect was due to inferences made about informants, some of the effect was seemingly independent of such inferences.

One possible source of these noninferential relearning effects is the formation of simple associations between mental representations of informants and traits. That is, while Don Carlston's insight was that attribution of traits to informants must necessarily produce links between mental representations of informants and traits, it is likely that other processes might also produce such associations. For example, such associations might occur if a trait is activated in the process of understanding and encoding a behavior, and then becomes associated with an informant simply because both constructs are simultaneously activated in working memory. Hence, if people encode a behavior by labeling it with a trait (e.g., that was cruel), if that trait is in working memory concurrent with the cognitive representation of the informant, and if the two are considered in conjunction with each other, a simple association might be formed between the person representation and the trait without any explicit impression formation processing. This reasoning is entirely consistent with logic articulated by Bassili (e.g., Brown & Bassili, 2002; Bassili, 1989a, 1989b).

Initial evidence for such simple associative processes was produced in two experiments reported in Carlston et al. (1995). In one of these studies (Carlston et al., 1995, Experiment 4), participants were told that the stimulus photos and descriptions were totally unrelated. That is, they were told that the photos depicted students at one university and the descriptions were generated by research assistants at another. In addition, participants were led to believe that these stimuli were randomly paired and that participants were being exposed to these pairings merely as preparation for the actual experimental task. Even under these conditions, relearning effects occurred. However, these relearning effects were substantially smaller than those observed in participants who were told that informants had described their own behaviors. This pattern of results is consistent with the notion that associative processes can occur under circumstances in which impression formation (intentional or otherwise) is unlikely. However, the fact that relearning effects were stronger when behaviors were allegedly enacted by the pictured targets is consistent with the idea that spontaneous inferences are also made to targets, under appropriate conditions.

A second study in Carlston et al. (1995, Study 3) turned out to have similar implications, though it did not seem so at the time. In this study, one group of participants was told that informants described themselves and a second group was told that informants described a third person. Carlston et al. found that relearning effects were larger in the self-informant conditions than in the other-informant conditions. Although this difference between conditions was not statistically different in this particular experiment, subsequent studies show consistent and significant differences in the magnitude of relearning effects in these self- and other-descriptive conditions (Skowronski, Carlston, Mae, & Crawford, 1998).

The fact that trait implications of descriptions become linked to third-party informants is a fascinating discovery that was given the name

Spontaneous Trait Transference (also see Mae, Carlston, & Skowronski, 1999). Though fascinating, however, the phenomenon posed a difficult problem for the interpretation of relearning effects. No longer could relearning effects be automatically interpreted as evidence that participants were making inferences about the informants to whom they were exposed. Instead, savings effects might sometimes reflect inferences made about behaviors—inferences that then became associated with cognitive representations of informants but were never really about them.

These two "routes" to savings were first outlined in Skowronski et al. (1998). A number of subsequent studies have explored the relearning effects that occur via these routes; the conditions under which such relearning effects increase or decrease in size; and the explicit trait judgments that accompany such effects (Carlston & Skowronski, 2005; Crawford, Skowronski, & Stiff, 2007; Crawford, Skowronski, Stiff, & Leonards, in press; Crawford, Skowronski, Stiff, & Scherer, 2008). One implication of these studies is that behavior need not prompt trait inferences about an informant at the time of encoding to have implications for later trait judgments. Though this has been demonstrated before (Hastie & Park, 1986), the mechanism those authors propose involves impressional processes that operate on recalled behaviors when judgments are ultimately made.

However, spontaneous trait transference research suggests a different mechanism for such post hoc inference making. This route involves the initial nonattributional formation of an association between the cognitive representation of a person and the trait implied by a behavior and the later use of that association to generate an inference about that person. This mechanism does not require that behaviors be explicitly recalled or even that they have logical implications for the judgment target. Thus, a target might induce others to perceive him or her as a bit smarter if he or she talks about an act of genius performed by some other person (Carlston & Skowronski, 2005).

A great deal of recent effort has been devoted to comparing the on-line inference and association-based routes to inference making. For example, Carlston and Skowronski (2005) observed that both negativity effects and evaluative generalization occurred in trait ratings of self-informants but not other-informants. They suggest that this is because inferential processes obey the logic described by attribution theories (e.g., discounting of relatively nondiagnostic positive behaviors) and implicit personality theories (e.g., the perceived co-occurrence of evaluatively congruent behaviors), whereas associative processes do not. Carlston and Skowronski also found that prompting participants to recall whether informants had described themselves or someone else strengthened inferences about this individual in the first instance but eliminated them in the latter. All of these results are consistent with the idea that trait inferences made of self-informants and of other-informants derive from different cognitive processes.

A research team led by Matt Crawford has also conducted a number of studies designed to document such differences. In one set of studies, building on the work of Brown and Bassili (2002) and Todorov and Uleman (2004), the Crawford team (Crawford, Skowronski, & Stiff, 2007) added a second photo to the stimulus display. In the self-informant condition, this photo was of a bystander who supposedly listened to the self-description; in the other-informant condition, this was supposedly the person whose behavior was being described. Inclusion of the second photo had no effect on savings effects or trait ratings pertaining to self-informants but eliminated transference effects (including both savings and ratings) for other-informants. One possibility is that, in the other-informant condition, the presentation of a picture of the person being described diverted attention away from the informant doing the describing. However, subsequent studies that directly measured attention revealed results inconsistent with this notion. Instead, in this condition, inclusion of the second photo seems to prompt inferences about this individual, disrupting the simultaneous consideration of the informant and the implied trait and thus interfering with formation of an associative linkage (Crawford et al., in press).

A second series of studies focused on the truthfulness of the descriptions. For example, some participants were instructed to try to determine whether a person shown in a videotaped interview was telling the truth or lying; other participants watched the videos without such "lie detection" instructions. The usual trait transference effects were obtained in participants' ratings of informants who described others, and this result was unaffected by the instructional set. In contrast, the trait inference effects obtained in ratings of self-informants were strongly affected by the instructional set. Specifically, such effects were reduced by lie detection instructions, as compared to the comparison condition. Crawford, Skowronski, Stiff, and Scherer (2007) replicated these trait-rating effects, found a parallel effect using the relearning measure, and demonstrated that these results were not simply a consequence of higher cognitive load in the lie detection condition.

In another set of studies, Crawford, Skowronski, Stiff, and Scherer (2008) paired each behavior description with a veracity cue (either "this statement is true" or "this statement is false"). The veracity cue was sometimes presented prior to the behavior and sometimes afterward.

When presented afterward, cues had no effect on inferences made about either self- or other-informants. However, when presented prior to the behaviors, the "statement is false" cue reduced spontaneous trait inferences about self-informants (as compared to controls) while having no impact on spontaneous trait transference to other-informants. Moreover, the "statement is true" cue increased spontaneous trait inferences about self-informants while having no impact on spontaneous trait transference. Again, such results suggest both that different cognitive processes underlie spontaneous trait inference effects and spontaneous trait transference effects and, more indirectly, that the processes of spontaneous trait inference involve the assignment of traits to actors.

ADDITIONAL EVIDENCE: SAVINGS AND BEYOND

The relearning method is not the only paradigm that has provided support for the idea that trait inferences can sometimes be linked directly to actors. For example, Todorov and Uleman (2002) provided converging evidence, using a false recognition paradigm. Participants were presented with actors' photos and trait-implying stories, some of which explicitly included a story-relevant trait term and some of which did not. Later, participants were presented with photo–trait pairs and asked whether the trait had been explicitly included in the story involving that actor. Todorov and Uleman reasoned that if participants spontaneously inferred the implied trait while reading a story in which the trait was not actually mentioned, and if that trait was linked to the actor, then participants might falsely recall the trait as having been explicitly mentioned in the text. This is exactly what Todorov and Uleman observed.

Importantly, false recognition was highest when the actor was paired with the exact trait implied by his or her story. Moreover, these effects occurred even when participants read the stories with the goal of memorizing the text. Hence, it seems that the assignment of traits to actors occurred spontaneously, even though participants were given alternative goals that were sometimes arguably antithetical to trait inference formation. Todorov and Uleman (2003) replicated and extended these findings, showing that they occurred even with brief exposures to the behaviors, when information processing was shallow, and despite a cognitive load during encoding.

Todorov and Uleman (2004) showed further that false recognition was more likely to occur with the actor's face than with other faces present at the time of encoding. To do so, they altered their earlier paradigm by adding an additional photo (e.g., a "bystander") to each stimulus set.

False recognition of the trait implied by the story occurred to a greater extent when participants were cued by actors' photos than when cued by other photos presented with each trait-implying story. These data are strongly suggestive of inferential processing about actors, but they are not definitive. Proponents of the associative viewpoint might suggest that the result might be a consequence of differential attention to actor faces and nonactor faces. That is, it may be the case that: (1) the only inference that is made is about the behavior, and (2) while encoding the behavior, people attend more to actor faces than to nonactor faces. This latter tendency would suggest that there should be a higher probability of linking the inference made about the behavior to an actor face than of linking the inference made about the behavior to a nonactor face. Hence, one may be able to explain the Todorov and Uleman (2004) results without hypothesizing that inferences are made about actors. However, it is also becoming clear that the accumulating data are making it increasingly difficult to maintain the association-only position.

More generally, the evidence provided by Todorov and Uleman in these three sets of studies converges with that provided by the savings paradigm. All of this research suggests that inferences are made during encoding of a story and that those inferences are linked to the actor producing the behavior. Todorov and Uleman's results point to the ubiquity of these linkages and the ease with which they seemingly occur. They also point to the fact that associations are made more strongly to actors than to nonactors. The remaining conundrum is to definitively demonstrate that these stronger associations are the result of inferences about the actor and not the result of inferences about the behavior that become associatively linked to the actor.

Other researchers have addressed whether people make spontaneous inferences about situations as well as about actors and whether these both can occur simultaneously. For example, in one study, Ham and Vonk (2003) showed participants sentences (e.g., "John gets an A on the test") that implied both actor traits (*smart*) and object properties (*easy*). They then employed a probe recognition task to examine the ease with which people could recognize terms relating to both of these implications. They theorized that if participants made a spontaneous inference about either the person or the object, probes relating to either of these would be easily recognized. This is the result that they obtained (but see Lupfer, Clark, & Hutcherson, 1990). In a second study, participants were asked to form impressions of the actor, the situation, or the whole event described by each sentence (which, again, had implications regarding both the actor and the object). Later, participants engaged in an associative learning task. Some trials on this task were essentially relearning trials—participants tried to learn pairings between traits and people or between properties and objects. Savings in relearning occurred for both traits and situations (compared to nonrelearning trials), and, as often found in previous studies using the relearning paradigm, the magnitude of savings was unrelated to participants' processing goals.

However, while persuasive with respect to the formation of linkages between people and traits, and between objects and properties, the Ham and Vonk studies (2003) leave open the question of whether these links occurred because participants labeled events during encoding and subsequently associated those labels with the enactors or with the objects, or whether during event encoding subjects assigned traits to enactors or assigned properties to objects. Additional research needs to be conducted to clear up this ambiguity.

One issue with all of the paradigms discussed here is that they rely on written behavior descriptions. The only exception is one individual experiment by Skowronski et al. (1998). However, even here, the stimulus was verbal. The experiment employed videotaped stimuli in which target individuals orally described their own behavior. One might therefore wonder whether spontaneous inference making is limited to such verbal stimuli. Such a limitation is plausible if past experience in trying to decipher verbal material were to lead to habitual tendencies to make inferences while processing verbal descriptions but such tendencies did not generalize to the processing of actual behavioral observations.

However, recent research suggests that this is not the case. Fiedler and Schenck (2001) showed participants static silhouettes of dyads interacting in ways that implied a personality trait for one of the dyad members. Later, participants were faster to identify masked trait words (and goal words, as well) when those words were preceded by the silhouette of the actor who behaved in a manner consistent with these words. A second study showed that this effect occurred even when participants were initially given a task designed to interfere with trait abstraction. In fact, Fiedler and Schenck noted that their data suggested that "focusing on the picture and refraining from abstract semantic interpretations . . . serves to enhance the STI" (p. 1543).

Fiedler, Schenck, Watling, and Menges (2005) replicated these findings with brief film clips. They also extended these results, showing faster identification of trait words pertaining to *both* members of an interacting dyad whose behaviors had trait implications. That is, when cued by the relevant target silhouette, participants identified traits implied by the clips faster than they did control traits. The effects were stronger for dyad members who enacted behaviors than for those who were the targets of those behaviors, suggesting that inferential activity was focused on the former. However, the fact that traits pertaining to both members of the dyad were more quickly identified suggests that some inferential activity was directed at the targets of behaviors, as well, although the nature of that activity (behavior labeling and association or assignment of traits to actors) remains unclear.

CONCLUSIONS AND FUTURE DIRECTIONS

In our view, there are a number of important implications to be derived from this line of research. First, it supports the claim that there is a distinction between two kinds of inferences that might be made at event encoding—one that is focused on labeling the behavior (e.g., that behavior was cruel) and a second that is focused on assigning a property to the behavior's perpetrator (e.g., Ed is cruel). Methods exploring spontaneous trait inferences need to distinguish between the two—as recent versions of the relearning method does.

A second implication is that spontaneous attributions to actors occur with surprising regularity, even in the absence of an explicit goal to derive inferences about such actors. This regularity may reflect the fact that understanding others is a task that we engage in regularly—so regularly that making trait inferences about others might be a chronically activated goal or even a habitualized cognitive activity.

Nonetheless, we still retain our belief that spontaneous attribution of traits to actors is not inevitable and can be altered by processing goals and environmental conditions. Recent results examining group membership and trait inference support this contention. For example, Wigboldus, Dijksterhuis, and van Knippenberg (2003) reported five experiments that examined the influence of stereotypes on the spontaneous inference of actor traits. They found that stereotype information appears to inhibit the formation of trait inferences from stereotype-incongruent information (for a similar finding, see Lupfer et al., 1990). Moreover, three savings experiments conducted by Crawford, Sherman, and Hamilton (2002) showed that a group member's behavior led to stronger trait inferences about him or her when this actor was a member of a low-entitative group (e.g., a collection of individuals). However, they also found that transference of traits from one group member to another was stronger when the actor was a member of a high-entitative group (e.g., a family).

Other recent studies, focused on individual differences, have also supported the idea that inference making is not inevitable and varies across inference makers. For example, Tiedens (2001) conducted studies suggesting that hostility and induced anger influence perceptions of targets' behaviors and the trait inferences drawn from them. Other researchers have found individual differences in spontaneous inference tendencies among those who differ in: (1) the strength or chronic level of activation of impression formation goals (McCulloch, Ferguson, Kwanda, & Bargh, in press); (2) the need to evaluate (Tormala & Petty, 2001); (3) the extent to which perceivers possess a repressive coping style (Caldwell & Newman, 2005); (4) the extent to which they are idiocentric (Duff & Newman, 1997); and (5) the extent to which they chronically access moral concerns (Narvaez, Lapsley, Hagele, & Lasky, 2006). Such results are suggestive but still paint an incomplete picture of spontaneous inference making. Future research needs to more intensively explore the conditions under which spontaneous trait attributions are made, documenting the processing goals, people, and environmental conditions that are especially likely to lead to the formation of such inferences.

A third implication of this line of research, though, is that spontaneous inferences need not be made *about* a target for that person to become associated or attributed with the trait implications of behavior. As suggested by the spontaneous trait transference effect, such effects can occur even when an informant describes the behavior of a third party. It is especially important to note that such informants not only become associated with the trait implications of behavior they describe, but that these associations also affect the trait ratings of the informant. Hence, under some conditions, people who describe smart behaviors are seen as smarter and people who describe dishonest behaviors are seen as more dishonest. Although not well documented, a similar process could occur for actors. That is, if conditions (such as alternative processing goals) prevent spontaneous attributions directly to an actor, those implications may nonetheless have an impact by creating an association in memory between the actor and the traits activated during behavior comprehension. One crucial goal for future research is to explore when such association-based impressions do (and do not) occur and how the inferences derived from such associations might differ from those produced by direct spontaneous inference or attribution processes.

A final implication is that many of these effects can occur without people's knowledge or awareness—at least at the time that judgments are made. Certainly, in spontaneous trait transference conditions, participants seem to have little idea that they are engaging in transference. Consequently, they do not seem to be able to easily correct their judgments to mitigate these effects (but see Carlston & Skowronski, 2005). However, a similar state of affairs may exist even when people make spontaneous inferences about targets at encoding. Our data suggest that these effects may cause "mental residues" that affect trait judgments even a week after exposure to the original event, and despite the fact that people consciously recall nothing about a target or that target's behavior (for additional evidence on this point, see Uleman, Blader, & Todorov, 2005). Such findings confirm the need for research methodologies that assess the action of cognitive processes without relying directly on subject reports of how they arrive at their judgments of others.

REFERENCES

Asch, S. E. (1946). Forming impressions of personality. *Journal of Abnormal and Social Psychology, 41,* 258–290.

Bassili, J. N. (1989a). Trait encoding in behavior identification and dispositional inference. *Personality and Social Psychology Bulletin, 19,* 200–205.

Bassili, J. N. (1989b). Traits as action categories versus traits as person attributes in social cognition. In J. N. Bassili (Ed.), *On-line cognition in person perception* (pp. 61–89). Hillsdale, NJ. Erlbaum.

Brown, R. D., & Bassili, J. N. (2002). Spontaneous trait associations and the case of the superstitious banana. *Journal of Experimental Social Psychology, 38,* 87–92.

Caldwell, T. L., & Newman, L. S. (2005). The timeline of threat processing in repressors: More evidence for early vigilance and late avoidance. *Personality and Individual Differences, 38,* 1957–1967.

Carlston, D. E. (1980). The recall and use of traits and events in social inference processes. *Journal of Experimental Social Psychology, 16,* 303–328.

Carlston, D. E., & Skowronski, J. J. (1986). Trait memory and behavior memory: The effects of alternative pathways on impression judgment response times. *Journal of Personality and Social Psychology, 50,* 5–13.

Carlston, D. E., & Skowronski, J. J. (1994). Savings in the relearning of trait information as evidence for spontaneous inference generation. *Journal of Personality and Social Psychology, 66,* 840–856.

Carlston, D. E., Skowronski, J. J. (2005). Linking versus thinking: Evidence for the different associative and attributional bases of spontaneous trait transference and spontaneous trait inference. *Journal of Personality and Social Psychology, 89,* 884–898.

Carlston, D. E., Skowronski, J. J., & Sparks, C. (1995). Savings in relearning: II. On the formation of the behavior-based trait associations and inferences. *Journal of Personality and Social Psychology, 69,* 420–436.

Crawford, M. T., Sherman, S. J., & Hamilton, D. L. (2002). Perceived entitativity, stereotype formation, and the interchangeability of group members. *Journal of Personality and Social Psychology, 83,* 1076–1094.

Crawford, M. T., Skowronski, J. J., & Stiff, C. (2007). Limiting the spread of spontaneous trait transference. *Journal of Experimental Social Psychology, 43,* 466–472.

Crawford, M. T., Skowronski, J. J., Stiff, C., & Leonards, U. (in press). Seeing but not thinking: Limiting the spread of spontaneous trait transference II. *Journal of Experimental Social Psychology.*

Crawford, M. T., Skowronski, J. J., Stiff, C., & Scherer, C. R. (2007). Interfering with inferential, but not associative, processes underlying spontaneous trait inference. *Personality and Social Psychology Bulletin, 33,* 677–690.

Crawford, M. T., Skowronski, J. J., Stiff, C., & Scherer, C. R. (2008). *The truth will out: Prior knowledge of description veracity influences spontaneous trait inferences but not spontaneous trait transference.* Manuscript in preparation.

D'Agostino, P. R. (1991) Spontaneous trait inferences: Effects of recognition instructions and subliminal priming on recognition performance. *Personality and Social Psychology Bulletin, 17,* 70–77.

D'Agostino, P. R., & Hawk, M. (1998). The transfer of actor–trait associations inferred from behavior. *Social Cognition, 16,* 391–399.

Devine, P. G., Sedikides, C., & Fuhrman, R. W. (1989). Goals in social information processing: The case of anticipated interaction. *Journal of Personality and Social Psychology, 56,* 680–690.

Dodge, K. A., Price, J. M., Bachorowski, J., & Newman, J. P. (1990). Hostile attributional biases in severely aggressive adolescents. *Journal of Abnormal Psychology, 99,* 385–392.

Duff, K. J., & Newman, L. S. (1997). Individual differences in the spontaneous construal of behavior: Idiocentrism and the automatization of the trait inference process. *Social Cognition, 15,* 217–241.

Dweck, C. S. (1999). *Self-theories: Their role in motivation, personality, and development.* Philadelphia: Psychology Press.

Fiedler, K., & Schenck, W. (2001). Spontaneous inferences from pictorially presented behaviors. *Personality and Social Psychology Bulletin, 27,* 1533–1546.

Fiedler, K., Schenck, W., Watling, M., & Menges, J. I. (2005). Priming trait inferences through pictures and moving pictures: The impact of open and closed mindsets. *Journal of Personality and Social Psychology, 88,* 229–244.

Funder, D. C. (1999). *Personality judgment: A realistic approach to person perception.* San Diego, CA: Academic Press.

Gilbert, D. T. (1998). Ordinary personology. In D. T. Gilbert, S. T. Fiske, & G. Lindzey (Eds.), *The handbook of social psychology* (4th ed., Vol. 2, pp. 89–150). New York: McGraw-Hill.

Ham, J., & Vonk, R. (2003). Smart and easy: Co-occurring activation of spontaneous trait inferences and spontaneous situational inferences. *Journal of Experimental Social Psychology, 39,* 434–447.

Hastie, R. (1984). Causes and effects of causal attribution. *Journal of Personality and Social Psychology, 46,* 44–56.

Hastie, R., & Park, B. (1986). The relationship between memory and judgment depends on whether the judgment task is memory-based or on-line. *Psychological Review, 93,* 258–268.

Higgins, E. T., & Bargh, J. A. (1987). Social cognition and social perception. *Annual Review of Psychology, 38,* 379–426.

Ho, C., Carlston, D. E., & Skowronski, J. J. (2008). Evaluative savings. Unpublished raw data.

James, W. (1890). *The principles of psychology.* New York: Henry Holt.

Jones, E. E., & Davis, K. E. (1965). From acts to dispositions: The attribution process in social psychology. In L. Berkowitz (Ed.), *Advances in experimental social psychology* (Vol. 2, pp. 219–266). New York: Academic Press.

Kanazawa, S. (1992). Outcome or expectancy? Antecedent of spontaneous causal attribution. *Personality and Social Psychology Bulletin, 18,* 659–668.

Kelley, H. H. (1967). Attribution theory in social psychology. In D. Levine (Ed.), *Nebraska Symposium on Motivation* (Vol. 15, pp. 192–238). Lincoln: University of Nebraska Press.

Lau, R. R., & Russell, D. (1980). Attributions in the sports pages: A field test of some current hypotheses about attribution research. *Journal of Personality and Social Psychology, 89,* 308–324.

Lupfer, M. B., Clark, L. F., & Hutcherson, H. W. (1990). Impact of context on spontaneous trait and situational attributions. *Journal of Personality and Social Psychology, 58,* 239–249.

MacLeod, C. M. (1988). Forgotten but not gone: Savings for pictures and words in long-term memory. *Journal of Experimental Psychology: Learning, Memory, and Cognition, 14,* 195–212.

Mae, L., Carlston, D., & Skowronski, J. J. (1999). Spontaneous trait transference to familiar communications: Is a little knowledge a dangerous thing? *Journal of Personality and Social Psychology, 77,* 233–246.

McCulloch, K. C., Ferguson, M. J., Kwanda, C. C. K., & Bargh, J. A. (in press). Taking a closer look: On the operation of nonconscious impression formation. *Journal of Experimental Social Psychology.*

Milner, J. S. (2003). Social information processing in high risk and physically abusive parents. *Child Abuse and Neglect, 27,* 7–20.

Narvaez, D., Lapsley, D. K., Hagele, S., & Lasky, B. (2006). Moral chronicity and social information processing: Tests of a social cognitive approach to the moral personality. *Journal of Research in Personality, 40,* 966–985.

Newman, L. S. (1991). Why are traits inferred spontaneously? A developmental approach. *Social Cognition, 9,* 221–253.

Newman, L. S. (1993). How individualists interpret behavior: Idiocentrism and spontaneous trait inference. *Social Cognition, 11,* 243–269.

Newman, L. S., & Uleman, J. S. (1993). When are you what you did? Behavior identification and dispositional inference in person memory, attribution, and social judgment. *Personality and Social Psychology Bulletin, 19,* 513–525.

Schneider, D. J., Hastorf, A. H., & Ellsworth, P. C. (1979). *Person perception* (2nd ed.). Reading, MA: Addison-Wesley.

Skowronski, J. J., Carlston, D. E., Mae, L., & Crawford, M. T. (1998). Spontaneous trait transference: Communicators take on the qualities they describe in others. *Journal of Personality and Social Psychology, 74,* 837–848.

Smith, E. R., & Miller, F. D. (1983). Mediation among attributional inferences and comprehension processes: Initial findings and a general method. *Journal of Personality and Social Psychology, 44,* 492–505.

Tagiuri, R., & Petrullo, L. (Eds.). (1958). *Person perception and interpersonal behavior.* Stanford, CA: Stanford University Press.

Taylor, S. E. (1982). Social cognition and health. *Personality and Social Psychology Bulletin, 8,* 549–562.

Tiedens, L. Z. (2001). The effect of anger on the hostile inferences of aggressive and nonaggressive people: Specific emotions, cognitive processing, and chronic accessibility. *Motivation and Emotion, 25,* 233–251.

Thomson, D. M., & Tulving, E. (1970). Associative encoding and retrieval: Weak and strong cues. *Journal of Experimental Psychology, 86,* 255–262.

Todorov, A., & Uleman, J. S. (2002). Spontaneous trait inferences are bound to actors' faces: Evidence from a false recognition paradigm. *Journal of Personality and Social Psychology, 83,* 1051–1065.

Todorov, A., & Uleman, J. S. (2003). The efficiency of binding spontaneous trait inferences to actors' faces. *Journal of Experimental Social Psychology, 39,* 549–562.

Todorov, A., & Uleman, J. S. (2004). The person reference process in spontaneous trait inferences. *Journal of Personality and Social Psychology, 87,* 482–493.

Tormala, Z. L., & Petty, R. E. (2001). On-line versus memory-based processing: The role of "need to evaluate" in person perception. *Personality and Social Psychology Bulletin, 27,* 1599–1612.

Trope, Y., & Gaunt, R. (2000). Processing alternative explanations of behavior: Correction of integration? *Journal of Personality and Social Psychology, 79,* 344–354.

Uleman, J. S., Blader, S. L., & Todorov, A. (2005). Implicit impressions. In R. R. Hassin, J. S. Uleman, & J. A. Bargh (Eds.), *The new unconscious* (pp. 362–392). New York: Oxford University Press.

Uleman, J. S., Hon, A., Roman, R. J., & Moskowitz, G. B. (1996). On-line evidence for spontaneous trait inferences at encoding. *Personality and Social Psychology Bulletin, 22,* 377–394.

Uleman, J. S., & Moskowitz, G. B. (1994). Unintended effects of goals on unintended inferences. *Journal of Personality and Social Psychology, 66,* 490–501.

Uleman, J. S., Newman, L. S., & Winter, L. (1992). Can personality traits be inferred automatically?: Spontaneous inferences require cognitive capacity at encoding. *Consciousness and Cognition, 1,* 77–90.

Uleman, J. S., Winborne, W. C., Winter, L., & Shechter, D. (1986). Personality differences in spontaneous personality inferences at encoding. *Journal of Personality and Social Psychology, 51,* 396–403.

Weiner, B. (1985). "Spontaneous" causal thinking. *Psychological Bulletin, 97,* 74–84.

Whitney, P., Waring, D. A., & Zingmark, B. (1992). Task effects on the spontaneous activation of trait concepts. *Social Cognition, 10,* 377–396.

Wigboldus, D. H. J., Dijksterhuis, A., & van Knippenberg, A. (2003). When stereotypes get in the way: Stereotypes obstruct stereotype-inconsistent trait inferences. *Journal of Personality and Social Psychology, 84,* 470–484.

Winter, L., & Uleman, J. S. (1984). When are social judgments made? Evidence for the spontaneousness of trait inferences. *Journal of Personality and Social Psychology, 47,* 237–252.

Winter, L., Uleman, J. S., & Cunniff, C. (1985). How automatic are social judgments? *Journal of Personality and Social Psychology, 49*, 904–917.

Wyer, R. S. Jr., & Lambert, A. J. (1994). The role of trait constructs in person perception: An historical perspective. In P. G. Devine, D. L. Hamilton, & T. M. Ostrom (Eds.), *Social cognition: Impact on social psychology* (pp. 109–142). San Diego, CA: Academic Press.

Zarate, M. A., Uleman, J. S., & Voils, C. I. (2001). Effects of culture and processing goals on the activation and binding of trait concepts. *Social Cognition, 19*, 295–323.

CHAPTER 14

First Impressions Based on the Environments We Create and Inhabit

SAMUEL D. GOSLING
SAM GADDIS
SIMINE VAZIRE

In May 1942, 1 year after the United States entered the Second World War, the Office of Strategic Services (OSS) began a program of assessments designed to identify candidates suitable for work behind enemy lines—they were looking for people who would make good spies. One of the assessment procedures was the "belongings test," in which candidates were required to describe individuals based solely on what they had left in their bedrooms—items included clothing, a timetable, and a ticket receipt (MacKinnon, 1977). The assumption underlying this test was that much can be learned about individuals from the spaces they inhabit. It would seem that the environments that people craft around themselves are rich with information about their personalities, values, and lifestyles. In turn, observers use the information available in environments to form impressions of the people who reside in them.

Many environments are very public and can be the first or only basis on which perceivers form impressions of others. A patient waiting to meet his doctor in the waiting room might look around for clues to the doctor's personality. A college student visiting her friend in his dorm room may look around his roommate's side of the room to form an impression of what the roommate is like. These days, it is not uncommon for two people who have never met to "google" each other or check out each other's profiles on MySpace or Facebook. Soon it will be commonplace to visit another's space in virtual worlds such as Second Life. Thus, our environments are increasingly providing the first glimpse we might get into someone's personality.

In this chapter we shall consider the links between people and the environments in which they dwell. We shall focus on living and working spaces, but we shall also consider other kinds of environments, like virtual and auditory environments, and geographic location. To understand why environments might provide clues to what people are like, consider the ways in which people can have an impact on their surroundings.

HOW PEOPLE AFFECT THEIR ENVIRONMENTS

Interactionist theorists have long recognized that individuals select and create their social environments (e.g., friendships, social activities) to match and reinforce their dispositions, preferences, attitudes, and self-views (Buss, 1987; Swann, 1984). Buss used the terms "selection," "evocation," and "manipulation" to delineate three broad classes of process by which individuals alter their environments. Selection refers to the process by which individuals choose to enter or avoid existing environments. For example, extraverts may choose friends, colleagues, and relationship partners who enable them to express their extraverted nature. Evocation is defined as the ways in which individuals unintentionally elicit predictable reactions from others. For example, the positive energy exuded by extraverts may elicit friendly enthusiastic reactions from those around them. Manipulation refers to the deliberate tactics used by individuals to alter their environments. Extraverts, for instance, may hold social gatherings to encourage and create new opportunities to meet and interact with other people. Assuming that personality is reasonably stable, one implication of all three of these processes is that the social environments that people create for themselves will be reasonably stable too. This idea was explored in a study of individuals who wore small audio recording devices for 2 days and then wore them again for 2 more days a month later (Mehl & Pennebaker, 2003). Results of the study suggested substantial stability in the social and physical environments people select—individuals were generally in the same places with the same people, doing the same kinds of things that they were doing 1 month earlier. Of course, it is possible that other factors, such as habit and social norms, not their dispositions, determined the stability of the participants' behaviors.

Interactionist theories can also be applied to physical environments as well as social environments. Humans spend many of their waking hours in their personal living and work environments, and they often decorate these places in ways that reflect their values, interests, experiences, and personalities. In most cases there is no straightforward functional reason why these spaces should be decorated at all. Is the rainbow pattern on the comforter really instrumental in ensuring that a bedroom occupant gets a good night's sleep? Is the alligator skull hanging from the bookshelf really needed to allow an office occupant to write effective advertising copy? Decoration is usually peripheral to the tasks supposedly central to living and work spaces, but people decorate them anyway. Moreover, people leave their individualized physical signatures in their spaces in the colors, patterns, motifs, and decor they choose.

To help understand the connections between people and the places in which they dwell, we next review and build on a model recently proposed to identify the reasons why individuals alter their environments (Gosling, Ko, Mannarelli, & Morris, 2002). Broadly, people alter their spaces for three reasons (see Figure 14.1): they want to affect how they think and feel, they want to broadcast information about themselves, and they inadvertently affect their spaces in the course of their everyday behaviors. The model was developed in the context of physical spaces such as bedrooms and offices; so, in the following sections we use these contexts to illustrate the three processes in more detail. Specifically we draw on data and experiences from a study of 83 bedrooms and 94 office spaces; in that study, the impressions of observers who had only seen the bedroom or office of a target were compared with self and peer reports about the occupant.

Thought and Feeling Regulators

Personal environments are the contexts for a wide range of activities, ranging from relaxing and reminiscing to working and playing. The effectiveness with which these activities can be accomplished may be affected by the physical and ambient qualities of the space. It can be hard to relax with a lot of noise around, and it is difficult to concentrate when surrounded by distractions. Such considerations influence where we go to perform an activity. Most people would find it easier to concentrate at the library than at the video arcade and easier to relax at the beach than at a nightclub playing Death Metal rock music. The environmental features conducive to one activity are not always the same as the environ-

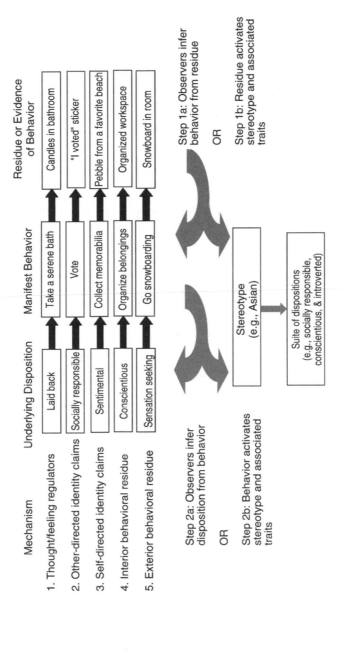

FIGURE 14.1. Mechanisms by which individuals affect their personal environments and processes by which observers use information in the environment to form impressions of the occupants. Adapted with permission from Gosling, Ko, Mannarelli, and Morris (2002). Copyright 2002 by the American Psychological Association.

ments conducive to another. A massage in a health spa is typically accompanied by gentle music, soft lighting, and a fragrant atmosphere, not by stroboscopic disco lights and a thumping bass.

We propose that a whole subset of items within an environment owe their presence to their ability to affect the feelings and thoughts of the occupant. Elements used to regulate emotions and thoughts could include photos of family, keepsakes, the color of the walls, and the CDs in the stereo. Each one of these elements can be used to affect how the occupant feels, serving such diverse purposes as allowing the occupant to reminisce about bygone happy times, focus on an important task, or get pumped up for a night on the town.

Identity Claims

One of the ways in which people make spaces their own is by adorning them with "identity claims"—deliberate symbolic statements about how they would like to be regarded (Baumeister, 1982; Swann, 1987; Swann, Rentfrow, & Guinn, 2003). Posters, awards, photos, trinkets, and other mementos are often displayed in the service of making such statements. Such signals can be split up into two broad categories, *other-directed identity claims* and *self-directed identity claims*, each reflecting their own particular psychological functions.

Other-directed identity claims are statements made by occupants directed to others about how they would like to be regarded. Bumper stickers on a bedroom door and pompoms in the university colors could be serve such a purpose, efficiently and publicly conveying the occupant's values. Obviously, it is crucial that one's intended audience understand the intended message, so these other-directed identity claims tend to rely on objects with shared meanings. By displaying culturally understood symbols, occupants of a space intentionally communicate their attitudes and values to others.

The specific content of other-directed identity claims may vary according to the identity of the anticipated "other," with different audiences evoking different self-presentational motives—items that impress your friends may not have the same effect on your coworkers.

In addition to making statements to others about how occupants would like to be regarded, they can also make self-directed identity claims, symbolic statements made for their own benefit, intended to reinforce their self-views. An expatriate Ethiopian living in the United States, with a strong sense of ethnic identity, may reinforce and affirm his self-view using Ethiopian iconography that resonates with his sense of self.

When identity claims are directed at the self, they can make use of symbols understood by others as well as items with meanings that are unclear to outside observers. As long as the items have personal meaning to the occupant, they can serve as effective self-directed identity claims. A pebble collected from a beach where the occupant had her first kiss could help the occupant connect to elements of her self-views formed during that period of her life. Self-directed identity claims and thought and feeling regulators overlap somewhat because both processes are designed by the occupant to affect how he or she feels.

Behavioral Residue

Many behaviors leave some kind of discernible residue in their wake. Given that large quantities of behavior are performed in personal environments, it is reasonable to suppose that these environments might accumulate a fair amount of residue. For example, the prototypically orderly act of organizing one's space may result in the residue of an alphabetized CD collection, whereas the creative act of doing some drawings may leave the occupant's charcoal sketches lying on the floor as its byproduct. The term "behavioral residue" refers to the physical traces left in the environment by behavioral acts. Sometimes it is the *lack* of an act that leaves a residue. For example, the dishes in the sink are the residue of the fact that you did *not* clean up after eating.

One central property of behavioral residue is the fact that it tends to reflect repeated behaviors. This property is an important part of what makes it so useful to observers. For something to be part of your personality, it should be typical behavior—something done repeatedly over time and across situations. A truly organized person does not just organize her books once; she keeps them organized, putting them back in their proper place, and she also organizes her CDs and keeps her filing drawers in order. Behaviors that occur repeatedly are more likely to leave a residue than are behaviors that occur only occasionally. This is why behavioral residue is useful: it typically reflects not just a single unreliable act but a whole pattern of acts, making residue a rather reliable source of information.

In addition to the residue of behaviors already performed, environments may also contain clues to *anticipated* behaviors; for example, a new deck of cards and a set of poker chips suggest an occupant is planning a game of poker. The metaphor of residue breaks down a bit for activities that have yet to be completed, but the general inference process is the same. Items in the space and their arrangement reflect potential or envisaged behavior.

In addition to containing remnants of past and anticipated activities within that space, personal environments also contain the residue of behaviors performed beyond the immediate surroundings. Material preparations for planned activities to be undertaken outside of the physical environment can provide all kinds of diagnostic behavioral information. A surfboard, snowboard, and skateboard stacked up against a bedroom wall suggest the room is occupied by a sensation seeker. This point is important because it emphasizes the breadth of information that is potentially available in a personal environment, extending well beyond the space itself.

Of course, only some acts leave physical traces in their wake. The act of sharpening all of one's pencils leaves a trace (i.e., sharp pencils in the drawer and pencil shavings in the trash can) in the environment, but the act of smiling does not. In addition, two different behaviors could result in similar environmental manifestations—a messy room could indicate sloth, or it could indicate a person who is overwhelmed with other responsibilities. Thus, although personal environments are inextricably tied to behaviors, it should be clear that personal environments are not the same thing as behavior. And because personal environments often contain a broad array of evidence in a single location, evidence in one area (e.g., the organized bookshelf) can be used to disambiguate the causes of evidence in other areas (e.g., whether the messy room indicates a slothful or temporarily overwhelmed occupant).

Note that the mechanisms described above are not mutually exclusive, and it may not always be clear to observers which mechanisms are responsible for which cues. For example, the snowboard in the corner of a room may indeed reflect exterior behaviors, but the occupant's decision to display the snowboard (rather than stow it in a closet) may also reflect a desire to make other-directed identity claims.

HOW WE FORM IMPRESSIONS FROM ENVIRONMENTS

The previous sections described the ways in which people affect their environments to reflect who they are and what they do. Because environments are such a rich source of potential information about a person, they are a promising context for examining first impressions. In the following section we examine the processes involved in forming impressions based on environments. How do observers detect and interpret environmental cues to form impressions of what a person is like? Can they form accurate impressions? We present the theoretical processes involved in these kinds of impressions, followed by several empirical examples from our own research on environment-based first impressions.

Processes Linking Observer Judgments to Environmental Cues

The lower section of Figure 14.1 illustrates how observers may form impressions about occupants via a two-step inference process, with the possibility that stereotypes could intervene at either step. If stereotypes do not intervene, observers first infer the behavior that created the physical evidence (Step 1a), and then they infer the dispositions that underlie the behavior (Step 2a). For example, they may infer from an organized workspace that the occupant organizes his or her belongings, and observers may associate such behavior with high levels of conscientiousness. However, stereotypes might be activated by residue in the environment (Step 1b) or by inferred behavior (Step 2b). In such cases, judgments about an occupant could be impacted by a stereotype that is associated with a whole set of traits, some of which may have no direct link to evidence in the environment. For example, an observer might notice some Asian books on the shelves, which activates stereotypes about Asians. This may result in the observer inferring a suite of traits stereotypically associated with Asians, such as being socially responsible, conscientious, and introverted.

How does the use of stereotypes affect the observers' judgments? When multiple observers hold similar stereotypes, as they might for common stereotypes such as those about sex and race, consensus among observers could be boosted (Kenny, 1991, 2004). Moreover, when there is some truth to these stereotypes, accuracy could be boosted (Lee, Jussim, & McCauley, 1995). Note that the stereotype-based inferences (Steps 1b and 2b) differ from Steps 1a and 2a in that observers using stereotypes may draw conclusions about traits for which they have no direct evidence.

Regardless of whether stereotypes intervene in the inference process, if observers make *similar* inferences, then consensus among observers' impressions should result. And if observers make *correct* inferences, then those impressions should also be accurate. However, observers may form inaccurate impressions by incorrectly matching evidence to the behavior that caused it or by incorrectly matching the behavior to the underlying disposition. Observers' use of invalid stereotypes would also diminish accuracy.

Research on impression formation has shown that observers do indeed draw on stereotypes when they form their impressions. For example, when forming impressions of others based on their working or living spaces, observers make use of gender and race stereotypes (Gosling et al., 2002); these broad stereotypes help form judgments in which the stereotypes have some accuracy (e.g., regarding gender differences in emotional stability) but hurt where they are inaccurate (e.g., regarding gender differences in agreeableness). Observers will also use narrower stereotypes, such as those associated with fans of specific music genres (Rentfrow & Gosling, 2007) or drivers of certain vehicles (Davies & Patel, 2005). For example, in one study, judgments of targets' extraversion levels were partially influenced by the amount of country music and hip-hop music in their top-10 records (Rentfrow & Gosling, 2006).

It is likely that the consensus and accuracy of impressions are affected by several parameters. For example, Kenny's (1994) weighted-average model (WAM) of consensus proposes nine parameters, such as similar meaning systems, to explain the extent to which observers agree about a target individual. Funder's (1995, 1999) realistic accuracy model (RAM) conceptualizes personality judgments in terms of four components—observers, targets, traits, and information. These components are associated with four basic questions that can be asked about personality judgments: (1) Are some *observers* better than others? (2) Are some *targets* more easily judged than others? (3) Are some *traits* more easily judged than others? (4) Do some kinds of *information* afford better judgments than others? These four questions can be combined to address more complex questions about interactions among the four components. For example, the idea of expertise translates into the question of whether some judges are more accurate at making judgments on the basis of one kind of information than on another? In the context of living spaces, we could ask whether student observers are more accurate at making judgments of students' bedrooms versus nonstudents' bedrooms—or whether females are better at judging the rooms of females than males.

HOW ACCURATE ARE FIRST IMPRESSIONS BASED ON ENVIRONMENTS?: SOME EMPIRICAL EVIDENCE

Physical Environments: Bedrooms and Offices

Although Gosling et al. (2002) did not test the specific processes in the model described above, they did examine impressions of people based on the spaces in which they live and work. In these studies, teams of observers were sent into 83 student bedrooms and 94 offices to see what they could learn about the occupants purely on the basis of the physical spaces in which they lived and worked. Data were obtained from three sources: (1) observer impressions of the occupants based purely on their personal environments, (2) criterion measures telling us what the occupants were really like, obtained from the occupants themselves and acquaintances who knew the occupants well, and (3) detailed documentation of the features of the personal environments (e.g., well organized) and the items (e.g., a desk calendar) contained in the rooms (Gosling, Craik, Martin, & Pryor, 2005a, 2005b).

The findings, summarized in Table 14.1, indicate that observers were able to form consensual impressions of occupants purely on the basis of their spaces. For example, observers showed substantial agreement about occupants' levels of extraversion, agreeableness, conscientiousness, and openness, but not their emotional stability. To determine which impressions were accurate, observers' impressions were compared with the criterion measures (i.e., self- and peer reports of the occupants). Observers formed generally accurate impressions for conscientiousness and openness, but their impressions of extraversion and agreeableness were less accurate. Clues to which room characteristics observers were using to form their impressions and which room characteristics were valid indicators of what the occupants were like were obtained by correlating the observer judgments and the criterion measures with the physical features of the personal spaces. The findings suggested that observers were correctly using characteristics such as the tidiness of the rooms and the variety of books to form impressions of conscientiousness and openness, respectively, but were incorrectly using characteristics such as how decorated and colorful the room was to form impressions of extraversion and agreeableness, respectively. Consensus and accuracy correlations from this study were consistently stronger than those found in most zero-acquaintance studies (see Kenny, 1994, for a review). In some cases, the environment-based consensus was stronger than that found in studies of long-term interactions (see Kenny, 1994), which suggests that personal environments contain rich and informative cues to occupants' personalities.

In addition to the Big Five personality traits, Gosling et al. (2002) also examined a number of personal characteristics that were not published in their report: wealth, political orientation, athleticism, intelligence, and attractiveness. In offices, consensus was strongest for wealth, next for political orientation and athleticism, and slightly weaker for attractiveness and intelligence. In bedrooms, consensus was strong for athleticism, political orientation, and wealth but weaker for attractiveness and intelligence. The level of accuracy also varied across traits. In offices, there was substantial accuracy for political orientation, closely followed by wealth and athleticism, respectively. Observers were less accurate in inferring intelligence and attractiveness, with the correlations failing to reach conventional levels of significance. In bedrooms, the observers' ratings of athleticism and political orientation were most accurate, with less accuracy found for wealth and intelligence, perhaps reflecting a restriction of range in this student sample.

TABLE 14.1. Judgments Based on Offices: Consensus and Accuracy

| | Interobserver consensus | | | | Observer accuracy (observer–self/peer corr.) | |
| | Mean pairwise r | | alpha | | | |
	Offices	Bedrooms	Offices	Bedrooms	Offices	Bedrooms
Personality—Big Five						
Extraversion	.39**	.31*	.84	.76	.24*	.22*
Agreeableness	.23*	.20	.70	.64	−.04	.20*
Conscientiousness	.42**	.47**	.85	.86	.24*	.33**
Emotional stability	.14	.08	.57	.38	.19	.36**
Openness to experience	.51**	.58**	.89	.91	.46**	.65**
Wealth	.52**	.32**	.90	.77	.37**	.28**
Attractiveness	.30**	.19	.77	.62	.18	.30**
Political orientation	.39**	.39**	.84	.82	.44**	.49**
Intelligence	.30**	.20	.77	.64	.23	.24*
Athleticism	.37**	.56**	.82	.90	.31**	.57**

Note: For offices (N = 94) and for bedrooms (N = 83), but Ns vary slightly across analyses due to missing data. Significance levels are not relevant for alphas and so are not reported here.

* $p < .05$ (one-tailed); ** $p < .01$ (one-tailed).

The accuracy correlations for the bedrooms were generally stronger than those for offices. We cannot determine what drove the differences, but the observers of both bedrooms and offices were students themselves; so, perhaps they were relatively well versed in the cultural meaning of the possessions and icons found in students' living spaces but less so in the meanings of cues in offices spaces. In Funder's (1999) terms, the observers may have had greater expertise in the bedrooms than in the offices. Other findings can usefully be conceptualized in terms of Funder's questions. For example, the finding that Openness was more easily judged than other traits and that this finding was unique to physical environments reflects a trait X information interaction.

There are a number of other possible explanations for why the accuracy correlations for bedrooms were stronger than those for offices. First, college is a time when individuals are negotiating identity issues; so, students may be particularly prone to self-expression. Second, people generally have the freedom to decorate their personal living spaces as they please, but office décor is often restricted by company guidelines. Third, individuals in offices, both voluntarily and because of extrinsic pressure and norms, are typically concerned about the positive and professional image they project. As a result, they may be pressured to arrange and decorate their offices in ways that are contrary to their actual preferences and personalities. Fourth, the rooms in our study of bedrooms were often multipurpose spaces where the occupants spent a great deal of their time, using them for a variety of activities such as working, sleeping, relaxing, and entertaining. Thus, the personal living spaces in the study of bedrooms may have been ecologically richer environments than the office spaces.

One concern often raised in the context of this research is whether occupants altered or tidied their rooms before the assessment team arrived. There are several reasons to think the rooms were not altered much. First, the rooms were assessed under conditions of anonymity and confidentiality, reducing the incentive to tidy the space. Second, we reminded participants that meaningful feedback (their primary incentive for participating in the study) depended on observers seeing the environments in their unaltered state. Third, the confidential ratings by the occupants' informants on how much they thought the rooms had been altered for the assessment indicated the rooms had hardly changed (Gosling et al., 2002). More informally, we noticed a difference between deeply tidy rooms and rooms that had merely been tidied. If an occupant does not live a tidy life—such as putting CDs back in their proper place when they have been played and buying supplies long before they run out—there is only so much the occupant can do in the short term to tidy it up. It takes consistent and persistent tidying behavior to have a deeply tidy room, but a hurried hour or even day or two of tidying can only produce, at best, a tidied room.

Other research on physical spaces has also identified links between individuals and their physical environments (Hata, 2004; Jones, Taylor, Dick, Singh, & Cook, 2007; Wells, 2000; Wells & Thelen, 2002). Moreover, researchers have begun to examine parameters that affect the accuracy of environment-based impressions. Hata (2004) found that personality assessments made solely on the basis of living spaces were more accurate when the occupants recognized their homes as expressive of their own personalities as opposed to when they did not identify with their living spaces. Wells (2000) found gender differences in the ways people personalize their offices; specifically, women tended to express their identities and emotions, whereas men more often expressed their achievements and status. Wells and Thelen (2002) also identified a range of cues associated with the personalities of the occupants. Specifically, extroverted employees were more likely than introverted ones to display items related to their friends and coworkers as well as items that displayed their intellect. Employees high in openness tended to display items related to the arts. Those scoring low on agreeableness and conscientiousness tended to display items relating to activities and hobbies.

A related area of research has looked into the impressions that are formed about others based on their possessions. With information about what an object is and the path it took to end up in its current location and state, observers may be able to infer something about the personality of the person who influenced that path, typically the current owner of the object. Alpers and Gerdes (2006) showed that participants could match photographs of car owners (from the waist up) to photographs of the cars they owned. Such inferences require observers to make judgments about the owners (what kind of person is that?) and about the cars (what kind of person would drive that car?) and then match the two sets of information.

Consistency Across Time: Are Environments Stable Reflections of Personality?

One common question is whether the same impressions would be elicited by a person's bedroom and his or her office. We have never been able to assess the bedrooms and offices of the same individuals, but we did have an opportunity to examine two offices belonging to a single occupant. Specifically, in 2002 the department of psychology at the University of Texas moved to a new building. We arranged for one group of observers to assess 35 offices before the move and another entirely different group of observers to assess the offices 6 months after arrival in the new building. As shown in Table 14.2, the consensus and accuracy correlations generally replicated those from the previous study of offices. Moreover the assessments based on one office correlated strongly with the assessments based on the other office.

Extending the Meaning of "Environment": First Impressions Based on Auditory, Virtual, and Geographic Environments

Environmental manifestations of personality are not limited to physical environments. As noted earlier, we craft our social environments to suit our personalities, and observers readily draw on social information when they form impressions of others. Indeed, observers will use information from environments as transitory as the people standing close to a target. Studies of stigmatization have revealed that merely associating with a stigmatized group can affect how individuals are perceived. In one study, Hebl and Mannix (2003) showed participants photos of male job applicants seated next to either an overweight or an average-weight female. An applicant's mere proximity to an overweight individual was enough to cause him to be socially stigmatized by the participants. The proximity effect was sufficiently strong that the same stigmatization occurred even when participants were told that there was no social relationship between the applicant and the overweight woman.

Observers are able to judge others on the basis of their environments and possessions because these contexts provide information about the people who own them. However, in addition to physical spaces (and the possessions that fill them) there are many other kinds of environments that could furnish information about others. Just as we craft our physical spaces, we also select and mold our auditory and social environments. Just as we physically dwell in houses and offices, we dwell virtually in online environments like virtual worlds, personal websites, and social-networking portals (e.g., MySpace.com, Facebook.com). Just as we leave traces of our actions, intentions, and values in our permanent spaces, we can also leave traces in other immediate surroundings such as our cars or clothing. Thus, many environments may be used by observers to figure out what we are like. Although Gosling et al.'s (2002) model was developed in the context of two studies of physical environments, it can easily be applied more widely. For example, the mechanisms linking individuals to their environments and the processes by which observers form impressions of others can all be applied to the domain of physical appearance—hair styles and clothing can be used to make identity statements, and clothing and accessories can provide evidence of past or anticipated behaviors. In other words, an individual's physical appearance may hold many clues to what he or she is like. And

TABLE 14.2. Judgments Based on Two Offices Occupied by the Same Person

| | Interobserver consensus | | | | Observer accuracy (observer–self cor.) | | Test–retest |
| | Mean pairwise r | | alpha | | | | |
	Office 1	Office 2	Office 1	Office 2	Office 1	Office 2	Office 1–Office 2
Personality—Big Five							
Extraversion	.20	.34*	.71	.88	.12	.32	.47**
Agreeableness	.16	.20	.66	.79	.16	.18	.50**
Conscientiousness	.20	.33*	.71	.88	.47**	.55**	.70**
Emotional stability	.13	.05	.60	.44	.22	−.17	.30
Openness to experience	.30	.35*	.81	.89	.49**	.29	.59**
Wealth	.38*	.30	.86	.84	.59**	.66**	.81**
Attractiveness	.16	.21	.65	.80	.09	.61**	.52**
Political orientation	.14	.27	.61	.85	.46**	.46*	.68**
Intelligence	.26	.22	.78	.81	.28	.24	.73**
Athleticism	.19	.18	.70	.77	.08	.45*	.42*

Note: $N = 35$, but varies slightly across analyses due to missing data. Significance levels are not relevant for alphas and so are not reported here.
* $p < .05$ (one-tailed); ** $p < .01$ (one-tailed).

as was the case with physical environments, observers may use this information to form impressions about individuals.

How accurate are first impressions formed on the bases of nonphysical environments? In the next section we describe some studies based on a very broad definition of "personal environment," extending the model from physical spaces to a range of new domains. This reinterpretation allows us to extend our conceptual model and research paradigm to a new range of real-world phenomena, such as the music individuals listen to, the way they present themselves online, and the language they use.

Auditory Environments

When students meet each other for the first time, in their efforts to get better acquainted they will often ask questions about one another's music preferences. In fact, over the course of a 6-week getting-acquainted exercise between pairs of students communicating via computer chat sessions, music was the topic most frequently talked about over the entire period (Rentfrow & Gosling, 2006). Furthermore, 9 of the top 10 dating websites ask users to provide information about their music preferences (Rentfrow & Gosling, 2006). These findings reflect the widely held assumption that knowing someone's music preferences can tell you something about his or her personality. Rentfrow and Gosling (2003) found support for this assumption. In a sample of 3,500 college students, music preferences were reliably related to various elements of personality, self-views, and cognitive abilities. For example, students who expressed a preference for a dimension that encompassed the jazz, blues, folk, and classical genres were higher on Openness and scored higher on a test of verbal IQ than did students who did not like those types of music. More importantly, a follow-up study showed that observers actually use music preferences to form impressions about others, and in many cases these impressions evidence considerable accuracy (Rentfrow & Gosling, 2006). Specifically, observers who formed personality impressions purely from listening to targets' top 10 songs showed strong agreement in their impressions. Pairwise interobserver agreement was strongest for openness (ICC = .38), followed by agreeableness (.37), conscientiousness (.30), and extraversion (.27), with little agreement for emotional stability (.11). The accuracy of the observers' judgments was assessed by correlating the aggregated observer ratings with targets' self-ratings. Given that the observers had access to nothing more than a CD of 10 songs, accuracy was surprisingly strong. The most accurately judged trait was openness (r = .47), followed by extraversion (.27), emotional stability (.23), and agreeableness (.21), with no accuracy for conscientiousness (−.01). To contextualize the magnitude of the accuracy correlations, we compared the trait accuracy correlations from this study with those of previ-ous zero-acquaintance research (summarized by Kenny, 1994). The com-parison showed that music preferences convey very different information from that conveyed through the stimuli used in past zero-acquaintance research (e.g., photographs, video recordings). In particular, music pref-erences provide more information about targets' agreeableness, emo-tional stability, and openness and less information about targets' extra-version and conscientiousness than do traditional zero-acquaintance stimuli (e.g., short video clips).

The fact that music appears so prominently in getting-acquainted contexts suggests that individuals are aware that their music preferences send signals about their personality. By advertising their music prefer-ences, people can make other-directed identity claims that convey to oth-ers how they would like to be seen (Hargreaves & North, 1997, 1999; North & Hargreaves, 1999). Certainly, contemporary student clothing (e.g., T-shirts) and decor (e.g., posters) hold many explicit clues to an in-dividual's music preferences.

Virtual Environments

As electronic forms of interaction continue to gain prominence in every-day life, new kinds of environments are catching the attention of social and personality psychologists. The Internet provides a diverse and data-rich medium for examining how people make judgments about others as well as how they manage the judgments others make about them. Two broad areas of this fast-expanding field are particularly relevant to im-pression formation.

First, researchers can examine the impressions (including first im-pressions) that are elicited on the basis of electronically mediated infor-mation; already researchers have examined the impressions that are con-veyed on the bases of various electronic or virtual stimuli, such as personal websites (Marcus, Machilek, & Schütz, 2006; Vazire & Gos-ling, 2004), online social networks (e.g., MySpace, Facebook; Gosling, Gaddis, & Vazire, 2007), email messages (Oberlander & Gill, 2006), Internet chatrooms (Markey & Wells, 2002), Internet Messaging, or IMs (Slatcher & Vazire, 2007), and virtual worlds (Yee & Bailenson, 2007; Yee, Bailenson, Urbanek, Chang, & Merget, 2007).

In our own work we have examined the impressions that are con-veyed on the basis of personal websites (Vazire & Gosling, 2004). Spe-cifically, observers rated 89 targets purely on the basis of their personal websites. Pairwise interobserver agreement was strongest for openness (ICC = .32) and extraversion (.32), followed by agreeableness (.28), con-scientiousness (.27), and emotional stability (.18). The accuracy of the observers' judgments was assessed by correlating the aggregated observer ratings with an accuracy criterion consisting of self and informant ratings of the target. The most accurately judged trait was openness ($r = .63$), followed by conscientiousness (.43), extraversion (.38), emotional stability (.31), and agreeableness (.28).

The second area of electronic interaction that is relevant to impression formation is in the domain of virtual worlds. In addition to understanding the connections between real people and their representations in virtual worlds (i.e., avatars), it will become increasingly important to understand how impressions are formed of virtual entities in their own right. For example, research will need to focus on the online identities created through immersive virtual worlds such as those found in games like EverQuest, World of Warcraft, and the virtual social network Second Life (Yee et al., 2007). As more interactions become entirely virtual in nature, it is important for social and personality researchers to examine the causes and consequences of the new social phenomena rapidly emerging in this domain.

Immediate Social and Physical Surroundings

Everyday observations of others draw on whatever information is available. For example, as noted earlier, merely associating with a stigmatized group can affect the impressions people elicit (Hebl & Mannix, 2003). Such findings suggest that mere location in terms of the people with whom individuals associate, the places in which they spend their time, and the activities in which they engage could affect how they are seen by others. Mehl, Gosling, and Pennebaker (2006) examined this possibility by instructing observers to rate targets on the basis of audio records of the targets' social environments collected naturalistically over a 2-day period. The records were obtained unobtrusively, using the electronically activated recorder (EAR), a computerized tape recorder, which records 30-second snippets of ambient sounds approximately every 12 minutes during targets' waking hours (Mehl, Pennebaker, Crow, Dabbs, & Price, 2001). These acoustic behavior traces have been shown to reliably capture peoples' locations (e.g., inside an apartment, in a public place) and activities (e.g., watching TV, attending a lecture, cooking, typing on the computer; Mehl & Pennebaker, 2003). In the Mehl et al. (2006) study, observers rated 96 targets purely on the basis of their EAR-derived audio recordings. The accuracy of the observers' judgments was assessed by correlating the aggregated observer ratings with the targets' self-ratings. The most accurately judged trait was extraversion ($r = .41$), followed by emotional stability (.30), conscientiousness (.27), agreeableness (.25), and openness (.21).

The physical location in which a person resides can also be conceptualized at a much broader level. The geographic region in which individuals live is associated with features of the physical and cultural environment, which can play a part in shaping the activities and interactions,
and hence the personalities, of the people who live there (Rentfrow, Gosling, & Potter, in press). For example, teenagers growing up in rural
neighborhoods will engage in activities quite different from those growing up in urban or even coastal neighborhoods. With no subways,
crowds, or strangers, people from a small town in Kansas seldom have a
chance to ride a subway crowded with strangers, and beach parties are
rare in places without beaches. An interest in contemporary art is easier
to nurture in a city with a thriving artistic community than it is in a
small country town. The effects of the environment in shaping people
are only part of the reason there could be geographic differences in personality, because there is a limit to how far people can adapt. When people have reached their limits and can no longer abide where they live,
they may move to places that better match their personalities. Thus, a
combination of environmental shaping and selective migration could result in geographic differences in personality. These differences, in turn,
could be used by observers to inform the impressions they form of others. Some recent studies have provided support for geographic variation
in personality. Even within the United States, there is evidence for regional variation in the values people hold (Rentfrow, Jost, Gosling, &
Potter, in press; Vandello & Cohen, 1999). For example, Rentfrow et al.
(in press) showed differences across U.S. states in mean levels of openness (these state-level openness scores predicted the percentage of votes
for Democratic and Republican candidates in the 1996-2004 presidential elections, even after adjusting for standard sociodemographic and
political predictors). In addition to suggesting that observers may reasonably rely on geographic location when they form their impressions of
others, the research also suggests that observers could make more finely
grained location-based judgments (e.g., for urban vs. rural dwellers). For
example, Kashima et al. (2004) found that in both Japan and Australia,
participants from rural locales were higher in collectivism than were
those living in metropolitan cities. Together these studies provide support for links between personality and very broad construals of the environments that people create and inhabit.

CONCLUSIONS

The studies discussed in this chapter show that people can and do form
impressions of others on the basis of the environments they create and

inhabit. Physical, auditory, virtual, and social environments provide observers with windows onto different traits. For example, social environments elicit the most accurate judgments for extraversion but physical, auditory, and virtual environments elicit the greatest accuracy for openness judgments (a dimension that tends not to elicit any accuracy in traditional zero-acquaintance contexts, such as brief interactions; Kenny, 1994). Now that the connections between individuals and their places are well established, future research should focus on elucidating the exact processes by which observers use environments in the judgment process. How much are judgments based on direct inferences (from the residue to the behaviors that caused the residue), and how much are they based on the use of stereotypes?

In addition to examining the parameters affecting impressions based on physical environments, social and personality researchers should position themselves at the forefront of the many new environments that are emerging. Our experience has taught us that, across contexts, similar mechanisms seem to underlie the links between people and the places in which they dwell (broadly construed). Thus, past studies of physical environments will continue to provide a useful starting point from which to examine the connections between people and the increasingly broad array of environments they create and inhabit.

REFERENCES

Alpers, G. W., & Gerdes, A. M. (2006). Another look at "look-alikes": Can judges match belongings with their owners? *Journal of Individual Differences, 27*, 38–41.

Baumeister, R. F. (1982). A self-presentational view of social phenomena. *Psychological Bulletin, 91*, 3–26.

Buss, D. M. (1987). Selection, evocation, and manipulation. *Journal of Personality and Social Psychology, 53*, 1214–1221.

Davies, G. M., & Patel, D. (2005). The influence of car and driver stereotypes on attributions of vehicle speed, position on the road, and culpability in a road accident scenario. *Legal and Criminological Psychology, 10*, 45–62.

Funder, D. C. (1995). On the accuracy of personality judgment: A realistic approach. *Psychological Review, 102*, 652–670.

Funder, D. C. (1999). *Personality judgment: A realistic approach to person perception.* San Diego, CA: Academic Press.

Gosling, S. D., Craik, K. H., Martin, N. R., & Pryor, M. R. (2005a). Material attributes of Personal Living Spaces. *Home Cultures, 2*, 51–88.

Gosling, S. D., Craik, K. H., Martin, N. R., & Pryor, M. R. (2005b). The Personal Living Space Cue Inventory: An analysis and evaluation. *Environment and Behavior, 37*, 683–705.

Gosling, S. D., Gaddis, S., & Vazire, S. (2007). Personality impressions based on Facebook profiles. *Proceedings of the International Conference on Weblogs and Social Media, Boulder, Colorado.*

Gosling, S. D., Ko, S. J., Mannarelli, T., & Morris, M. E. (2002). A room with a cue: Personality judgments based on offices and bedrooms. *Journal of Personality and Social Psychology, 82,* 379–398.

Hargreaves, D. J., & North, A. C. (Eds.). (1997). *The social psychology of music.* Oxford, UK: Oxford University Press.

Hargreaves, D. J., & North, A. C. (1999). The functions of music in everyday life: Redefining the social in music psychology. *Psychology of Music, 27,* 71–83.

Hata, T. D. (2004). Inferences about resident's personality in Japanese homes. *North American Journal of Psychology, 6,* 337–348.

Hebl, M. R., & Mannix, L. M. (2003). The weight of obesity in evaluating others: A mere proximity effect. *Personality and Social Psychology Bulletin, 29,* 28–38.

Jones, R. M., Taylor, D. E., Dick, A. J., Singh, A., & Cook, J. L. (2007). Bedroom design and decoration: Gender differences in preference and activity. *Adolescence, 42,* 539–553.

Kashima, Y., Kokubo, T., Kashima, E. S., Boxall, D., Yamaguchi, S., & Macrae, K. (2004). Culture and self: Are there within-culture differences in self between metropolitan areas and regional cities? *Personality and Social Psychology Bulletin, 13,* 816–823.

Kenny, D. A. (1991). A general model of consensus and accuracy in interpersonal perception. *Psychological Review, 98,* 155–163.

Kenny, D. A. (1994). *Interpersonal perception: A social relations analysis.* New York: Guilford Press.

Kenny, D. A. (2004). PERSON: A general model of interpersonal perception. *Personality and Social Psychology Review, 8,* 265–280.

Lee, Y., Jussim, L., & McCauley, C. R. (1995). *Stereotype accuracy: Toward appreciating group differences.* Washington, DC: American Psychological Association.

MacKinnon, D. W. (1977). From selecting spies to selecting managers: The OSS Assessment program. In J. L. Moses & W. C. Byham (Eds.), *Applying the assessment center method* (pp. 13–30). New York: Pergamon.

Marcus, B., Machilek, F., & Schütz, A. (2006). Personality in cyberspace: Personal web sites as media for personality expressions and impressions. *Journal of Personality and Social Psychology, 90,* 1014–1031.

Markey, P. M., & Wells, S. M. (2002). Interpersonal perception in Internet chat rooms. *Journal of Research in Personality, 36,* 134–146.

Mehl, M. R., & Pennebaker, J. W. (2003). The sounds of social life: A psychometric analysis of students' daily social environments and natural conversations. *Journal of Personality and Social Psychology, 84,* 857–870.

Mehl, M. R., Gosling, S. D., & Pennebaker, J. W. (2006). Personality in its natural habitat: Manifestations and implicit folk theories of personality in daily life. *Journal of Personality and Social Psychology, 90,* 862–877.

Mehl, M. R., Pennebaker, J. W., Crow, M., Dabbs, J., & Price, J. (2001). The Electronically Activated Recorder (EAR): A device for sampling naturalistic daily activities and conversations. *Behavior Research Methods, Instruments, and Computers, 33,* 517–523.

North, A. C., & Hargreaves, D. J. (1999). Music and adolescent identity. *Music Education Research, 1,* 75–92.

Oberlander, J., & Gill, A. (2006). Language with character: A corpus-based study of individual differences in e-mail communication. *Discourse Processes, 42,* 239–270.

Rentfrow, P. J., & Gosling, S. D. (2003). The do re mi's of everyday life: The structure and personality correlates of music preferences. *Journal of Personality and Social Psychology, 84,* 1236–1256.

Rentfrow, P. J., & Gosling, S. D. (2006). Message in a ballad: The role of music preferences in interpersonal perception. *Psychological Science, 17,* 236–242.

Rentfrow, P. J., & Gosling, S. D. (2007). The content and validity of music-genre stereotypes among college students. *Psychology of Music, 35,* 306–326.

Rentfrow, P. J., Gosling, S. D., & Potter, J. (in press). The geography of personality: A theory of the emergence, persistence, and expression of regional variation in basic traits. *Perspectives in Psychological Science.*

Rentfrow, P. J., Jost, J. T., Gosling, S. D., & Potter, J. (in press). Statewide differences in personality predict voting patterns in 1996–2004 U.S. presidential elections. In J. T. Jost, A. C. Kay, and H. Thorisdottir (Eds.), *Social and psychological bases of ideology and system justification.* New York: Oxford University Press.

Slatcher, R. B., & Vazire, S. (2007). *It's not just who you are, it's how you act: Influences of global and contextualized personality traits on relationship satisfaction.* Manuscript under review.

Swann, W. B., Jr. (1984). Quest for accuracy in person perception: A matter of pragmatics. *Psychological Review, 91,* 457–477.

Swann, W. B., Jr. (1987). Identity negotiation: Where two roads meet. *Journal of Personality and Social Psychology, 53,* 1038–1051.

Swann, W. B., Jr., Rentfrow, P. J., & Guinn, J. S. (2003). Self-verification: The search for coherence. In M. R. Leary & J. J. P. Tangney (Eds.), *Handbook of self and identity* (pp. 367–383). New York: Guilford Press.

Vandello, J. A., & Cohen, D. (1999). Patterns of individualism and collectivism across the United States. *Journal of Personality and Social Psychology, 77,* 279–292.

Vazire, S., & Gosling, S. D. (2004). e-Perceptions: Personality impressions based on personal Web sites. *Journal of Personality and Social Psychology, 87,* 123–132.

Wells, M. M. (2000). Office clutter or meaningful personal displays: The role of office personalization in employee and organizational well-being. *Journal of Environmental Psychology, 20,* 239–255.

Wells, M., & Thelen, L. (2002). What does your workspace say about you? The influence of personality, status, and workspace on personalization. *Environment and Behavior, 34,* 300–321.

Yee, N., & Bailenson, J. N. (2007). The Proteus effect: The effect of transformed self-representation on behavior. *Human Communication Research*, *33*, 271–290.

Yee, N., Bailenson, J. N., Urbanek, M., Chang, F., & Merget, D. (2007). The unbearable likeness of being digital: The persistence of nonverbal social norms in online virtual environments. *Journal of CyberPsychology and Behavior*, *10*, 115–121.

Index

f indicates figure, *t* indicates table